To Rosemarie,
my forever friend,
always, Tea

"You Have Been Kind Enough to Assist Me":

Herman Stern and the Jewish Refugee Crisis

By Terry Shoptaugh

Institute for Regional Studies
NDSU

Library of Congress Control Number: 2007937543
ISBN 978-0-911042-69-6

Printed in Canada.

Published by the North Dakota State University
Institute for Regional Studies
P.O. Box 5075, Fargo, ND 58105
www.ndsu.edu/ndirs

"You Have Been Kind Enough to Assist Me": Herman Stern and the Jewish Refugee Crisis
By Terry Shoptaugh

Contents

Acknowledgments

Close to one hundred thousand European Jews found refuge in the United States before the onset of the Second World War. This story is about how one man living in a small town in North Dakota, by dint of his energy, determination, refusal to be discouraged, help at critical moments (for he well knew that he could never have succeeded as he did without the help of a special friend in Washington), he managed to pluck more than a hundred German Jews away from the clutches of the Nazis. It was a remarkable achievement. Then when, after the Holocaust, historians argued, with justice, that America could have done more, this man was content to express his gratitude that with help he was able to do something.

It is in that same spirit that I need to express my own gratitude. I wanted to tell the story of this man and how he changed the lives of so many by what he did. I could not have done it without the cooperation of those men and women who shared their stories about those times. I am indebted to all of them: Tea Eichengruen Stiefel, Hilda Jonas, William Mueller, Margaret Steiner, Lore Moser, William Spier, Michael Stern, Lotte Henlein Ullman, and Thomas Maier.

I also thank relatives and friends of Herman Stern, who shared with me many insights about this very private man: Edward and Richard Stern, his sons; John and Rick Stern, his grandsons; Cheryl Stern Seltzer, his granddaughter and her husband Robert Seltzer; Myer Shark; Nathan Crosby; K. B. Cummings; James Hetland; Lee Isensee; Dean McConn; Roy Sheppard; David Walker. Many other residents of Valley City who knew Stern shared memories with me one evening after a talk at Barnes County Historical Society. To all of them my deepest thanks. Special thanks also to Michael Morrissey, Tenessa Gemelke, and the very helpful staff at the Washington State Holocaust Education Resource Center for their assistance in conducting some of the interviews.

I owe a debt of thanks to reference archivists at the National Archives for their help in providing copies of important State Department cables and reports relevant to my research. Temple Beth El in
Fargo, North Dakota kindly allowed me access to their records. Linda
Mack Schloff, the author of an excellent book on Jewish life and
culture in the upper Midwest, gave me help with the contents of the
Jewish Archives of the Upper Midwest, deposited at the University
of Minnesota. Wes Anderson, director of the Barnes County Historical Society in Valley City, helped in more ways than I can summa-
rize, everything from finding elusive bits of information in the local
newspapers to showing me around the town and helping with illus-
trations. Darel Paulson performed his usual magic with the photographs we were able to gather. Sandy Slater and her staff at the Elwyn
B. Robinson Department of Special Collections, University of North
Dakota, were tireless in answering my numerous requests for materials from the Herman Stern Papers.

I owe a very special thank you to the late Paul Wellstone, U.S.
Senator for Minnesota, who helped me gain access to some impor-
tant State Department personnel files, held at the National Personnel
Records Center in St. Louis.

Five individuals were indispensable to me in the completion of
this book. Janet Daley, former editor of *North Dakota History* (now
the director of the North Dakota Humanities Council) was the first
person to urge me to do a book on Herman Stern and never ceased to
encourage me to see it through. Gisela Nobel greatly helped the research by translating the many German-language letters in Mr. Stern's
Papers. As project director for the Minnesota Humanities Commission, Jane Cunningham helped me obtain a Works in Progress grant
so I could complete the writing. And Korella Selzler, my assistant at
Minnesota State University Moorhead cheerfully carried out the thank-
less task of proofreading and retyping my chapters.

Finally, there is really no adequate way I can thank my wife
Deborah for enduring it all while this book was written. There is a
story about the wife of George Bernard Shaw, who once told a friend

she took up her knitting whenever Shaw talked about what he was writing at the moment. The knitting kept her hands busy, Mrs. Shaw said, because otherwise "I'd strangle him to shut him up." Deborah knows how Mrs. Shaw felt.

The Stern Family in Germany

Samuel Stern (1842-1919)
m. Minna Strauss Stern (1848-1928)

Moses (b. 1872)*

Adolf Stern (b. 1873)
m. Dora Kann

2 children

1. Gustave (b. 1901)
   m. Gertrud Vasen
   2 sons

2. Julius (b. 1903)
   m. Herta Landsberg
   2 sons (born in U.S.)

Salli (1875-1919)

Julius (b. 1877)
m. Frieda Falkenstein

3 children

1. Gustav (b. 1906)
2. *Ludwig (b. 1907)*
3. Alice (b. 1909)

Gustav (b. 1880)
m. Selma Lewisohn

2 children

1. Klara (b. 1915)
2. Erich (b. 1918)

Dora (1883-1934)

Jettchen (b. 1884)
m. Hugo Henlein

1 child

Lotte (b. 1925)

Herrmann (b. 1887)**
m. Adeline Roth
(in United States)

2 children

1. Richard (b. 1913)
2. Edward (b. 1914)

* *Names in Italics* indicates person was murdered in the Holocaust
** Herrmann Stern changed his name to "Herman" after immigrating to the United States in 1903

Chapter One
A New Life in North Dakota

Herman Stern was born in 1887 in Oberbrechen, a town of about two thousand people in the Hesse district of Germany. The Sterns were one of a small number of Jewish families in Oberbrechen. Herman was the youngest of eight children. His father, Samuel, made a living by growing fodder on a small piece of land, dealing in cattle, and inspecting slaughtered meat to insure it was kosher. Herman recalled that "Father used to go down to the cattle market where he helped the Bauern [farmers] to pick up cattle for their own use. The Bauern houses were built right next to each other and our home was in a rather crowded yard." The residence itself was what Herman called a "very modest two-story house," attached to the barn and a wooden gate which served as entry to a tiny courtyard framed by a small stable for the family's wagon and horses, a little chicken coop, and a few tiny pens for rabbits. Along the street were several more homes, each one much like its neighbors. The cobblestone street was near Oberbrechen's principal Catholic church, which young Herman occasionally attended with his non-Jewish friends.

Samuel Stern was a "very religious" man, a cantor at a synagogue in a nearby town. His wife, Minna Straus Stern, had a grandfather or great-grandfather who had been a rabbi. But the piety of the Sterns was leavened by poverty. Before Herman was four years old his parents began sending him out to walk along the road leading into Oberbrechen, to pick up loose grain that had fallen off wagons. This "gleaning" of grain, he once told his grandson, provided the family with something more to eat, together with the vegetables grown on the little piece of land they owned and some meat from the chickens and rabbits. Although Samuel raised and bred cattle, his family rarely ate beef. Cows were more items for trade than property for food.

1

As Herman grew older, he began to help out in the vegetable garden, where, among other things, his father grew tomatoes, which were "quite unusual to have" at that time. Herman also went into the nearby woods to pick wild berries. As he grew older he took care of the cows, a chore he hated because the "beasts" kept trampling on his feet. Older still, he took on heavier tasks, both on the farm and in hiring himself out about the village. All the children worked; the oldest brother, Moses, a merchant sailor shipping out from Hamburg, occasionally sent money home to help the family make ends meet.[1]

Herman constantly dreamed of a better life. Many years after leaving Germany he told an interviewer that he "never felt at ease" with his life in Oberbrechen. Partly this was because of the poverty, partly also because as the youngest member of the family he felt that he was never free from having to constantly answer the summons of someone else, taking orders from parents and all of his brothers and sisters. Once a year, a unit of the German army held maneuvers outside Oberbrechen. While as a child he enjoyed the spectacle of the soldiers marching through town - "we would march ahead of them" and play with toy wooden swords. His youthful excitement about soldiers cooled a few years later when soldiers came to his father's home during the annual maneuvers, to see if they could find quarters for their officers. He remembered that they were arrogant and "acted very unpleasant" toward his family.

Herman avidly listened to his mother talk about her brother Henry Straus, who had gone to America in the late 1800s. These stories fired him with a desire to "know more about America," where there were many opportunities, where a man could have fewer constraints and might be allowed to do as he pleased.

But visions of a richer life across the Atlantic had to be set aside in the face of the pressing need to find a living. Herman attended his basic eight years of schooling in Oberbrechen and generally did very well in his classes. But he later admitted that he looked forward more to the school breaks when children were released to help relatives with their haymaking and potato harvests. Herman went to Mainz and became an apprentice to one "Herr Kaufman," a tailor in one of the city's larger clothing firms. As one of three apprentices, Herman spent two years learning the tailors' trade. He lived in the firm's attic receiving room and board for his work, but no pay. He ate his meals with the other apprentices in a small room adjacent to the more opulent dining room of the firm's proprietors, but he found the quality of the food he received to be much poorer than what the proprietor's enjoyed.

When Herman was not working, he would go with the other apprentices to look about Mainz, taking walks along the Rhine and visiting the city's fine library. The business was only a couple of blocks away from the Mainz Opera, so the apprentices often walked over to the opera house where they might hear some of the star vocalists practicing. Sometimes, for a few small coins, they could watch a performance in the "standing room" gallery. Herman also enjoyed Mainz's annual festival. But he again found the presence of soldiers in this large fortress city unsettling. The arrogant officers "went where they pleased and they made me feel very uncomfortable." He also did not like Herr Kaufman, who had a "very nervous temperament."

Then, late in 1902 or early 1903, a different opportunity came knocking when Morris G. Straus, Henry Straus's nephew, came from America to visit Minna. Straus had followed Henry Straus to America in the 1870s, learned the clothing trade in Cincinnati, and since 1879 had owned a clothing store in Casselton, North Dakota. Straus and his wife Fredrecka had returned to Germany to find someone he could trust to help him with his growing business. He quickly became interested in Herman, who was about thirty years his junior.

Herman later remembered how he and Straus came to an arrangement: "After I had been [at Mainz] two years, my cousin M. G. Straus, came over to Germany to visit and my mother notified me of that. So I came home one Sunday and Mr. Straus was there, and one of the first questions he asked me was 'how would you like to go to America with me?'" Given the stories the young man had heard, "it was easy for me to make up my mind to come" [to the United States]. But how could he get out of his apprenticeship? Kaufman agreed to let Herman go in return for one thousand marks. "Of course we did not have such money, so I had to wait until later. Morris suggested I serve my year [i.e. remainder of the apprenticeship agreement] and come, but I was restless." Straus returned to North Dakota, promising to wait until young Stern was free to go.

Youth overrode patience. Herman kept thinking about Straus's offer, and Kaufman soon complained that he "didn't have my mind on my work, that I was dreaming about America." I wrote to Morris Straus that if he would send me [a loan of] $75, I would come. He sent me the money soon, so I got quietly ready to go and went home to tell the folks, who hated to see me go. It was the High Holidays and my parents were very unhappy. In my eagerness to get away, I used that date to have enough time from my job at Mainz to get away." Stern's use of such terms as "get away" and getting "quietly ready to go" suggest that his break from his apprenticeship was a one-sided affair. Herman's son Edward later said that "Dad told us that when he packed, he had someone who worked with him bring his suitcase to the train, and he ran away from his job."[2]

Herman, barely sixteen years old, sailed from Hamburg on October 1, 1903, bound for New York. When Stern arrived in New York, Mrs. Straus's brother met him and gave him sixteen dollars for a train ticket to North Dakota. He scarcely had time for more than a glance at the huge city before boarding the train. "I couldn't talk any English, so he taught me the denominations of the money, bought me a box lunch and put me on the train, and I went to Casselton, North Dakota." Crossing half the continent in a matter of two days, Stern watched from the window as the train passed through one city and town after another. He was thrilled when the porter of the train was kind and attentive to him, giving him an extra pillow and a blanket. But then when he arrived in Casselton he couldn't understand why the porter was suddenly cold and formal. Only after he mentioned it to Straus did he come to understand that the porter had expected a tip, something he had never seen in Germany. It was his first lesson in American customs.[3]

Stern went to work immediately upon arrival in Casselton. Straus had his store on Casselton's Front Street, almost directly across from the Northern Pacific depot, an ideal location for doing business with salesmen and travelers as well as residents. Straus began teaching his young protégé the finer points of the clothing trade. Stern later recalled at a gathering of businessmen that he started his job with no more English than what was needed to help a customer. "I knew what to say when a customer said 'how much?' and I also knew what to say when he said 'too much'." Stern was fortunate in not having to cope with a sliding-price system, which was still quite common in many retail stores: a laboring-class customer might pay fifty cents for a shirt, while a local lawyer might pay a dollar or more for the same item. Since prices were not posted for each item of clothing, haggling, or "bickering and bartering" as Stern later termed it, was normal: "We expected a customer to say 'you want eighteen dollars, I'll give you twelve dollars.' Finally we'd settle for fifteen dollars." Straus, however, had decided to sell all his items at set prices that he had posted. Haggling still occurred, but Straus attracted more customers because his prices were clearly marked.[4]

Stern learned to study each type of cloth and recognize the strengths and drawbacks of various fabrics. He spent much time making alterations to suits and slacks. He learned how to select the proper accessories for a suit, to wrap a package with just enough paper, no more, wasting no string in tying it up. His English improved and he came to know each of the customers, how to treat them and make suggestions to them. He learned how to keep the accounts, how to make displays, how to manage the stock. Of course he made mistakes. One time he accepted a check from an unreliable customer and received a rebuke from Straus when it bounced. Overall he did well and the Strauses liked his eagerness to please; Mrs. Straus "became my second mother." But he missed his parents in Germany enough to use part of his first pay to send a birthday present to his mother in Oberbrechen.

In 1907, Straus purchased a second store in Valley City, about forty miles west of Casselton. While he moved to Valley City to reorganize it, he gave charge of the original Casselton store to Stern. Valley City had been established in 1872 at the site where the Northern Pacific line crossed over the Sheyenne River. The Northern Pacific's engineers had been too busy to worry about colorful names and so had marked the site on their maps simply as "Second Crossing," but the inhabitants quickly changed this to Valley City because the town was nestled among a number of rolling hills. Because more than a dozen bridges spanned the meandering Sheyenne, the inhabitants gave their town the nickname "City of Bridges." In its early years, Valley City had most of the characteristics of a frontier community. The rest of the town was a mix of small shops, clapboard homes, a few churches, and unpaved streets. Straus Clothing in Valley City was located on Fifth Avenue, on the ground floor of the Kindred Hotel. Like the Casselton shop, this one was located so that someone disembarking from one of the many trains into town almost had to pass by the door.

However, 1907 was poor time to take on another store. A financial panic, beginning with over speculation in the nation's largest banks, built over the year into a full-fledged depression when banks began hoarding currency and calling in loans to cover their losses. Cash became especially scarce in rural areas. "You couldn't get a five dollar bill or a ten dollar bill at a bank," Herman Stern remembered. "There wasn't any currency available for several months in the fall of 1907. There was in those days the big bonanza farm, the John Dalrymple farm . . . they imported many workers from Norway every year [for the harvest]. And this money panic came just about the time many of these men came in with their checks. And the poor fellows, I still remember some of them, they couldn't get a dime. They couldn't get a bank to give any money to them [for their paychecks]." It took nearly five years for North Dakota agriculture to fully recover from this panic.

So perhaps it was not surprising that, in 1910, sick and worn out from three years of struggle to keep the new store in operation during tough times, M. G. Straus decided to return to Casselton. Herman, having recently obtained his American citizenship, admitted that he had "made a great many mistakes that make me blush," while managing the original store, but was very pleased that Straus was choosing him to take over. He moved to Valley City and set to work. At some point during the year he also returned to Germany and visited his parents and siblings. The only item in Stern's papers attesting to this quick trip is a photograph of him and his parents, with his five brothers and two sisters, taken outside one of his brother's homes. As the twenty-three old Herman smiled toward the camera, his pride of his success in America was only too visible.

At first he had only one assistant in the Valley City store, making it necessary for him to put in sixteen-hour days at the store. He usually had his lunch and dinner in the shop so as not to miss a customer. If a train was due to arrive at the station after the store's normal closing time, he would stay open late: a passenger might need another pair of socks.

He worked endlessly to cut costs. In selecting his stock, Stern followed a rule that Straus had drilled into him: too much inventory was "only to the benefit of your wholesaler . . . that isn't worth anything in our work." A customer entering Stern's store in 1907 would have found a stack of standard black work shirts, "almost the uniform of the working man." Made from suedine, they sold for fifty cents apiece. For more formal wear, there were dress shirts for seventy-nine cents; a Trump shirt, the top-of-the-line dress shirt, cost a dollar. All dress shirts had replaceable linen collars, which sold two for a quarter. An inexpensive tie with a celluloid collar sold for fifteen cents, and a man could get "a pretty good suit of clothes for ten dollars, a good suit of clothes pretty decently made." For the town's leading citizens there was the Kuppenheimer suit, "sixteen to eighteen ounce fabric, a suit you would never wear out." These cost sixteen-fifty. Shoes ranged in price from three to five dollars. You could generally identify a man's economic status from his shoes, because farmers and poorer folk seldom had the money for shoes to wear only for special occasions. Postcards made by itinerant photographers in the early 1900s invariably depict farm families wearing their best Sunday clothes with well-worn shoes.[5]

In 1912, Herman married Adeline Roth, the younger sister of Straus's wife Fredrecka. Stern had known Adeline for some time. Adeline had grown up in Cincinnati, where her father owned a successful business manufacturing shirts. Then in 1904, Mr. Roth fell ill with cancer. Selling his business, he moved with his family to Casselton to live with Fredrecka and Morris Straus. When Roth died within the year, Adeline and her mother remained in Casselton. Then in 1907, Adeline, who was eighteen, accompanied the Strauses to Valley City. While Morris put his new store into shape, Adeline took classes at Valley City Teachers College. From the time she was very young, she had been interested in art, so she took drawing and painting classes, thinking perhaps that she might become an art teacher. But then she had met young Stern.

When Adeline and Herman married on June 4, 1912, the local wedding announcement noted that she wore a family heirloom tulle veil that had been worn by four previous brides in the Roth family. The groom, as befitted his calling, was "faultlessly attired and the handsome couple was much admired by all who saw them. The gifts were elaborate and there were many checks for large amounts." Stern purchased a small house in Valley City for their residence. Their first son, Richard, was born in March 1913.[6]

Marrying Adeline allowed Herman to become part of a family for the first time since leaving Germany nine years before. It was a family, moreover, that had deep roots in both American mainstream culture and American Judaism. The Roth family history in America began in 1853, when Morris Roth emigrated from Germany to Philadelphia. Morris's family was much like the Sterns in that they came from the villages of the Hesse region. Their surname had originally been Bernheim, but since so many of the Jewish families from Hesse had that name, Morris's grandfather Moses decided to change it. Family history has it that Moses had a great shock of red hair and used that for his choice of Roth as the new family name.

Like Herman Stern, Morris Roth was sixteen years old when he left for America. Before he departed, his father, Benjamin, had given him a lengthy letter in which he imparted to his son twenty-four "rules" to follow for a good life. "Consider them," Benjamin Roth wrote, "as a bequest from your father and strive to live according to them as much as you can." Most of these admonitions to Morris were standard fare for the time: to guard carefully his money, but not to the point of jeopardizing his "clean conscience;" to avoid "loose women," "drunkards and ruffians," "slanderers and hypocrites;" avoid also gambling, alcohol and tobacco; practice "self-possession" and try to emulate his mother's "forbearance and endurance throughout the long years of her continuous sufferings and pains."

On the matter of faith, Benjamin urged his son to cling to his heritage: "Never give up the religion which you have inherited from your fathers! Neither money nor seduction, neither splendor nor expectations of honor, neither friendships nor love of a girl should ever influence you to change your religion. You will meet situations and conditions which make it difficult to observe or even prevent you from carrying out some of the ceremonies of our religion, all of which by the way, you should maintain as much as possible . . . keep away from [Christian] missionaries. You possess too little knowledge of our Holy Scriptures, and you could be influenced by their words and fall into error. . . . I was capable [of resisting missionaries of other faiths] since I had a thorough education in the Holy Scriptures when I was young."[7]

In America, Morris went to Milwaukee where he sold notions. Then in 1855, after his brother Solomon joined him, the two men opened a general store in Monroe, Wisconsin. In 1861, Benjamin Roth died in Germany. Morris returned to Germany briefly to settle his father's estate and while there, he also took a bride, a woman named Bertha Mainhardt. Morris then returned to America with Bertha. But instead of going back into the store operation with his brother, he dissolved their partnership and became a tobacco broker for a number of years. After that, he moved his family to Cincinnati where he built and managed a shirt factory. He did well and the family prospered.

The Roth's had four children, the oldest being their daughter

Fredrecka, and the youngest being Adeline. Everyone who knew Fredrecka called her Rickie. It was Rickie who married Morris Straus in 1894, whom she had met through a mutual friend. It was also Rickie who had made the arrangements for her father and mother and Adeline to move to North Dakota in 1903, once Morris Roth learned he had cancer. Herman Stern's sons believe that he had been 'selected' as a prospective husband for Adeline, and if this is true then Rickie was in all probability the person who acted as match-maker.[8]

Herman Stern had lived for nine years in the United States when he married Adeline. But he quickly discovered that the Roths, with almost six decades of experience in America, could teach him still more about American ways. For example, Herman had concentrated so much on his work that he had seldom socialized with other businessmen in Casselton. Now, in Valley City, he became active in a number of community groups, the kinds of organizations that were cornerstones of Midwestern harmony and cohesiveness. Soon after his wedding, for example, Stern became a leader in the local Boy Scouts. He apparently did this at the urging of Adeline, and while his store benefited from the fact that he now began to carry official Scout uniforms, Stern himself was most drawn to the movement because it reminded him of similar groups for young men in his native Germany.

Stern also joined local business groups and clubs, and began helping to raise money for civic improvement programs. He avoided political groups and movements of all kinds, however. He had an almost religious commitment to neutrality in politics. He quietly voted Republican but followed the dictum that a clothier never sold a lot of suits with "active" political opinions. Consequently, while the Non-Partisan populist movement was remaking North Dakota's political landscape between 1915 and 1925, Stern never uttered a public word about the governmental and financial issues that were brewing at that time.[9]

When Stern took over the Valley City store, there were only about four other Jews living in the town, all part of the small family of a traveling salesman. Practicing one's Judaism, or maintaining any Jewish identity at all, was a challenge that Stern would have to face with his own individual resources and resolve.

He worked hard to be considered just one of the members of the business community. But he did not forget his heritage. Nor did Adeline forget hers. Before coming to North Dakota, the Roths had been members of the influential congregation of Rabbi Isaac Wise, one of the most important figures in the Reform Judaism movement. Adeline reflected this in the way she raised her sons. Edward and Richard remember well how both of their parents reminded them of their Judaism. "Mother's father was not very devout," Dick remembered, "but she didn't want us to act just like all the other kids." Their schoolmates put up Christmas trees in December, but in the Stern household there were candles for Hanukah Adeline also refused to serve pork; both boys vividly remember how one summer former president William Howard Taft came to Valley City for a Chautauqua presentation and stayed overnight at Stern's home. "Taft was a big man and he asked for a breakfast of bacon and eggs," noted Ed. "Mom made all the eggs we had, but she wouldn't get any bacon."

Herman and his family did not observe a regular Sabbath. But about once every year, Adeline and Herman took the boys to the Twin Cities for Yom Kippur services at one of the larger synagogues. Ed was never too happy about the trips: "I just sat and fidgeted because I couldn't understand much of the service." When the boys came closer to their tenth birthdays, their parents prevailed upon the Congregational minister in Valley City to spend Saturday mornings teaching them the Old Testament. The boys found the lessons tiresome, and "tried to get out of that whenever we could." Reluctant as they were to sit through the lessons and the services, Herman's sons slowly absorbed something of their heritage.[10]

In all other ways, the Stern boys lived the typical lives of most children growing up in a Midwest town. Born just sixteen months apart, Dick and Ed (whose childhood friends still call him "Eddie") were buddies as well as brothers, the more so because when he was about five Dick became quite ill. Both of the boys had the measles when Dick, running outside in the cold air of the winter, contracted pneumonia. It was severe enough for Adeline to take him and Eddie to California for two months, so Dick could recuperate in the warm sunshine. He recovered, but the pneumonia weakened his lungs for several years. Eddie, although younger, became Dick's self-appointed protector against any bullies in school. The boys also went through most of their schooling together because Eddie did so well in the fourth grade he was advanced to the sixth grade the next year.

For recreation the boys liked to play ball with their friends, fish, swim in the river, and see movies at the Rex Theater (but only at the first-run theater, because the theater for the second-run features was in Herman's view a "disreputable" place). Herman never allowed his sons to hunt, something that most every boy did at that time and place. "Dad had gone on one hunting trip with some of the other men in Valley City. One of the men was careless and misfired his shotgun. That scared Dad to death. He didn't let us go hunting after that." As they grew older, Herman set the two boys to tending the vegetable garden he kept on a plot of ground north of town. "He insisted that we weed it properly and if we didn't he punished us, about the only time our mother didn't hand out the punishments."

They did from time to time "get into a bit of mischief." Ed remembered one time when he and Dick were caught throwing a chunk of ice at the windows of an empty house: "Dad made us pay for that from our savings. We earned money by working at the store. I swept the walk outside and helped with the inventory." On another occasion, Ed admitted that he "pilfered some firecrackers at Carl Olson's store, but I'm sure Carl, if he saw me, never told my dad because they were good friends." Eddie loved fireworks and looked forward to every July 4 celebration, "which began about 5:00 a.m. when the American Legion fired off a Civil War cannon. Then Dick and I would spend the day blowing up milk bottles with firecrackers, which annoyed the neighbors. One time I threw one into the basement of the Lutheran Church. I got into real trouble for that."

Neither Ed nor Dick was old enough in 1914 to remember the

beginning of World War I, but both remembered when America entered the war in 1917. "Mother and Dad spoke German to each other anytime they wanted to talk about something they didn't want us to hear," Ed remembered, "but they never used German in public." Before 1917, the overwhelming view about the war in the upper Midwest was that it was something that the United States should stay out of. When war did come, those same people expressed their patriotism by threatening any German-American in the area who did not buy war bonds or display the American flag. The United States Congress voted overwhelmingly to restrict immigration to the United States by requiring prospective entrants to pass a literacy test. When President Woodrow Wilson refused to sign the bill, Congress passed it over his veto. This was the beginning of a decade of ever more restrictive immigration legislation.[11]

If his sons thought the war an exciting time of patriotic speeches, marches, whistles and sirens, he saw it differently. He knew from letters he received in 1914 and 1915 that his brothers Adolf and Julius were in the German army and that brother Salli was in the Landsturm (reserves). Moses had been at sea when the war began and was now interned in Australia, but was well. At the height of German victories, Adolf had written to tell Herman that "if the British and French once more try to take the offensive, then they will be finished . . . we are unbeatable." But he also admitted that many German men were dying in the battles. A man named Bernard, who had planned to marry his sister Jettchen, had been "killed in action." For months, Jettchen was "crying all day." Many of Herman's old friends had also been killed. All the men in the service sent home what they could from their pay, but prices were rising. Adolf's wife Dora, less confident of the war's outcome than her husband, asked Herman if he could send some money to help them.

Now that America had entered the war, driving a wedge between the land of his birth and the country he had made his home, Herman was unable to receive more letters from Germany. All he could do was wait, and assure his neighbors of his patriotism by contributing to war bond drives and quietly attending local rallies. When the farmers ran short of suitable labor and were faced with trouble at harvest, "the businessmen [in Valley City] banded together and day after day we went out [to help] so the farmer could get his grain threshed." Business was good, on the whole, for the war increased the need for American grain in Europe and elsewhere. Wheat prices in North Dakota rose from sixty-five cents a bushel in 1914 to more than two dollars in 1917. The farmers had more money in their pockets, and they spent it. Business at Herman's Valley City and Casselton stores grew.

The war created one problem that affected the quality of clothing that Stern had to sell. As he recalled years afterward, "the United States chemists had not been able to invent any fast dyes [for coloring clothing]. All our fast dye had come from the Fatherland, directly from Germany. One of our customers would come into the store in those days and ask for a suit of clothes. The quality was terrible, the prices were terrific. In other days you could buy a suit for sixteen dollars and fifty cents . . . but in 1917 it jumped up to seventy-five dollars, and the fabric - well, we wouldn't think of putting anything like that in our store today." Despite this "very, very inferior merchandise," the stores could not help but make money. The Straus business rose more that ten percent in 1917 and another ten percent in 1918.

As the war was drawing to an end, Stern also joined a relief effort to provide food, medicines, and other vital necessities to people in Europe. Many men, women, and children on that war-torn continent were starving by 1918, a result of the war's devastation, coupled with Great Britain's blockade of German trade. In reaction to this, notable Americans had established several groups to collect and send humanitarian aid to Europe. One of these organizations was the American-Jewish Relief Committee. A North Dakota chapter of the Committee was organized in Fargo and Stern agreed to serve on its central board, together with Rabbi Benjamin Papermaster, Alex Stern, and a number of other prominent men in the state. The state committee successfully raised money, which they forwarded to the national headquarters in New York. They would continue to do this good work until the mid-1920s.[12]

By the fall of 1918 Germany was tottering. The allied armies penetrated the final German defense line in France, killing thousands of German soldiers and taking a quarter million more as prisoners. Now they were on the verge of invading Germany itself. In October, large numbers of German sailors mutinied, refusing to put to sea for a final battle against the British fleet. German soldiers began to disobey their officers. As October ended, the chief of the German Generals staff told the Kaiser that defeat was inevitable. Germany *must* ask for an armistice. Wilhelm abdicated a few days later and a new German government was formed to ask the allied powers for terms. On November 11, the war came to an end.

Only now could Stern get more news about his brothers and their families. All his brothers had survived the war, but Germany was prostrate. The people were facing mass starvation from the British naval blockade, which would continue until Germany signed a peace treaty. Germany's economy was ruined, the value of the people's wages evaporating under the heat of inflated prices. Returning soldiers could find only the most menial work. Some joined mercenary units called *Freikorps* and fought either for various factions in a chaotic battle for power or went to other countries and fought for pay.

The Spanish influenza was spreading across Europe, and Germany suffered from it greatly. Thousands, convinced that their civilization was collapsing, embraced pure hedonism. "The German people, starved and dying by the hundred thousand, were reeling deliriously between blank despair, frenzied revelry, and revolution," wrote a Berlin diary of these months. "Berlin had become a nightmare, a carnival of jazz bands and rattling machine guns." Early in 1919, Stern received the sad news that his father had passed away, likely a victim of the flu. His brother Salli, barely home from the front, died a few months later.[13]

As devastating as the flu epidemic was, it was overshadowed by the wreckage of German defeat. In May 1919, the victorious British, French and Americans presented the new German government with the Treaty of Versailles, which contained a clause stating that Germany had started the war, took full responsibility for its destruction, and would pay an unspecified amount of reparations to the winning countries. Germany would also cede territory and reduce its military to a mere 100,000 men who could not be armed with the most modern weapons — aircraft, submarines or tanks. This treaty was not a starting point for negotiations, the Germans were told; they would accept it or the allied troops would invade. The new German chancellor, who had taken over when Kaiser Wilhelm abdicated, refused to accept the ultimatum. He resigned, calling the treaty an instrument for turning the German people into "slaves and helots." His replacement however, knowing that Germany could no longer put up a fight, directed that the treaty be signed and accepted.

Signed it was, but the majority of the German people never accepted it. Nor did millions of them ever really accept the new parliamentary-style government that had, however reluctantly, accepted the treaty. In the words of one historian, the new German constitution became a "document in search of a people" to support it. Almost overnight, large numbers of Germans spoke out in favor of rejecting the commitments of the Versailles Treaty and restoring Germany to its prewar glory. Many of these rabble-rousers ignored the facts behind the chaos and the mutinies and claimed that Germany had not *really* lost the war. Their soldiers, who had been winning in the field, had been betrayed at home – Jews and communists were generally singled out as the traitors. So the argument was made to excuse the defeat.

In the years to come, these rationalizations and prejudices were to be fed by envy. Germany's acculturated Jewish population was to contribute much to the new republican Germany and would benefit from it. Walter Rathenau, a most able man and an acculturated Jew, became the foreign minister and had some success in reducing the war's bitterness between Germany and its neighbors. The new German constitution gave Jews greater freedoms in society and education; they were admitted to universities in greater numbers than ever before, entered the professions more easily and became major figures in a cultural renaissance in the arts, music, and film.[14]

Such successes only further infuriated anti-Semites. Joined by opportunists who saw a chance to ride into power on the back of race hatred, they made Jews into a favorite whipping boy for all those who refused to accept that Germany had lost the war. Three months after the Versailles Treaty was signed, a group calling itself the National Socialist German Workers Party, a fledging organization whose members espoused a vague combination of German nationalism and rabid anti-Semitism, welcomed a new member. He was an ex-soldier who had great ambition, a belief that he was destined to lead Germany back to greatness, and a burning hatred of all that was Jewish. His name was Adolf Hitler.[15]

Notes

1. Here and below, Herman Stern, interview by Duane Crawford, March 21, 1971, interview tape contained in the Herman Stern Papers, Elwyn B. Robinson Department of Special Collections, Chester Fritz Library, University of North Dakota (hereafter Stern Papers). Also Edward Stern, interview with Shoptaugh, October 1993, Oral History Collection, Northwest Minnesota History Center, Minnesota State University Moorhead, supplemented by notes made by Herman Stern in 1979 for his son Edward. Edward later transcribed these notes and shared them with the author. Named "Hermann," Stern Americanized the spelling of his name in 1903, and this form is used throughout this narrative.

2. Herman Stern interview by Duane Crawford, Stern Papers, supplemented by an interview with Al Thal, June 1, 1974, transcript copy at the Barnes County Historical Museum, Valley City, ND. Stern wrote a slightly different version of this story in about 1976, in notes he made for a group compiling a history of Judaism on the Great Plains. In these notes he wrote that after Kaufman refused to release him, "I decided to go without permission, made quietly preparations to go after receiving the fare from cousin Morris to bring me to New York. Because of the shortness of time I was not able to go to Oberbrechen to bid my parents & family goodbye." These undated notes are in the Jewish Historical Project file, Box 15, Stern Papers.

3. Stern-Thal transcript, p. 3, and Edward Stern Interview, pp. 4-5, 10; Obituary of Herman Stern, Fargo Forum, June 22, 1980. Background on Straus comes from an undated pamphlet, "Straus of North Dakota," published around 1979 when Straus Clothing celebrated its 100th anniversary. The pamphlet was prepared with the assistance of Herman Stern, then 90 years of age. A copy of the pamphlet is in the collections of the Clay County [Minnesota] Historical Society. In a newspaper article in 1975, Stern also said he "ran away" from his apprenticeship in Mainz: "Stern: A Life of Satisfaction," Fargo *Forum*, April 27, 1975. At the time Straus opened his store in 1879, Casselton was part of Dakota Territory; ten years later, the Territory was divided into the states of North and South Dakota.

4. Herman Stern, transcript of a 1968 speech made at a marketing seminar in Fargo, Marketing Seminar file, Box 12, Stern Papers.

5. Stern-Thal transcript, p. 3, and Stern, marketing seminar transcript. The Valley City store was originally Sternberg Clothing, owned by Adolf Sternberg, whose wife was Fredrecka Straus' aunt. When Sternberg died in 1907, Straus bought the store. On the bonanza farms and their impact, see Hiram Drache, *The Day of the Bonanza* (Fargo: North Dakota Institute for Regional Studies, 1964).

6. "Roth Family History," prepared by Adeline Roth Stern in the 1960s, copy given to author by Edward Stern; Obituary of Morris Roth, [1905], and Stern wedding, June 7, 1912, clippings from *Casselton Reporter* in Stern family scrapbook. A pamphlet history of Straus Clothing, prepared in the 1980s, suggests that one of the reasons Morris Straus went to Germany and recruited Herman Stern was the hope that he would be "a prospective suitor for Mrs. Straus' young sister Adeline." Adeline Roth was still living with her parents in Cincinnati when Straus went to Germany, but since her father was by then quite ill, it may be that Straus anticipated his in-laws would soon be living in North Dakota.

7. Here and below, "Roth Family History," and letter of Benjamin Moses Roth to his son Morris Roth, 1853. Italics have been added for emphasis. Morris received a similar letter from his mother, Lena Bickart Roth, who counseled, "certainly nobody thinks highly of somebody who does not keep his faith." Both letters, in translation, are in the Stern scrapbook.

8. The Roth Family History notes that Straus chose Casselton for his store on the advice of another Roth relative, the half-sister of Fredrecka's mother. This half-sister was the wife of Adolph Sternberg, yet another immigrant from Hesse. Sternberg's son was the owner of the clothing store in Valley City that Straus purchased on the death of Sternberg in 1907. The elaborate family connection in all this underscores the importance that American Jews often placed on family in both social and business matters.

9. Edward Stern interview, p. 17. On Stern's interest in Scouting and local civic groups, see numerous comments in *Barnes County History* (Dallas: Taylor Publishing Co., 1976).

10. Edward and Richard Stern, videotaped interview with Wes Anderson, July 24, 2004, Barnes County Museum, and Edward Stern interview, pp. 11-12. Richard incidentally remembers that Herman had some knowledge of Hebrew. He also remembered only one occasion when someone at school made a "derogatory remark" to him about being Jewish. Edward remembers no incidents of anti-Semitism.

11. Bruce Larson, *Lindbergh of Minnesota: A Political Biography* (New York: Harcourt Brace Jovanovich, 1973) nicely summarizes the region's reluctance to become involved in the war; Joel Watne, "Tolerance and Conformity: The Fargo-Moorhead Area in the First World War," (MA thesis, Moorhead State College, 1967) describes several persecutions of German-Americans during the war.

12. Adolf and Dora Stern to Herman Stern, November 21, 1914 and April 10, 1915, Adolf Stern file, Box 9, Stern Papers (unless stated otherwise, all further documents from the Stern Papers are found in Box 9). See also Herman Stern transcript 1968 marketing seminar speech, Marketing Seminar file, Stern Papers; Papermaster, "Reminiscences," p. 26.

13. Otto Friedrich, *Before the Deluge* (New York: Harper and Row, 1972), esp. pp. 55-56.

14. Walter Laqueur, *Weimar: A Cultural History* (New York: Putnam and Sons, 1974), esp. pp. 72-77. The acculturated Rathenau was murdered in 1922 by a cadre of ex-soldiers, for what they called his "Jew crimes" against Germany.

15. Richard Watt, *The Kings Depart* (New York: Simon and Schuster, 1969), pp. 309-314; Klaus Fischer, *Nazi Germany: A New History* (New York: Barnes and Noble, 1998), pp. 54-65, 115-23.

Chapter Two
"Be More Than Tolerant"

By 1920 Stern was becoming well known in North Dakota business circles, and in Valley City as a businessman who was a booster for the community. He was also a leader in the Boy Scout movement. He had come far since he got off that train in Casselton in 1903. Still a fairly quiet and self-contained person, Stern did not socialize much with other businessmen. Adeline belonged to several women's groups in Valley City and so became better known in the community, while Stern was seen as someone who "dedicated himself to his business." He went to lunch with other merchants when they discussed ideas to improve the community and was always willing to make suggestions or help out. Away from work he usually kept to himself, spending evenings at home with his family. Several of the merchants who knew him for decades commented that he seldom really relaxed and almost never drank alcohol. One man remembered that, as Stern became active in the local Rotary group, he would invite new Rotary members to his home for an evening and serve hors d'oeuvres made by Adeline, and "even serve a glass of wine." But he almost never drank himself. Another recalled one occasion when one of Stern's fellow merchants was celebrating improvements to his store. "They talked Herman Stern into taking a drink. Herman said, 'I never, I don't drink. But I will take one in honor of Al.' He did, and he held a drink toasting Al. He took one little tiny sip, set it down, and never took any more, because he really didn't drink at all."[1]

Anyone who knew him well knew that he had many relatives back in Germany and that he still kept in close touch with his brothers. They also knew that he was Jewish and that he was not very active in his faith. In fact, he was not well known within the Jewish community of the state. There were three very active Jewish communities within a few hours drive of Valley City. There was a small but close-knit Jewish community in Devils Lake, a larger and thriving one with its own synagogue in Grand Forks and a third community, which was less cohesive, in Fargo. The Sterns apparently never attended worship at any of these closer sites, yet they would drive to Minneapolis for the annual High Holidays. As Eddie Stern remembered about the closer North Dakota communities, "we didn't know much about them."

This was ironic, because when Stern turned his energies to helping German refugees escape from the National Socialists in the 1930s, he found these Jewish communities to be among his firmest and most helpful allies. For this reason, it is important to look at the development of these communities in some detail.

When Jewish settlers first entered the Dakota Territory in the 1880s, they were confronted by a raw, enormous frontier. In 1882, about ten immigrant families, of Russian and Romanian origin, aided by a loan from the Hebrew Emigrant Aid Society, established the Painted Woods farming colony north of Bismarck. Bad luck, drought and debt plagued the colony, forcing most of the colonists to leave by the end of the decade. Some of them moved to a second colony of Jewish farmers that had gathered near Devils Lake a few months after the Painted Woods colony dissolved. Conditions at Devils Lake were hard, too. A young woman who came to Devils Lake in 1894 was shocked by the hard-scrabble appearance of other girls she met: "They wore men's shoes and a rough looking garment. Only common peasants wore such clothes in Russia. I was dismayed to see such attire worn by Jewish women. It was indecent. Poor as I had been all my life, I had always worn a dress like any self-respecting Jewish woman."[2]

As might be expected, these settlers found it very difficult in such circumstances to maintain all their traditions. The harvest season in Dakota interfered with Sabbath traditions, as one daughter of an early settler remembered: "there were [only] just so many days for sowing and reaping and harvesting before the first frost took over. Most of the Jewish farmers asked God's indulgence and continued working feverishly seven days a week." A farmer's income was so unstable in the 1880s and 1890s that many Jewish homesteaders could not afford candles for the Sabbath. Only a handful could find the funds necessary to build a proper ritual bath. The climate sometimes made it difficult for fathers to quit working on the Sabbath and provide their sons with regular instruction in Hebrew and Jewish Law. Likewise, distances between homes made it very difficult to gather enough men for a minyan. One man, who traveled eighteen miles in sub-zero weather in order to make up a sufficient number for his nephew's bris, suffered severe frostbite and lost part of each foot.[3]

Until 1891, there were no rabbis in North Dakota. The small settlements and individual families had to rely on brief visits from rabbis, *schochets* and *mohels* from St. Paul or Minneapolis for most ceremonies. The first permanent rabbi was Benjamin Papermaster, a native of Lithuania, who had received his Judaic education at the renowned Yeshiva in Kovno. After receiving his *Kabalah* in 1890, Papermaster was persuaded by his mentor at Kovno to leave Europe for America, "to serve a community completely as a teacher, schochet, mohel, cantor, etc." He agreed, largely because he knew that by taking his sons to America he could save them from Russian military service. Arriving in New York in January 1891, Papermaster learned that he would go on to Fargo, North Dakota, and became rabbi for the nascent Jewish community there.

But when he reached Fargo, Papermaster discovered "not even a semblance of a Jewish community in Fargo." Almost all of the fifteen or so Jewish families in Fargo were of German background, and were, in Papermaster's view, little interested in "proper Judaism." They seldom conducted essential ceremonies: "It was with the greatest difficulty that a minion was gathered for a yahrzeit." Papermaster decided he must return to New York and look elsewhere, but before he left he met with Alexander Stern (not related to the family of Herman Stern), who had moved to Fargo in 1880 and opened a clothing store. Alexander Stern suggested that Papermaster take a look at Grand Forks, north of Fargo, before leaving. There were some sixty Jewish families there, Stern said, many of them Ukrainians, and they had been asking for a rabbi for some time. Perhaps the people in

New York had meant to tell him of that town instead of Fargo? Papermaster agreed to visit Grand Forks and see the situation for himself.

In Grand Forks, the young rabbi met Benjamin Greenburg, former justice of the peace at the Devils Lake colony. Greenburg introduced Papermaster to several other Jewish men in the community and after several discussions with them Papermaster decided to stay. He realized the challenges were formidable – he barely understood the Yiddish or Hebrew of many of the residents and worried about being the "only Lithuanian in a community of Russians." But he agreed to give it a try and promised that he would "adjust himself to their ways and practices as was consistent with his knowledge, training and views."[4]

The match worked, partly because soon after taking the post, Papermaster learned that his wife, back in Lithuania, had died while he was in New York. In 1892, he married Chaya Levonton, his brother's sister-in-law, after she and his four sons made their way to America. Over the next few years, he was able to persuade a number of other relatives to cross the Atlantic and make their new homes in Grand Forks. Papermaster was instrumental in helping to buy land for a proper Jewish cemetery outside the town, helped establish a Hebrew school, naming it the Talmud Torah School, and organized the synagogue, which was later named Temple B'nai Israel. In addition, he traveled frequently to provide services for Jewish families across the length of the state, so frequently that he knew many of the conductors on the Great Northern Railroad by their first names.

As the years went by the rabbi (who actually preferred the title "reverend" because it was "American") was a decisive force in holding the congregation together. He said that while he inclined toward the "liberal views of the house of Hillel in America," he rejected most of the Reform movement's tenets because he believed that these violated the *Shulchon Ahruch*, a long-used compilation of 613 'rules' of Jewish faith that he had carefully studied in Kovno and brought with him to America.

In dealing with doctrinal disputes, Papermaster relied increasingly on pragmatism. When one of his congregation died and the family wanted the man buried in a business suit rather that the traditional white shroud, the cemetery committee would not grant permission to have the man buried in the consecrated ground. Papermaster helped the family buy land adjacent to the cemetery and summoned a Reform rabbi from St. Paul to conduct the service. On another occasion when one of his conservative members rebuked him for not checking carefully to see that everyone maintained a kosher home, Papermaster drew on American traditions and replied "the Lord did not send me to Grand Forks to spy on members to make sure that they did not mix meat with milk. People must remember that this is a free country and what they do in their kitchens is their business." The rabbi also decided to refuse a salary from the congregation and live off fees for his services, so as to "preserve his freedom" to do what he thought best to hold the Jewish community together. With only a few exceptions, he succeeded.[5]

In Devils Lake, a sense of community was easier to maintain, partly because many of the Jews who settled there were related. The family of Herman Shark was a good example. Born in a Jewish village in Lithuania in about 1875, Shark immigrated to the United States in 1900, largely because he wanted to escape from Russian persecution. Making his way to St. Paul, he worked at a number of odd jobs – delivery driver, furniture sales, whiskey sales – before he met and married May Glickson, another Lithuanian immigrant. Since May had a brother who owned a men's clothing business in Devils Lake, North Dakota, the couple moved there and Herman went to work in his brother-in-law's store. After some years of working and saving his money, Shark opened his own business. For help, he employed a man who wanted to marry one of May's sisters. "He lived with my parents," Shark's son recalled. "After he had saved up enough money to get married, they got married and then he opened his own store," also in Devils Lake. Thus all three of the major clothing stores in the town were tied to one family. "These families who came over from Europe . . . for security, they stuck together very, very close, extremely close."[6]

Family ties helped weld Jews in Devils Lake into a small, fairly

Orthodox congregation. For years, they worshiped in one of the county buildings. "They held the High Holiday services in the district courtroom, and the judge would never call a term of court until he first called up one of the Jewish men to find out when the High Holidays were," remembers Shark's son. "They would take over the courthouse and bring the Torah scrolls in for Rosh Hashanah, and then for the intervening week they would have the room locked up. They would leave the scrolls there and keep the key, and then they would have the room for Yom Kippur. After Yom Kippur, they could use it again for court." This continued even after a rabbi (who also acted as *schochet*) was hired to serve the community.[7]

Fargo's situation was a bit different. Most of the early Jewish settlers in Fargo were men like Alex Stern — of German background, proprietors of their own businesses. About twenty years after the town was founded in 1871, Jews from Poland, Lithuania, and other eastern European states began to settle in Fargo. Many of these families had been part of the agrarian colonies and had migrated to Fargo in search of work. According to a study of early Jewish history in Fargo, these men and women, for the most part, found poorly paying laboring jobs, which placed them well below the economic level of the Jewish storekeepers who had established a niche in Fargo's business elite. They lived mostly in small shacks on Front Street, near the banks of the Red River. Firmly Orthodox, they established the Fargo Hebrew Congregation in 1896 and bought a small plot of land on the north edge of town for a consecrated cemetery.

Descendents of some of the earliest members of the congregation told interviewers: "the German Jews did not become involved in religious affairs [at the Fargo Hebrew Congregation], with the exception of attendance at High Holiday services." This was partly due to the fact that few of the German Jews knew any Yiddish, the language used for the services.

Max Goldberg, a Fargo grain trader at the turn of the 20th century, told his grandson that, even though he was Lithuanian in origin, he was put off by the Orthodox worship: "to be an observant Orthodox Jew, you are to have prayer in the synagogue on the Sabbath. If it is

35 below zero and you live two miles from the synagogue, it doesn't make a lot of sense. It makes no sense if you live[d] in Prairiewood or West Fargo to walk five miles to synagogue. . . . if we were going to have a Jewish community in Fargo that was going to survive in this era of the twentieth century, Orthodoxy simply would be a much more difficult path to trod." Embedded in this statement was the fact that the original Jewish settlers in Fargo, and the synagogue they had built, had ended up in a small, relatively poor area near the river, while successful men like Goldberg and Alexander Stern by 1910 were living in better homes on Fargo's east or south side. Goldberg and several others thus had limited contact with the Hebrew Congregation.[8]

Thus, three Jewish communities in North Dakota, one cohesive and Orthodox community, another that was divided between those who were Orthodox and those who thought Orthodoxy primitive, and a third that did not always agree on doctrine but maintained harmony with strong leadership. These three communities pretty much mirrored the situation of American Judaism around 1900. Before 1850, most Jews living in the United States were either recent immigrants from one of the German states or descendants of German Jews. Judaic practices, as a result, tended to reflect Judaism as it was practiced in Germany.

German Judaism had by no means been a unified monolith. Just as there were many German states before 1871 there were also differences in doctrine and ritual. In Jewish communities where influence of the eastern European yeshivas was strong, Orthodox practices remained strong. In other areas, especially those parts of Germany where the ideas of the Enlightenment and the Rights of Man had had great impact, practices began to change. By the 1840s, as one authority has noted, "almost all German Jews gave up the Yiddish language without any regrets. . . . But were the kosher food laws, which created a certain distance between Jews and non-Jews, still relevant? Should Jewish worship be westernized so as to appear less exotic and 'oriental' to the contemporary Christian and acculturated Jew? Did the belief in the messianic ingathering of the Jewish people retain its validity?" Jewish thinkers and community leaders debated these questions, giving rise to a reform movement that German Jews who crossed the Atlantic to America carried with them as part of their cultural baggage.[9]

As these new arrivals spread across the United States, tripling the American Jewish population between 1850 and 1860, the reform ideas they brought with them began to have a powerful impact on Judaism in the United States. Congregations that had already begun to experiment with different forms of worship made further changes, while traditional congregations began to permit women to leave the galleries and side-benches and join the men in worship. These transitions did not always occur smoothly; there were many disputes, many arguments, and a number of schisms. In one extreme case, in Portland, Oregon, in the 1870s, a rabbi who wanted to replace the venerable *Minhag Ashkenaz* (German Jewish prayer book) became so angry toward those who opposed his plan that he tried to shoot one of them.[10]

Most disputes did not degenerate into such violence. But they were emotional enough, and moreover frequently were intensified by the greater freedoms that America offered to those who migrated from Europe. As Naomi Cohen explains in her groundbreaking work on the development of Reform in America, "German Jews in the United States consciously and sometimes painfully recognized the religious differences that set them apart from fellow Americans." Confronted with such mundane matters as being prevented by local laws from working on Sunday or inviting Gentile neighbors to dinner without violating dietary laws, Jews in America asked themselves how far could a Jew take on the trappings of American culture before he no longer was a Jew?[11]

One person who tried to answer this question was Isaac Mayer Wise, the rabbi whose congregation the Roth family had attended when they lived in Cincinnati. Born in Germany, extremely well educated, both in rabbinical studies and the literature of the Enlightenment, Wise came to America and began to advocate many of the reform ideas he had absorbed in Europe. He drafted a prayer book to replace the *Minhag Ashkanaz,* calling it the *Minhag America* and publishing it in German, Hebrew and English. He also published a journal, the *Israelite,* in which he urged rabbis to recognize "whatever makes us [Jews] ridiculous before the world" and discard it. He urged congregations to use English in their worship, helped create the Union of American Hebrew Congregations, and then in 1875 played a major role in founding Hebrew Union College in Cincinnati, "for the training of teachers, ministers, and rabbis" in ideas that would help American Jews recognize the "affinity between Judaism and Americanism."[12]

The American commitment to the separation of church and state gave impetus to the urgings of Wise and others. Separation allowed immigrants the opportunity to enter into American society as individuals, rather than as part of a communal group. Jews follow their own inclinations. As one eager young immigrant put it, "Everyone can choose freely whether or in which synagogue he wants to be enrolled." Remarks like this worried Jewish traditionalists who feared the seductions of a fast-growing and wide open nation would lure Jews away from their faith altogether. As one east coast elder complained: "a [Jewish] youth would rather not be recognized as a Jew, and never thinks of visiting a Synagogue." While this was not universally true, Jews who made up the second and third generation in America did show a growing tendency to discard customs that had made their faith a palpable part of their daily lives.[13]

There was anti-Semitism in the United States. Popular images of Jews, as expressed in newspapers, magazine articles, fiction and drama, contained a goodly share of stereotypes of Jews as greedy, scheming, and manipulative. Certain Protestant churches in America launched organized efforts from the 1860s on to convert Jews to Christianity. Their success in these undertakings was limited. Forms of "social anti-Semitism" were pervasive. Jews were excluded from many clubs and organizations and many of the highest ranks of business and government were not really open to them. As Herman Shark's family discovered, they might be denied, by formal or informal methods, the right to live in some neighborhoods.

But the extent of these discriminations was relatively limited compared to most other places. The American press also regularly portrayed Jews as hard working, energetic, successful, and good citizens. As an editorial writer noted in the *Washington Sentinel* in 1854, "the liberal institutions of this favored land induce many [Jews] to live among us. The Jew here has the same privileges, social, religious, and political, that any other class enjoys. . . . All the professions that ambition delights in, all the pursuits that the love of gain inclines to, are open to the Jew as to any other man."

In America there were no organized pogroms against Jews, no government actions to restrict their political or religious rights under the Constitution, almost no overt violence against temples, Jewish societies or large Jewish communities. No political parties existed with anti-Semitism as a cornerstone of their principles. No organized efforts were made to drive them from the nation. In short, many of the kinds of threats that Jews had known in other lands did not really exist in America, and so did not promote a compelling need for a strong Jewish unity. Jewish immigrants, both Orthodox and Reform, generally agreed that their freedoms and opportunities for a good life were unparalleled in the United States. Agreeing on this, they had the safety and freedom to disagree among themselves as to what to retain from their traditions and what to eliminate.[14]

There was another, less happy, aspect of pluralistic Judaism in the United States. Throughout their short national existence, Americans had shown strong streaks of a nativism that could turn ugly in a heartbeat, manifesting in periodic waves of anti-foreign or anti-ethnic prejudice. In the 1700s the good Puritan townsmen of Boston had celebrated an event they called "Pope Day" by beating one another's heads in to capture an effigy of the pope that they could then burn while howling anti-Catholic imprecations. In the 1850s a political party briefly gained national influence by campaigning for stricter immigration laws to slow the influx of Germans and Irish.

In the 1870s a number of candidates for office pandered for votes by denouncing "strangers in the land." The second half of the 19th century witnessed an outpouring of textbooks that had been designed to impel students, especially young immigrants, to discard their ethnicity and embrace "American" ways. Immigrant students were punished during this era for speaking their native languages in class and rewarded for successfully memorizing poems and speeches that celebrated the Anglo-Saxon past of the young nation.

None of these latter actions had specifically targeted Jews. Rather, suspicions of Jews reflected something less coherent, an unsettling element in the American psyche, a dark suspicion of "outsiders" who simply seemed too "different" for a people of western European, Christian roots to feel as trustworthy. Those who harbored these kinds of fears probably took some comfort in the 1885 platform statement of the American Reform rabbis, which avowed: "we consider ourselves no longer a nation, but a religious community and therefore expect neither a return to Palestine . . . nor the restoration of any of the laws concerning the Jewish state." Here was a promise that Jews had no "Rome," no Masonic hall, no home country that could demand from them a divided loyalty.[15]

In turn, this paranoid aspect of American life frightened Jews, some of them leaders of prominent Jewish organizations, some Orthodox and some Reform, who worried about latent American hostility toward the "outsiders." Thus, more Jewish leaders counseled American Jews to be an active part of the towns and cities in which they lived. In a special report on the role of the rabbi, for example, the Central Council of American Rabbis urged Jews to remember: "In our American life the rabbi is a citizen of his community as well as the spiritual head of his congregation. . . . it should be his pleasure as well as his duty to represent his congregation in the various charitable, municipal and social activities that interest the community at large. His congregation expects this, for he must not only be in the world but of it." How much such implicit promises that Jews were loyal to their greater American communities may have quelled the fears of nascent anti-Semites is uncertain.[16]

These fears – of Americans toward those who were different, of

Jews that their neighbors might suddenly turn hostile, as so many neighbors had done for centuries – carried into the 20th century. When, after the Great War of 1914-1918, a disillusioned America recoiled from the rest of the world, including the world's immigrants who sought entry into the country, American Jews began to detect signs of growing anti-Semitism in the United States, they worried that, once again, they might be accused of being part of some "Jewish conspiracy."

And when a terrible wave of anti-Semitism erupted in war-torn Europe after 1918 and grew worse in the years following, fear, with prejudice and uncertainty as its consorts, hobbled the ability of all Americans, Jewish and Gentile, to meet the crisis.

Herman Stern took his family to High Holiday services in Minneapolis. He had little to do with the active Jewish communities in Devils Lake, Grand Forks, and Fargo, where the majority of active worshipers were more Russian in culture and more Orthodox in practice. This had been reinforced by his marriage to Adeline Roth, whose own Reform ties to the Cincinnati congregation of Isaac Mayer Wise would have made it difficult, if not impossible, for her to begin attending Orthodox services.

Had the Reform movement not existed in America, would Stern have abandoned Judaism altogether? Given his upbringing in Germany and insistence on having his sons learn about the faith, that seems very unlikely. There were others who did so. An authority on American Jewish life in small-town America has noted that Jews who lived in small towns with overwhelming Gentile culture often did become ambivalent about their faith, leading sometimes to outright rejection of it. Others often took a sort of "Be quiet! Don't call attention to us" approach, particularly if signs of anti-Semitism existed in the Gentile community. The third most frequent response in towns like Valley City was the "ambassadors to the *goyim*" approach — working to convince one's neighbors that Jews were good citizens. It is quite easy to recognize Stern in this last role, what with his leadership in many community groups, his role in establishing the

Greater North Dakota Association, his work in scouting, and so on.[17]

As a businessman, Stern preferred finding straightforward solutions to problems. Others could debate finer points of doctrine or argue about purity of faith or worry about who belonged in which group and why and how. Like many immigrants, Stern lived his life with his heart in two different places. He had his life and friends and family in America, and there were those he had left behind in Germany. As the months followed the end of the Great War, and as he heard from his brothers and read the news about the collapse of the Imperial order – about the strikes, the influenza and the food riots, about the Spartacist revolt crushed by *Freikorps* brutality, about the creation of a republican government that was founded mainly on exhaustion and the desire for peace - he felt the tug of his old homeland, the need to get over there and check on his family.

He thought also about the meaning of conflict and community. At some point in the 1920s, Stern began writing a little pamphlet that he later printed with the title "Good Rules to Achieve Pride of Accomplishment" and gave to members of the Boy Scout organizations he worked with and to every person who came to work for him. The rules were in large part about how someone succeeded in business, in particular sales: to be organized, be enthusiastic, resourceful, look good and be confident. But they also addressed the issues of character and how one should fit into his community. Some of what he wrote was derived in part from the advice that Benjamin Roth had given to his son back in 1853 (which had come into the possession of Adeline on her father's death). Old Roth had advised Morris to be industrious, practice "self possession, honor his faith, keep his humility and avoid vices."

Stern, in similar language, admonished his readers to work hard, keep learning and "constantly strive to better yourself," be "humble in the eyes of God," and remember character was based on learning and "the early cultivations of religious training and reverence to God" (adding to this a quote from Abraham Lincoln). In his last rule, Stern wrote "be more than tolerant, be understanding. In dealing with people, learn to respect and understand their position. Judge an individual not on his race, creed, or economic standing; judge him for what he is." In the coming years, Stern would show just how far he was willing go in obeying this principle.[18]

Stern realized that he would never understand all that was going on in postwar Germany simply by reading the news or getting letters from his brothers. He decided that as soon as he could square away some of his obligations at home, he must return to Germany and see what was happening for himself.

Notes

1. K. B. Cummings, interview with Michael Morrissey, July 16, 1999, transcript, p. 4; Roy Sheppard, interview with Michael Morrissey, August 5, 1999, transcript, pp. 7, 12-13.

2. *Rachel Calof's Story: Jewish Homesteader on the Northern Plains,* ed. by J. Sanford Rikoon. (Bloomington: Indiana University Press, 1995) p. 22. This edition of Rachel Calof's memoir also contains Rikoon's essay "Jewish Farm Settlement's in America's Heartland," with valuable detail on the North Dakota Jewish colonies.

3. Jason Zevenbergen, "Establishing a Jewish Community: A Study of Jewish Immigrant Homesteaders in North Dakota, 1880-1920," ms. In the Merrifield Competition Papers, Elwyn B. Robinson Department of Special Collections, Chester Fritz Library, University of North Dakota.

4. Benjamin Papermaster's experiences as recoded by his son in the "Reminiscences of Rabbi Isadore Papermaster" (ca. 1950), typescript copy in rare book collection of the Grand Forks Public Library.

5. Papermaster, "Reminiscences." From frequent remarks in this manuscript, it is evident that Benjamin Papermaster told his son Isadore several times that he was pleased that his congregation had only a small minority of German Jews among its members, apparently because he feared their Reform inclinations could eventually break up the Temple. Yet, a year before his death in 1934, Benjamin also remarked that after dealing with several Reform rabbis he thought "Reform Judaism may exert a better influence on Jewish life in this country than I formerly believed."

6. Myer Shark, interview with Shoptaugh, June 8, 1999, transcript, pp. 1-5.

7. Jewish relations with the rest of the Devils Lake residents were generally good. Myer Shark remembers two incidents in his childhood, one where a neighbor complained to his father that he did not want Myer chatting with his daughter, and an incident when his family bought lots on which to build a house, and one of the other residents did not want Jews for neighbors; Shark transcript, pp. 12-16.

8. Robert J. Lazar, "From Ethnic Minority to Socio-Economic Elite: A Study of the Jewish Community of Fargo, North Dakota" (PhD thesis, University of Minnesota, 1968), pp. 68-78; Robert Feder, interview with Mathias Geiger, October 26, 1990, OHC-NMHC; *Temple Beth El, Fargo, North Dakota: The First Fifty Years, 1942-1992* (np. 1992), pp. 7-8.

9. Robert M. Seltzer, *Jewish People, Jewish Thought: The Jewish Experience in History* (New York: Macmillan Publishing Co., 1980), pp. 544-545. Exactly where the line lies between "acculturation" (the adoption and acceptance of many values and practices from the dominant culture) and "assimilation" (the discarding of a traditional culture, potentially including its religion, for the dominant culture of the host nation) is a subject of enormous scholarly debate. But the issue of how far Jews could accept American culture without losing their "Jewishness" was a matter of practical concern, and intense debate, among American Jews in the late 1800s and early 1900s.

10. I. Harold Sharfman, *The First Rabbi: Origins of Conflict Between Orthodox and Reform, Jewish Polemic Warfare in Pre-Civil War America* (1988), pp. 427-30.

11. Naomi W. Cohen, *Encounter with Emancipation: The German Jews in the United States, 1830-1914* (Philadelphia: Jewish Publication Society of America,1984), pp. 162-163

12. James G. Heller, *Isaac M. Wise: His Life, Work and Thought* (New York: The Union of Hebrew Congregations, 1965). pp. 303-06, 564-66; Jacob R. Marcus, "The Americanization of Isaac Mayer Wise," 1931 address reprinted in Marcus, *Studies in American Jewish History* (Cincinnati: Hebrew Union College Press, 1969), pp. 180-94; Cohen, *Encounter With Emanicipation,* p. 171.

13. Naomi W. Cohen, Jews *in Christian America: The Pursuit of Religious Equality* (New York: Oxford University Press, 1992), p. 45-46; Howard M. Sachar, *A History of Jews in America* (New York: Alfred A. Knopf, 1992), p. 104.

14. Louise A. Mayo, *The Ambivalent Image* (Rutherford, NJ: Farleigh Dickinson University Press, 1988) is a comprehensive study of how Jews were portrayed in 19th century American literature and press. See also "The Jews, As Citizens," *Washington Sentinel,* May 21, 1854, reprinted in Morris U. Schappes, ed., *A Documentary History of the Jews in the United States, 1654-1875* (New York, Schoken Books, 1971), pp. 342-344. The only official act ever taken specifically against Jews by the Federal government occurred in 1862, when General Ulysses S. Grant issued a military order banning Jews from his district during the Civil War. President Abraham Lincoln immediately had the order rescinded.

15. Ray A. Billington, *The Protestant Crusade* (Chicago: Quadrangle Books ed., 1964), pp. 18-19; John Higham, *Strangers in the Land* (New Brunswick NJ: Rutgers University Press, 1955), pp. 35ff.; Cohen, *Encounter with Emancipation*, pp. 167-68.

16. Cohen, *Encounter with Emancipation*, pp. 193-94.

17. Ewa Morawska, *Insecure Prosperity: Small Town Jews in Industrial America, 1890-1940* (Princeton, NJ: Princeton University Press, 1996), esp. pp. 216ff.

18. Herman Stern, "Good Rules to Achieve Pride of Accomplishment," [np., nd] numerous copies in Stern Papers.

Chapter Three
Early Appeals for Help

B rief notes on a photograph indicate that Stern made a brief trip to Germany in 1920. He probably arrived during the last months of the great world-wide influenza epidemic and perhaps that was the reason why the visit was rather short. But the main reason no doubt was the pressure of the business. Morris Straus's health had been slowly failing since he moved back to Casselton in 1910. In 1913 he had decided to give Stern the title of "Vice-president of Straus Clothing." Stern's primary job was still to run the Valley City store, but as vice-president he began making more decisions for both stores. For example, he suggested to Straus that they should prominently display their "One Price to All" policy. So signs in English, Norwegian, and German were placed in the stores and in the local ads assuring customers "they could expect honest pricing, equal treatment, and no 'free' neckties that had been previously built into an inflated price."

Stern also took over the buying trips to Chicago. After the World War, as economic changes in the country decreased the importance of salesmen who had come to the store, Stern began traveling to New York to select suits and other items for the stores. For his own part, Straus cut back on the time he spent at the business. Early in 1920, he decided to retire. He offered Stern a chance to buy into the ownership of Straus Clothing and take over management of the entire operation.[1]

Stern could not let this opportunity pass. A more leisurely visit to Germany would have to wait. He took some of his savings, bought a half-interest in both the Valley City and Casselton shops, and agreed to a partnership agreement in which he would manage the stores and split the profits with Straus. Satisfied with the details, Straus and his wife sold their Casselton home and moved to California. For his part,

Stern sold his home in Valley City and moved into a new home built for him on the corner of 7th and Helena Streets, just two blocks north of the downtown business. Stern walked home for lunch when he had the time. The new home was large: two full stories, a full basement and a sizeable attic space. Much of the yard was devoted to flower gardens. Adeline used the flowers in art projects and to decorate the house, while Herman was reminded of his childhood in Germany when he would wander the woods picking wild flowers. He continued to put in long hours at the shop and traveled frequently to Casselton to check on business there. He also began making plans for two new stores in Lamoure and Carrington, to open later in the 1920s.[2]

Finally, after seeing to every detail in the new partnership, Stern went to New York. On January 14, 1922, he boarded the *SS Hudson*, a liner of the old Hamburg-American ship line. The fourth day out, the ship ran into storms that continued, with increasing intensity, for six days. "It is not an altogether pleasant sensation to be thrown from one corner of your cabin to another," he later recalled of the voyage. The storms finally subsided and, after a brief stop in Ireland, the *Hudson* sailed into Bremerhaven.

Prior to this, Stern had made only one other trip home, in 1910. Now, when he arrived in Germany, he found much that had changed in the twelve intervening years. Moses, the oldest brother, was now living with his mother and his sister in Oberbrechen, where he farmed the family land. Adolf, just a year younger than Moses, now lived in Duisburg. He had returned from the German army to his old occupation as a cattle trader, in business with his brothers-in-law, Fritz and Salli Kann. Herman's sister Jettchen was about to marry a man named Hugo Henlein, who also dealt in cattle. Julius and Gustav, the remaining brothers, were making ends meet as well.

Stern visited all of them. His mother spent most of her time "thinking of the past" and chided Herman to write more often. One of his brothers told him that during the whole of the war, "a great many people were not in sympathy with the war and [had] hoped for a downfall of the Prussian militarism." His brothers also assured

him that most of the German people were happy with the new constitutional government of Germany. Herman invited Moses to come to
America, but Moses declined because he said it would be too hard on
his health. After spending about three weeks in Germany, Herman
returned to America.

When Stern returned to Valley City, he was full of optimism for
his old homeland. He made a speech about his journey at a spring
meeting of the local Rotary. He told his listeners that Germany was
quickly recovering from its defeat in the war. "Business is boom-
ing," he assured them, "there is beautiful merchandise of every description and the stores are crowded with buyers" who were trying to
make up for the wartime shortages. The German factories were "recovering very fast, every factory is busy and working overtime fill-
ing contracts for foreign countries and supplying the large demands
at home." In addition, there was "also very lively buying from the
Scandinavian countries, Holland, and Switzerland." Germany, further, had a trade advantage over much of the rest of Europe because
its devaluated money permitted it to export its goods while limiting
its imports. He admitted, however, that "the German businessman is
working under very high tension — while his profit in paper dollars
are enormous, yet he realizes that his business is not on a sound basis
until the value of the mark stabilizes." But he felt certain that the
inflation in Germany would soon fade, leaving the country in the
same strong economic position it had enjoyed before the war.

Stern noted further that, to his "pleasure and surprise," he found
that "the rank and file of the German people [were] very democratic
and very fair in their remarks with reference to America entering into
the war [against Germany]. . . they realize America was justified . . .
the German people regretted the sinking of the *Lusitania* very much."
In short, Stern was so sanguine about Germany's future he went so
far as to say that its present government was "made up of democrats
and centrum parties [and that] the military is not represented." He
concluded his remarks by predicting that before too long Germany
and the United States would again be firm and lasting friends.[3]

Stern had no idea that behind the scenes Germany actually was in political and social turmoil. In 1919, the Social Democrats, in order to stave off an attempted coup by communists, had made a fatal bargain with the *Reichswehr* (the small postwar German army) for support. The soldiers crushed the communists brutally and the army thereafter had substantial influence over the government's policies and decisions. The election of one of the war's heroes, General Paul von Hindenburg, to the presidency strengthened its hand even more. True republicanism was further weakened by the fact that the government could only function through a series of coalition governments in which the Social Democrats generally dominated, but also invariably had to make expensive concessions to its coalition partners in order to keep the system from relapsing into authoritarianism. The voters often distastefully referred to the legislative process as *kuhandel* – cattle trading.

When Stern returned to Germany for another visit in 1924, he must have noticed that conditions were not as good as he had hoped two years before. Wild inflation in 1923 had all but wrecked the country's economy, destroying people's savings in a matter of weeks. This had weakened the ordinary citizen's faith in the government and had opened the way for a number of extremist movements. Membership in the German Communist Party had grown tremendously. Right-wing organizations had also expanded and gained new respectability, especially among disillusioned ex-soldiers and young men who saw no future in supporting the Republic. One of these groups was the National Socialist German Workers Party, the Nazis. By this time, Adolf Hitler had become the undisputed leader of the Nazis. Even though he was at that moment in jail for attempting a coup in Munich, the fact that he had received only a short prison sentence for an act of treason only underscored the Weimar government's weakness.

Anti-Semitism had grown in Germany after the war. Many anti-Semites were drawn to the banner of Nazism. Hitler had told a German journalist in 1922 that as soon as he held power in Germany he intended to "have gallows built in rows" on which "Jews will be hanged indiscriminately." He said he would keep ordering hangings "until all Germany has been completely cleansed of Jews." Hitler and his followers blamed the Jews for all of Germany's woes. The defeat in the war, the divisions in German society, the growth of the communist movement, the problems in the economy – all were laid at the feet of the Jews. Hitler made it clear that his Nazi movement intended to destroy what he saw as a pervasive Jewish conspiracy that was keeping Germany from its rightful domination of Europe.[4]

There were many who took Hitler's propaganda at face value. In 1923 and 1924, Jewish businesses were wrecked by mobs that blamed them for the inflation. Jews in both rural and urban areas were killed. A Jewish teacher later wrote of this period that "anti-Semitism, with all its well-known signs, fully showed itself at a time when Hitler and his movement were still the object of curiosity or of casual jokes." Anti-Semitism proliferated in books, essays, pamphlets, and newspapers but one did not have to read to become acquainted with these poisonous screeds. A song sung by storm troopers in the streets contained the verse "Crack the Jew pack on their heads and win the future. Our colors will snap proudly in the wind when Jewish blood streams down our sabers." Nazis broke the windows of synagogues, affixed signs to public places that said "Jews Enter at Risk to Your Life," kicked over Jewish gravestones, and assaulted Jews in the streets. Many joined the party precisely because it gave them a chance to act out their prejudices through violence.[5]

Anti-Semitism rose even in the towns where Stern's brothers lived. During the inflation of 1923, peasants refused to sell their foodstuffs for the worthless paper money, sneering "we don't want any Jew-confetti from Berlin." In *Der Sturmer,* the vile anti-Semitic newspaper of Julius Streicher, stories of Jews kidnapping Christian children for ritual killings found favor in rural districts. If Herman's brothers talked with him about local tensions, they probably dismissed these things as temporary; things would get better as the economy improved. But police files show that the mayor of Stern's home village of Oberbrechen later remembered that local anti-Semitism did increase, although he believed the "tension between the Jewish residents and their neighbors [before 1933] was not racial in nature, but stemmed from the ordinary tensions of everyday life in the village." This was hardly a comforting explanation.

There were reasons for regarding the future of Jews in Germany with confidence, however. In the republic they had more freedom than ever before, were admitted to universities in greater numbers, made their way in German society more easily. Something that troubled traditional Jews and angered anti-Semites also gave comfort to those who wanted to be assimilated: by 1927, 64 of each 100 Jewish marriages in Germany were to Gentiles.

Before leaving for home, Herman visited with a childhood friend named Alfred, caught up on each other's lives and swapped old stories. Later he sent Alfred two hundred dollars to help him pay debts.[6]

Returning to Valley City, Stern was as energetic as ever. In 1924, he purchased land in central North Dakota, near the town Stanton, where he began a farm. Over the years he added additional land until he had over seven hundred acres. He hired tenants to live on the property and cultivate the crops, which consisted mainly of wheat and other small grains, and divided the profits with them. Stern traveled to the farm frequently to check on the property, and also simply to enjoy the rural surroundings that reminded him of his German childhood. The farm was not very profitable in the early years, but over time Stern did make a considerable amount of money from it. When his sons were old enough he made them partners with shares of their own in the farm. Herman loved farming, and he could never understand why neither of his boys showed much interest in the minute details of agriculture.[7]

An idea for advancing North Dakota took root in his mind in February of 1924, while he was in New York. He bought a newspaper there and read an account in it of the bitter winter being endured on the Great Plains. The article, Stern remembered later, had said that in North Dakota wolves had been driven by the cold into "coming down from the hills," prowling around farms, even entering the towns where they posed a danger to the local citizens. To him this was sensationalism, portraying North Dakota as a primitive place inhabited by simple people experiencing terrible lives. The part about the wolves especially angered him. He was certain that the writer had made it up,

Returning to Valley City, Stern formulated a plan. In March, he gave a talk at the Valley City Town Criers Club. Recounting what he had read in New York, Stern said that the state should organize a group to "tell the truth about North Dakota." Jumping at the suggestion, the club members sent invitations for a larger gathering to businessmen, members of the press, and elected officials in the state. The response was favorable. In May, representatives from eighteen counties and thirty-five towns, including Governor Ragnvald Nestos, executives from the Northern Pacific Railroad and the Soo Line, and H. D. Paulson, editor of the Fargo *Forum*, met in Valley City. The group agreed to form the Greater North Dakota Association: essentially a state chamber of commerce. The GNDA's first task would be to carry out "an extensive advertising and publicity campaign . . . for the better development of the state and its natural resources." The assembled body selected Stern to act as president of the GNDA until by-laws could be written and a regular election held.[8]

Stern did much of the work on the Association's by-laws, but despite having originated the idea, he was not elected to the GDNA presidency when the first election was held. That honor went to John Carley, a Grand Forks businessman who was better known across the state. Stern was making his name known in ever-wider circles, however, and by remaining active in the GDNA, he would make valuable contacts. Two men he met through the Association would become especially important to him. One of these was James Milloy. A Canadian by birth, Milloy came to North Dakota when quite young to work for an uncle who had a farm in Bottineau County. He later wrote for a small-town newspaper, then moved to Minot where he became the secretary of the local chamber of commerce. While there, he helped reorganize and expand the state's Automobile Association, doing such an impressive job that he was chosen to be the secretary of the Association. When the Greater North Dakota Association absorbed the Automobile Association a little over a year later, Milloy was hired to be the GDNA's secretary. Milloy quickly formed a firm friendship with Stern.[9]

The other man that Stern became friends with through the GNDA was Gerald Nye. Nye had been active in North Dakota politics for some time. He had cut his teeth as the editor of a newspaper that championed the rural poor, and then lost a close election as a candidate for Congress in 1924. Although Nye by temperament and association was a Republican on most issues, he supported enough of the local and statewide measures of North Dakota's then-powerful Nonpartisan movement to win votes from many farmers and working-class voters. In 1925, he was appointed by the governor to the U. S. Senate to fill out the term of E. F. Ladd, who had died with more than a year to go on his term. Nye quickly proved his mettle in balancing conflicting voting blocs and earned the Republican Party's nomination for the position, then handily won the election in 1926. In Washington, he joined with the Republicans when voting on most issues, but won reformist approval at home by publicizing some of the abuses of the Teapot Dome scandal and chairing a special committee to investigate the campaign expenditures of his fellow senators. In 1932, moved by the devastation wrought upon North Dakota farmers by the Great Depression, he joined other Republican senators in refusing to endorse Herbert Hoover for reelection, although he did not go so far as to join his Senate colleague William Langer in supporting Franklin Roosevelt. In all, he showed enough adeptness on the political tightrope to keep his Senate seat for many years to come.

Stern family lore has it that Nye and Stern first met in 1925 when Nye needed to buy a good suit before leaving for Washington. That may be true, but their real friendship was forged during the early years of the GDNA. Nye corresponded with Stern and others about some the Association's initiatives and sought Federal support for these whenever he saw an opportunity to do so. Before the end of the 1920s, he and Stern had dropped the formal salutations in their letters and simply wrote to each other as "Dear Herman," and "Dear Spike," the latter being Nye's nickname.[10]

Neither Stern nor Nye nor Jim Milloy could possibly have guessed that, having come together to better the fortunes of their state, they were destined to carry out a task that was at once smaller and greater: saving the lives of over a hundred people.

Later in the 1920s, Stern agreed to help one of his nephews leave Germany and come to America. This was Julius, the younger son of his brother Adolf. Born in 1903 in Duisburg, Julius always seemed to be in the shadow of his brother, Gustave. Two years older than Julius, Gustave was a very talented musician. He played piano with deftness before his fifth birthday, had an excellent ear for pitch, and decided while still very young that someday he wanted to be a conductor. He achieved his dream by studying music theory in Leipzig, where he also directed the choir at the city's finest synagogue. After studying voice in Cologne, he returned to Duisburg and found a position as a conductor with the Duisburg Opera Company. His father, who had been in a choral society for many years and occasionally served as cantor in Temple services as Duisburg, was delighted. As for his mother, whose family also had background in music, Dora was thrilled beyond measure; "my son the conductor" became a frequent phrase in her conversations.

Not that the younger son was completely without talents of his own. Julius had a fine voice himself. There was nothing he enjoyed more than a chance to sing at Temple services. He could not, however, make a living by singing. Because he understood numbers well, had a decent head for business and a good deal of charm, he tried his hand at selling. In the early 1920s he visited America and worked for his uncle at Straus for about three years. Returning to Germany in 1926, he tried his hand as a salesman in one of the larger cities. He did well enough, but was not really satisfied with his situation. In 1927, he wrote to his Uncle Herman that he wanted to return to the United States. Herman wrote back, apparently promising him another job at the store in Valley City.[11]

The American government had by that time further restricted immigration by establishing a complex formula: "an annual quota of any nationality [which] shall be two per cent of foreign-born individuals of such nationality resident in [the] continental United States as determined by the United States census of 1890." What this meant in plain English was that no more than 153,774 persons could immigrate to the United States per year; because millions of German-born people had been living in America in 1890, about 26,000 of these immigrants could be from Germany. Since times were still good in 1927, Julius was able to apply for and receive an entry visa without too much difficulty. By early 1928, Julius was in Valley City, living in the Stern's home and working in the store.[12]

The details of what occurred then are unclear, but the general picture can be discerned from letters that the two men exchanged a few months later and from recollections by Herman's and Julius's son. Julius did his job at the store, but his heart was not in the work. It seems he had hoped he and his uncle might operate the store as partners, but Herman insisted that Julius would have to work as an ordinary salesman for some time and thoroughly learn the business before he could have a share in the operation. This made perfect sense to the elder Stern, for he had had to do this before becoming a partner with Straus. But Julius probably found the arrangement somewhat demeaning.

Julius also had difficulties with the stolid pace of the Stern home. Herman devoted almost all his waking hours to the business and civic activities. About the only leisures he permitted himself were gardening and listening to the kinds of classical music he had enjoyed when he lived in Mainz. Adeline enjoyed her arts and crafts and read, and while she and Herman listened to the radio, neither much enjoyed the modern jazz styles or the emerging big bands. Adeline permitted no alcohol or tobacco in her home. This was hard for Julius, for he was a regular smoker, and, as his son noted years later, "he liked to have a drink after work." Unable to find that drink in the Stern house, he began going to a small tavern in Valley City. But Adeline objected to this as well, because she thought that by "frequenting a saloon," he harmed Herman's image in town. Before too long, Adeline and Julius were hardly speaking to one another.

Julius decided to try his luck elsewhere. Sometime around March of 1928, he left Valley City and moved to Chicago where he found

another job, probably in a clothing store. But that did not work out
either, for in early April he wrote Herman a letter pleading for help:
"I am getting crazy here, I earnestly don't know what to do, I am so
nervous just from worrying." The money he was making in Chicago
was not enough "to live on and eat right." He was behind in his hotel
bill, his one suit was fraying, and he did not want to write to his
parents for help because that would "make them feel bad." He asked
Herman to take him back at the store in Valley City and promised to
"do anything you want me to." He followed up two weeks later with
a second letter saying that most days he could afford only one sandwich and some coffee and promised that if his uncle helped him with
enough money to settle his debts, he would return to Valley City and
"try to make up for it."

Stern replied to his nephew with a blunt letter. He would help, he
wrote, and he would set aside Julius's "old faults" and take him back
at Straus on the assurance that he was "ready to buckle down and be
really the kind of businessman that will reflect credit to your father,
and mother, ourselves, and the store with which you will be associated." Stern understood that "working for a relative was not an easy
task" but he insisted that if Julius returned he would have to agree to
certain stipulations:

"I realize you are no longer a boy, but on the other hand you must
prove to me that you can and are willing to do the things that I expect
of you. And for that reason, Adeline and I are to be consulted on any
matters of importance that may come up. There is another stipulation
that I am going to make, which is – you will receive enough money
to make a decent living, but the balance of the money that you are
going to earn here must be kept in the business, so that you really can
accumulate something for yourself, but in the event that you do not
make good here, and it will be necessary for us to part again, which I
hope will not be the case, you would forfeit the money that has been
accumulating for you in the store."

Stern promised to send money to help Julius settle his debts – but
only after he agreed to the terms. He wanted a detailed list of everything Julius owed, then would have a friend in Chicago pay them off.[13]

Julius accepted the deal and returned to Valley City to work at the store. But again it did not work out. Julius found Adeline's rules just as confining as before. The tension in the Stern house distressed Herman, who also was not satisfied with what he perceived as Julius's lack of zeal for the business. Julius, in turn, grew increasingly unhappy. On one occasion he asked Herman to lend him some money against his next paycheck, but Herman refused. Frustrated, feeling that he was being treated unfairly, Julius decided it was time to leave. In mid-1930, Adolf Stern, Julius's father, sent Herman a brief telegram stating that he had heard from Julius, who was "homesick." Adolf was sending money to pay for Julius's passage home. Julius left for Germany soon after. After this unfortunate experience, neither Herman and Julius, nor Herman and Adolf, were ever completely relaxed with one another.[14]

Stern was clearly disappointed in how the arrangement with his nephew had turned out, so much so that when he began receiving similar requests from other relatives in Germany just a few years later, he at first hesitated to commit himself wholeheartedly to helping them leave Germany.

When Julius Stern returned to Germany in mid-1930, he probably found it hard to recognize the nation he had left about three years before. The worldwide depression was cutting a cruel swath through the German economy. Over three million Germans were unemployed by the end of 1930. The figure rose to nearly four-and-a-half million a year later. Hard times brought about the end of the coalition governments dominated by the Social Democrats. More and more Germans abandoned what faith they once had in the Social Democrats and in democracy itself, turning to the extremist parties for solutions to the crisis. The Communist Party in Germany grew to unprecedented numbers. As its ranks swelled with thousands of angry men out of work, middle-class Germans fled into the arms of the right. National Socialist membership rose from about 120,000 in mid-1929 to almost 400,000 by the end of 1930.[15]

Matters, economic and political, grew steadily worse over the next two years. Unemployment rose to six million men and women. A new government was created with Heinrich Bruening, a member of the Catholic Centre Party, as chancellor, and most of the cabinet posts parceled out to members of other parties – but none to the Nazis. When Bruening failed to muster enough votes to push his program for economic recovery through the Reichstag, President Hindenburg granted him emergency powers under the constitution to enact it by decree. Conditions only worsened. Hoping that the voters might now finally unite behind one political force, Bruening called for new elections. But again the voters scattered across the ideological spectrum: ten parties each won over a million votes but no one party had a majority. Another coalition government was inevitable. It was certain to be unstable as well.

The National Socialists did well in the election, their candidates wining six million votes. Where the party had previously only twelve deputies in the Reichstag, now it had one hundred and seven, enough for Hermann Goering, a fighter pilot hero in the late war and a friend of Hitler's, to be made President of the Reichstag. The Nazi Party was a political force to be reckoned with. But Hitler rejected all offers to join a coalition government unless he was given the chancellorship in it. He began to think about running for the presidency when von Hindenburg's term (or the 83-year old general himself) expired. His storm troopers (popularly called Brownshirts because of their uniforms) prowled the streets, staging mass demonstrations, attacking Jews, engaging in bloody brawls with the Communists and Social Democrats.

Bruening's government fell. He was replaced as chancellor by Franz von Papen, another Catholic Centre man of conservative inclinations. Papen had charm and wealth, but little else beyond a reputation for prizing ease above work and a reputation for intrigue. Papen's government faltered and collapsed, and was replaced by one of the German Army's more political generals, Kurt von Schleicher. Schleicher, like Bruening and Papen before him, could not achieve much without Hindenburg's emergency power of decree. Wanting somehow to make use of the Nazi's growing strength without having to deal with Hitler, Schleicher tried to divide the party by intriguing with some of its lesser leaders. This failed completely, and the Nazi strength kept growing.

Hitler challenged Hindenburg for the presidency in 1932, and while the old war hero won with about fifty-three percent of the vote, the contrast between his obvious frailty (he stood for another term reluctantly) and Hitler's frantic energy was marked. Hitler had been born in Austria, had only recently obtained his German citizenship, had been in prison, and had never held an elective office or compiled any record in government. He repeatedly refused every cabinet post offered to him, saying he would have the chancellor's role or nothing. The Army worried that his burgeoning ranks of storm troopers might attempt a coup, which would provoke a civil war. But millions now thought he was the answer to Germany's troubles. Nazi Party membership was approaching 800,000 as 1932 drew to a close. Schleicher's effort to hold together a stable government collapsed.

As a genuine expression of representative government, the Weimar Republic was already dead. Hindenburg's readiness to allow the chancellors to rule by emergency decree had all but killed it. All that remained now was for the Army, the Nazis and the opportunists to inter the corpse. Papen suggested that perhaps Hitler could be named chancellor while the rest of the cabinet would be packed with 'responsible' men who would 'control' him. Schleicher, for reasons of his own, backed the idea and went to work to persuade Hindenburg, who loathed Hitler, to appoint him chancellor. Hindenburg's son, who admired Hitler and was in fact being given large sums of money from the Nazis' party coffers, helped sway the old man into agreeing to the plan. Papen would be made vice-chancellor and trustworthy conservatives who were not Nazis, would make up the cabinet. Neither Schleicher nor Papen, nor any of the others who went along with this fantastic scheme seem to have heard the English children's rhyme about the lady who blithely thought she could ride on the back of a crocodile.

Hitler was now poised to receive the power he had been seeking for the past decade. It is appropriate to ask, then, what part did the Nazi's anti-Semitic rhetoric play in his rise to office?

The roots of anti-Semitism ran deep in Germany. But this was true throughout Europe, not just the German states. Jews were persecuted throughout the Middle Ages over the entire continent, with Churchmen attacking them as "Christ-killers," Christian merchants denouncing them as unfair competition, and peasants engaging in periodic pogroms against them by burning their segregated villages and neighborhoods. Many of the things said and written against the Jews later could be found in the literature of Europe's medieval era. When Martin Luther, angry that few Jews had accepted his offer of conversion, wrote in the 1540s, "Let the magistrates burn their synagogues and let whatever escapes be covered with sand and mud. Let them be forced to work, and if this avails nothing, we will be compelled to expel them like dogs," his diatribe was hardly novel. Which did nothing to stop the Nazis from quoting him endlessly four hundred years later.[16]

The nineteenth century, however, witnessed the emergence of a very different kind of anti-Semitism in Europe, a type that was horribly intertwined with the attempts of many thinkers and statesmen to define their national characters. Germany first: in the early decades of the 1800s, writers from Johann Fichte to Ernst Arndt to Friedrich Jahn contributed to the creation of the idea of the "Volk." "Volk," wrote Jahn were the good, loyal people who made up the essence of any state: "A state without Volk is nothing, a soulless artifice; a Volk without a state is nothing, a bodiless, airy phantom, like the Gypsies and the Jews." By selecting Jews and Gypsies as examples of wandering peoples, Jahn was suggesting that they lacked the character, or perhaps even soul, to become a Volk. Jahn essentially denied the universal equality of all humans that had been annunciated by the French Revolution. Since German Jews, stirred by the Revolution's message of equality, had begun to press some of the German states for full rights of citizenship, Jahn's choice could hardly be random. The popularity of his works among German conservatives was hardly coincidence either.

Later writers and patriots, trying to further define what it meant to be "German" or "French" or whatever, began to draw on the so-called "racial science" that emerged after the works of Charles Darwin became widespread. Arthur de Gobineau, a French aristocrat, was one of the most influential progenitors of the idea that, since life was a matter of struggle, in which the "fittest" survived, then it stood to reason that racial differences determined the progress of people. History, Gobineau wrote, showed that "all civilizations derive from the white race," an assertion for which he provided no real evidence whatsoever. Gobineau further believed that the purest members of his "white race" were those of "Aryan blood." Gobineau was not especially prejudiced against Jews, but his widely distributed essay on racial inequality, with its core belief in the superiority of "Aryan blood," drew the attention of many other writers, including some in France, Britain, the United States and Germany. When the Dreyfus Affair exploded in France at the end of the nineteenth century, the French publicists who most viciously attacked the "Jew Dreyfus" were often also admirers of Gobineau. Similarly a member of the British ruling class, writing about the "unfortunate" decline of the "true-blooded" aristocracy in the late Victorian era, admitted that she and her friends thought anyone who advocated social changes were "too clever" to be acceptable in society; they especially despised Jews "not because we disliked them individually, for some of them were charming and even brilliant, but because they had brains and understood finance."

In Germany, it did not take long for some to draw heavily on race and Volk in their expositions of Germany's problems, prospects, and potential. One such result was that of Wilhelm Marr, a journalist who had not found much success and believed that Jews in the German publishing industry had somehow blocked his career. Probably the first person to use the term "anti-Semitism," in his 1873 pamphlet "The Victory of Judaism over Germandom," Marr argued that the "race" of acculturated Jews were subverting traditional German culture. They would corrupt "all [German] standards ... dominate commerce, push themselves ever more into state services." He feared they would eventually take over the German nation.

Germany had unified in 1870, but its first years as a nation were troubled. Economic difficulties in Europe in the mid-1870s had imposed hard times on thousands among the poor and the small business owners. Finding it hard to make ends meet, worried about their futures, many of these men and women turned to the works of Marr and others to seek an explanation for their plight; Marr's pamphlet went through twelve editions before the 1870s ended. Others who were not even inconvenienced by the depression of that decade found that identifying the Jews as a menace to the decent-but-hard pressed "volk," the "true" Germans, was good politics. For example, Adolf Stocker, chaplain to the German emperor, discovered that he could attract more followers to his conservative Christian Social Workers political movement by attacking the Jews in Germany.[17]

Signs of a growing distrust of Jews continued into the 1880s and 1890s, with the circulation of an "Anti-Semites Petition" to restrict further immigration of Jews into Germany, the creation of further explicitly anti-Semitic parties like Stocker's, and occasional riots. The flow of literature and propaganda filled with anti-Jewish invective also continued unabated. While most of these activities were usually sparked by some local or regional concern, the trend was disturbing. As historian Oded Heilbronner has observed, "a revival of political anti-Semitism" across the nation was now a real possibility because, as the German government began to suspect that war with France and Russia was inevitable, it was only too likely that "the conservatives and the national [patriotic] associations might make use of it [anti-Semitism] at a suitable opportunity." While this was exactly what happened in 1914, it should not be forgotten that it happened in France, in Britain, and in Russia as well as in Germany.

But it was Germany that lost the war, Germany that was assigned blame for it in the Versailles Treaty, Germany that had to pay reparations, Germany that struggled through the 1920s with crippling inflation and unstable government. It was Germany that in 1933 embraced Adolf Hitler, the megalomaniac who accepted the arguments of the Volk and German racial superiority, without doubt or reservation, Hitler the consummate anti-Semite who came to the twisted conclusion that German success required the total destruction of the Jews. Would France or Britain have succumbed to their own versions of Hitler had they lost the war and seen their nations brought so low? Perhaps. But something that never happened can ever be proven. Germany lost. Germany succumbed to Hitler.[18]

He met with Papen and agreed to accept the chancellorship with the restrictions on cabinet selections. He told his subordinates later not to worry; he would find a way to alter the cabinet at a suitable moment. His appointment was announced on January 30, 1933, after a brief meeting with Hindenburg. That night, the storm troopers marched for hours, wielding torches, singing their songs, cheering both Hindenburg and Hitler as they stood looking down on the processions from windows in the Chancellery. That same night, Egon Hanfstaengl, the son of one of Hitler's first supporters, rushed up to an old friend and exclaimed, "Kurt! We've done it, we're in power!" Kurt stared at him quizzically and then said "I'm glad for you." It took the puzzled Hanfstaengl a moment to remember that, as a Jew, his friend Kurt could hardly be delighted with Hitler's triumph.[19]

Notes

1. In his 1971 interview with Crawford, Stern commented that before World War I, Straus chose stock for the stores primarily from traveling salesmen "who in those days would come to the store with six or eight large trunks filled with complete lines of suits and shirts, not just swatches of cloth. Mr. Straus would go to Chicago once or twice a year. But after the war, I'd make two or three trips a year to Chicago and New York to select things for the stores."

2. "Straus of North Dakota," (ca. 1979) company pamphlet in the collections of the Clay County Historical Society, Moorhead, Minnesota.

3. Moses and Dora (sister) to Herman Stern, March 3, 1922, Moses Stern file, Stern Papers; "Herman Stern Gives Talk on Trip to Germany," undated clipping (annotated as 1922) in Stern Scrapbook, Box 8, Stern Papers. A photograph of Herman with his family in Germany, dated 1910, is the only extant documentation of his earliest visit home.

4. Gerald Fleming, *Hitler and the Final Solution* (Berkeley: University of California Press, 1984), p. 17; Eberhard Jaekel, *Hitler's Weltanschauung: A Blueprint for Power* (Middletown, CT: Wesleyan University, 1972), pp. 52-61.

5. Theodore Abel, *Why Hitler Came to Power* (New York, Prentice-Hall, 1938); Michael Kater, *The Nazi Party: A Social Profile of Members and Leaders* (Cambridge, MA: Harvard University Press, 1983), pp. 19-71; Kater, "Everyday Anti-Semitism in Prewar Nazi Germany: The Popular Bases," *Yad Vashem Studies* 19 (1984), pp. 133-135.

6. Examples of the anti-Semitic writings and songs in the 1920s can be found in Laqueur and in H. G. Adler, *The Jews in Germany* (South Bend, Ind.: University of Notre Dame Press, 1969), ch. XVI, while the "Jew-confetti" remark is in Piers Brenden, *The Dark Valley* (New York: Alfred A. Knopf, 2000), p. 32. See also Kater, "Everyday Anti-Semitism," and Menahem Kaufman, "The Daily Life of the Village and Country Jews in Hessen from Hitler's Ascent to Power to November 1938," *Yad Vashem Studies*, XXII (1992). The September 13, 1925 letter from Stern's friend Alfred (no surname given), thanking him for $200, is in the German Correspondence file, Stern Papers.

7. See the records for the farm in the Farm Correspondence files, Box 5, Stern Papers.

8. "Tell the Truth about North Dakota – A Good Slogan," news clipping in Stern scrapbook, Box 8, Stern Papers.

9. Biographical information from "Milloy, Once Minoter, Who Became Look Officer, Dies," ca. March 1971, undated obituary in James Milloy file, Box 15, Stern Papers.

10. Wayne S. Cole, *Senator Gerald P. Nye and American Foreign Relations* (Minneapolis: University of Minnesota Press, 1962), supplemented by Edward Stern interview and correspondence in Stern Papers.

11. Much of the information here and below comes from a conversation with Larry Stern, Julius's son, in March 2004, and letters in the Jay Stern file, Box 16, Stern Papers. Documents in the Stern Papers alternately refer to Gustave Stern, Adolf's son, as "Gustave" and "Gustav." So too, does the State department correspondence. Because Herman Stern had a brother named Gustav and yet another nephew named Gustav (the son of brother Julius, and often referred to as "Little Gus" by family) I have chose to use Gustave for this nephew to reduce some of the confusion in identities.

12. The language of the immigration quota system is from President Calvin Coolidge's Proclamation on Immigration, based on the 1924 Act of Congress "to limit the immigration of aliens into the United States." By drawing on the 1890 census of nationalities, the 1924 law was intentionally designed to favor western Europeans over eastern Europeans, Asians and Africans since the proportions of these peoples in the 1890 population were much lower.

13. Julius Stern to Herman Stern, April 7 and April 27, 1928, Herman Stern to Julius, May 10, 1928, all in the Julius Stern file, Stern Papers, supplemented by conversations with Julius's widow in 1997 and with two others who preferred not to be identified. In some of these conversations, it was speculated that Julius had gone into debt because of gambling, but I have found no corroborating evidence for that claim. Stern's proposal to Julius, offering a share in Straus through what was in effect a payroll deduction plan, is the first recorded instance in which Herman Stern made such an offer. In later years, he made similar offers to his best salesmen, allowing the employee to purchase a share in Straus through deductions from his wages and giving him a percentage of the profits in return. Stern then took the money from wage-savings and expanded the business.

14. Adolf Stern telegram to Herman Stern, July 16, 1930 in Julius Stern file, Stern Papers.

15. Here and below, Alan Bullock, *Hitler: A Study in Tyranny* (revised edition, 1973), pp. 151-245; Roger Manvell, *The Hundred Days to Hitler* (New York: St. Martin's Press, 1974).

16. In this section I have relied largely on Lucy Dawidowicz, *The War Against the Jews,* esp. ch. 2; George G. Iggers, *The German Conception of History* (Middletown, CT: Wesleyan University Press, 1968); Peter Pulzer, *Jews and the German State* (Oxford, Blackwell, 1992); and Oded Heilbronner, "From Antisemitic Peripheries to Antisemitic Centres: The Place of Antisemitism in Modern German History," *Journal of Contemporary History* 35 (2000), pp. 559-576. The Martin Luther quote is from his essay, "Concerning the Jews and Their Lies," 1543.

17. An excellent analysis of Gobineau's racial theories, and the flaws in his reasoning, is Michael D. Biddiss, *Father of Racist Ideology: The Social and Political Thought of Count Gobineau* (New York: Weybright and Talley, 1970). Dawidowicz, p. 44n, notes that many European political movements used "Christian" in their name to denote anti-Semitism as part of their platform.

18. Heilbronner, pp. 572-576, hypothesizes that the traumas of Germany after 1918 created a "devaluation of life" in Germany and in effect dehumanized enough Germans to make Hitler and his monstrous movement acceptable. See also Gerald Feldman, *The Great Disorder* (New York: Oxford University Press, 1993).

19. Egon Hanfstaengl's encounter with his Jewish friend is recounted in John Toland, *Adolf Hitler* (New York: Doubleday and Co. 1976), p. 396. Egon's father, Ernst 'Putzi' Hanfstaengl, who broke with Hitler in 1937 and fled to England wrote a memoir, *Unheard Witness* (Philadephia: Lippencott, 1957), that gives some insight into the origins of Hitler's anti-Semitism. For the best examination of that subject, in English, see Robert S. Wistrich, *Hitler and the Final Solution* (New York: Modern Library, 2001).

Chapter Four
"Injustice Has Ever Been the Jew's Lot"

As the situation was deteriorating in Germany, Herman Stern received a second request for help from one of his relatives in Germany. In 1932, Klara Stern, the daughter of Herman's brother Gustav, living in the village of Gerolzhofen, hinted that she would like to come to America. Klara was seventeen years old in 1932. She had completed her schooling in a secretarial training program, but she could not find a job. Writing to her uncle in fluent English, she noted that all was well with the family, particularly her brother Erich, who was attending a secondary school, and was "the best pupil in his form." But as she was unable to find any work, she did not know what to do. She concluded by saying that she would come to America "with pleasure! But I have no money to pay for ships."

Exactly what Herman replied to this is unknown, but he clearly did not offer to help her leave Germany. It would have been difficult for him to help in any case. The Great Depression that had begun in 1929 was taking its toll across the nation and North Dakota was no exception. Jobs were extremely scarce and unemployment was high. Farmers were losing their land in record numbers because they could not make enough money to pay the property taxes. With the farmers going under, business in the towns was naturally poor as well. Stern had no job to offer Klara. He owned men's clothing stores, employed only men in them, and was struggling to keep his stores in Casselton, Lamoure, and Carrington afloat as it was.

It would also be more difficult for Klara to obtain permission to come to the United States. In 1930, President Herbert Hoover ordered the Department of State to provide him with a report concerning the impact of immigration on the American job market. The State Department responded with a recommendation for restricting immigration visas more severely. The report argued that "where there is not any reasonable prospect of prompt employment for an alien laborer or artisan who comes hoping to get a job or live by it, the particular consular officer in the field to whom application for a visa is made (upon whom the responsibility for examination of the applicant rests) will before issuing a visa have to pass judgment with particular care on whether the applicant may become a public charge."

Hoover accepted the recommendation and issued an executive order to all consulates that "if the consular officer [in any country] believes that an applicant [for a visa] may probably be[come] a public charge at any time, even … a considerable period [after] his arrival [in the United States] he must refuse the visa." The directive offered no guidelines for making a distinction between applicants who wanted to come to America "hoping to get a job" and those who might be fleeing political or religious persecution. The number of visas issued for immigration to America soon dropped to about one quarter of what had been issued before.[1]

Given these circumstances, and Stern's previous experience with the now-departed Julius, one can guess that he hesitated to extend another helping hand. Almost a year would pass before Klara sent him another letter about coming to the United States. Much would change in Germany in that time, but Stern did not seem worried at first about Adolf Hitler's hatred of the Jews. Trading letters with a business associate about two months after Hitler became chancellor, Stern remarked that the French and British press probably exaggerated the tales of Nazi persecution of Germany's Jews.[2]

Despite Klara's assurances that "all was well," the situation for Jews in Germany was in fact becoming more dangerous every day. When Schleicher and Papen had fashioned the cabinet that they believed could tether Chancellor Hitler, they had not wanted Hitler's lieutenant, Hermann Goering, to have any real power in the national government. And so they allowed him into the cabinet only as a "minister without portfolio." But they did not object when Hitler made Goering the Minister of the Interior for the State of Prussia, an appointment that gave him effective command over all the police in Prussia, the largest of the German states. Papen, as Commissioner (in effect governor) of Prussia, perhaps thought he could handle Goering. If so, he was completely wrong.

One of Hitler's first actions as chancellor was to issue a decree for new elections in March. Goering's power in Prussia made him a priceless asset as the electioneering began. He began replacing some of the police commandants with loyal Nazis and giving "auxiliary police" commissions to storm trooper units. Before long, the police in Prussia were taking no action when Brown Shirts assaulted political opponents in the streets of Berlin and elsewhere. Goering went so far as to specifically order the Prussian police not to interfere with storm troopers as they broke up Communist and Social Democratic rallies. Papen, despising Communists and Social Democrats as much as Hitler, took no action to curb Goering.

Behind the scenes, Goering quietly created a second force of "political police" within Prussia. As he later explained, "This [secret police] is the first instrument which is so much feared by the enemies of the [Nazi] State . . . We had to proceed against these enemies of the State with complete ruthlessness . . . and so the concentration camps were set up, to which we sent first of all thousands of officials of the Communist and Socialist Democratic Parties." The new force began rounding up political opponents immediately. The new force was called the Geheime Staatspolizei (secret national police), but this was quickly shortened to "Gestapo."[3]

While Goering was busy with police matters, the new chancellor took steps to reassure the German Army. Some of the army leaders worried that Hitler would try to supplant the army with his own SA, which had more than three times the size of the one-hundred thousand strong military force allowed under the Treaty of Versailles. Meeting with a group of general officers on February 3, Hitler promised them that he would never wish to replace the traditional army. Instead he intended to rebuild it and restore it to its former glory. According to notes kept by one of the generals he promised that he would "Battle against [the] Versailles [Treaty]" and make the "Armed forces [the] most important [National] Socialist institution of the State . . . no fusion of Army and SA intended." But this would take time,

Hitler cautioned the generals. First, he needed to effect a "Complete reversal of the present domestic political situation . . . Extermination of Marxism [in Germany] root and branch. Adjustment of youth and the whole people to the idea that only a struggle can save us and that everything else must be subordinated to this idea. . . . Training of youth and strengthening of the will to fight by all means. Death penalty for high treason. Tightest authoritarian State leadership. Removal of the cancer of Democracy!" Once this was accomplished, he promised, he would see to it that "National Service [military conscription] must be reintroduced." Most of the generals were delighted with Hitler's promises, so much so that in the months ahead it was they who took the initiative to have soldiers address Hitler as "Mein Fuhrer" and use the term "Heil Hitler" as a greeting. More ominously, the army added to its standard uniform a patch consisting of an eagle gripping in its claws a globe of the world, with a swastika covering the globe.[4]

This was just the beginning of the Nazi revolution. On February 27, less than a week before the new elections, the Reichstag Building was destroyed by an obvious act of arson. Many believed then and after that Nazi agents had planned the job. Guilty or not, Hitler and his party quickly took advantage of the outrage. Goering rushed to the scene of the fire and, while the massive building was still burning, announced to several onlookers that communists, who would now attempt a coup against the government, had set the blaze. "At this moment I knew that the Communist Party was the culprit," he later wrote. Under his direction, the police began arresting Communist Party leaders wholesale. Auxiliary policemen raided trade union offices to look for evidence of complicity in the fire; they usually smashed up the premises in the process. Hindenburg approved of these measures by giving Hitler an emergency decree after the fact. The newspapers of the Communists and the Social Democrats were shut down with police decrees, while conservative newspapers followed the Nazi lead in calling on the voters to "stamp out Communism" and "crush Social Democracy!" The organizations of both of these parties were shattered, and frightened voters went to the polls ready to cast their lot for a strong law and order government. When the elections were held on March 5, the Nazis won forty-four percent of the vote, enough of a plurality to allow them to cast off the restraints that Papen and Schleicher had try to put on Hitler.

Hitler reshuffled the cabinet, adding to it a new Ministry for Propaganda and Public Enlightenment. He named Joseph Goebbels, his longtime press chief for Berlin, to head this ministry. Goebbels began taking control of the newspapers, radio, film, and cinema in Germany. When an English correspondent asked Hitler if this meant that the right of expression was to be permanently denied, he disingenuously said that, while he was "only too anxious for the normal state of affairs to be restored," he could not do so yet because "our laws are too liberal for me to be able to deal properly and swiftly with this Bolshevik underworld."

When the newly elected Reichstag met, Goering, now acting in his role as President of the Reichstag, wheedled enough votes from members of the German Nationalist Party and the Catholic Centre Party to push through a special "Law for Removing the Distress of the People and Reich." The new law granted Hitler, as Chancellor of the government, the power to enact new laws by "means other than the process laid down in the Reich Constitution" for the next four years. In other words, the Chancellor could rule by decree. Hitler's word was now law.[5]

The Nazis had been busy destroying the Social Democrats and the Communists, but were not so occupied as to forget about the Jews. Articles appeared in Nazi-owned newspapers suggesting the Jews had inspired the Reichstag fire. A particularly vicious one was printed in *Der Sturmer,* published in Nuremberg by Julius Streicher, who was already known within the party as "Jew-baiter number one." The article charged that the fire had been part of a Jewish plot to stage an uprising against Hitler's government: "seized with terror, rage and hatred, [Jews] made a last attempt to regain its power in Germany." In order to explain how the approximately 525,000 Jews in Germany, less that one percent of the population, hoped to carry out their coup, Streicher's staff simply charged that "Communist subhumans were to be the tools [of the Jews]. The burning of the Reichstag was to be the signal for the attack . . . The Jew is guilty. He is guilty of arson in Berlin."

Inspired by such invective, storm troopers enrolled as "police auxiliaries," went on a rampage. The SA's anthem ended with the refrain "march on with steady, quiet feet," but now they trampled down anyone they pleased. A young Jewish woman who had been seen taking photographs of Nazis celebrating the March election victory was arrested on suspicion of being an agitator. She and her father were taken to a local jail where she was held in a cell with prostitutes while her father was beaten in a nearby room. A Jewish theater director in Breslau was seized and beaten with truncheons and whips; Jewish shop windows were broken in Wiesbaden and their owners clubbed; a British journalist in Berlin reported that gangs of young men combed the streets for victims: "many Jews were beaten by the Brown Shirts until blood ran down their heads and faces. Many fainted and were left to lie in the streets, until they were picked up by friends or passersby and brought to hospitals."[6]

Nazi leaders denied that these attacks were directed or encouraged by the government or the party; they were, rather, "spontaneous" actions by German citizens against the "Reich's enemies." Conveniently overlooked in this explanation were the Nazi press agitations. Also overlooked was the unsettling fact that with Hitler's triumph, thousands of opportunists – many of them young and ambitious men from the best families and universities – were rushing to join the National Socialist Party; pundits termed those applying for party membership after the election victory the "March violets." Eager to gain respect from the old guard, anxious to work their way up the party ranks, these budding flowers joined the attacks on Jews with gusto. One group of young SAs, accompanied by students, stormed the State Art School in Berlin, attacked and ejected three Jewish instructors and then trashed the offices of other faculty.[7]

On top of these physical threats Hitler's government and German society heaped legal and social persecutions. The Nazis were already burning the books of Jewish writers in public bonfires, but this was not enough. Soon after becoming Chancellor, Hitler appointed the composer Max von Schillings to be the new president of the Prussian Academy of Arts, which in Germany was a government position. Sixty-five years old and a very sick man, Shillings understood what Hitler expected from him, and until his death in July, Shillings signed and sent dozens of letters to writers, musicians, and artists who were Jews to inform them that their membership in the Academy had been voided.

On April 7, a law was promulgated "for the Restoration of the Professional Civil Service." Designed ostensibly to "simplify" the government's administration, the essential purpose of the new law was to be found in the short phrase: "civil servants who are not of Aryan descent are to be retired." Jews in the German civil service were quickly dismissed, their jobs quickly filled by Nazi Party members.[8]

These persecutions certainly did not go unnoticed. Foreign correspondents reported them to their newspapers and wire services in France, Britain, and the United States. But extensive coverage was limited mostly to the larger newspapers and magazines with a substantial Jewish staff; *Time,* for example gave almost no space over to the attacks on Jews, while *Nation* and *The New Republic* published a number of articles. It was possible for an American Jew like Adolph Marx to be surprised by the level of anti-Semitism he discovered when he visited Germany in mid-1933. Better known to moviegoers worldwide as "Harpo," the most frenetic of the Marx Brothers comedy team, Marx was in Hamburg about six months after Hitler took charge. Walking down one of the streets he confronted "the most frightening sight I had ever seen – a row of stores with Stars of David and "*Jude*" [painted on them], and inside, behind half-empty counters, people in a daze, cringing like they didn't know what hit them and didn't know where the next blow would come from." Marx went back to America soon after but the memory of what he had seen kept haunting him. "I hadn't been so wholly conscious of being a Jew since my bar mitzvah."[9]

One New Yorker was so distressed by the scant attention given to the Nazi attacks that he wrote an essay that echoed the outcry against the Dreyfus Affair at the turn of the century:

"Today half a million men and women, like Dreyfus, are tortured and imprisoned, deprived of rank and dismissed from office, judged on false evidence, convicted by a biased court, condemned because they are Jews. But where is the outcry? Where is the cry of anguish that humanity and decency are violated in every action of the Nazis, that liberty and truth and justice lie prostrate under the juggernaut of rapacious fanatics?"

What did the world intend to do about this seeming abandonment of Germany's Jews?[10]

For that matter, what did Jews in America intend to do? At first, not very much. In New York City, a group of Jewish veterans of the late war gathered and staged a march to city hall where they asked the mayor to join them in protesting the actions of Hitler's government. He fobbed them off with polite remarks and no commitment. Similar demonstrations in other cities met generally with the same response. In Washington, Congressman Samuel Dickstein (democrat from New York) said that when Congress convened he would call together the House Committee on Immigration, which he chaired, and ask them to support a resolution to lift the prevailing immigration quota restrictions in this situation and allow German Jews, who had relatives in America and were "fleeing from persecution," to come to the United States.

But when Dickstein asked American Jewish leaders to come to the capitol and testify on behalf of his plan, a curious thing happened. Almost all of these leaders hedged on the support they gave him. The American Jewish Committee, for example, privately asked Dickstein to allow his plan to "die a natural, quiet death." Stephen Wise, the dynamic leader of the American Jewish Congress, undercut Dickstein's plan in public. Testifying before the House Immigration Committee, he said that while he and his group would support a loosening of immigration restrictions for *all* potential immigrants, he would not ask the government to provide "special amendments to

American immigration laws" solely for the German Jews.

Did the American Jews not care about what was happening in Germany? Many in fact did care. Wise also said to the Committee that while he did not know if Hitler actually planned to kill all the Jews in Germany, he expected the Nazis "economically and morally to exterminate the Jewish people." But at that moment Wise was more worried about America's Jews. He feared that if the immigration laws were altered specifically to help German Jews it would trigger an anti-Semitic backlash in depression-ridden America. Most American Jewish leaders, even those who were his mortal enemies on most other issues, agreed with Wise that they could not risk a backlash against Jews in America by charging headlong into a fight to protect the Jews of Europe. Deserted by those he expected to be his greatest allies, Dickstein could only admit defeat and withdraw his resolution.[11]

Congress clearly would not act, but what would the President do? Herbert Hoover still had a few weeks left in his term when Hitler became chancellor. But, humiliated by his 1932 election loss to Franklin Roosevelt, Hoover had taken no real interest in what was happening in Germany during the last weeks of his administration; his Secretary of State, consequently, had instructed the American ambassador in Berlin simply to use his "discretion" and "talk the matter [of the Jewish persecutions] over with the German Government and acquaint them with the apprehension and distress that is being felt here [in the United States]." The ambassador in turn was expecting the incoming Roosevelt administration to replace him with someone else. He made only a token effort when he met with the German Foreign Office, complaining that some American citizens had been "subjected to indignities" by overzealous storm troopers. After receiving reassurances that "the mistreatment of these foreigners might have been instigated by *provocateurs*," he went away satisfied that Hitler would soon restore order: "in view of the good discipline generally obtaining with the Nazi ranks," he wrote back to Washington, Hitler's insistence on law and order "should bring about a cessation of the anti-Jewish demonstrations."

Those who hoped that president-elect Franklin Roosevelt would do more than this would also be disappointed. Roosevelt had won the presidential election in 1932 by a record vote and conceivably could have used this mandate to make changes in a foreign policy that rested on a conviction that the American nation should be as uninvolved as possible in the rest of the world's problems. But from the moment of his inauguration, Roosevelt was focused almost entirely on domestic policy, especially the challenge of battling the economic crisis in America. He did not take any steps to pursue international agreements against aggression, nor did he make more than a half-hearted attempt to deal with either world trade barriers or the ominous signs of international rearmament.

As for the problems in Germany, Roosevelt did not share with Jewish leaders a report he received from his Consul General in Berlin, which predicted that the Jews in Germany would inevitably be "eliminate[d] . . . from all positions of importance, influence, or profit in the country." He did not direct his diplomats to lodge any strong protests with the Nazi government. During the spring and summer of 1933 he did not give Samuel Dickstein, whom he knew quite well, one word of encouragement in the latter's plan to amend the immigration laws.[12]

Hoping that they might be able to spur Roosevelt to do more, a commission of scholars and legal experts, brought together by the American Civil Liberties Union, sent him a letter urging that some of the procedures that the consuls used in handling visa applications could be changed without Congressional approval. One suggestion focused on the provision that persons who wanted to enter the United States had to demonstrate that they would not become a "public charge" in America. After receiving Hoover's 1930 order, consular officers had regularly interpreted this to mean that the applicant had to show that he had sufficient funds or property *from his own resources* to take care of himself. But several legal experts, including Judge Joseph Proskauer, who was prominent in the American Jewish Committee, had already pointed out that for many years visas had been issued when a relative in America posted a bond for someone overseas. Why, then, could not the State Department give a new order to the consuls that they must issue the visa once such a bond was posted?

The State Department resisted this argument, claiming that it was all very well for someone in America to post a bond and make a promise to look after an immigrant in America. But if they backed out of the obligation, what could the government do about it? Only the consul, State argued, saw each applicant face to face, and only he could form an opinion of the applicant's character. The consul's decision, they said, would be "based principally upon the peculiar mental and physical characteristics of the alien application, brought out upon a personal examination and interrogation of the latter, rather than upon a mere lack of money or of the connections in the United States by which a living might be made or support found." State's critics countered that the use of such terms as "peculiar mental and physical characteristics" and "interrogation" betrayed insensitivity to the plight of the Jews and came close to mirroring the prejudices of the Nazis.

In the end, Roosevelt pressured the State Department to make some concessions. In late June, State assured the American Jewish Committee that "every reasonable effort is being made to insure sympathetic and considerate treatment of aliens applying for visas in Germany." Assistant-Secretary Wilbur Carr soon after issued a circular to the consuls that they should not interpret the phrase "likely to become a public charge" too literally when dealing with visa applications: "All evidence of assurance of support [by American sponsors] is material and must be given due consideration." Carr also reminded the consuls that the guidelines for sponsorship already indicated that a promise of support from a "close relative" – a son, daughter, sibling, spouse or parent – should be accorded greater weight than that of a "distant relative" or someone who was not related to the applicant. This was not to say that a visa must be issued automatically, Carr noted, but if a close relative in America could show that he or she had "permanent employment" and some savings – a "margin of resources," with which to help out an immigrant if that person had difficulty – then the Consuls could place this applicant in the "first-preference class" for a visa.

Despite all its discussion of "preference" classes, its reminders about "close relatives" and all the rest, a careful reader of this circular might have noticed that it contained advice only, no firm order, nothing to limit the consul's discretion. An historian who has examined this moment in time very closely has concluded that the State Department had chosen a strategy of "facilitating the admission of the few [German Jews] with close relatives already in the United States" while maintaining the "old barriers" against the majority who might want to come to America. The consul could still make the final decision to grant or deny the visa, and he could take his time doing it, more time that a German Jew could afford.[13]

While these maneuvers over immigration were going on in Washington, Herman Stern's sister Dora was keeping him informed of the developments in Germany. Just six weeks after Hitler became chancellor, she wrote to tell him that planting on the family land would be delayed because Moses was recovering from a broken leg due to falling on ice the previous winter. Neighbors were helping them slaughter goats from their small herd so they could try and sell the hides. She mentioned that many of the "young people" were talking about leaving Germany because they saw little chance for them in the future. A month later, she wrote again to tell Herman that he could probably get "any number of young people" from Germany to come over and work in his stores.[14]

In October 1933, Herman's brother Gustav wrote to the American consulate in Stuttgart asking for information on how a person could apply for an American visa. Gustav likely sent this letter not only for Klara but for her brother Erich as well. Among the new laws that the German Reichstag had passed the previous spring was the "Law Against the Overcrowding of German Schools and Universities." This devious piece of work decreed that the number of "non-Aryan" students in any public school could not exceed five percent of the total number of students, and so thousands of young Jews were summarily dismissed from their schools. One of these was Erich Stern.

Erich had not been able to find any decent work since. His sister Klara had not had much luck either. The events of the past few months had triggered Gustav's decision to contact the Stuttgart Consulate.

In reply to Gustav Stern's inquiry, Hugh Teller, the vice-consul at Stuttgart, all but ignored Washington's advice to be more sympathetic to applicants who had close relatives in America. He wrote in a discouraging tone that the "present difficult economic situation" in America meant that before anyone could hope to obtain a visa, he or she would have to provide documented proof that they would not "become a public burden" in the United States and that this would probably be very difficult to do. Gustav promptly forwarded the letter to Herman and asked him if he could do anything to help.[15]

Herman had, in fact, already written to North Dakota's Senator Gerald Nye to request his help and had sent a letter to the "Department of Immigration" assuring them that Klara could live in his home and "be no charge to the government." While this second letter was being sent on to the State Department, Nye contacted the Immigration and Naturalization office of the Department of Labor to ask that up to date information on the immigration process be sent to Stern. He promised Stern that he would write to the Stuttgart Consulate and send a letter of support to Klara as well. North Dakota Governor William Langer (Stern addressed him as "Governor Bill") also promised to write to Stuttgart attesting to Stern's ability to provide a home for his niece. Stern was confident that with the aid of Langer and Nye, Klara would have no difficulty obtaining a visa. He was so certain that he advised Klara to prepare to leave Germany within a few days.[16]

He was much too optimistic. The same day he wrote to Klara, American immigration officials from the State Department and the Department of Labor were posting letters to him, outlining the mind-numbing paperwork he would have to do before his niece bothered to pack a valise. These packages included an explanation of the immigration quota system and the requirements for affidavits attesting to Stern's ability to financially sustain his niece after she arrived in America; supporting affidavits from banks and business associates;

yet more affidavits for Klara and her family to fill out, attesting to
her health and character; and instructions for sending all these to the
American Consul in Stuttgart. The officials in Washington cautioned
Stern to expect a "lengthy process" before action would be taken,
and even then a visa could be denied.

Stern, however, sat down and carefully read the copy of the Labor Department pamphlet "General Information Concerning United
States Immigration Laws." While slogging his way through this, he
came upon the section on "Students," and learned that if a person
came to America "for the purpose of study," they would be treated
"as a nonquota immigrant and are therefore exempt from the quota
in the issuance of immigration visas." Like Archimedes in his bath,
Herman might well have cried "Eureka!" Within a matter of days, he
had obtained support from Carl Allen, president of the Valley City
State Teachers College, for enrolling Klara into the school.[17]

Matters proceeded more smoothly after this. Stern completed all
the paperwork he needed and sent copies both to Washington and the
Consulate in Stuttgart. Then he wrote to the National Council of Jewish Women in New York for advice on how to book passage for her
on an American ship. Klara Stern went to Stuttgart to submit her
own paperwork, completed a battery of written and physical examinations, and then returned to Gerolzhofen to wait. The Consulate
took action on her application fairly quickly, possibly because of the
support from Senator Nye and Governor Langer. She received her
visa on the first of December.

Stern meantime made arrangements with an American steamship
company to buy a ship ticket for her. He had, as well, asked friends in
New York to meet her when she arrived in New York port and see to
it that she boarded the right train for Chicago. For good measure, he
persuaded two of his wife's relatives in Gary, Indiana, to meet Klara's
train in Chicago and see to it she made the right connection to Valley
City. Then he penned notes thanking Nye and Langer for their help.
Stern had always been a stickler for small detail. In this matter he
went so far as to supply his New York friends with an itinerary for
Klara when she got to the big city: "Mrs. Stern and I would both love

to have her stay with you and see something of New York, specially the most interesting buildings and Rockefeller Center and Radio City. It is also possible that Klara would enjoy going to Temple Emanuel. If I am correct, such modern temples are not found in Germany."

Klara sailed from Hamburg on the last day of January and arrived in New York eight days later. After what must have been a whirlwind tour of New York, she boarded a Pennsylvania Railroad train for Chicago, transferred to a Burlington train there for St. Paul, then made the final leg of the journey to Valley City on the Northern Pacific line. Herman and Adeline had her room ready and waiting. She would not be able to start classes at Valley City State Teachers College until late March when the last quarter of the school year would begin. In the meantime, she received a letter of welcome from Senator Nye, addressed to "Mr. [sic] K. Stern," expressing his "distinct pleasure" in helping her come to America.[18]

Klara was at the college for about three terms, taking classes in stenography and accounting, as well as advanced English and American history. She also joined one of the campus literary societies and sang second soprano with the campus Madrigal Club. Although enrolled in the Class of 1938, she did not receive a degree before going to work for one of the clothing wholesalers in Chicago in the summer of 1935. By then, she had helped her uncle lay the groundwork for sponsoring others in Germany so that they, too, could come to live in the United States. These included her brother Erich and some of her cousins.[19]

There was no question that Stern planned to help others leave Germany. He had embraced the idea of rescuing members of his family from the reach of Hitler's persecutions, had committed himself heart and soul to this as a cause. Of that there can be little doubt. In one of the letters that Stern wrote to his friends who met Klara when she debarked at New York port, Stern mentioned that he and Adeline had recently listened "with great interest" to a radio address by James MacDonald, the League of Nations Commissioner for Refugees. MacDonald's radio address, which repeated remarks he had made in Geneva before the League, had warned that "very far-reaching differences" between the rising dictatorships and the more democratic nations, as exemplified by the Nazi persecution of German Jews, was creating a refugee crisis that would threaten both the world's economic recovery and its peace. "This gentleman surely is doing a noble work," Stern remarked to his friends.[20]

It was about at this same time that Stern obtained a transcript copy of another broadcast, this one by Rabbi Albert Gordon who had a weekly commentary slot with the largest radio station in Minneapolis. In this particular address, Gordon read excerpts of a letter he had received from a listener, who, admitting he had been born in Germany, referred to the situation in Germany and commented, "Who will deny that there is cause for censure [of the Jews] in many directions . . . injustice has ever been the Jew's lot. That seems to be his fate, to suffer and endure. It is surely not to the credit of your people to hold high so many of the vile things in life for the gain of money. Constantly, I read Jewish names when crimes are charged, whether in the field of booze or kidnapping. The sort of moving pictures highly extolled by advertisement to get the income are in the hands of Jews." The man concluded his letter with the remark that he "look[ed] more leniently on Hitler's way of driving a hard bargain."

Gordon systematically denied the writer's allegations and dismissed as offensive his "use of a personal incident or particular case as proof that all Jews are guilty of crimes against society and that therefore they ought to be militated against." This was the approach of Hitler, a tactic leading "the German people . . . to violate every bit of decency and decent feeling," to the point of making that nation "a menace to civilization." But, Gordon went on, such examples of "deep-rooted prejudice and lack of tolerance" could equally well happen in America. "Good-will between the various religious and national groups is not to be obtained by joining forces with another group in an effort to fight a third . . . As long as people will permit themselves to be deluded by the fears that their neighbors are planning to destroy them, nothing but intolerance can rule their hearts and minds."[21]

From Herman Stern's remark to his friends about listening to

James MacDonald, it was clear that he was following the situation in Germany very carefully. By acquiring and saving Gordon's broadcast transcript, Stern may also have been worried that some Americans could react to the plight of Germany's Jews by threatening Jews in America; precisely what American Jewish leaders had feared when they hesitated to be drawn into discussions about liberalizing the immigration laws. But unlike the national leadership, Stern had chosen to face the challenge. He had helped his niece leave Germany. He had learned the process for sponsoring someone for an American visa. If others in Germany turned to him for help, he was prepared to act.

Notes

1. David Wyman, *Paper Walls: America and the Refugee Crisis* (New York: Pantheon Books, 1968), p. 4, italics added; Klara Stern to Herman Stern, May 5, 1932, Klara Stern File, Stern Papers. For North Dakota during the Great Depression, see Catherine McNicol Stock, *Main Street in Crisis: The Great Depression and the Old Middle Class on the Northern Plains* (Chapel Hill: University of North Carolina Press, 1992).

2. Stern did not begin keeping copies of his correspondence to his German relatives until the second half of 1933, which was when he began actively obtaining information about how to sponsor relatives for American visas. Consequently, the earliest letters he sent to Klara and others are not preserved in the Stern Papers. Stern's remark about Hitler in 1933 is paraphrased in Willard C. Lyon to Stern, March 21, 1933, copy given to Shoptaugh by Edward Stern.

3. Here and below, Manvell, *The Hundred Days to Hitler,* esp. pp. 124-25; R.J. Overy, *Goering the 'Iron Man'* (Boston: Routledge and Kegan Paul, 1984), pp. 23-28.

4. J. Noakes and G. Pridham, *Nazism, 1919-1945: Foreign Policy, War and Racial Extermination* (Exeter, UK: University of Exeter Press, 1997), vol. 3, pp. 628-29; Ernest May, *Strange Victory* (New York: Hill and Wang, 2000), pp. 31-32, for army response to Hitler.

5. The only limits the Enabling Law of March 1933 placed on Hitler's power were a statement declaring the "rights of the Reich President [Hindenburg] … unaffected" and a provision preventing him from doing away with the Reichstag. Manvell , *The Hundred Days to* Hitle,r (p. 224) offers the strongest argument that the Nazis themselves set the fire at the Reichstag, citing a secondhand remark by a highly placed storm trooper that he would be "a bloody liar" if he denied Nazi involvement in it. Overy (p. 25) cites German scholars to the effect that the Nazis were not involved and merely took advantage of the fire.

6. Marion Kaplan, *Between Dignity and Despair*; Victor Klemperer, *I Will Bear Witness* (New York, Random House, 1998), p. 18; Michael Wildt, "Violence Against Jews in Germany, 1933-1939," pp. 181-82, in David Bankier, ed., *Probing the Depth of German Antisemitism* (New York: Berghahn Books, 2000). A translated copy of the *Der Sturmer* article, "The Guilty," is on the Calvin College German Propaganda Archive website (www.calvin.edu/academic/cas/gpa/index.htm).

7. Michael Steinberg, *Sabers and Brown Shirts: The German Students' Path to National Socialism* (Chicago: University of Chicago Press, 1977), pp 131-140. In 1923, cultural historian Arthur Moeller van den Bruck, from whom the Nazis took the term "Third Reich," had forecast that the youth of Germany would eagerly rebel against the Weimar Republic in order to "purge itself of any guilt that clings to the nation" from defeat in the Great War. "There are no young liberals in Germany to-day," he wrote, "there are young revolutionaries; there are young conservatives. But who would be a liberal?" (*Germany's Third Empire,* translated by E.O. Lorimer, p. 111).

8. Saul Friedlander, *Nazi Germany and the Jews: The Years of Persecution* (New York: HarperCollins, 1997), pp. 11-12. The 1933 Civil Service law exempted from dismissal Jewish "civil servants in office from August 1, 1914, who fought at the Front for the German Reich or its Allies in the World War, or whose fathers or sons fell in the World War." This was only a temporary expedient to prevent the possibility that veterans' organizations would withdraw support to Hitler.

9. "Back to Barbarism," *Nation,* April 12, 1933, p. 388; Harpo Marx's account is cited in Roy Hoopes, *When the Stars Went to War* (New York; Random House, 1994), p. 6.

10. Johan J. Smertenko, "J'Accuse," *The New Republic,* May 31, 1933, pp. 74-75.

11. Rafael Medof, *The Deafening Silence* (New York: Shapolsky Pub., 1987), pp. 22-27; Arthur D. Morse, *While Six Million Died* (New York: Random House, 1967), pp. 113-14.

12. *Foreign Relations of the United States* (hereafter *FRUS*), 1933, vol. II, pp. 320-28.

13. Medof, p. 27; Arthur D. Morse, *While Six Million Died*, pp. 122-24; Bat-Ami Zucker, *In Search of Refuge: Jews and US Consuls in Nazi Germany, 1933-1941* (London: Vallentine Mitchell, 2001), pp. 86-93; Cyrus Adler and Aaron Margalith, *With Firmness in the Right* (New York: American Jewish Committee, 1946), p. 366.

14. Dora Stern to Herman Stern, March 26 and May 1, 1933, Moses Stern file, Stern Papers.

15. Teller to Gustav Stern, October 7, 1933. This and the following correspondences are all in the Klara Stern file, but Gustav's letter to the Consulate is not extant.

16. D. H. McArthur to H.S., September 19, 1933; H.S. to "Department of Immigration," September 27, 1933; H.S. to William Langer, October 10, 1933; H.S. to Klara Stern, October 10, 1933.

17. Henry B. Hazard to H.S., October 10, 1933; U.S. Department of Labor, Bureau of Immigration, "General Information Concerning United States Immigration Laws," (May 1933 edition) p. 7; Carl Allen to H.S., October 10, 1933. The American immigration laws, together with the visa regulations and how they could be interpreted, are conveniently gathered in Michael N. Dobkowski, ed., *The Politics of Indifference: A Documentary History of Holocaust Victims in America* (1982), pp. 235-257.

18. Details from correspondence is in the Klara Stern file, including the quoted letter from Stern to Mr. and Mrs. M[erle] S. Ward, February 2, 1934, and Nye's welcome letter, dated March 13, 1934. It is interesting to note that, while Stern had sought to obtain for Klara a non-quota visa as a student, Leon Dominian, the Stuttgart Consul informed Gerald Nye that "Miss Stern was granted a quota immigration visa on December 1, 1933" – Dominian to Nye, December 2, 1933.

19. Klara Stern's transcript, at the Valley City State University Archives, and copy of the VSTC 1935 Yearbook.

20. H.S. to Mr. and Mrs. M. S. Ward, January 18, 1934; "Debate at Geneva," *New York Times,* January 7, IV, 4:7.

21. "As I See It," Talk by Rabbi Albert I. Gordon over WCCO [Radio], December 3, 1933, transcript in Klara Stern file.

Chapter Five
"Get Your Children Out"

Jews in Troisdorf knew nothing of anti-Semitic persecution before the coming of Hitler. Hilda Levy's family and friends assured her that "never [before 1933] did anything like this happen." Through most of its existence, Troisdorf was just one of many towns on the east bank of the Rhine. For over two hundred years visitors had gone to Troisdorf to see its one and only attraction, the cathedrals. There was the St. Hippolytus Troisdorf which had been founded about the year 1000 AD, and the magnificent St. Lambertus Bergheim, whose congregation dated even further back, to a hundred years before Charlemagne was crowned Holy Roman Emperor in 800 AD. They would walk through the cathedrals, admiring the architecture, the echoes of Medieval grandeur; they would stay overnight at one of the inns and then move on while Troisdorf quietly rusticated.

Then in the mid-1800s the railroads came, steel rails that were pulling together the German states into one mighty nation. There were three major rail lines running through Troisdorf by 1871, the year of Germany's national unification. The rail lines made Troisdorf an ideal site for factories that sprang up, one after another, too fast for the inhabitants to comprehend it all. A steel plant by Mannstaedt–Werke forged the sinews of modern cities from Ruhr coal and Austrian iron ore. An explosives plant, Dynamit Nobel, was built by the man who invented dynamite and would later endow an international peace prize in his own name. Within a couple of decades, Troisdorf was a bustling industrial town of ten thousand residents, most of whom owed their livelihood to the factories. During the First World War, Troisdorf's plants produced gunpowder, steel, small arms and other supplies for the German Army.

After Germany's defeat in 1918, Troisdorf suffered through the hard times like the rest of the country, then enjoyed a return to pros-

81

perity in the middle 1920s before unemployment rose again with the Great Depression. Throughout this period the heavily Catholic population sent members of the Catholic Centre Party to the Reichstag. Even after the mysterious fire destroyed the Reichstag in March 1933, the voters continued to cast their ballots for the Centre Party. A few of the young men in Troisdorf joined the Nazi Party before 1933. But even when Hitler became chancellor, party ranks rose only slightly. For the remainder of 1933, the local SA bullies confined themselves to harassing a few local communists among the industrial workers, of whom one was eventually arrested and sent to a concentration camp. The tiny number of Jews in Troisdorf – no more than forty – were left alone.[1]

Hilda Levy's father, Samuel, owned a small butcher shop in Troisdorf. He had taken over the business from his father about the time Hilda was born in 1911. It was a tiny shop, going back in the family's hands for several generations. The Levys sold a variety of sausages and other products to their mostly Catholic neighbors and carried some kosher products for their more Orthodox Jewish friends. The family lived in the same building, just behind the storefront; sixty years later Hilda could still vividly recall the sharp odors of the sausages and cabbage wafting back into the small parlor where she, her father, her stepmother Hedwig, and her stepsister Ruth, rested and talked at the end of each day. A most courteous, soft-spoken man, Samuel was well liked by everyone. Hilda, who had inherited a more impulsive temperament from her late mother, remembered how her father counted among his friends practically everyone at the synagogue in Siegburg, where the family went for worship, and nearly everyone who came into his shop; Samuel's friends among Troisdorf's Catholics would later help save his daughter's life.

Completely non-political, the Levys gave little thought early in 1933 as to how Hitler's appointment as chancellor might affect them. It was not until the first day of April 1933, that they saw the first shadow of dark days to come. As Hilda remembered it, she and Samuel finished their morning breakfast and went into the shop to open for business, only to discover a young SA trooper in full uniform standing outside by the entryway. This man spent the entire day urging every person who approached the shop "kauf nicht bei Juden" — do not buy from Jews. Most of the men and women ignored him, but he was back again the next day.

The SA trooper's actions were part of an attempt by the Nazis to stage a nationwide boycott of Jewish-owned businesses. There had been local attempts to intimidate Jewish shop owners before this, including one in March in Duisburg when "a civilian accompanied by an armed member of the SS gained forced entry into the furniture store of the Polish Jew AAC, who apparently had antagonized his competitors by underselling them. The SS man accosted the Jew with his fists and left him covered with blood." But Hitler, angry at American and British press criticism of his anti-Semitic policies, and seeing an opportunity to blame this on an "international Jewish conspiracy," had ordered this national boycott. Since Hitler wanted this to appear as a spontaneous *aktion* of the German people against the "non-Aryan" Jews, the Nazi Party, not the government, issued the actual order for an organized boycott of Jewish shops. It was difficult to sustain the appearance of spontaneity however, after party newspapers announced to its members on March 29 that "Action committees are to be formed immediately for the practical implementation of a boycott of all Jewish shops, Jewish goods, Jewish doctors and Jewish lawyers . . . the principle must be that no German will any longer buy from a Jew, or allow Jews or their agents to recommend goods."[2]

Many Germans, like those of Troisdorf, ignored the boycott and continued to buy what they wanted at Jewish-owned stores. But there were many others who supported the boycott, like the woman who came into a Jewish chemist's shop with two uniformed SA and loudly proclaimed that "she had brought with her some goods she had purchased a few days before, and demanded that the chemist should return her money [saying] 'I did not know you were a Jew, I don't want to buy anything of Jews'." Another German woman recalled later that she and her mother went into a boycotted fabrics shop: "It was so terrible – such a very large store and completely empty. The owner came over to us. He was so thankful that someone came. My mother really had nothing to buy but wanted to show him, I'm still coming. So she bought two small spools of thread . . . but it was so sad."[3]

Hitler had given instructions that the storm troopers were only to make demonstrations; they were not to attack the Jews. He did not want to give the British or American governments cause to file an official protest. Despite his wishes, the Nazi boycott effort was accompanied by considerable violence. Any Jew who spoke out was beaten. Several were killed. Many were bullied into selling their businesses, often at ridiculously low prices, to "Aryan" buyers. Many German businesses, supported by the president of the Reichsbank, wanted the boycott called off because it was disrupting business too much. Most of the members of Hitler's own cabinet urged him to end the boycott. He refused to do this without first using the boycott to strengthen his image as a defender of the German nation against "foreign interference."

After a few days more to allow the SA to let off steam, the Nazi boycott of Jewish shops was called off on April 4, the German foreign minister assuring the American consul that it would not be renewed. Goebbels blandly announced that because of the action "outrageous foreign propaganda [against the Nazi government] had been stopped." This was not true: the boycott actually had increased criticism of the Nazis in the American and European press, so much so that one foreign correspondent in Germany suggested that without this press attention the Nazis might have begun a "mass slaughter" of the Jews then and there. Hitler was not yet ready to order wholesale murders. But his ultimate intentions were clear — he told the Italian ambassador at this time that he wanted history to remember him as the one who "exterminated the Jewish pest from the world."[4]

Having dropped an overt national boycott for the time being, the Nazis simply altered their tactics. Contrary to the promise given to the American consul, they continued "informal boycotts" against Jewish business by creating signs bearing the words "German Business" — seals of approval in effect that were displayed on non-Jewish shops.

The Reich government also began to enact legal restrictions of Jews in the professions. On April 7, less than a week after the boycott, Hitler authorized his Ministry of Justice to issue a decree barring Jewish lawyers from practicing their profession. The decree exempted from the ban Jewish lawyers who were veterans of the First World War, after President Hindenburg warned Hitler against persecuting Jews who were veterans. While bowing to Hindenburg's wishes, the chancellor, again seizing the chance to portray himself as champion of the "volk," wrote to the old president that in the long run Germany could not tolerate "an alien body that was never entirely amalgamated with the German people." Hitler then argued that his measures were part of a "cleansing process [that] is only intended to be the restoration of a certain healthy and natural relationship, and secondly, to remove from certain positions important to the state those elements which cannot be entrusted with [decisions involving] the existence or nonexistence of the Reich." Hitler ordered drafting of further decrees to restrict Jews in the areas of medicine, education and other walks of life. A recent history of this era notes that from this moment on Jews in Germany worked under a "boycott of fear," if they worked at all.[5]

To underscore the point that "Semitic ideas" were of no account in the new Germany, Nazi groups in several cities staged public burnings of books written by Freud, Marx, Tucholsky, Thomas Mann and other authors. In Berlin books were pulled by SA troopers aided by excited university students and carried in trucks and cars to a central bonfire on the Opernplatz. Men and women marched around the fire, wearing the caps and badges of their student groups; some also wore Nazi armbands. They cheered as each author's work was thrown on the flames. Goebbels spoke, declaring "Jewish intellectualism is dead. National Socialism has hewn the way. The German folk soul can again express itself. . . . The old goes up in flames, the new shall be fashioned from the flame in our hearts."

The book burnings and legal bans were part of the program the National Socialists called "Gleichschaltung," a composite term meaning both "equal" and "consolidation." Gleichschaltung was an all-encompassing undertaking initiated by the Nazis in order to bind nation and party together so that National Socialism might achieve full control over every aspect of German society – in essence, a totalitarian system through which Hitler's government would determine political and economic life, education, the family, everything. And where would the Jews fit into this design? Nowhere. There would be no equality for them under Gleichschaltung. No Germany either. As an "alien body," as Hitler called the Jews in his letter to Hindenburg, they were to be removed from German society through a "cleansing process." They would be ostracized, driven out of Hitler's Germany. If they did not, or could not, leave — there was Hitler's vision of himself as exterminator.[6]

Herman Stern's brothers and sister worried about the Nazi threat but resisted the idea of leaving. Dora Stern wrote her brother in America that she and Moses felt confident they would be "better off" in Oberbrechen because they could grow vegetables in their garden and raise goats. Adolf talked briefly of leaving for America or Palestine, but she doubted he would do so. She had been told that those who were trying to get to Palestine were discovering that they could take almost nothing with them, while those who had gone there had written that it was hard to find work. Dora admitted that her sister-in-law Selma had urged Gustav that they should leave, but Gustav was resisting the idea. Their son Erich, however, wanted to come over and join his sister Klara in America.[7]

Adolf Stern lived in Duisburg with his wife Dora. So did their son Gustave with his own family, while Julius, home from North Dakota since his disagreements with Herman and Adeline, visited frequently between his travels on various business ventures. Adolf, or any of his family, may or may not have known about the assault on the Jewish owner of the furniture store in March, referred to above; Duisburg was a sizeable community and more than two hundred Jewish families lived there, scattered throughout the city. If he did know of it, Adolf could well have decided that the attack implied no threat to him. "AAC," the store owner was a Pole, one of the "eastern Jews"

(Ostjuden) who had come to Germany after the war's end and obtained residency. The Nazis had brutalized eastern Jews frequently in the 1920s, and many German Jews believed that the party's anti-Semitism was primarily aimed at the Ostjuden. And, like his brothers, Adolf had served in the German army during the war. He thought the Nazis might leave veterans alone.

But there was one thing that Adolf could not ignore: how his son Gustave had been treated soon after the Nazis took power. It will be recalled that Gustave was a conductor with the Duisberg Opera Company, which made him a civil employee. He also occasionally served as a repetitor for the local theater, had directed chorale societies in Krefeld, and taught voice to a number of pupils. Gustave and his wife, Gertrude, lived comfortably in one of the finer sections of Duisberg. Their son Hans was not yet three years old when Hitler became chancellor. "Overnight, I lost everything," Gustave later recalled. The Duisberg Opera, yielding to pressure from the local Nazi leadership, dismissed Gustave from his job almost a month before Hitler's government promulgated its Law for the Restoration of the Professional Civil Service, which stated that "civil servants who are not of Aryan descent are to be retired." Gustave's voice students quickly ceased taking his classes as well. Bereft of his means to make a living, convinced that this was only the beginning of the Nazi persecutions and that it would get worse, Gustave decided there was no alternative but to leave the country.

They were among the first German Jews to heed the danger of the Nazis and leave their homeland. "The 31st of March 1933, we left for Holland." Gertrude's parents were already living in Holland. Her father, having foreseen the Nazi victory in 1932, had moved a good deal of his savings into Dutch and French banks. He had also invested in French businesses and recently built a small sausage-casing factory in Paris. He and Gertrude's mother were packing to move to Paris when Gustave, Gertrude and Hans arrived in Holland. Gustave could find no jobs for a musician and briefly feared that he and his family would become impoverished. "My father-in-law said, 'Why don't you come with us?' We didn't have anything so I had to go. In

Paris I had the power of attorney for my father-in-law and had to manage the factory. He died very early, maybe a half year after we were there. I had to take over the place because it was a family property. . . . I met some people in music [in Paris] and played a few times in radio recitals, but otherwise did not do much in music."[8]

Gustave's comment that he and his family "didn't have anything" references a significant factor in emigration from Germany at this time. While Hitler and his cronies were anxious to drive out the Jews, they had no intention of letting anyone leave German without penalty. In 1931, the German government had established a special tax to stem the flow of capital out of the depression-wracked country. Anyone who wanted to transfer money for a foreign bank or business, or applied for an exit visa to emigrate, had to open his finances to the government for a thorough inspection. After inspecting all accounts and property, including an estimate of personal property, the government confiscated twenty-five percent of the person's net worth as a "flight tax." Only then could the emigrant leave for another country. Hitler continued the tax after taking power, but the Nazis also added a special touch – when they examined the property and accounts of Jews, they undervalued everything. Further, the Jewish applicant for a visa usually lost even more when he found he could not sell his property at anything near its assessed value, yet still had to pay the tax based on that value. Finally, when converting the emigrant's marks to another currency, the Reich government pegged the mark at a higher value than its true market rate, thus denuding his savings even further. Thus men like Gustave bought their freedom while, through confiscations and blatant manipulations, the Nazis obtained money for the German treasury.[9]

Gustave and his family rented a small apartment in Paris. It was a modest place, for they had far less money now than they had had in Duisburg. At first they did not worry. They expected the Nazi tide to crest and recede: surely civilized Germans would not accept the crass Hitler and his thugs for long! Adolf and Dora kept in touch through letters in which they shared bits of news about the family but (for fear they might be accused of acting as spies) carefully wrote little

about what was happening in Germany. Gustave was also circum-
spect in his replies. As the months turned into years, with no change
in Germany, they began to accept their new lives. Gustave manfully
struggled to meet the challenges of the sausage-casing business,
Gertrude kept a wary eye on expenses, and Hans learned French.
Hans entered school, his mother changing his name to Jean so as to
make him more acceptable to his classmates. Jean soon forgot how
to speak German. In 1936, the Sterns had a second son, naming him
Michel. By 1938, Gustave was resigned to spending the rest of his
life in France.

Back in Germany, Hitler was tightening his and his party's grip
on the whole nation. With his powers to issue emergency decrees, he
began removing from office elected and appointed officials who refused to support his plans or who were married to "non-Aryans."
"Practically all office holders, high or low, other than National Socialists, have been removed," the American embassy in Berlin informed Washington, and "practically all new appointments have been
men from the National Socialist Party . . . it may be definitely said
that the National Socialist Party is the legal constitutional government." Frederick Birchell, the *New York Times'* resident correspondent in Berlin, prowled about the city, talking to government officials and ordinary citizens, to Nazis and non-Nazis, and came to much
the same conclusion. The National Socialists, he wrote, were moving to "ensure a successful Third Reich" through "'gleichgeschaltet,'
a wonderful word in the Nazi vocabulary meaning 'co-ordinated in
the spirit of the new Germany.' Successively, the Nazis must take
over not only the Reich itself but everything in it. . . . In every business establishment throughout the Reich there [is being] installed a
Nazi cell to bring it into harmony with 'awakening Germany'."
Birchell added that efforts were underway to "sweep" all "non-Aryans" out of "the hospitals, the universities, the theatres and cinema
plants [i.e. studios], and all publishing concerns."[10]
Hardliner anti-Semites like Julius Streicher wanted Hitler to issue another decree banning marriages between Jews and non-Jews.

But the Fuehrer (as he was increasingly being called even by non-Nazis) decided the time was not yet ripe for so radical a step. In the meantime, the party sent the SA into the streets to warn young women not to be seen associating with Jewish men. If a woman ignored this warning, then the Nazis promised that her "name will be put down in the register of those women who possessed no race pride" and eventually "a visible sign will be etched or branded on the face of such persons, as a sign for every German man."[11]

On April 25, another restriction was promulgated with the "Act Against the Overcrowding of German Schools and Institutions of Higher Education," which stated that "the number of non-Aryan Germans . . . who may be admitted to schools, colleges and universities, must not exceed a number proportionate to the Aryan students in each school, college or university compared to the percentage of non-Aryans within the entire German population." As a result thousands of Jewish boys and girls were not permitted to remain in school. But Hitler went further by ordering that in all matters of curriculum and teaching, German public schools must now follow the dictates of the Reich Ministry of Education. In the New Order of Learning, students would be inundated with images of Hitler as the savior of Germany. They would begin each day with the statement "Heil Hitler," continue it at the start of each class, and repeat it during discussions, in answer to questions, until they had said and heard it dozens of times before leaving for home. History lessons were rewritten to make Nazism appear the apotheosis of German development and culture, to emphasize that communists and Jews had subverted Germany during the Great War, and that its destiny was to dominate Europe. All teachers were required to wear the swastika when in their classrooms.

To reinforce this indoctrination of German superiority and Nazi supremacy, and further insure that his racial ideas were implemented in every public classroom, Hitler appointed Bernard Rust, a longtime member of the party and an "old comrade" of his, as Minister of Education and Culture. Rust spent a large part of his first months in office directing the revision of virtually every textbook to be used. These were hastily issued before the new term of school began. A prime component of the texts, indeed the entire curriculum, was "racial science" (*Rassenkunde*) lessons at every grade level. This Nazi attempt to "prove" scientifically the racial superiority of the Aryans frequently used the Jews as the counterpoint to Aryan virtues. As one German scholar wrote after analyzing hundreds of such texts, "the universal Jew was [depicted as] evil pure and simple. The Aryan represented the good. Race mixing was the greatest sin." Thus "racial science" and anti-Semitism joined hands in making learning a near-religious experience.[12]

The American consul in Berlin informed Washington that through the Education Ministry's new guidelines "racial hygiene has been elevated to primary importance in the curriculum of schools and universities. Particular emphasis is being placed on the evils of miscegenation." He added his belief that one of the prime goals of the racial classes was to "reduce the German Jews to the position of ignominy to which they were subjected to during the Middle Ages." In point of fact, it was going to be even worse than that, especially for those Jewish children who remained in the public classrooms.

Jewish grade-school students, for example, had to sit and listen to classmates read from the best-selling Nazi novel *Poisonous Fungus*: "Inge looks up . . . her eyes stare into the face of the Jewish doctor. And this face is the face of the devil . . . Behind the thick spectacles gleam two criminal eyes. Around the thick lips plays a grin, 'Now I have you at last you little German girl!'" Barely adolescent students reading, at a teacher's directions, passages from a vulgar screed in order to humiliate their own classmates – a few years before, it could have been a satirical scene in one of Weimar's innovative cinema directors. Under Hitler it was instead a deadly serious bit of political theater: hate your neighbor, he's not really a person.[13]

Alfons Heck, a non-Jewish student who was in the Hitler Youth, noted in his autobiography that his racial science classes were even more anti-Semitic than the party lessons he learned outside of school. His teacher, Herr Becker, was a Nazi with a sadistic cunning: "Herr Becker seldom beat the Jewish children like he whipped us. Instead, he made them sit in a corner, which he sneeringly designated as 'Israel.' He never called on them, which I perceived as a blessing, but we quickly realized that he wanted us to despise the Jews." It took little time for children across Germany to absorb the lesson. In one Berlin school, non-Jewish children began bringing soap and water to school in order to clean off their desks, "where the Jewish children had sat." A later study of Nazi education found that a Jewish child in a small town was more likely to be victimized by his or her class-mates because in a setting where everyone knew everyone else, "non-Jewish children, even if they had wanted to, did not dare to be seen with Jews."[14]

Tea Eichengruen learned the cruelties fomented by racial science only too well. Tea and her family lived in the town of Dinslaken, north of Duisburg. Her mother, Elly Kann Eichengruen, was a cousin of Dora Stern, Adolf's wife, living in Duisburg. Elly had married Hermann Eichengruen around the end of World War I. Hermann's business was furs and hides. Each day he would leave Dinslaken and ride out into the countryside with his driver to buy hides and furs from local farmers. These were then brought back to the outbuild-ings of his property, where hired men would tan the hides and clean and brush the furs before he sold them to clothing manufacturers. Elly owned her own business, a millinery shop in Dinslaken. She employed about half a dozen women to make the hats she and her workers fashioned and sold in the shop, together with handkerchiefs, scarves, and small notions. "My mother was always the most pro-gressive person. The woman who was her directress, the main [staff] person in this workplace, was a dwarf with a hunchback. It didn't bother my mother one iota." In addition to Tea, born in 1920, the Eichengruens had a son, Erwin, born in 1924.

They enjoyed a good life in Dinslaken, which had about 23,000 inhabitants in 1930. Tea remembered that during the 1920s her par-ents employed a nanny and another woman who was both cook and housekeeper. Both women lived in the home, "There were separate quarters for them – I hate to use the word, but they were servants." There were only about two hundred Jews in Dinslaken, including the Eichengruens. The Eichengruens were, on the whole, more German than Jewish. They honored religious holidays and attended weekly services at the small synogogue in Dinslaken, and occasionally went to the larger Temple in Duisburg. Because the new German government had granted greater rights to German Jews, Tea's parents were Social Democrats, and flew the Weimar flag at holidays. Some of the neighbors flew the flag of Imperial Germany, but Tea could not remember heated arguments over politics or any slurs against Jews before 1933. "We were what you would call conservative Jews," Tea remembered. "We did not have a kosher household .... [We] were first and foremost *Germans* of Jewish religion."[15]

Tea saw kosher foods for the first time in the latter 1920s, when Hermann's father died and his mother came to live with the family. Hermann's mother had grown up among Orthodox Jews in one of the rural German villages west of the Rhine. She continued to follow many of the old customs and insisted on a kosher diet, something that Tea's mother had no idea how to prepare. So the Eichengruens hired an experienced cook to provide proper meals for the old woman. Tea would watch the cook go about her work with fascination. She enjoyed listening to stories that her grandmother told her about her own childhood. As a child will, she thought some of her grandmother's ideas were simply old fashioned, but when her grandmother died about 1930, she missed her greatly.

Finding a kosher cook had been easy for the Eichengruens because there were a number of Ostjuden families living in and near Dinslaken. Most of the heads of these families were small merchants or industrial workers. Many followed Orthodox practices and had retained the traditional beards, forelocks, and distinctive clothing. Ostjuden made up one in every five of the half million strong Jewish population in Germany, but they were not particularly welcomed by many German-born Jews. This was true in the case of Tea's family: "We thought of Eastern Jews as having come in [to Dinslaken] as beggars, a few peripherally as merchants . . . they were treated differently, and not very well by us German Jews. I'm ashamed to say it but it definitely was true."

The Nazis had been very shrewd in making the Ostjuden the focus of some of their most virulent anti-Semitism during the early months of Hitler's government. They had learned over the years that it was "easy to mobilize the xenophobic animosity of broad sections of the [German] population against such an 'alien' group of Jews." The first Jews arrested and placed in a concentration camp after Hitler took power were the Ostjuden. In July 1933, the Reichstag approved another law that revoked the citizenship of anyone who had been naturalized between November 9, 1918 and January 30, 1933, a move specifically aimed at the Ostjuden.[16]

Probably because they believed that the anti-Jewish rhetoric of the Nazis was directed primarily toward Ostjuden, Tea's parents did not immediately see Hitler's government as a threat to them. When the boycott came in March, Elly Kann was not overly alarmed. Tea returned from school that day and found "storm troopers placed at the entrance to my mother's business – they had the brown cap, the boots, the swastika, the whole nine yards. They no longer wanted people to patronize Jewish establishments. This wasn't only at my mother's store, it was at all the Jewish stores up and down the two streets where [Jewish] businesses were located." But when the boycott was abruptly called off, Elly and her husband felt that perhaps the demonstration had been aimed at the eastern Jews who were so different from the cultured German Jews. "The business probably suffered," Tea remembered, "but I don't think there was anybody laid off until my mother sold the store [two or three years] later. My mother enjoyed doing the work. I don't know that she had to do it financially, she just liked it."[17]

Not until Tea began her first year at the *Gymnasium* (the German equivalent of high school) in 1934 did her parents recognize the seriousness of the Nazi's hatred of all Jews. Tea had always loved school. "My first eight years were at a Jewish school. We had three elementary schools in Dinslaken – Jewish, Protestant and Catholic. After I was at the Jewish school, I went on to the 'high school,' which was separated by gender. I went to the girls' high school, boys went to the boys' high school. I know I was fourteen when I was asked – when we [Jews] were all asked to leave. Because the new law against 'overcrowding' limited the number of Jews allowed to attend public schools, we could no longer attend school in Dinslaken. My parents found – I don't know how they managed to do this – but they found a private business school in Duisburg, the town where Adolf and Dora Stern lived. I could go to that school. I either rode the streetcar or the train [to Dinslaken] and commuted to this school."

The mandatory racial science lessons were taught at this private school, but Tea was more fortunate than other young Jews in this respect. "I was the only Jewish student and was treated actually respectfully. The teacher was a decent guy. I was dismissed from the room when he had to discuss the 'Jewish question'." It was when she returned to Dinslaken that she came face to face with the impact of daily lessons about the "evil Jew." "After I had left school [in Duisburg] one day, I came home and saw my closet friend Liselotte Schulze. She was wearing her Hitler Youth uniform, for the girl's organization. We were standing two feet apart. She turned around and said nothing, and I turned away. That was the moment when I came home and told my mother, 'I don't want to stay here anymore. If Liselotte cannot speak to me, no one else will and I want to get out'."[18]

But leaving Germany was out of the question. "My mother understood. My father was totally aghast at the thought of a fourteen or fifteen year old leaving, or wanting to leave, Germany. Hermann, another veteran of the Great War, thought that the German people would wake up to the insanity of Hitler's movement and drive the Nazis from office; all they had to do was wait. Frustrated and angry, I made the decision that if I was going to be hated because I was a Jew, I would *be* a Jew." She had often spent Saturdays at the Jewish orphanage in Dinslaken. As a small child she played with the children there. Then, when she was older, she read stories to them. Many of the children in the orphanage were Polish or Russians, whose parents had fled those countries and come to Germany. Since Hitler had become chancellor, "more children came into the orphanage because more children had lost their families, often because their parents had been killed by Nazis or had fled again, leaving them behind." Now, rejected by her non-Jewish friends, she began to spend more time at the orphanage, talking to the director, who was Orthodox. "Dr. Rothschild, the director, had a very rational religious outlook and he could explain things to me [about Judaism] in a way that made great sense."

While Tea was embracing Judaism as a way of defying the Nazis, the Eichengruen household suddenly was enlarged by another tragedy. Mrs. Eichengruen's brother, Rudolf Kann, was an attorney living in Essen. Like his sister and brother-in-law, he was a Social Democrat. In 1934, he agreed to take a case defending a communist who had been accused by the police of committing a crime. "This was a very well known communist," Tea remembered, "although I don't remember his name, but I do know the trial was a big thing." Some members of the Nazi party considered it a big thing that Kann would defend any communist. Angered, they called Kann and made "threats to his life." He decided he and his wife must "leave immediately" before the Nazis made good their threat. He and his wife, Selma, crossed into Switzerland. Their two sons, Manfred and Herbert, were left with the Eichengruens. Tea was not certain how to feel about this. "Manfred was a year older than my brother, who was ten, and Herbert was about nine." While the household was large enough for all four children to live there comfortably, the strain of the constant Nazi menace was taking its toll on everyone.[19]

In 1935, Nazis again began pressuring people not to shop at Jewish-owned businesses in Dinslaken. Elly Kann slowly lost most of her customers. She sold her millinery shop – at a fraction of its true value – to a buyer who met the Nazi requirements for being a German of "pure blood." Tea could not "remember ever having met the people who bought the shop, or knowing who they were, but we continued to live upstairs in the building." Through all of this Tea had been putting on some pressure of her own, alternately telling her mother that they should leave Germany and then urging her to adopt a stronger sense of Judaism. "I wanted to be kosher [as her grandmother had been] and didn't want to do things on the Sabbath, and so forth. My mother thought this was not necessary. Finally she said,

'Look, if you want to stay here, you live the way we live. If that doesn't suit you, you can move to the orphanage.' Of course, I didn't want to do that." But still Tea kept thinking that if she and her family were going to be ostracized in their own country, the only solution was to leave. But leave for where?

All across Germany, Jewish families were facing persecutions ranging from petty humiliations to mortal dangers, day to day trying to gauge the seriousness of the Nazi threat. Christopher Isherwood, a British writer living in Berlin until 1934, recorded the mounting fear among Jews as they struggled with their dilemma: "Almost every evening, the SA men come into the café [Isherwood and friends frequented]. Sometimes they are only collecting money; everybody is compelled to give something. Sometimes they have come to make an arrest. One evening a Jewish writer, who was present, ran into the telephone box to ring up the Police. The Nazis dragged him out, and he [also] was taken away. Nobody moved a finger."[20]

Hitler and his henchmen had said that they wanted the Jews out of Germany. Was this just posturing for momentary gains or the purpose of gaining more public support, or did the Nazis mean it, so much so that they were prepared to kill those who did not leave? Could more reasonable men in the government or the Nazi party restrain the most radical anti-Semites? Should the Jews leave Germany now, before it was too late? In the first year of Nazi rule, very few did. Only 37,000 of the more than half million Jews in Germany emigrated that year, only a little more than 500 of them going to the United States. Even with the American immigration restrictions, far more could have obtained an entry visa, especially after Roosevelt pressured the State Department to be more lenient in its review process.

Years later, those who had the benefit of hindsight were quick to ridicule the vast majority who did not recognize the threat and leave at once. Another writer, Arthur Koestler, had spent two years on the staff of the liberal newspaper *Vossische Zeitung,* before leaving Germany a few months before Hitler took power. In his 1952 autobiography he wrote that the Jews he had known in Germany had "reacted to the approaching apocalypse according to their varied temperaments. There were the professional optimists and the constitutional optimists. The former fooled their readers; the latter fooled themselves. There were those who said 'they can't be as bad as all that.' And those who said: 'They are too weak, they can't start anything.' And those who said: 'You are frightened of a bogey, you've got persecution mania, you are hysterical.' And those who said: 'Hatred doesn't lead anywhere, one must meet them with sympathy and understanding.' And those who said simply: 'I refuse to believe it'."[21]

Koestler's observations were no doubt accurate. It was easy, however, to relate such things years later with an after-the-fact wisdom. No one in 1933 or 1934 could have presented convincing evidence that Hitler ultimately intended death for every Jew that came under his control. And every Jewish man and woman, who hesitated to give up everything they had made of their lives and leave Germany, could offer sensible arguments for their choice. Jews who owned businesses would lose them at a fraction of their true value; one could not be certain that he or she would ever see friends or relatives again; who could know for certain how long Hitler would remain chancellor. The Nazis had altered many of their policies while climbing to the pinnacle they now held. Could it not be that they would do so again at some point in time?[22]

In the hopes of preserving something of the Jewish presence in Germany, major Jewish organizations counseled their members to remain in Germany, to wait before acting hastily. The Central Organization of German Citizens of the Jewish Faith (known as *Centralverain*) recommended that Jewish newspapers and groups should try to reassure the Nazis by expressing their loyalty and patriotism. Numerous publications did offer such statements, while several Jewish organizations, generally those who supported conservative political goals, published statements approving of Hitler's intention to suppress communism. The *Deutscher Vortrupp* (German Vanguard), for example, made the argument that it was the duty of German Jews to remain loyal to their country, "even to a Nazi state that wanted to throw them out." *Deutscher Vortrupp* representatives condemned Zionists and liberal Jewish ties to Weimar politics, and attempted to make an alliance with conservative veterans groups in order to persuade non-Nazis in Hitler's cabinet that the majority of Jews would be loyal to the state.

The Nazis turned a deaf ear to these overtures. The party continued its campaign to paint the Jews as a grave threat to Germany, and as the months went by, more and more Germans came to believe the claims. While the Jewish groups searched for other ways to reassure their countrymen, it fell to individual families to decide what they must do.[23]

As we have seen, of the three families who faced these agonizing questions, the Gustave Sterns elected to leave immediately, for France, hoping that circumstances in Germany would eventually change for the better, allowing them to go home. The Eichengruens elected to stay and wait on events, overruling their daughter's wishes to leave. The Levys also decided to remain. That did not mean that all the members of the Levy and Eichengruen families accepted this, however.

In Dinslaken, Tea was still determined to leave Germany at the earliest opportunity. Even though she knew her mother tacitly supported her wishes, she knew no one would permit her to go anywhere alone when she was just fifteen years old. However, she also knew that plans being made at the orphanage might serve as her way out: Dr. Rothschild was engaged in delicate negotiations with Hitler's government to take many of the orphans to live in Palestine.

The Nazis were willing to grant Rothschild exit visas so he could do this. But since Great Britain administered Palestine under a League of Nation mandate, and Her Majesty's government were strictly limiting the number of Jews allowed to immigrate, Rothschild had to have the permission of the British government to enter the Holy Land. But if he could accomplish this, Tea in turn was confident she could convince her father to let her go with them. If that did not work, then she had another possible way out. She had come to know Adolf and Dora Stern fairly well while going to school in Duisburg. Dora sympathized with her desire to leave, and said that perhaps Adolf's brother in America might be able to help her – when she was older.

Meanwhile, in Troisdorf, Hilda Levy was looking for her own way to leave Germany. A friendly policeman in Troisdorf had advised Samuel Levy to "get your children out, get them away" from Germany as soon as possible. At the age of twenty-four, Hilda could easily leave on her own, but the Levys had no money for the travel expenses. She also knew that other countries were less likely to grant an entry visa to a single woman. But she had met a man named Sally Jonas at a Jewish organization social. Jonas, eight years older than Hilda, had sold his small business under Nazi pressure in 1933. Hilda had persuaded her father to take him on as an apprentice in the butcher shop. Hilda had decided that Sally would make a good husband. He now lived in the Levy home. He had two aunts living in the United States. One was Fredrecka Straus, whose late husband had begun the Straus clothing chain in North Dakota. Fredrecka's sister was Adeline, the wife of Herman Stern.[24]

Notes

1. Hilda Levy Jonas, interview with Shoptaugh, October 24, 1997. Information on Troisdorf from "Troisdorf unter dem Hakenkreuz" (Troisdorf under the Swastika), Bonn news service story filed in 1987 and preserved at http://www.floerken.de/texte/tdf-ns.htm.

2. The order for the boycott, published in the *Voelkischer Beobachter,* March 29, 1933, is available in many collections of Holocaust documents. See also Avraham Barkai, *From Boycott to Annihilation: The Economic Struggle of German Jews, 1933-1943* (Hanover: University Press of New England, 1989), pp. 13-25; Edwin Black, *The Transfer Agreement* (NY: Macmillan, 1984), pp. 11-39. While Black's has much useful detail on the boycott, he overestimates the possibility that Britain and the United States could have applied trade restrictions to drive Hitler from power in early 1933.

3. Daniel Goldhagen, *Hitler's Willing Executioners: Ordinary Germans and the Holocaust* (New York: Alfred Knopf, 1996), p. 90; Alison Owings, *Frauen: German Women Recall the Third Reich* (New Brunswik, NJ: Rutgers University Press, 1993), p. 199.

4. Karl A. Schleunes, *The Twisted Road to Auschwitz: Nazi Policy toward German Jews, 1933-1939* (Urbana: University of Illinois Press, 1970), pp. 62-91; Black, pp. 13, 59-61. During the boycott George Gordon, the American *charge d'affaires* in Berlin, gave the State Department the impression that the anti-Semitic actions since Hitler became chancellor were largely the work of Goebbels and Goering, and that Hitler himself was acting as an "element of moderation in the Nazi Party." This misperception of Hitler's intentions in regard to Germany's Jewish population was to adversely influence American diplomacy with Germany throughout the decade. See Gordon's reports of March 25 and April 2, 1933, in *FRUS,* vol. 151, pp. 331-33, 347-50.

5. George Gordon to Acting Secretary of State, July 8, 1933, in *FRUS,* vol. 151, pp. 354-56; Hitler to Hindenburg, April 5, 1933, in *Documents on German Foreign Policy* (hereafter DGFP), vol., 1, pp. 253-255; Saul Friedlander, *Nazi Germany and the* Jews, p. 29.

6. "Burning, Students Supervise Event," *New York Times,* May 11, 1933; Klaus Fischer, *Nazi Germany: A New History,* (NY: Continuum Press, 1995), pp. 278-284; Helmut Krausnick, "Stages of 'Co-ordination,'" in *The Path to Dictatorship* (NY: Praeger, 1966).

7. Dora Stern to Herman Stern, December 1, [1933], Moses Stern file; Dora Stern to Herman Stern, July 15, 1934, Klara Stern file, Stern Papers.

8. Here and below, Gustave Stern, interview by Dr. Eric Offenbacher, October 29, 1979, Jewish Archives Project transcript, Washington State Holocaust Education Resource Center, Seattle, pp. 5-6.

9. David Wyman, *Paper Walls* (New York: Pantheon Books, 1985 ed.), p. 28. Marion A. Kaplan records that over eight years, the Nazis raised "as much as 900 million marks from the Reich Flight Tax alone," *Between Dignity and Despair* (New York: Oxford University Press, 1998), p. 70-71.

10. George Messersmith (consul General) to Secretary of State, April 10, 1933, in *FRUS,* vol. 151, pp. 222-227; Birchall, *The Storm Breaks: A Panorama of Europe and the Forces that Have Wrecked Its Peace* (New York: Viking Press, 1940). pp, 137-139.

11. Edgar Ansel Mowrer, *Germany Puts the Clock Back* (New York: William Morrow and Co., 1933), pp. 223-24.

12. Eve Nussbaum Soumerai and Carol D. Schulz, *Daily Life During the Holocaust* (Westport, CT: Greenwood Press, 1998), pp. 40-42; Gilmer W. Blackburn, *Education in the Third Reich: Race and History in Nazi Textbooks* (Albany: State University of New York Press, 1985), pp. 75-76.

13. George Gordon to the Acting Secretary of State, July 8, 1933, *FRUS*, vol. 151, pp. 354-56; Soumerai and Schulz, p. 42. In issuing the Act Against Overcrowding of German Schools, the Nazis argued that the Jewish professors and students "unfairly dominated" higher education. This was another lie. The number of Jews teaching in German universities had increased during the Weimar era (from 69 professors in 1910 to 114 in 1932) but as a percentage of the total it had fallen (6.9 % in 1910, 5.6% in 1932). The percentage of German Jewish students in universities had also declined: in 1930 only 4.3 % of the students professed themselves as Jewish. That was less than half of the percentage in the 1880s. See Peter Pulzer, *Jews and the German State* (Cambridge: Harvard University Press 1992), p. 276,278.

14. Alfons Heck, *A Child of Hitler: Germany in the Days When God Wore a Swastika* (Frederick, Colorado: Renaissance House, 1985), p. 13; Kaplan, *Between Dignity and Despair*, pp. 93-94.

15. Here and below, Tea Eichengruen Stiefel, interview with Shoptaugh, March 17, 1998, Oral History Collection, Northwest Minnesota History Center, Minnesota State University Moorhead, transcript, p. 4, 11; *Encyclopedia of Jewish Life Before and During the Holocaust*, ed by Shmuel Spector (New York: New York University Press 2001), vol. 1, p. 311 for Jewish population of Dinslaken.

16. Friedlander, *Nazi Germany and the Jews,* pp. 18-19; Deborah Dwork and Robert Jan van Pelt, *Holocaust: A History* (NY: W.W. Norton, 2002), p. 73. See also David Clay Large, "Out with the Ostjuden: The Scheunenviertel Riots in Berlin, November 1923," in Christhard Hoffmann, et. al., eds. *Exclusionary Violence: Antisemitic Riots in Modern German History* (Ann Arbor : University of Michigan Press, 2002).

17. Stiefel interview transcript, pp. 22-23, 30-31.

18. Stiefel transcript, pp. 12-16. The girl's variation of the Hitler Youth was the *Bund deutscher Madel* – German maiden's group.

19. Stiefel transcript, pp. 38-40. Rudolf Kann died in Switzerland in 1936, possibly from peritonitis, although some suspected he was poisoned by Nazi agents. Kann's wife, Selma, then returned to Germany and took her sons to live in Holland. Sometime in 1940 or 1941, after Germany occupied Holland, the three were arrested and deported to camps in Poland. Documents from the German Ministry of Justice, copies of which were sent to the Stiefels in 1951, confirm that Selma and Manfred Kann died at Auschwitz, and Herbert Kann died at Sobibor.

20. Christopher Isherwood, *The Berlin Stories* (New York: New Directions Books, 1954), pp. 203-204. See also Jonathan Fryer, *Isherwood* (New York: Doubleday and Co, 1978), pp. 133-34.

21. Kaplan, *Between Dignity and Despair*, pp. 72-73; Koestler, *Arrow in the Blue: An Autobiography* (New York: MacMillan Co., 1952) pp. 250-51.

22. One of the arguments offered for staying in Germany, coming from rabbis, intellectuals, and others, was the argument that the Jewish people must accept the will of God, remain in Germany, and "bear witness" to the persecutions of the Nazis. A good example of this can be found in the diaries of Victor Klemperer, *I Will Bear Witness* (New York, Random House, 1998).

23. John V. H. Dippel, *Bound Upon a Wheel of Fire* (New York: Basic Books, 1996), pp. 64-69.

24. Hilda Jonas transcript, pp. 3-5. Several studies offer direct testimony and psychological findings to the effect that Jewish "women usually saw the danger signals first" and urged their families to leave Germany. Marion Kaplan, provides an excellent summary in *Between Dignity and Despair,* pp, 62-67.

Chapter Six
"You Have Been Kind Enough to Assist Me"

While life for the Jews in Germany was quickly deteriorating, Herman Stern had problems of his own in America. The depression had cut deeply into his business, particularly in his newest stores in Lamoure and Carrington.

Herman had opened the Lamoure store in 1927, buying out an already-existing clothing shop and converting it to carry the lines of clothes that had sold so successfully in Casselton and Valley City. Herman's son Eddie had followed the fortunes of the Lamoure store first hand. He and brother Dick had been driving a truck, making deliveries from Valley City to the other stores, since he was fourteen. "I'd drive over those gravel roads in every kind of weather, even when it was icy. I guess I never thought about it too much and so never skidded off the road," he remembered. In the late 1920s, the shop in Lamoure and the shop in Carrington, which had opened about the same time as the Lamoure store, had been growing. But after the 1929 stock market crash "business was getting slower at all the stores and really poor at Lamoure and Carrington."

Many of the farmsteads around both of these towns were now deserted. The farmers who had lived on them had been ruined by the low prices for their crops and livestock. Stern, true to his father's profession as a cattle dealer, carefully followed cattle prices in North Dakota as a sign of the state's overall economic health. He noted that by 1930, farmer's were "getting less for their cattle than in cost to transport them to market." Grain prices were equally bad. The farmers could live on the land with vegetables, some chickens and hogs, but they had to pay their taxes and mortgages. When they lacked the money for this, the banks foreclosed on them.

Some of the farmers tried to stem the tide of foreclosures by joining a populist group called the Farm Holiday Association. While

Association leaders lobbied state legislatures to obtain legislation to postpone tax payments, the rank and file attended farm auctions and tried to intimidate anyone from placing a bid on the property. Sometimes the intimidation worked and an Association member would buy the farm for a few dollars and then sign the deed over to the farmer who had lost it. Sometimes this strategy failed. In any event, few people had the money to buy the land under any circumstances. So the farms lay empty. And with the decline of their customer bases, business at the Lamoure and Carrington stores fell sharply.

By 1933, Eddie's dad decided he had to cut his losses and close the two stores. The towns, he decided, were "too small to do profitable business" with "the type of merchandise we handled." In short, there were no longer enough buyers who could afford the higher prices of the Kuppenheimer suits, Arrow shirts, and other quality merchandise that Stern carried as his main stock. Rather than try to sell the shops, Stern closed the Lamoure store, gave inventory from both shops to the man he had hired to run the Carrington store to help him organize his own store. In return, the man "sold" back to Stern his shares in Straus Clothing. Stern then turned to preserving his remaining shops.[1]

This would not be easy. His customer bases in Valley City and Casselton had also declined. His merchandise had always been more expensive than that of his largest competitor in Valley City, Montgomery Ward. Stern used his advertising to attract white-collar customers, with dress shirts for one or two dollars and suits for about thirty dollars. Ward's targeted blue-collar families, offering work shirts for as low as forty-nine cents, union suits for ninety-eight cents and house "frocks" for less than thirty cents. Stern carried work clothes as well, but he could hardly cut his prices low enough to match a chain store like Wards.

Stern was carrying more of his customers on credit. "Some of our best customers had always been teachers," he later explained to an interviewer. Teachers tried to look their respectable best and so had frequented Straus. But with the hard times, teachers in North Dakota were suffering terribly. As Stern pointed out, "the bank failures had made it very hard for teachers to get cash for their paychecks." Even worse, many teachers were not being paid by check but with vouchers that some local merchants would honor on the promise of being paid later. Stern accepted the teacher's vouchers but could not convert these into cash for his own needs.[2]

Stern was growing increasingly frustrated with Roosevelt's New Deal, in particular the number of regulations that the Federal programs required from the states in exchange for Federal aid. In 1937, the state legislature passed an Unemployment Insurance Act which provided some benefits to workers who lost their jobs during economic downturns. The act spared the smallest operations from its requirements but any business with at least eight employees had to abide by its provisions. Stern, together with several others, used his position in the Greater North Dakota Association to attack the law. The act "would never have been brought to our statute books had it not been for the instigation of the Federal Government," the GDNA secretary wrote to a manufacturer's association. "There is considerable dissatisfaction with the Act," he added, but doubted that it could be overturned until unemployment compensation ceased to be "one of the dominant interests of the Federal Government." Stern and many others also disliked the New Deal's agricultural policies, none more than the limits placed on crop acreage for wheat and other staples by the U.S. Department of Agriculture. The idea behind the plan was to raise prices by lowering production, but many felt the plan was unfair. The GNDA urged numerous business and farming groups to sign petitions against the plan and paid for hundreds of radio ads calling it an unfair restriction of the farmer's freedom to run his own business.[3]

Worried that in hard times the merchants would get desperate and fall into cutthroat competition, Stern looked for new ways to unite the business interests in his community. Back in the 1920s, he had helped organized the Valley City Town Crier's Club, a group that would "develop a general fellowship between competitors in business." Now he feared that all sense of fellowship would disappear. So he and several of the other businessmen met to discuss what could be done to maintain the old sense of unity by working to keep the businessmen in touch with one another. One way to do that, they decided, was to carefully limit the cost of luncheons at the Rotary Club: "we kept the price of the lunch down to forty cents, no more, because some of the men wouldn't come if the price was higher than that."

Stern himself was doing well enough to afford to pay more than forty cents for lunch, but he handled his money carefully just the same. In 1930, both of his sons had graduated from Valley City High School and entered college. Dick had expected to go to the Massachusetts Institute of Technology, but with the depression, he had to settle for the University of North Dakota, where he studied civil engineering. Eddie's path to a profession was more convoluted. "Mom and Dad wanted me to go to the University of Pennsylvania, probably hoping I'd meet a nice Jewish girl, but by then I had my eye on this Valley City girl, so I talked them into letting me go to UND with Dick for a year. Then I told Dad I wanted to help him at the store, that way I could keep seeing the girl." Neither Eddie nor Dick knew at the time how much Herman worried about the cost of their tuitions. "It was a pretty tough time to see them through college," he later told an interviewer. "College was much cheaper then, but a thousand dollars looked mighty big in those days."[4]

All in all, Stern had plenty to worry about. Enough, that when Klara contacted him about coming to live in America, he could easily have said he was sorry but could not take on any further obligations by sponsoring her. But he had not done that. Instead, he had signed the papers, took her into his home in February 1934, enrolled her at the local college, and later helped her find a job.

He also must have told Klara that he was willing to help other relatives leave Germany, because in 1934 and 1935, he prepared paperwork for sponsoring four others. One was Klara's brother, Erich. A second was a distant relative who wanted a chance to pursue her art. The third was a total stranger, a man who knew Klara but had never met Stern. The fourth was someone that Stern knew only too well. Indeed, it must have tested Herman's resolve considerably to consider helping young Julius Stern come to America a second time.

Klara received letters from her brother Erich almost as soon as she settled into Herman's home in Valley City. His uncle had submitted an affidavit for a visa on his behalf by May of 1934, scarcely three months after Klara's arrival. By June, Stern was contacting shipping lines to secure a ticket for Erich's passage. In October 1934, Klara sent Erich a long letter assuring him that he would like America. "You will be happy when you come here," she wrote, "if you have money," and Herman, she promised would help him find a good job. Erich must have written her that he hoped to be able to stay in New York, for she wrote to tell him "Uncle thinks you should live here [in Valley City]. New York will be too expensive." She noted that when he arrived a woman named Blumenthal, who Stern knew in Oberbrechen and who had emigrated years before, would meet his train in Chicago and see that he made the connection to North Dakota. "Uncle [Herman] is very nice and does speak German, so you need not be anxious."

Stern had hoped to meet Erich's ship in New York, but when his departure was delayed, as frequently happened, he asked one of the partners of Sonneborn Brothers, one of Fifth Avenue's finest shops "for boy's and student's clothes," to meet Erich and get him on the train. "I would suggest a first class ticket from New York to Chicago," he wrote, "and a coach ticket from Chicago to Valley City. There is considerable saving on the coach ticket west of Chicago." He sent the man a "blank check" and asked him to fill in the proper amount "after you have taken care of his railroad fare and other expenses." Erich made the crossing in early November and arrived in Valley City about three days after reaching New York.[5]

Erich Stern lived with Herman and Adeline for several months, working at least part-time in the Valley City store. Sometime in the summer of 1935, he decided that he wanted to move to Chicago. Stern evidently hoped that Erich would stay in North Dakota, but by mid-1935, Erich wanted to go, partly because Klara lived in Chicago, and also because he wanted to become more independent. From a series of letters he wrote to Herman and Adeline in the early months of 1936, one can obtain insights into the lives of young German immigrants in Depression America. When Erich arrived in Chicago, sometime in the autumn of 1935, he found a job at a store called Father and Son Shoes. As he wrote to Adeline later, he was paid "the first few days one dollar and later on 75 cents," this for a work day that began at 10:30 am and ended at 11:00 pm. He admitted that he did not like the job but "had to keep that since anything better couldn't be found."[6]

Erich could not have survived on his pay were it not for the fact that he was living with a family named Bromberg, who were relatives of the Sterns. He was paying them a small rent. He noted in one letter that his sister Klara was saving more money for her own rent by "teaching small children" in the evenings and hoped he could find something similar. It is evident that Stern was sending the Brombergs some money. In one of Erich's letters to his uncle he mentions the letters that Herman sent to Mrs. Bromberg and remarks "they make a secret out of what is going on . . . but I think that I can see pretty good what about [sic] it is. It's ok to have sent that check to Br. I will try to save a little every week to pay you back."

He obviously did not enjoy living with the Brombergs. Louis Bromberg was at best working only part time: "I don't know what Mr. Br. is doing. He must be doing something since he is going downtown every day." Erich complained that both Mr. Bromberg and his son Morris "seem to think that what mine is, is theirs. Besides using my toothpaste, shaving lotion, etc., I caught Morris wearing my underwear, ties, and esp. sox." This led to an argument with Mrs. Bromberg, when he wanted her to darn socks that he said Morris had put holes in. It also inspired Erich to conceive a little plot of revenge. Knowing that Morris wanted to have good dress shoes, Erich offered to get him a pair from Straus at cost, and then, as he wrote Herman, "charge him a little more than you charge me." Herman firmly refused to allow this.

With no money to speak of, Erich's social life was spent at some of the German-American clubs in Chicago. At one group he called the "Club of German Newcomers," he remarked that he could meet others and listen to talks about the city and "American interests." At a second ethnic club, he met some young men and women who had "just came over from Germany." He generally had to speak German with these recent immigrants. This, plus the tendency of these new arrivals to continue their "German customs," bothered him: "I hate that stuff, especially since I want to use my English." He wanted to take some night school classes as soon as he could, probably to improve his chances of finding a better job.

In response to Erich's letters, Herman sent him new clothes (which the Brombergs kept borrowing), lent him some money and sent Eddie and Dick to visit him and help him meet others in Chicago. Stern himself went to Chicago in early February to help Erich find a better job. It appears that he succeeded, for Erich was working in the stock room of Kuppenheimers at a salary of fifteen dollars a week. Stern had urged Erich and Klara's parents to leave Germany. But knowing that the children did not have the resources to make a convincing case to the State Department that they could sponsor their mother and father, he had decided to add his own name to the affidavits. This heartened Erich considerably. He "hope[d] my folks will be here soon." But there were still a great many barriers standing between Gustav and Selma Stern and the shores of America.

A second young man who Stern agreed to help at this time was a young German Jew named Leon Hayum, a tailor who had seen the handwriting on the wall the moment Hitler was named chancellor. By February 1933, he had immigrated to Luxembourg, living there with his fiancé, a woman named Ida, who was also a cousin of Klara Stern. Leon wrote a letter to Klara, who was still in Germany. He asked if her Uncle Herman could help him and Ida. "I am not able to make a living here in Luxembourg," he wrote. "I only get a monthly work permit [i.e. renewable by the Luxembourg government each month upon application] here, foreigners are not permitted to set up a business of their own." As a result, he was doing piecework for established clothiers and did not have sufficient money. He and Ida had thought of moving on to Palestine, but he believed that there would be more than enough Jewish tailors there already, and so he hoped Klara would show his letter to her uncle after she got to America.

Proud of his craftsmanship, he wanted Herr Stern to know that he had saved some two thousand marks for ship passage and would "gladly" repay any debts he might have to assume. Also, that he was "well trained for my career as a tailor for men and ladies" and had received high marks on his journeyman examination. "Ida and I are used to a hard life. It is a point of honor with me to work my way up. What we need is work, and we hope one day to become American citizens. Your uncle's sponsorship would be our stepping stone."[7]

Klara showed Hayum's letter to Herman when she came to Valley City. Stern must have been impressed with the young tailor's resolve. He sent to the State Department an affidavit to sponsor both Leon and Ida for residency visas. By that time, Leon and Ida had married. But the American consul in Anvers, Belgium, where Hayum went to apply for his papers, rejected Stern's affidavit on the ground that Ida was not a close relative; "friends or distant relatives," the consul wrote, could not be held legally responsible for someone if he became a public charge.

Stern refused to accept the consul's ruling. Once again he appealed to Gerald Nye. Nye in turn sent a cable to the American consul general in Antwerp, giving his assurance that Stern was the kind of man who would honor his moral commitment to take care of the Hayums should it be necessary. Whether the State Department accepted the assessment of Stern's character or not, they decided not to risk upsetting Nye. Leon Hayum and Ida received their visas within a month of Nye's cable.[8]

Leon and Ida made their crossing in September. As with Erich Stern, an employee of Sonneborn's met them in New York and sent them on their way to Valley City. Stern had found an apartment for them and gave Hayum a tailor's position at Straus, paying him forty dollars a week. Hayum, who decided he would be "more American" with the name Leo, worked at Straus for some three years. Stern clearly liked the young man and hoped he would stay at the store. But in 1938 or 1939, Hayum moved on, realizing his dream to open his own shop in Florida. As will be seen, Stern by then was sponsoring four other relatives of Hayum's.

The first judgment of the American Consul in Belgium, that Stern could not be held liable for a "distant relative," provides a glimpse of how the State Department continued to deal with the Jewish crisis in Germany. In 1933, President Roosevelt had requested the State Department to look more sympathetically upon applications for visas from German Jews. Within State itself, there were those who accurately assessed the danger of the Nazi threat. George Messersmith, the Consul General in Berlin, warned his superiors as early as the fall of 1933 that the Jews in Germany were in grave danger. "There has been nothing in social history more implacable, more heartless and more devastating than the present policy in Germany against the Jews," he wrote to the Undersecretary of State.

A few weeks later, Messersmith went further, warning Secretary of State Cordell Hull that any statements by Hitler about moderating the German government's anti-Semitism should be considered "complete illusions." The Nazis, he warned, had taken latent anti-Semitism in German society and fed it remorselessly with their propaganda. He warned Hull that the persecutions would continue and that the American government would be faced with an ongoing crisis concerning German Jewish refugees. The British ambassador warned his government essentially the same thing in his own analysis: "it is certainly Hitler's intention to degrade and, if possible, expel the Jewish community from Germany."

Yet, even after accurately foreseeing the crisis, Messersmith opposed any steps that would lead to a major increase in German immigration to the United States. As one recent study of the consular service's reaction to the German Jewish crisis concludes, "applicants for visas at the Berlin consulate-general during [Messersmith's] tenure (1933-34) found a sympathetic ear, [but] he showed no disposition whatsoever to bend the rules in their favor. Some were granted visas, but many others who could have received them were turned away."[9]

In defense of their actions, consuls argued that, after all, they were only following the law as Congress had written it. With historically high unemployment, how could they open the doors wide to immigrants, even those who were threatened in their home countries? Their supporters in the press and Congress agreed with this reasoning and added another argument: if German Jews were granted a special status to enter the country, how long would it be before the precedent encouraged Poland or Rumania or some other nation to launch pogroms against its Jewish population and call on America to grant them wholesale entry as well? Such arguments found favor with a large part of the American public. Some groups were already charging that large Jewish-owned businesses were denying jobs to "100% Americans" while hiring refugees "just off the boat."

And so, despite the dangers in Germany and despite Roosevelt's request for greater flexibility, consuls had continued to be parsimonious when reviewing the individual applications. They habitually turned to the "likely to become a public charge" clause of the 1917 Immigration Act as their justification for rejecting an application, even if an American citizen signed an affidavit promising to care for an immigrant if it became necessary. As seen in the consul's action in the case of the Hayums, many State Department diplomats doubted that American sponsors could be held legally accountable if an immigrant did indeed become a "public charge."

Late in 1935, the White House ordered the State Department to stop leaning on the "public charge" clause (often referred to as the LPC provision) as a reason for rejecting visa applications. In the wake of continued Nazi persecutions, Roosevelt pressed Cordell Hull to inform consuls that they should show "the most generous and favorable treatment possible under the laws" when receiving applications from German Jews. A few months later, the head of the State Department's Visa Division sent the Undersecretary of State a memo giving his own view that, based on the visas that had been issued because of sponsors, if American Jews promised to help an immigrant if necessary, "the likelihood of their becoming a public charge is very remote."

Neither Roosevelt's wishes nor the visa division head's view made much difference. American consuls continued to reject thousands of immigration applications on the grounds that the applicants would simply join the ranks of the unemployed in the United States. American Jewish organizations complained about this practice throughout the 1930s, to little avail. Immigration from Germany rose only a modest ten to twenty percent a year between 1933 and 1936. Success like Stern's only underscored the importance of a Gerald Nye: the one certain way to get the State Department to set aside its own obstacles was to have friends in high places.[10]

American public opinion regarding the crisis and divisions made it even more difficult to break down the State Department's intransigence. American correspondents had since 1933 worked to provide their readers with an accurate picture of the Nazi campaign of vilification against their Jewish countrymen. They had braved the displeasure of Nazi officials, courted expulsion from the country, and even risked arrest in order to report the horrors they had witnessed. H. R. Knickerbocker, correspondent for the *New York Evening Post,* was expelled for suggesting that the Nazis were determined to go to war to reverse the defeat of 1918. "The German people as a whole have disavowed and repudiated the Versailles Treaty," he wrote, and as a result "warlike years lie ahead for Europe. American investments on this continent are investments in a battlefield . . . Germany [is] in the midst of . . . the first period of the 'Hitler era'."

In some cases, the correspondents had had to face the doubts of their own editors and publishers. When Edgar Ansel Mowrer of the *Chicago Daily News* referred to Germany as an "insane asylum" in one of his dispatches, his publisher, Frank Knox, thought he was worn out and should be replaced. Knox visited Germany himself a few months later and decided that Mowrer was not exaggerating at all. But even as the correspondents were shown to be right, many papers, together with thousands of their readers, continued to doubt their reports. The *Minneapolis Tribune* in 1935 opposed proposals to renew business boycotts against Germany because, it argued, Americans had "little accurate information" about Nazi policies regarding its Jewish population.[11]

Many smaller newspapers, particularly those in middle America, seldom carried much international news. A great many never carried any news at all about the treatment of the Jews in Germany. After its three stories on the boycott in March 1933, the *Valley City Times-Record* printed virtually nothing on the subject of Germany's Jewish population for the remainder of the 1930s. The Fargo *Forum*, North Dakota's largest newspaper, carried only a few such stories during the decade, while the *Moorhead Daily News*, the largest paper in western Minnesota, had even less. These few examples could be found duplicated across the country. Under such circumstances, the fact that most American readers did not see the need to discuss whether the immigration procedures should be revised is hardly surprising.

Some American Jewish groups tried to call greater attention to the Jewish crisis in Germany. But their efforts were hampered because the many organizations could not reach a consensus on what exactly they should do. The American Jewish Congress, which had played a critical role in organizing the protests in 1933, wanted all the major Jewish organizations in the United States to join them in a major lobbying effort to press for a liberalization of the immigration laws. They also wanted to renew the boycott of American businesses against Germany, in the hope that the Nazis would behave in a "more civilized manner."

These suggestions appealed to many, but the leaders of the venerable American Jewish Committee argued against both proposals. They did so partly because they did not want to jeopardize their excellent rapport with Franklin Roosevelt. Jews in America had generally voted Republican before the late 1920s. But in 1928, a large number of Jews gave their support to Al Smith, the Democratic candidate for president. They gave their votes to Roosevelt in still greater numbers in 1932. A year later, as the crisis in Germany developed, the American Jewish Committee argued that a campaign to pressure the administration would create a backlash, antagonizing friends in the government while encouraging anti-Semitism in the United States.[12]

The Committee leaders also warned that another boycott would goad Hitler into even greater brutalities. In response, the American Jewish Congress suggested that all the major Jewish groups poll their memberships on these questions. But the Committee refused to participate, saying that such a "referendum" would make America Jews look like a "state within a state" and raise questions about their loyalty. The B'Nai B'rith sided with the Committee on this, both arguing that it was best for Jewish groups to gradually nudge the public toward greater sympathy for the growing number of Jewish refugees. With both the Committee and B'Nai B'rith opposed to it, the idea of polling the members of national Jewish organizations was dropped.[13]

Debates such as these mostly were carried out in the larger urban areas. To the big groups, and to Washington, the thoughts of small-town businessmen men like Herman Stern on what Americans should do about Germany were all but unknown. In Stern's case, it is noteworthy that before late 1938, he only contacted the Joint Distribution Committee or the Hebrew Immigrant Aid Society regarding specific individual cases, mostly to obtain information about ship tickets. Whether it was directed to Nye or anyone else, he generally used the telling phrase, "you have been kind enough to assist me" in these letters, always making it clear that he assumed full responsibility for those he sponsored.

For Stern, helping German Jews come to the United States was a personal matter. As he explained to an interviewer many years later, "We, my wife and myself, felt that it [sponsoring others for visas] was something that should be done. We felt that, as far as I was concerned, it was just an accident that I came to this country. And we felt we certainly had a responsibility to make it possible for other people to continue to live and have an opportunity to enjoy this great country of ours, which was so good to us." Although he came to realize before many others that his relatives in Germany were in mortal danger – he wanted them to "continue to live" – his greatest motivation in the early years was gratitude to Morris Straus for bringing him to America. He wanted to give Klara and Erich and others the opportunity to "enjoy this great country of ours." Adeline, whose own parents had emigrated from Germany, had fully agreed with him in this. They felt strongly enough about it to sponsor even a stranger like Hayum.[14]

Trudl Hermann was little more known to them than Hayum. A distant cousin, Hermann had studied voice in Germany and had hoped to sing in one of the many opera companies – that was before Hitler came to power, and she was dismissed from her voice training. Her voice teacher, however, thought enough of her to provide a letter attesting to her talent, and she appealed to Stern for help in getting to the United States so she could resume her intended career. Stern provided the necessary affidavit, and Trudl made it to New York, where she eventually became a voice teacher herself.[15]

Herman's and Adeline's determination to help was probably most severely tested in 1935 when they received another request for help from their nephew, Julius Stern. The memory of the difficulties when Julius had lived with them in the late 1920s no doubt still rankled. But Julius's letter left no doubt as to why he was again appealing to them. There was nothing left for Jews in Germany, Julius wrote. In every city he went to find work, he was confronted with signs that said "No Jews Wanted," "No Jews Work Here," or simply "No Jews." Recently, Julius had run into some Nazis and "got some hits on my shoulder from an S.S. man." Adolf and Dora had begged him to write Herman to see if he could return to America. Trying to allay any skepticism from his uncle, Julius wrote that he was "pretty sure I'll find a job to take care of myself. Of course I won't be a burden to you. Of course, you must know better yourself, whether you can send me a certificate [i.e. affidavit]. . . . Times are changing and *people* change *too*."

Herman waited a considerable time before replying with his decision (by which time he had heard from others making the same request). In the end, he agreed to provide an affidavit. But he left Julius in no doubt as to what the Sterns would and would not do to

help him. "You understand, Julius, that there is no room in our organization for you. Eddie will soon be out of school and he plans to
come back to Valley City. I believe you will find it possible to locate
in New York or somewhere else in the East." In the meantime, Herman
urged Adolf and Dora to come to America. But Adolf did not want to
face the need to leave his homeland, even though he was having a
very difficult time continuing his cattle business. He was trying to
offset his losses in Germany by investing in a dairy farm in Belgium.
For the moment he was willing to endure the "upsetting things [that]
are happening."[16]

When Erich Stern worked at Straus Clothing, he lived at Herman
and Adeline's home, as had Klara. Herman had found an apartment
in Valley City for the Hayums to live in while Leo worked at Straus.
By the middle of 1935, he was planning to sponsor several other
relatives so that they, too, could leave Germany. He hoped that some
of them would decide to make their homes permanently in North
Dakota. This was not just because he wanted some of his Old World
family to stay near him: as the man who initiated the Greater North
Dakota Association, as someone who habitually looked for opportunities to develop his community, he wanted to help his state grow
and thrive.

What better way to do that than by bringing to North Dakota
more hardworking German immigrants? He had known many such
men and women when he had started working in Casselton in 1903.
He was confident that new immigrants from Germany would help
bring an end to the depression and then contribute to better times for
North Dakota and the nation.

Stern did not seem to be worried that not everyone would be
happy he was sponsoring refugees from Germany. North Dakota had
been developed just six decades before, mostly on the labors of a
large immigrant population, a mixture of primarily Germans (from
Germany proper and Russia), Ukrainians, Scandinavians, and other
Europeans. There had been some prejudices visited upon these immigrants in the early years, to be sure, with the native-born seizing

the bulk of elective offices and investment plums. But as the years went by, matters shifted to a more equal balance. Old World voters blocked temperance groups from enacting a prohibition law, ethnic pride organizations flourished, and second generation Norwegians and Germans began to win more seats in the Legislature. In general, everyone got along, which is not to say there were no instances of anti-Semitism in the state. When populism was in full flower before World War I, the Non-partisan League had hawked a book "exposing the Jewish-banking conspiracy" against the farmers. In the 1920s, local Ku Klux Klan groups in Fargo and Grand Forks had hurled invectives at Catholics, Jews and foreigners. And as Nazis gained in popularity in Europe, some German-language newspapers in both North Dakota and Minnesota defended the Nazi anti-Jewish policies and added some slurs of their own.[17]

Herman Stern was well aware of some of this. He could hardly have been ignorant of the indifference that many newspapers showed to the plight of the German Jewish population. When an associate of Hitler published a "case for anti-Semitism" in a French newspaper, some papers and magazines agreed with his claim that Jews were "a foreign nation" distinct from the country they lived in. The State Department was filled with personnel that were "social anti-Semites," persons who did not necessarily wish Jews harm, may even have considered some individual Jews as friends, but did not like or wish to associate with them as a whole. Beyond this there were the more vicious anti-Semites like Father Charles Coughlin, whose radio broadcasts drew as many as fifteen million listeners a week, and the American fascist groups like the Silver Shirts.

In 1938, when the dangers to Jews living under Hitler should have been obvious to anyone, Congress still refused to alter the immigration laws on the grounds that it would further harm the economy. Large numbers of Americans applauded when Congressman Martin Dies asserted that "our unemployment problem was transferred to the United States from foreign lands, and if we had refused admission to the sixteen and a half million foreign born in our midst, there would be no serious unemployment problem to harass us." Poll after poll showed that there was little public support for changing the immigration laws to allow more German refugees to enter the country. This was enough to keep the doors firmly shut.[18]

Stern knew much of this. While keeping silent about it for the moment, he would later express his resentment in a most dramatic way. But if he feared that by helping his German relatives he would himself become a target of anti-Jewish anger, he refused to let it deter him. In fact, in the middle of 1935, he let it be known that he would sponsor others and began to advise his brothers to think about leaving Germany themselves. His courage and determination were timely. The lives of Jews in Germany were becoming much more precarious.

Notes

1. Here and below, Herman Stern interview by Duane Crawford, 1971; Edward and Richard Stern 2004 interview by Wes Anderson.

2. Straus and Montgomery Wards ads in *Valley City Times Record,* April 6, 1933; Stern-Crawford interview, 1971, Stern Papers; Linda Mack Schloff, *And Prairie Dogs Weren't Kosher*(St. Paul: Minnesota Historical Society Press, 1996) p. 51.

3. See M. O. Ryan to James L. Donnelly, August 8, 1938, GNDA Abbreviated Statement of Current Activities, August 31, 1938, and other documents in the Grasshopper Plague file, Box 2, Stern Papers.

4. *Bits and Pieces From Valley City – City of Five Names* (np. 1983), p. 60; Stern-Crawford interview, 1971; Richard and Edward Stern interview, 2004.

5. Klara Stern to Erich Stern, October 29, 1934 [translated]; Victor Kolasinski (Roosevelt Steamship Company) to Herman Stern, October 29, 1934; Herman Stern to Louis Sonneborn, October 24, 1934; all in Klara Stern file, Stern Papers.

6. Here and below based on conversation with Edward Stern, November 2004, and letters of Erich Stern to Adeline Stern, January 7, 1936, and Erich Stern to "Dear Uncle" [Herman Stern], February 8, 1935 [sic], February 13, March 1, and March 8, [1936], all in Klara Stern file, Stern Papers. It is clear from the continuity of detail that these were all written in early 1936 and the February 8 letter is misdated.

7. Leon Hayum to Klara Stern, February 11, 1933 [translated], Hayum-Schafheimer file, Stern Papers.

8. Gerald Nye to Stern, June 4, 1935 and Stern to Nye, July 8, 1935, both in Hayum-Schafheimer file, Stern Papers.

9. Richard Breitman, *Official Secrets* (New York: Hill and Wang, 1998), pp. 20-23; Zucker, *In Search of Refuge* (London: Vallentine Mitchell, 2001), pp. 173-75.

10. Henry L. Feingold, *The Politics of Rescue* (New Brunswick, NJ: Rutgers University Press, 1970), pp. 15-17; David Wyman, *Paper Walls,* (New York: Pantheon Books, 1985 ed.) pp. 4-7; Zucker, *In Search of Refuge*, pp. 143-47. In 1939, Harry Schulman, a law professor at Yale, provided the American Jewish Committee with an analysis of the immigration legislation and gave his opinion that an affidavit indeed was not a "legally enforceable obligation." He did note that the affidavit was "a solemn avowal of responsibility," one that he felt "doubtless creates a moral obligation which the affiant is expected to perform." As we shall see, Stern did indeed take his commitments very seriously.

11. H. R. Knickerbocker, *The German Crisis* (New York: Farrar and Rinehart, 1932), p. 251; Deborah E. Lipstadt, *Beyond Belief: The American Press and the Coming of the Holocaust, 1933-1945* (New York: Free Press, 1986), pp. 20-39.

12. "The Jewish community in general advocated the proposition that the federal government was responsible for the welfare of all Americans and believed in social security, unemployment insurance, favorable labor legislation, and progressive taxation. . . . Because Roosevelt identified with the [ethical and charitable] ideals cherished by Jews, they gave him their overwhelming support": Martin Plesur, *Jewish Life in Twentieth-Century America: Challenge and Accommodation* (Chicago: Nelson-Hall, 1982), p. 84.

13. Feingold, pp. 9-13; "B'Nai B'rith and the German-Jewish Tragedy," *B'Nai B'rith Magazine,* May 1933; Max Kohler, "The United States and German-Jewish Persecution: Precedents for Popular and Government Action," *Bulletin of the Jewish Academy of Arts and Sciences,* no. 1 (1933).

14. Stern-Crawford interview, 1971.

15. Claire Hermann to "Herr Stern", January 30, 1934, Trudl Herman Howell file, Stern Papers.

16. Julius Stern to Herman Stern, September 7, 1935, Adolf Stern to Herman Stern, September 15, 1935, and Herman Stern to Julius Stern, April 13, 1936, all in Julius Stern file, Stern Papers.

17. "Great Conspiracy Exposed," *Non-Partisan Leader,* November 2, 1916, endorsing the 1916 work, Henry L. Loucks, *The Great Conspiracy of the House of Morgan and How to Defeat It*; Jonathan F. Wagner, "Nazi Propaganda Among North Dakota's Germans, 1934-1941," *North Dakota History*, vol. 54 (1987), pp. 15-24; Frederick Karl Knudsen, "Southern Minnesota Reaction to Policies of Nazi Germany, 1936-1939," (MA thesis, Mankato State College, 1969), esp. pp. 29-47.

18. Ernst zu Reventlow, "The Case for Anti-Semitism," *Living Age*, July 1934; Lipstadt, *Beyond Belief,* p. 127; Zucker, *In Search of Refuge*, pp. 170-79; Martin Dies, film clip in "America and the Holocaust: Deceit and Indifference," written and produced by Martin Ostrow in 1994 as part of the PBS "American Experience" series.

Chapter Seven
"Perhaps You Are Chosen to Become For Us All a Place of Refuge"

On August 2, 1934, Hitler became the absolute master of Germany. The day had begun with the death of Paul von Hindenburg, the eighty-seven year old war hero and president of the nation. The day ended with the merger of the president's powers to those of the chancellor, and with Hitler assuming the title of German *Fuehrer* (Leader). To put the seal on his absolute rule, Hitler had the entire army swear an oath to "render unconditional obedience to Adolf Hitler, the Fuehrer of the German nation and people."

Hitler's path to such totalitarian power had been strewn with duplicity and blood. In October 1933, he had given the world notice that Germany would withdraw from the League of Nations, on the grounds that the League tolerated well-armed nations like France while supporting the disarmament of Germany under the treaty of 1919. He was already planning the rearmament of Germany. A few months before Hindenburg's death, he had made a bargain with the German army. Since the *Reichswehr* officer corps also wanted to see the Versailles Treaty scrapped, they found it possible to conclude a bargain with the Nazi chancellor: Hitler would curb his SA and the military would accept him as Supreme Commander of the Armed Forces. In late June of 1934, Hitler purged the high leadership of the SA by having them murdered by party firing squads on charges of conspiracy to commit treason. The military kept their end of the bargain when they directed their troops to swear the above oath. Did the generals and admirals suspect the appalling crimes they would commit in honor of their pledge?

Jews may have privately enjoyed the purge of the SA, their tormenters. Some hoped that this might be a sign that the Nazis would temper their anti-Jewish rage. Since the one-day boycott, Hitler had heeded the warnings of his economic advisors to move carefully in relation to the largest Jewish-owned businesses. If these were disrupted, it might not only inhibit economic recovery, it might interfere with Hitler's plans to rearm the German military. The SA was still allowed to demonstrate and to harass the small shopkeepers, like Samuel Levy and Elly Kann.

Now, with the SA hobbled, might things get better? Most Jewish leaders doubted it. Editors of Jewish publications were advised to write nothing about the purge – one poorly chosen word could have led to a charge that they were displaying *deutschfeindlich* – hostility to German ways. It was better to keep quiet. In private, some Jewish leaders thought things might get even worse. If Hitler could order the slaughter of old Nazi comrades, what might he do to them in the end?[1]

That was the crucial question. After the boycott, Hitler's government had concentrated its efforts on gaining full control of all levels of government in Germany, and on ruthlessly breaking the communists. Dachau and the other early concentration camps were established primarily to hold communist party leaders. The SA's bully-boys continued to amuse themselves in humiliating Jews or tried to enrich themselves by extorting a Jew to sell out his or her business. But after the first spate of legislation banning them from many official jobs and limiting their participation in education, Hitler's government had moved more slowly concerning the Jews.

Part of the delay was essentially bureaucratic – determining who, exactly, was a Jew. In the summer of 1933, a committee created in the Ministry of the Interior to prepare a law to exclude Jews from German citizenship quickly became bogged down on this issue. The Nazis tried to break the logjam by announcing in March 1934, that Jews were not German citizens, but still did not explain what "Jew" meant in this context, nor what rights Jews had lost. Most of the actions taken in 1933 and 1934 to ban Jews from theaters, restaurants, swimming pools and other public facilities had been local, inspired by Nazis in most cases, but not directed by the central government.

Not that the Jews had been forgotten by Hitler's inner circle –

when Heinrich Himmler, as head of the Munich state police forces, spoke to the press about the purpose of the camps, he made a point of saying that the camps would be used to keep Jews in "protective custody" when they were "exposed to the anger of the people" because of their poor "behavior towards the national Germany." At the same time, Himmler's subordinates took care to identify policemen who needed to be "educated" in the New Order's racial policies. Special classes for this purpose were established. If a policeman showed himself to be strongly in sympathy with the Nazis, he was offered a chance to join the SS.[2]

Joseph Goebbels had also been busy. As Minister of Propaganda, Goebbels had full control of German radio and cinema, and he used his power eagerly. When "Hans Westmar," one of the first Nazi-inspired feature films, was released in 1934, it contained several anti-Semitic scenes. Goebbels arranged to have a booklet distributed to schools so the students could discuss the film. The booklet urged teachers to point out that communists in the movie were "supported by Jews spewing forth hatred; Jewish intellectuals seducing credulous workers; and Jews who were nothing more than murderous rabble, criminals and receivers of stolen goods." The Nazi-controlled press added their own invective with continuous anti-Semitic editorials and such special efforts as *Der Sturmer's* multi-part "expose" on Jewish ritual murders of Christian children.[3]

In 1935, a new wave of street violence erupted. In Munich, SA members smashed windows of Jewish-owned shops and beat those who dared to shop in the stores. In Berlin, similar depredations occurred; a German writer whose wife was Jewish noted in his diary that when Jews were attacked in the streets, "nobody came to their help, because everyone is afraid of being arrested." The agitations continued into the summer, spreading across Germany. Some of this was carefully organized by SA leaders and Nazi officials, but some appears to have been spontaneous violence, initiated by groups of Germans who were frustrated because they had not yet gained any benefits from the slow pace of economic recovery.

Hitler and his inner circle were not entirely happy with the outrages that were not sanctioned, so much so that in April, Deputy Fuhrer Rudolf Hess issued an order that party members could demonstrate but were not to attack individual Jews. Some SA members ignored the order. Some within the Nazi hierarchy, including Himmler and Schacht, urged Hitler to quell the violence before it harmed the revival of business and threatened foreign trade. Others, including Goebbels and Streicher, pressed the chancellor to immediately confiscate all Jewish property. Hitler vacillated for weeks before deciding on a compromise measure. He would follow Schacht's advice to protect economic recovery by ending the street violence. At the same time he appeased Streicher, Goebbels and the other radicals by bringing forth legislation to further restrict Jewish life in Germany.

Hitler chose to use the annual party rally in Nuremberg to announce his new legislation. This was the perfect stage for him, surrounded by thousands of party worshippers who would applaud his histrionic harangue and accept any lie, any exaggeration, or any absurdity from his lips. He began by justifying his decision, made earlier in the year, to ignore the Versailles Treaty and expand the army: threats from abroad, engineered by Jews and Communists, made this a "defensive" necessity. The Jews were, in fact, the cause of all the world's woes, he warned, and Germany must respond to threat with new laws to prevent unrest due to Jewish provocations. These laws, he said, "were guided by the hope of possibly being able to bring about, by means of a singular momentous measure, a framework within which the German *Volk* would be in a position to establish tolerable relations with the Jewish people." If this failed, he warned, and "intra-German and international Jewish agitation proceed[ed] on its course," then the "National Socialist Party" would find a "definitive solution" to the Jewish menace. The party faithful cheered every utterance.

Hermann Goering followed Hitler to the rostrum to read the Nuremberg Laws, as they came to be known. Signed by Hitler, the laws should have made clear that Jews had no future in Nazi Germany. One law made the Nazi flag the national flag, and a second stated that German citizenship was limited to those of "German blood." The third law, "for the Defense of German Blood and Honor," got down to the heart of the matter by stating frankly that "the purity of German blood is the condition for the survival of the German *Volk*," and that Jews were not members of the *Volk*. The law forbade marriages between Jews and the *Volk* and further forbade any sexual relations between Jews and non-Jews. Jews were also not allowed to employ as domestics any German women under the age of forty-five. In private, Hitler told an assistant that with these laws he wanted to isolate Jews in Germany into "a ghetto . . . [where] the German people [can] look on as one looks at wild animals."[4]

While some of Goebbels' minions tried to reassure the foreign press that these new laws were not intended to drive all the Jews from Germany, a major subordinate of Himmler suggested otherwise. Kurt Daluege, head of the German Order Police – which would one day play a major role in the murder of thousands of Jews in eastern Europe – met with, and excoriated, foreign correspondents for criticizing Nazi racial policy, saying that Jews promoted swindles, fraud, drug sales, and gambling among otherwise loyal Germans. He then said that Nazi policy was moving "in the direction of a general purge" of the Jewish population. It was left to the reporters to decide what Daluege meant by the remark.[5]

Despite the obvious hostility of Hitler's government, Jewish emigration out of Germany had been modest up to this point. About thirty-seven thousand had left in 1933. Then the number had dropped to about twenty-three thousand in 1934. Such low numbers could have been a reflection of the Nazi preoccupation with other matters during that time, but even in 1935, with the renewal of street violence and the introduction of the Nuremberg Laws, only twenty-one thousand left. Most of these emigrants went to neighboring countries, primarily France, Holland and Belgium, or to Palestine, where the British government permitted about ten thousand to enter each year. About seven thousand Jews left Germany and went to the United States each year from 1933 through 1935. Extensive American publicity about a "flood" of Jewish immigrants thus was completely misleading.[6]

Among Herman Stern's relatives in Germany, a good many were moved by the Nuremberg Laws to reconsider their futures. Herman's brother Adolf was one of these. Adolf's business as a cattle dealer had not suffered as egregiously as that of other Jewish businessmen. Since bargaining over livestock usually took place in small villages or in the rural countryside, away from prying eyes of the party, it was still possible to bargain amiably in the old way, haggling over details until the deal was struck and then sealed with a glass of schnapps. Indeed, a Gestapo report prepared in that same September of 1935, complained that German farmers still "preferred" to deal with Jewish cattle dealers and that "sterner measures" should be taken to induce rural Germans to stop this practice.

These sterner measures usually consisted of various forms of intimidation, reinforced by the rapid growth of the Nazi party across the countryside after 1933. As the Jewish owner of a mill explained to an interviewer, "the local Nazi appeared in my office with two of his henchmen. Before sitting down, he took out his revolver and put it on the table." The Nazi leader then proceeded to present demands as to which workers should be promoted and which should be dismissed. Another tactic was for tax officials to repeatedly examine a business's records for any error that could be used to arrest the owner or confiscate his property. Nazis also offered inducements to workers or neighbors of Jews – a better job or a chance to move up in the party – in return for the person denouncing a local Jew "of sabotaging the ideas and will of the Fuehrer." Eventually one's customers disappeared and one's neighbors began to avoid you. Some variation of this was used on Adolf Stern, because by the middle of 1936, about the time that his son Julius left for America, he was worrying about his finances.[7]

Adolf did not, however, contact his brother Herman for help with this problem. Instead he turned to Fritz and Sally Kann, the brothers of his wife, Dora. The Kann brothers were also cattle traders and had on many occasions joined Adolf in business ventures. And like Adolf, they found their livelihood threatened by the Nazi revolution. But in 1936, events occurred that threatened Sally Kann's very life.

Sally's daughter, Erika, was very young at the time of the incident but vividly remembers what happened: "Adolf Stern, my father
Sally, and [Uncle] Fritz Kann were business partners. One day somebody called [my father] 'dirty Jew' and my father just hit him." Sally's
horrified neighbors warned him that he must hide immediately; otherwise he might be killed by storm troopers before he could even be
arrested. One man urged him to flee Germany and Erika remembers
that "the same day he crossed the border into Belgium, where he had
a cousin [living]. We [i.e. Erika and her mother] followed later."
Erika's uncle Fritz remained behind to help Adolf try to keep the
business going.[8]

But the business continued to decline, prompting Adolf to write
Herman that he and Fritz were "only losing money" and had decided
to give up cattle trading. They would now try to take advantage of
Sally's residence in Belgium. They would open a dairy business near
Antwerp, financing it with some of their own savings and the rest
with "a partner who is bringing with him the missing capital." Who
this partner was and how Adolf and Fritz managed to get funds into
Belgium is unclear. Whatever the method, Sally rented land in the
village of Wommelgem, where he "open[ed] … a creamery, produc-
ing and delivering kosher milk."

By November 1936, Sally Kann's farm consisted of pasture land,
a stable, a home for himself and his family, and a herd of forty cows.
It would have been possible for Sally to openly send money back to
Adolf and Fritz. The Nazis did not prohibit this, they simply took a
large share in taxes. Adolf himself recognized that the Belgium farm
might not solve his financial difficulties for very long. As he wrote
his son Julius, "Who knows whether things will work out here …
well, we'll have to see."

Julius made his way to America in November of 1936. He had
hoped to sail with one of his cousins (whose own story follows) and
they had talked of finding jobs together in New York. But the cousin's
departure had been delayed, so Julius traveled alone. Upon arrival in
New York, Julius learned that his Uncle Herman had made an arrangement for a possible job for him in Chicago, so he moved on to

the Windy City and went to work in the clothing trade. Julius seems to have taken this second opportunity in America more seriously than his first trip in 1928. Perhaps it was the sobering advice his father had given him before he left: "you are 33 years old, having lived and enjoyed your life with pleasure. Now do turn a new leaf and start a new life, with a new outlook, built on new principles: be more saving, always telling the truth, be diligent, God fearing . . . Do take my words to heart, do become a man, act as a man, brace up as a man, so your parents and your family can be proud of you. You are gone now, and we have to see how to get by." To further impress Julius of the situation, Adolf added the chilling words "perhaps you are chosen to become for us all a place of refuge, for I believe in Europe there is nothing to gain in the next decades."[9]

Now we must turn to the experience of Julius's cousin, one of the three Gustav Sterns in the family. Before the decade was over, these three caused confusion among the record keepers in the State Department's visa office. The first and oldest was Herman Stern's brother, who lived with his family in the village of Geraldshofen. Then there was Adolf's oldest son Gustave, still living in Paris. The third was the son of Herman's brother Julius. In order to distinguish him from the others, his relatives habitually referred to him as "little Gustav," even when he was thirty years old.

Like so many others in his family, little Gustav had concluded that any future he might have in Germany was now utterly worthless. Following Julius's example, he asked his American uncle for an affidavit of support for an immigration visa. The announcement of the Nuremberg Laws had left Herman Stern convinced that all of his closest relatives should leave Germany. Accordingly, in late October 1935, Stern forwarded to Washington affidavits for Julius and little Gustav, for Adolf and his wife Dora, for Gustave and his family in Paris, and for the parents of Klara and Erich – Gustav and his wife in Geraldshofen. Furthermore, he sent a letter to Senator Nye asking that since Nye had been "kind enough to assist me in securing visa[s] for German relatives," could he now write a note of assurances to the

State Department? Nye obliged with a letter addressed to Samuel Honaker, the Consul in Stuttgart, expressing a "hope that everything possible may be done to expedite matters" for the Stern relatives.[10]

Samuel William Honaker, who was to become something like Stern's nemesis in the years ahead, was a career foreign service officer, having been with the State Department since 1913. He had been born in Florida in 1887, the same year Stern was born in Germany. He grew up in a respectable middle class family, attended a private boarding school, received his higher education at the University of Virginia, where he did well, earning high grades, joining the right organizations, and quarterbacking the Cavalier football team in his senior year. Upon his graduation in 1912, with both Bachelors and Masters degrees, University President Edwin recommended him as having "achieved wide distinction as an athlete and as a leader among his fellows." He looked the part of a leader, having piercing eyes, a patrician nose, a firm chin and slightly waved hair that he combed into a pompadour. A leader but not a politician: his State Department file photograph is of a serious, unsmiling bureaucrat. Among his accomplishments was a talent for languages, including French, German, Spanish, Portuguese, and Italian.

With these credentials it was only natural for Honaker to join the State Department, which he did in late 1913. His first consular appointment was as a clerk in the main consulate at Rio de Janeiro, Brazil, where he impressed his seniors. After several years in Rio, the department moved him around, seasoning his experience with assignments in South Africa, Turkey, Portugal, Jamaica, and Iran. In 1929, he was named Consul General to the Berne office in Switzerland, where he did well, then took the same position in Glasgow, Scotland. In 1934, he became the Consul General of Stuttgart, just in time to face the rising torrent of Jewish families seeking refuge from Hitler.[11]

The Stuttgart Consulate was housed in two floors of an impressive brick and stone office building at 19A Koenigstrasse. For many years, the visa office of the consulate had been located in separate offices, on Eberhardstrasse. But, as the 1936 inspection report of the

consulate noted, the drop in immigration because of the "strict application of the Public Charge Clause" beginning in 1930, allowed the
State Department in 1931 to move the visa operation into the
Koenigstrasse building and thus reduce its rental expenses. Soon after, the consulate in Cologne was closed, with the visa work of that
location also being transferred to Stuttgart. Now with the increased
Nazi persecutions, the Stuttgart Consulate was where more than forty
percent of the Jewish population had to apply for an American visa.
It was soon evident that it was "too small for the [post-1933] renewal
of immigration activity and inadequate to house the copious files
[being compiled]." Although Honaker was able to obtain additional
space in the building for processing visa requests, he soon complained
that the volume of immigration requests was too great for his existing staff.[12]

Honaker's principal assistant in visa matters was Hugh M. Teller.
Seven years younger than Honaker, Teller was born in Michigan, but
grew up in the District of Columbia. After graduating from high school
in 1914, he spent some time in the Coast Guard, mostly in drafting
coastal maps. He later studied commercial art but gave it up to attend
Georgetown University's School of Foreign Affairs. Graduating with
a foreign-service certificate, he joined the State Department and was
posted to Stuttgart, probably because he was very fluent in German,
his mother having been born there. He had been in Stuttgart ever
since. After 1930, he was in charge of the visa section.

There is one other thing of interest about Teller. As he noted in a
1945 application to rejoin State after military service, he had while
in Stuttgart traveled extensively throughout western Europe where
he "collected information of a political character" and summarized
what he had learned from "many contacts established during my long
period of residence." During the war years he served as the visa
division's head of "Anti-American Activities Section," with a duty
of recommending what alien residents should be restricted from traveling in America because they might be "engaged in activities of a
subversive or dangerous nature." He consulted regularly with FBI
and Immigration and Naturalization Service agents, and military in-

telligence officers. In his spare time he acted as an expert on "visa fraud" for the Justice Department. Small wonder his State Department file photograph is of a grim, moon-faced man, with spectacles and a thin mustache, who looks like he was planning to give someone the third degree.[13]

As a result of the Nuremberg Laws, the number of visa applications submitted at Stuttgart more than doubled from what it had been in 1934 and early 1935. Honaker, as his subsequent reports and correspondences with applicants and their American sponsors made clear, was not inclined to meet the requests for visas with much sympathy. He was also apparently a very limited administrator. At least that was the opinion of the senior State Department official who wrote the 1936 inspection report for the consulate at Stuttgart. Of Honaker, the inspector wrote that he "has not the personality to inspire in his subordinates that urge which brings from them the better effort . . . He is somewhat unsympathetic in nature, adopts arbitrary methods in his office management, treats his subordinates rather mechanically. . . . In his delegation of duties to subordinate officers in charge of sections of the office, he has also neglected to follow up these subordinates to assure that the tasks delegated have been carried out in proper form. He has, in short, paid little attention to the details of his office." The inspector also noted, "in justice" that Honaker's staff members were rather "inferior" and as the volume of requests for immigration visas grew, had "contributed large in letting the office down."

It is clear that in the matter of visas, Honaker had essentially turned almost all the responsibility over to Hugh Teller, explaining to Washington that Teller had "assumed practically full responsibility for the work of the visa section." If Teller was already developing his interest in security measures and possible fraud, then it is probable that he was no more sympathetic toward those requesting visas than Honeker. And, in fact, the inspector of the consulate noted in his 1936 report that Teller "has not learned fully that visa immigration work requires breadth of view in addition to application in a routine way of laws and regulations."[14]

Herman Stern soon learned that Teller and Honaker were going to present a considerable number of obstacles to his efforts to get his relatives out of Germany. While the passports for Julius and little Gustav had moved through the system fairly readily, with Gustav arriving in New York a few weeks after Julius had left for Chicago, neither Adolf nor his son Gustave was prepared yet to leave Europe. The consulate placed Herman's affidavit for them on file.

Herman's brother Gustav and his wife Selma were anxious to leave. They had written to him scarcely a week after the Nuremberg Laws were announced to assure him that they were selling their furniture ("secretly," in order to prevent a visit from bargain hunting party members), trying to buy clothes suitable for the North Dakota climate, and asking questions as to where they might live in Valley City. All of this, however, came to an abrupt halt when the consulate denied a visa on the ground that Gustav had once seen a heart specialist. Herman appealed to Nye for help, an action that appears to have greatly annoyed Honaker. He sent Stern a coldly worded letter that he had given the visa application "every proper consideration," but Gustav's heart ailment "renders him unable to become self-supporting." As far as Honaker was concerned, that was the end of the matter. But to Stern, this was just the first round.[15]

In the meantime, Stern was busy helping others. Neither of his oldest brothers, Moses or Julius, was willing to leave Germany. Moses had written to Herman soon after the Nuremberg Laws were announced with reassurances that he could still make a living. If he decided he should leave, it would probably be to Australia, where he knew people and had some "possibilities." But he advised Herman to help their sister Jettchen, and her family, to get out.[16]

Jettchen's family did indeed want to leave Germany. In a letter sent to Stern in late September of 1935, Jettchen's husband, Hugo, made clear their anguish. "We would like to leave from here, but to where?" he wrote. "Dear Hermann, you wrote once about a farm, we'd be very interested in it, because here we do not have any livelihood any more. If you have the intention to send for us, please describe the living conditions on a farm. Does one have farm workers?

I do not know anything in regards to plowing and planting. Can one make a living by raising cattle and horses? This would be difficult for me, both of us are over 50." Hugo admitted that he would get very little for his property because so "many Jewish homes are for sale," and he worried that none of the family knew much English. But "we cannot continue this way." Stern sent an affidavit to Washington within days of receiving the letter.

Jettchen had met Hugo Henlein about eight years after her fiancé had been killed in the Great War. They married in 1924 and a year later had their only child, a daughter they named Lotte. A couple of year's later, Hugo's aunt came to live with them when she could no longer care for herself. Hugo had been a cattle dealer, living in Bad Schwalbach, a spa town located in the Taunus Mountains, about fifteen kilometers northwest of Wiesbaden. As a spa town, Bad Schwalbach's population fluctuated with the seasons. The permanent Jewish population was about one hundred souls, and most of these were strongly Orthodox; in fact, the members of the community instructed their young not in German but in *Juden-Deutsch*, a variant of Yiddish.[17]

Lotte Henlein remembered her childhood in Bad Schwalbach as pleasant, but somewhat poor. "We didn't have a shop, but in those days you were permitted to use the house. In the back there was a barn and there were cattle there. Then in earlier days we had a horse there, too." The Henlein house had been built by Lotte's grandfather, Ferdinand, in 1874. The family had a small kitchen, dining room and parlor on the ground floor, three or four small bedrooms and a bath on the upstairs floor (first floor, European) and the same on the second floor, which they rented to another family.

As soon as Lotte was old enough, about six, she earned a little extra money at the spas. The vacationers "played tennis and they needed someone to pick up the tennis balls, so you could go earn yourself a few marks." Lotte remembered when one of her friends received a gift from one of the tourists. "This was Edith Falk, her father had a bakery, a not too prosperous bakery, either. She got a nice box of candy as a gift, and we were so disappointed because she didn't offer us a candy. She took it home, gave it dutifully to her parents, who put it in the store for sale. Nobody was doing really well."

Of course that did not stop children from having good times. "This is where you were born, this is where you lived. And you had your friends and you were playing with them. We played ball and then we had marbles, the same type of thing that children would do anywhere. We jumped rope and had story books in German." Lotte's friends were both Jewish and Christian. Jews did not live in just one part of the town; it was too small for that, perhaps three thousand people. The Jews had a small synagogue for worship. "It was Orthodox. We were all comparatively Orthodox. I don't remember any name on it at all. Levi Spier was a relative of ours, he used to lead some of the prayers."

Lotte began school in 1931 and enjoyed it. She had paid no notice to public events before January 1933, but clearly remembered her parents' nervousness when Hitler was made chancellor. After that she saw, for the first time, a Nazi uniform and a swastika. The earliest demonstrations were probably organized by SA troops from Wiesbaden. Then, "all of a sudden, it wasn't as if they came here, it was people in the town who joined the Nazi Party. Then they got into the uniforms, then they started marching, then the songs came. Then they had a place where they put up posters." The posters stayed in her mind the rest of her life. "They said that we [the Jews] were their enemies and noted all the things we 'did to them,' said mean and horrible things. The man who wrote much of this was [Julius] Streicher. The posters had caricatures with those horrible hawk noses and such."

Lotte's father was almost immediately ruined by the Nazi revolution. He had sold some cattle, for which he was still owed money. But "those who owed him didn't pay." Instead, they assaulted him. "My father said they came into the house and wouldn't pay. Now the basement was right by the kitchen door and there was a staircase down to the cellar. One of them gave him a push, and by the grace of God he didn't break his neck." A few of Hugo's buyers continued to do business with him, secretly. "He had to take [the cows] out in the evening and meet them somewhere in the woods so nobody could see them. Sometimes I went along with him." Her dad gave her a heavy stick to drive the cows, but also for protection. "Papa would always say to walk in the middle of the road if it got dark so you see danger coming either way. You'd take a stick to protect yourself. I never forgot the things he taught me." The money from these nocturnal transactions was welcome, but not really enough to live on.

"In a way, I might say, it was a good thing that it happened early, because my father realized then the situation was to a point where he couldn't remain there. No one was really anxious [to leave]. You'd live there all your life, and they were already in their fifties. They married late and I came late in their lives. Well, it's difficult to make another move somewhere else. And [Mother] certainly didn't want to be a burden somewhere else, so it was with mixed feelings [that we thought about leaving]."

The final spur to go was Lotte's experiences at school, where every lesson now began with a required "Heil Hitler." "The children had been brought up [for two years] to hate us, and since nobody could restrict them, you could get slapped around. And God forbid if the teacher left the room for a minute." Her second year teacher, a true believer in Nazism, often singled her out for punishment, striking her with a ruler when she was not quick enough with an answer. Her teacher in her third year, in 1935, was no Nazi. He understood what was happening in Germany and tried to shield Lotte and the other Jewish student in the class. "If he left, there would be a bit of a rumpus in the room. Herr Blum would come back and ask what was happening. Gunther Steinhardt and I, the two of us got blamed. The teacher knew this wasn't so but there wasn't anything he could do about it, because then they would report him." After Lotte had been slapped a few times by other students, her father had had enough. "My father took me out of school when things got to the point where I used to come home crying and everything. He said, 'this is the end. They're not going to kill my daughter.'" He sent his first letter to Herman Stern soon after.[18]

Dieter Ackerman, another Jewish student at the school, was six years old when Lotte was ten. Having begun public school in 1935, he could not remember, as an adult, any non-Jewish playmates. All other children "were so influenced as to not have anything to do with us." Since they could "only find safety with each other," Jewish students banded together, which allowed the older Lotte to provide him and others with some security. But that was limited, as he later recalled. "German schools allowed an hour for religious instruction. It was divided, with Protestants together, Catholics together, and Jews together. Every time we had this class, older boys, wearing their Hitler Youth uniforms, would come in, saying they had forgotten a book or something, and disrupt the class, "laughingly tear[ing] up things on our desk and so forth."

The cruelest treatment came from Dieter's next-door neighbor, Frau Roerich, who lived between the Ackerman's and a small Jewish-owned bakery further down the street. When Dieter was sent to fetch bread from the bakery, he had to "pass her place on the sidewalk. She would stick her foot out and make me say "Heil Hitler" before I could get by. She taught her daughter to do the same thing, and push me down if I didn't heil Hitler." While many of the Jews in Bad Schwalbach, who were "well assimilated," resisted leaving, some began to do so. "I would find out that someone I knew had just left." One of these disappearances from his shrinking world was Lotte.[19]

It took a year for the Stuttgart Consulate to investigate the Henleins, study the paperwork, consisting primarily of the application and financial statements, Herman Stern's affidavit and financial statements (already on file with the previous affidavits he had sent for Klara and the others), conduct the medical and mental examinations of Hugo, Jettchen and Lotte, and approve a visa for them to live in the United States. Originally, the family expected to take Hugo's aunt with them. Carolina Henlein had lived in the home all her life, first with Lotte's grandfather, her brother, then with Hugo and his family. Her mind had faded somewhat and she really did not understand what had happened with the Nazi triumph. "When the [SA] marchers marched on the streets," Lotte remembered, "she would sit way out by the window and look, and then she would ask what it was about. Well, she didn't know, and they didn't bother to tell her." Hugo worried that she would find it very hard to leave Bad Schwalbach, but, perhaps mercifully, Aunt Carolina died in mid-1936, before the visa was approved in Stuttgart.

While waiting, the Henleins struggled with money. "Dear Hermann, it is not our extravagance, but, unfortunately, we have become very poor. We wanted to wait for your letter and wanted to try to sell our house, so - as much as possible - to pay off our debts." Hugo had assured the consul staff in Stuttgart that he had enough savings to take care of the family in America: "I would only in an emergency, ask someone from over there [for help]." But he admitted to Stern that he had written to a Jewish aid committee in Cleveland, to see if relatives of a great-great grandfather who had gone there almost a hundred years before, could share the burden of sponsorship with Herman. He also advised Stern not to contribute money to any of the American aid campaigns. "Nothing [from the donations] gets to us people here." He asked if Stern could send a thousand marks to help, assuring him that they would purchase only the most vital necessities. "Be thankful to God, that you are not and never will be in such a situation." Stern did send some money, how much is uncertain.[20]

While waiting for a decision in Stuttgart, Lotte borrowed a book, *A Thousand Words of English*, from a friend of the family. Many of the neighbors stopped saying hello "or looked at us in any way or form, because they were afraid." When they went to the synagogue, a Nazi sat in the rear to listen if "something would be said against the government." Local Nazis, now present in greater numbers, organized a boycott against the Jewish merchants. "There was this poor little vegetable shop where the [Jewish] owner got up at three in the morning, went to Wiesbaden to buy some fruits, vegetables and so forth. And there were two Jewish hotels there, too. They had two hotels, the Rosens. They had storm troopers in front of all of them."

Finally, the visa was approved, almost a year to the day since the Nuremberg Laws had been announced. Hugo had never been able to sell his house. He simply signed it over to a local bank to pay his remaining debts. The family packed some clothes, personal possessions, and pots and pans into some battered suitcases. Other Jewish families in Bad Schwalbach and nearby towns were leaving too. Some however, who had filed papers to leave, had changed their minds. Hitler had ordered a moratorium on anti-Jewish demonstrations during the 1936 Olympic Games, which were held in Berlin, and as a result, some Jews, hoping that the worst was now over, decided to stay in Germany.

Before leaving Bad Schwalbach, they went around to say goodbye to some of their few remaining friends. Lotte went to pay her respects to the Marxheimers, who had a daughter who had suffered persecutions with her in school. Living next door was Herr Blum, the teacher who had tried to protect her. Blum came over to see her, "at night through the back way [of the Marxheimer house, so he would not be seen]. I cried that I had to say goodbye. And he said to me, I'll never forget it, 'Don't you cry, you're lucky to get out of here. I wish I knew a way my two sons could get out of here. God knows what will happen to us yet.'"

They sailed from Hamburg to the United States on the *SS Washington*. Lotte mostly remembered the Halloween party on board, with "apples hung on strings" in the ship's main lounge. Halfway across the Atlantic, Hugo went for walk on the deck and crossed over to the rail. He, too, had fought in the World War, on both the Russian and French fronts. A gas attack late in the war had severely damaged one of his lungs, inflicting him with respiratory problems thereafter. Pausing at the *Washington's* rail, he took out of his coat pocket a military medallion he had worn on his uniform. After looking at it for a moment, he dropped it over the side.[21]

Elsie Sternberg, a cousin of Adeline Stern, met the Henleins in New York harbor. The port authorities refused to let them leave until they disposed of a kosher salami they had purchased in Hamburg and brought onto the ship. They had never reached the point of starvation in Bad Schwalbach – "there was always food on the table" – but the years of making ends meet had left their mark. "Papa said, 'What?

Throw out food?' Out of the question. So we bought rolls and we sat there [in the port authority] and then ate salami and the rolls."

That done, Elsie Sternberg took them to Pennsylvania Station and put them on a train bound for Chicago. As they rolled westward, they were amazed at the extent of the American countryside. "There was no end to it. My mother couldn't get over that there was no end to it." They paused in Chicago for an overnight stay, with Klara. "Klara took us to her place and we visited with her, and Eddie's brother Richard," who had a job with Rierson Steel. "'This is your other cousin,' she said. And then [in the morning] it was time to board the train for Valley City." The next afternoon, Herman and Adeline met them at the train station and took them to a large house on Third Avenue, built in the 19th century and converted into a dozen small apartments in the early 1930s. It was three blocks south of the Stern's own home, and the apartment space was much smaller than their home had been in Germany. But to eleven-year-old Lotte, now safe after all the months of persecution, "it was a small paradise." Since it was the beginning of winter, one of the worst in the decade in fact, Herman bought them winter coats and boots.

Stern had found a temporary job for Hugo, taking care of cows for a local dealer. Later, he helped Hugo start a junkyard out on the west edge of town. Ed Stern remembers that Herman "didn't want to get him into a job that would take a job from someone else, they didn't want to cause any hard feelings. The railroad would let you start a junkyard alongside the tracks because they could stop and pick up the scrap metal." Henlein's Yard allowed the family to get by.

Lotte entered school almost immediately where she was admitted into the sixth grade but sent to the first grade classroom for a time each day to learn beginning English grammar. "I've never forgotten this, all the teachers stayed after school, took turns to work with me on my English. Who would do that in today's age?" Lotte also joined the Girl Scouts, which Stern felt would help her with her English and also teach her more about America.

Some of her sixth grade classmates, of German ancestry, would try to speak German to her. "They'd come in and say 'guten morgen,' whatever they'd heard from the parents, but they didn't really know the language." Adeline also admitted that speaking with Jettchen and Lotte allowed her to improve her own half-forgotten German. But, although the transition to America was difficult, it was nothing compared to the feeling of safety, the sense that you were seen as an ordinary person. "Oh, God, it was heaven on earth. [In Germany], you're called a dirty Jew, you killed their God, you did everything under the sun that got you a slap and smack and you were insulted from top to bottom. And here you got invitations to a birthday party, and it was Halloween time, every-thing. I didn't know what hit me."[22]

Notes

1. Dippel, *Bound Upon a Wheel of Fire,* pp. 149-51. Noakes and Pridham, *Nazism, 1919-1945: The Rise to Power*, vol. 1, pp. 177-87, has a selection of important documents on the purge of the SA. See also May, *Strange Victory*, pp. 28-32.

2. Robert Gellately, *Backing Hitler* (Cambridge: Oxford University Press, 2001), p. 21; Breitman, *Official Secrets*, pp. 29-30.

3. David Welch, *Propaganda and the German Cinema* (New York, I. B. Tauris, 2001 ed.), pp. 61-71; Saul Friedlander, *Nazi Germany and the Jews,* pp. 123-24.

4. Dippel, pp. 163-65; Friedlander, pp. 141-44.

5. Breitman, p. 30. Daluege was not the only Nazi to imply at this time the possibility of ultimate extermination of the Jews. Friedlander, p. 144, notes that Walter Gross, head of the Nazi Party Racial Policy Office, subsequently testified that ten days after the Nuremberg rally, Hitler told him that if Germany were to find itself in another two-front war, he was prepared to accept "all the consequences" for settling the Jewish question.

6. Dippel, pp. 160-61, 176-77; Zucker, *In Search of Refuge*, pp. 46-48.

7. Gellately, *Backing Hitler*, pp. 121-22; Frances Henry, *Victims and Neighbors: A Small Town in Nazi Germany Remembered* (Massachusetts: Bergin and Garvey Publishers, Inc., 1984), pp. 22-28. See also Robert Gellately, *The Gestapo and German Society* (Oxford: Clarendon Press, 1990), p. 105, for further information on Nazi efforts to suppress Jewish cattle dealers and other Jewish rural entrepreneurs.

8. Erika Bachar-Kann, letter to Shoptaugh, January 24, 1999.

9. Adolf Stern to Herman Stern, August 22, 1936, Adolf Stern file; undated telegram to Julius Stern from Herman Stern, Julius Stern file; Adolf Stern to Julius Stern, November 14, 1936, German Correspondence file, Stern Papers.

10. Affidavits for Stern relatives, with Stern to Nye October 24, 1935 and Nye to Samuel Honaker, October 28, 1935, in Adolf Stern file, Stern Papers.

11. Honaker's Application for Appointment with letters of recommendation and employment summary card, all from his State Department personnel file. I am very grateful to the late U. S. Senator Paul Wellstone for his assistance in obtaining copies of these documents under the Freedom of Information Act.

12. "Report of Inspection, Consulate, Stuttgart, Germany, September 16-October 8, 1936," by J. Klahr Huddle (hereafter cited as 1936 Stuttgart Inspection Report), RG 59.4.5, National Archives.

13. Hugh Marlow Teller personnel file, obtained from the State Department through the FOIA.

14. 1936 Stuttgart Inspection Report.

15. Gustav and Selma Stern to Herman Stern, September 24, 1935 and February 9, 1936, and Samuel Honaker to Herman Stern, March 20, 1936, Adolf Stern file, Stern Papers. All correspondence concerning Gustav was for some reason filed with the Adolf Stern letters.

16. Moses Stern to Herman Stern, September 16, 193[5], Moses Stern file, Stern Papers (the latter part of the date is badly smeared, but the context, when compared to the Hugo Heinlein letters, make it clear this was in 1935).

17. Hugo Henlein to Herman Stern, September 22, 1935, German Correspondence file, Stern Papers; "Bad Schwalbach," *Encyclopedia of Jewish Life Before and During the Holocaust*, vol. 1, p. 77.

18. Lotte Ullmann, interview with Shoptaugh, June 26, 2000, transcript, pp. 7-14.

19. Thomas Maier (nee Dieter Ackerman), interview with Shoptaugh, October 1, 2004. Dieter's mother married Eugen Ackerman in 1938, after which the family emigrated to Colombia, making their way to the United States, by way of Panama and the Canal Zone, in 1941. He could not find or talk to Lotte Henlein Ullmann again until 2004.

20. Ullmann transcript, pp. 13,20; Hugo Henlein to Herman Stern, November 10, 1935, German Correspondence file, Stern Papers.

21. Ed Stern believed that the medallion Henlein threw overboard was the Iron Cross that he was awarded, but that cannot be correct because Alan Ullmann, Lotte's son, has his grandfather's medal, which is a "Merit War Cross" awarded to German combat veterans of the Great War. The item Henlein disposed of may have been a veteran's pin that many Great War veterans wore on their suits after the war.

22. Ullmann transcript, pp. 17-33.

Chapter Eight
The Senator, the Rabbi, and the anti-Semites

On September 4, 1934, Gerald P. Nye walked into the large caucus room of the Senate Office Building, sat down, picked up his chairman's gavel, and called to order the first public hearing of the Senate's Special Committee Investigating the Munitions Industry. Nye's Committee, as this one would come to be called, was about to begin grilling the representatives of the "merchants of death." These hearings, which produced almost fourteen thousand pages of documentation in the committee's published reports, ultimately determined Nye's place in history. Alongside the munitions investigation and the reputation Nye gained from it, his part in saving German Jews from the Holocaust would remain unknown.

Ironically, Nye twice had refused the chance to lead an investigation of the armaments industry, something that several peace groups had been pressing Congress to do for years. Nye agreed to do it only after the venerable Senator George Norris urged the duty upon him and pointed out that, with no real munitions businesses in North Dakota, he was unlikely to antagonize many of his constituents while he would gain some national prominence. It is also worth noting that the State Department endorsed the selection of Nye as the committee's chairman – at least at first.

Once he took up the challenge, Nye threw his customary frenetic energy into the effort. For weeks at a time, the special investigating committee delved into business secrets of dozens of major munitions manufacturers, ship builders, banks, and arms sellers. Its hearings harvested a flood of favorable publicity from across the nation. The committee's findings, published in a series of reports in 1935 and 1936, left a lasting impression with the public that munitions companies had routinely bribed government officials worldwide in order to sell their merchandise, raised the cost of defense, exerted improper leverage within the departments of War, Navy, Commerce, and State, and wrecked prospects for peace by acting "to goad and frighten nations into military activity." These findings, and the perceptions they left in the public mind, had enormous influence on the neutrality legislation that Congress passed between 1936 and 1939.

The committee also made Nye a celebrity, as Norris had predicted. He began to travel on nationwide speaking tours, gave hundreds of interviews, and became a major player in the Senate. His reputation in Washington was greatly enhanced. There was even brief talk of him being the Republican candidate for president in 1936.

Naturally, Nye made enemies. The State Department, having come to regret his part in the munitions investigation, resented his implications that the department cooperated too closely with the armaments industry. Secretary Hull remembered some of Nye's remarks with such bitterness that he singled the North Dakotan out for special criticism in his autobiography. But for all that, Nye's popularity as a result of the munitions investigation was so widespread that Hull hesitated to cross him. This was a situation that undoubtedly helped Herman Stern and those he sponsored for American visas – at least for a time.[1]

Stern and his German relations continued to benefit enormously from Nye's support of his affidavits. In 1936 and 1937, he succeeded in obtaining entry visas for more than two dozen men, women and children. In some cases, the family ties were tenuous at best; in other cases he acted as a co-sponsor to help convince the State Department to issue the necessary clearances.

The family of Sally and Hilda Jonas, living in Troisdorf, was such a case. Early in 1936, the Gestapo had briefly imprisoned Hilda's father, Samuel Levy, for "seditious remarks," which probably meant someone had overheard him utter a complaint about their intimidations. Hilda and Sally Jonas were married the same year. Toward the end of the year, and probably at Hilda's prompting, Sally's mother wrote a letter to Fredrecka Straus. She, in turn, asked her brother-in-law how she should help Sally and his family. Herman took it from there, preparing visa applications and affidavits that he sent to Fredrecka for her signature. Fredrecka indicated in this paperwork that she intended to have the Jonases live with her in her "ten room house" in California.

That is not how it turned out, for when Sally and Hilda received their visas in 1937, they left Germany for Holland, with their four-month old son Walter. Boarding a ship in Amsterdam, they made their way to New York, then to Valley City and met Stern, who had found a temporary job for Sally at one of the local butcher shops. A few months later he got a better job at the Land O' Lakes Creamery. Hilda picked up some extra money by cleaning homes, and the family lived in the small apartment house where Stern had found a place for the Henleins. At night, a teacher from Valley City State College gave them both English lessons. In time, Sally changed his name to Solly. Over the next year, Hilda sent some letters to Troisdorf and learned from the replies that her father had been forced to give up his butcher shop. He and her stepmother and Ruth were now sharing a small apartment in Cologne with a couple of other Jewish families; through such forced movements the Nazis were creating de facto ghettos.[2]

Each time Stern sponsored someone like Sally Jonas, he opened his door to another extended family of distant relatives, or semi-relatives, all looking for a way out of Germany. Hans Benjamin, for example, was apparently a cousin of one of Stern's sister-in-laws. When he contacted Stern to ask for an affidavit, Stern readily complied, referring to Benjamin in his affidavit as a "second cousin," which probably stretched the true relationship considerably. By the end of 1937, Benjamin was in the United States, living in Richmond, Virginia and working at a clothing factory. The letters exchanged between Benjamin and Stern indicate that Stern knew some members of Benjamin's family but had never met the young man.

Similarly, in 1936, Stern began corresponding with a man named Solomon Reichenberg, who had apprenticed with Stern in Mainz back in 1902. Reichenberg remembered helping Herman take his "suitcases to the train station, it was really a juvenile frivolity of the two of us to pull such a trick [helping Stern leave without a release from his master in Mainz]. He now asked Herman if he could somehow help his son Manfred. "Regarding the future of the young Jewish people here," he wrote, "one thing is for sure, they *have no* future. . . I am convinced, once he is with you, you'll not regret that you helped him to come to America. I know it is difficult to sponsor people who are not related to you. But my wife's maiden name is also Stern, maybe are related, perhaps not directly."

Relative or not, Stern agreed to help. After waiting some months to see his earlier sponsorships safely through the process, he sent an affidavit for young Reichenberg. The Stuttgart Consulate, after some hesitation, granted the visa early in 1937. Manfred's father could not "find the words" to express his gratitude: "I would do anything for you . . . in Germany there are only a very few who would have done what you did." Manfred boarded a ship in February, intending to see an old friend of his father's, living in Brooklyn, about a job. If things worked out, he hoped to convince his mother's American relatives to sponsor his parents.[3]

Soon after this, Stern took an enormous risk, when he sent an affidavit on behalf of a Julius Haas, referring to Haas and his wife as cousins "who desire to come to America to join me." However, Stern also wrote a letter to a man in New York, Sigmund Steeg, informing Steeg that he had sent the affidavit for Hass, and pointedly telling him that "the relationship [I have] given in affidavits sent to the Haas family is "Cousins." Steeg's reply contains another curious remark: "In order to further assist them to spend their rotten marks in Germany, I have made the statement that the family would settle in Valley City . . . kindly remember that the family is locating in Valley City and please reply to any inquiry accordingly." Stern replied a few days later asking Steeg to "persuade *your relatives* to buy their passage on [a] U.S.Line boat."

It is fairly evident from these letters that the Haas family was related to Steeg but, at best, a distant relative to Stern. One can further surmise from the letters that Stern knew Steeg fairly well and they had agreed to act as co-sponsors for Julius Haas and his family. They took special care to keep each other informed as to exactly what information they had supplied on their respective statements, particularly that the family intended to "join Stern" in Valley City. In fact, Haas and his wife and two sons made their home in New York after leaving Germany with their visas.

The significance of this was twofold. First, recall that in 1933, the State Department had advised its consuls they could provide "first preference" for a visa to applicants who had a "close relative" in the United States with sufficient wealth to care for them should that become necessary. The 1933 circular to consuls had stipulated that "distant relatives" should not be accorded this consideration because the American sponsor might not, in the end, grasp the nettle and take care of them. Exactly what Steeg's relationship to the Hass family is unclear, but he must have feared his affidavit alone on their behalf would be rejected. Stern entered into the matter as a co-sponsor, and because of Nye, his special friend in Washington, his co-sponsorship probably carried the day.

The second significance was that Stern meant what he promised in his affidavit. Whatever State Department's officials thought of the risk of allowing a distant relative (let alone a non-relation) to sponsor an immigrant, he would provide Haas and his family with support if it became necessary. This was substantiated not only by what Stern did for others he sponsored, but also from the fact that in 1943, in the midst of the war, he filed papers with the National Council of Jewish Women and the State Department, promising to help Mrs. Haas support two other members of the Haas family, cousins who had made it to England prior to 1939 and still resided there as "stateless persons."[4]

Word of Stern's success in successfully sponsoring German immigrants was getting around. His brother Adolf asked if he might be able to sponsor a young couple in Duisburg, Eugen Schwarz, a young doctor who had lost most of his practice after the Nazis forbade Jewish physicians to treat "Aryan" patients, and Schwarz's fiancé, Hanna Kann, a niece of Adolf's wife. Eugen had a brother living in America, who could not "at this point be their sponsor," and another brother in Holland who would give them some money "so you would not have any expenses because of them . . . it will give you satisfaction helping them to start a new life – you have helped so many already!"

Adolf's son, Gustave, also wrote to Herman from Paris, asking if he might help Ludwig, the brother of Alice and little Gus. Ludwig had gone to Paris soon after the Nazis were swept into power in March 1933. Since then, Ludwig had worked in a factory in Paris as a laborer, but now was likely to lose his job. Gustave doubted Ludwig would be able to find another job. "Paris is for all Germans very difficult. Since the unemployment here is great, he won't get a work permit anymore. He cannot return to Germany, he would end up in a concentration camp." Because Ludwig was strong and a "diligent worker," could Herman help him get an American visa and perhaps "place him on a farm?" In passing, Gustave remarked that the sausage casing factory he managed was not "going too well," that anti-Semitic incidents in France were on the rise, and that he and his wife were expecting another child.[5]

Stern was just then struggling to get the Stuttgart Consulate to reverse its ruling about his own brother Gustav. Gustav had suggested to Klara that perhaps he could "send for mother alone," but Herman would not hear of bringing Selma over without her husband. He urged Gustav to obtain another opinion about his heart and new X-rays. In the meantime, he would try to get Nye to stoke the fires in Washington. And he also pledged to do what he could for Eugen Schwarz, Hanna Kann, Ludwig, and others.

Stern's sponsorships had evolved into a major operation. It was probably not a coincidence that the number of affidavits he provided grew significantly in 1936, for this was when both of his sons graduated from college, which reduced his expenses considerably. He kept careful track of his affidavits even so, and made every effort to obtain the best deals on such matters as ship and train tickets, which he frequently arranged for those he sponsored. Like a good salesman, he also tried to cultivate the good will of the consul staff in Stuttgart, sending short notes from time to time to thank Honaker and his aides for the "very courteous treatment accorded to [relatives] when their visa was issued." On one occasion he sent along a case of "North Dakota honey" in "personal appreciation" for their work.

Acutely aware that this time he was investing in lives, not merchandise, he carefully attended to every detail of a refugee's trip, sending out numerous letters and telegrams to ensure that each new arrival would be met in New York port at the proper time, seen to the right train, and so forth. He combed through his lists of friends and business associates to find work for the immigrants, kept in touch with them, advised them, sent them small gifts, and, if necessary, lent them money. He and his wife both worked hard to help them learn English and adapt to American customs, with Adeline often explaining such things as American slang, table manners, and minor details of behavior that were so important in this so-much-more-egalitarian society.

Herman advised the Henleins, the Jonases, and the other immigrants who had children, to enroll their sons and daughters in the Boy Scouts and Girl Scouts, which he saw as a perfect instrument for teaching "American ways." Recognizing that many of these men and women were thrilled to have escaped the Nazis, and yet in tears to have left behind all they had known, he urged them to embrace the United States as their new home. He promised them that they were welcome by the American people.

But was he right in this last assurance? There were many signs that Americans were not altogether happy to see refugees coming to America.

Gerald Nye had used his influence to help Stern snatch these men and women from the clutches of the Nazis. At the same time, however, Nye believed that the United States should stand as aloof as possible from the problems and tensions of Europe. It was a view that was, on the whole, reflected by most of Congress. In the spring of 1935, Nye used his committee's findings to introduce bills that would prohibit American munitions and armaments companies from selling their goods to nations at war, prohibit American lenders from lending money to belligerents, and prohibit American citizens from traveling on the ships of belligerents. Loans and arms sales from 1914 to 1917 had tied the United States more closely to Britain in its war against Germany. The death of so many Americans aboard the *Lusitania* had done more to bring America into the war than any other incident. Nye and his supporters were trying to close the door on the past by creating forms of hindsight legislation.

But in 1935, Hitler was repudiating the Treaty of Versailles. Germany was beginning again to enlarge its army and navy. Hermann Goering was building a new German air force. Japan had seized Manchuria from China in 1931, and tensions between the two nations were heating up again. Most recently, Italian troops had invaded Abyssinia. Commentators were forecasting new and devastating wars in Europe and Asia. Measures designed to keep the nation from becoming enmeshed in such wars were precisely what most of the American people wanted. Thus, after debates and amendments to allow the president some discretion on how to implement these prohibitions, the bills were combined into the Neutrality Act of 1935. It was passed by huge margins in both houses of Congress. Roosevelt, sensing the public mood with his usual acumen, pledged that he was "definitely committed to the maintenance of peace and the avoidance of any entanglements which will lead us into conflict."[6]

The American mood was clear: no one wanted Europe's or Asia's problems to become their problems. This only discouraged efforts to help those who wanted to escape from the growing tyranny of the Nazis. In addition, there were signs that the mood was buttressed by a surge of anti-Semitism around the country. Hitler's success in Germany had inspired the creation of a few American fascist organizations, the most prominent of which were the Silver Shirts and the German-American Bund, which had limited influence nationwide but received publicity well beyond their numbers. The head of the small Silver Shirts unit in Minneapolis, for example, told journalist Eric Sevareid that the Jews were planning a revolution in America and that men had best prepare to "die defending [one's] Christian home." In the northeast, a group called the Friends of New Germany, which was allied to the Bund, tried to imitate the Nazis and organize boycotts of Jewish businesses. The efforts had only limited success but still "exacerbated anti-Semitism in their neighboring communities."[7]

Additional anti-Jewish outbursts, which again received considerable attention from the press, were connected to the 1936 presidential campaign. The opponents of the New Deal gathered their forces in the vain hope of unseating Franklin Roosevelt. The Republican Party chose as their standard bearer Alfred Landon, the governor of Kansas. Landon had gained a reputation as a champion of populist causes, and his closest advisors included some of the most progressive Republicans in the nation. But among the many true conservatives who spoke in favor of Landon's candidacy were some who managed to work into their messages an odious term that had been bruited around since 1933 – the "Jew Deal." Sadly, some responded to this sordid style – as one woman wrote to Mrs. Roosevelt, "my husband says that the Jews are bringing ruin on this country the same as they did in Germany. . . . They are all criminals, my [unemployed] husband says. My poor children are starving and your husband is responsible, as he has given everything to the Jews. My husband and all the Christian neighbors are going to vote the Republican ticket."[8]

The Union Party, made up of a shaky assortment of Roosevelt haters, ambitious men on the make and downright quacks, was, if anything, even worse. The key figures in this unwieldy coalition were Frances Townsend, a longtime advocate for America's elderly, and Father Charles Coughlin, an extremely popular Catholic priest whose weekly radio address was one of the most listened to programs on the air. Both Townsend and Coughlin had dabbled in the political arena for years; both had initially praised Roosevelt but had turned on him after he refused to support ideas they had brought forth for bringing the nation out of the depression. Now they had joined hands to form a third political party that they hoped would, if not sweep them into power, at least unseat "that man in the White House."

Townsend, a basically decent man, harbored no ill will toward Jewish people. But Coughlin was a different story. He repeatedly denied that he was in any way anti-Semitic, but his speeches and radio addresses suggested otherwise. In a February 1933 broadcast, he spoke of how "the progeny of Father Abraham readily acquired the evil habit of dealing in usury." On another occasion he termed Wall Street bankers "modern Shylocks [who had] grown fat and wealthy." There were enough such references that he attracted listeners because they believed he was anti-Semitic. A poll taken in the mid-1930s concluded that two-thirds of the more than three million men and women who listened to his radio show "regularly," recognized such remarks as anti-Jewish and approved of them.[9]

As the 1936 campaign got under way, these perceptions became inextricably linked with the Union Party. How could it be otherwise when Coughlin, who dominated the party, accepted the help of Gerald L. K. Smith, a former minister and for years the premier hatchet man for Louisiana's "Kingfish" boss, Huey Long? Smith never made a secret of his hatred of Jews. In the campaign he traveled across rural America with a stock performance that began with "I'm here to make a speech against the vermin that are trying to destroy America," and went on to attack immigrants, capitalists, and Jews in equal measure. Then there was "Big Bill" Thompson, a former mayor of Chicago, who was the Union Party's candidate for governor of Illinois. In the midst of the campaign, Thompson decided to court votes at the annual picnic of the Chicago Nazi Clubs, where, after shaking hands and kissing a few infants, stepped up to a microphone and said he was going to drive the "Reds and Jewish bankers" out of the country.

With Coughlin, Smith, and Thompson grabbing much of the press attention, the party's actual presidential candidate, who was personally chosen by Coughlin, was almost forgotten. It was William Lemke, a two-term congressman from North Dakota, who had gained national attention for his proposal that the Federal government refinance all farm mortgages. Lemke was not known for anti-Semitism, and indeed later endorsed Zionism and agreed to be a sponsor for the American Jewish Congress's work for European refugees. He signed on with Coughlin largely from bitterness after Roosevelt had quashed his farm mortgage bill. Coughlin's reasons for the choice of Lemke were never entirely clear. Apparently he hoped that Lemke would draw enough votes from the farmers to bring FDR down. If so, the strategy failed completely. In November, the Union Party received only two percent of all the votes cast and won not a single electoral vote. Roosevelt won a second term in one of the biggest landslides in American history.[10]

The Union Party collapsed, with Lemke returning to Congress for a few more terms and Townsend fading into obscurity. Coughlin and Smith however, would be heard from again, and if their listeners were fewer, that meant they simply shouted even louder.

North Dakotans had never known a year like 1936. After a particularly brutal winter of low temperatures and heavy snow, the spring thaw produced seas of mud, and planting was delayed. Summer brought the hottest weather in memory, with temperatures rising above one hundred degrees for days on end – the record was 121 degrees on July 6. In addition there was no rain, so what had been mud was now endless clouds of dust. The crop yields that fall were pitiful. New Deal price supports had helped raise wheat to a dollar a bushel for the first time in the decade, but what good was that when farmers were getting less than eight bushels of wheat per acre? All in all it was a horrible year.[11]

When the farmers suffered, so did the businesses, and Straus Clothing was no exception. Stern had to cut back on his inventory and lowered his prices in order not to lay off more of his salesmen. It helped that Eddie, having graduated from the Wharton School of Business, was returning home to join the operation. Eddie suggested that maybe he could buy a Ford he saw on the local dealer's lot. But Herman said no, not so much because of Henry Ford's open and virulent anti-Semitism, but because Eddie could make do with the family Buick. Herman himself used it only for out-of-town meetings. He would have his fiftieth birthday in 1937, but he still had the vigor to walk to work and back each day, even if it was twenty below zero.

Those quiet walks gave him time to think. Even with additional paperwork, and more pressure from Nye, the Stuttgart Consulate was still refusing to grant a visa to Herman's brother Gustav. Gustav and Selma were now leaning toward the idea of going to South America, on short-term visas, where they could wait and hope that an American visa would come through before their temporary visas expired. Herman understood the desperation that drove them to this risky step. But he also knew that if time ran out for them in South America, they could be deported back to Germany, and then inevitably sent to camps.

He had had happier success in sponsoring Eugen Schwarz and his fiancé Hanna. They, with Hanna's mother, Regina Kann, had received their visas and made it to New York near the end of 1936. Eugen had married Hanna at Christmas time. Thanks to some money that Regina had managed to have transferred to Holland, all three were living fairly comfortably. But Eugen had not been able to find work as a physician. Despite his recent training, and excellent letters of recommendation from prominent doctors in Germany, the New York authorities had refused to give Eugen a license to practice medicine. On top of this disappointment, Hanna's mother disliked America almost from the moment she stepped out off the ship, and was now talking of returning to Europe. Herman thought this would be a very foolish move, but he could not convince Regina to change her mind.[12]

There were other pending requests on his mind. One of these was the visa applications of Erich Falkenstein and his wife Ruth. Erich Falkenstein, another of the ubiquitous cousins who had asked Stern for his help, was a dentist living in Mulheim, which was very close to Duisburg. Having been denied the right to treat non-Jewish patients soon after the Nazis gained power, he had contacted Stern in 1936 and asked for help. Stern's affidavit for Falkenstein went off to Stuttgart near of the end of the year.

The Stuttgart consulate's visa section was just then in the process of being reorganized; Washington, in response to Samuel Honaker's call for help in coping with the rising tide of visa applications, had dispatched to Stuttgart a most efficient young consul, Herve Joseph L'Heureux. L'Heureux, as his name implied, was of French-Canadian ancestry, a native of New Hampshire. He had joined the State Department in 1927 after spending several years as a clerk in the

Washington office of U.S. Senator George H. Moses. Since 1930 he had been serving in the consular office at Windsor, Canada, where his supervisors had made note of his fine management skills.

Taking charge of the visa section at Stuttgart in January 1937, L'Heureux lost little time in taking stock of the visa situation. He notified Honaker that the visa staff interviewed an average of sixty visa applicants each day, that Hugh Teller needed an assistant, "with a good working knowledge of German," and that much of his own time would have to be spent writing "careful and complete replies" to "inquiries from the Department, from Senators and Members of Congress and from other interested persons." L'Heureux's years in working for a senator had taught him the wisdom of keeping these men fully informed. In all, L'Heureux was confident that if he could get the additional help he requested, the visa section could increase its workload and "handle 70 to 75 visa applicants per day."[13]

L'Heureux was given some more help for the visa section, and it does appear that the staff was able to speed up its handling of the applications during the next twenty months. Whether or not more visas were actually approved is debatable, but Herman Stern was pleased by the efficiency with which Stuttgart quickly cleared some of the visa requests for his relatives, beginning with the long-standing delay over Gustav and Selma Stern. In 1936, Samuel Honaker had denied them a visa on the grounds that Gustav had a heart condition. Since then, Herman had kept up a steady correspondence with Honaker, arguing that he was "already supporting" Gustav and Selma by sending them money, so it would "simplify matters greatly" if they were in the United States. Nye also sent additional letters to Honaker. It is very likely that after he arrived in Stuttgart, L'Heureux was able to persuade Honaker that this was one of those cases when it was a good idea to respond to the desire of "Senators and Members of Congress," because suddenly in February 1937, Stern was informed that, having passed a new physical examination, Gustav was now being awarded a visa, as was Selma. When the couple got to the United States, they moved to Chicago to be near their daughter Klara.[14]

Another case that was handled to Stern's satisfaction was that of

Erich Falkenstein. This, too, was handled within a few months, and Stern was particularly pleased to receive a polite letter from L'Heureux telling him that the Falkensteins would soon be invited to appear for their physical examinations and that "their cases will be given every consideration." The Falkensteins received their visas and immigrated in the late summer.[15]

A third set of visas was readily given to the Moser family. Moritz Moser lived in the city of Neuwied, northwest of Koblenz, with his wife Bette and young daughter Lore. A prosperous wholesaler of watches and clocks, Moser had decided to emigrate after the Nazis proclaimed the Nuremberg Laws. His daughter, Lore, was very small then, about four years old, too young to understand the danger. In fact, she at first found the Nazis exciting: "I remember when the Nazis came and marched through the streets, you know, and singing, all their military songs. There was one—not a military song—it had my name in it. "Lore, Lore, Lore," you know, about pretty girls and so on. And I heard them singing and I wanted to go down and see that and play, and my parents shut the shutters and said, 'No, you cannot do that.'"

She understood better when the Nazis refused to let her go to one of the public schools. "The German Jewish community in Neuwied established a school for all the Jewish children, and it was a one-room schoolhouse. There were children from six to sixteen, in one room, and the teacher was the rabbi. I have to tell you, I learned a great deal in those couple of years, and he was just very tough, very difficult, because he had to be a disciplinarian and all. If you were bad, you had to come in front of the room and he would strike your palms with a stick. I would get home and my father would be out-raged and go the next day to see him, and the teacher would say, 'But your daughter keeps talking.'" After listening to the rabbi explain what was going on in Hitler's Germany, Lore began to understand why her father said he "saw the handwriting on the wall" and they should leave.

Moritz made the decision, but it was Bette Moser, who had known Herman Stern when they were young, who said, "Gee, I know someone in America. He's in North Dakota, in Valley City," and wrote to him." Stern supplied one affidavit and a relative of Moritz's who lived in New York provided a second one. The Mosers were called to Stuttgart for their examinations in the fall of 1937. The day before they left, Bette was very nervous about this and thoroughly terrified Lore. "I was a nail-biter as a child. My mother said, 'We are going to go to another city where you're going to be examined, and we're all going to America. If you don't stop biting your nails, they won't let you come with us.' So when the time came to be examined, I had to go into a doctor's office, and I was so frightened and so fearful, that my heart was racing. The doctor said, 'We'll have to do some further examinations.'" Bette broke down at the news, explaining what she had said to Lore, and begging the doctor to let them calm Lore down. "And so we had to wait a few hours and they took me out to lunch and bought me ice cream and told me that of course I would always come with them. When we went back, of course, my heart was fine." Germany in 1937 was a place where life-or-death decisions could rest on a dish of ice cream.

After receiving their visas, the Mosers sailed to New York in December of 1937. They found an apartment in Washington Heights, fairly near the home of Moritz's relatives. Before obtaining the visas, Moritz had used some of his savings to purchase "china and stemware and all kinds of things, hoping to sell it when we got here, so we would have some money. But when we got here, the Depression was still going, so nobody wanted to buy anything." Moritz found his first job as a delivery boy while Bette cleaned homes for a time before getting a job at Longines Watch Company. Less than nine months after they arrived, Moritz had enough money to purchase a half-interest in a small restaurant on Washington Street and Third. The restaurant did well enough for Moser to buy out his partner at the end of 1940. Within a few years, Lore began making a little money of her own by baby sitting and working at a bakery. "I've always worked, always. So you never really had much of a childhood, but neither did all the other refugee children."

Even though it was Moritz's relatives who helped them day-today, Stern helped as well. He made a point of visiting them every time he went to New York. "He made sure I was going to the right school," Lore remembered. "It wasn't just 'well, you're here now, you're on your own. He helped us. I think he was that way with everybody."[16]

By now Stern was convinced that it was too dangerous for any Jew to remain in Germany. But he still could not persuade most of his brothers to leave. Moses still lived in Oberbrechen, but not at the old family home – that had been sold, for a pitifully small sum, after their sister Dora died in 1934. Moses now lived with neighbors who had taken him in and let him raise goats on their land. Since the people of Oberbrechen, most of them, remained friendly, he was content to stay. At the end of 1935, a recent immigrant from Montbaur had written to Stern to warn him that his brother Julius "has no income whatsoever," and the situation would only get worse. Yet, Julius insisted he would remain, that he was too old, at sixty-five, to move and learn English. Besides, as he asked his brother-in-law Hugo before the Henleins left for America, "where else would life be as fine as in Germany?" Adolf, too, was resisting Herman's entreaties to immigrate.[17]

How could Herman convince them to see the danger of remaining? A frank statement warning them might make matters worse if Nazi censors opened the letter. All he could do was offer his help and hope for the best. In the meantime, he had not forgotten the problems of North Dakota. The recent drought troubled him deeply. As farmers gave up or lost their mortgages because they could not pay their property taxes, the number of empty farmsteads around the state was at an all time high. State officials were giving voice to fears that unless something was done, the state's population might decline alarmingly. This was one of the reasons that William Lemke had made his proposal for a mortgage protection law. But with Congress rejecting it, what should be done now?

Mulling over these things, Stern began to wonder if the refugee problem might be used to help the state's fallow acres – could enough German Jews be brought over to settle on some of the empty farmsteads? As a young man in Casselton, he had been impressed by the hard-working farmers in that part of Cass County, many of them of German ancestry; he had complete confidence that a new wave of German immigrants from the rural villages he knew as a child could succeed in the same way. Could a large enough area of empty lands be found for a new village? If so, could funds be raised for a large enough down payment? Could some kind of organization be created to arrange visas for dozens of refugees instead of a family or two?

In order to find the money, he might get help from one or more of the larger American Jewish groups. He had met a few prominent Jewish leaders on his trips to New York. When he helped Klara get her visa in 1934, he had corresponded with some of the Joint Jewish Distribution Committee's people, and raised some money for their efforts. Reviving this connection might put him with touch with others.

The other major obstacle would be the State Department. In 1936, as in the years before, the total immigration of Germans into the country was well under the established quota – less than six thousand of the twenty-five thousand allotted. Herve L'Heureux, whose father had immigrated to the United States from Quebec, appears to have been more sympathetic toward visa applicants. But most of the consuls, who a frustrated writer characterized as having "little respect for members of those races customarily dismissed by Anglo-Saxons as inferiors," continued to turn a deaf ear to entreaties for granting more visas.[18]

Rabbi Stephen S. Wise could attest that such insensitivity existed even among America's own Jews. Wise, the guiding spirit of the American Jewish Congress, had played a large part in organizing the boycott against German imports in 1933. A few months after that, he had met some of the refugees in Paris who had fled the Nazi persecutions. "Through their eyes, I have looked in the depths of hell," he wrote to a friend. He returned home and decided that he must "devote every minute of my time" to make Americans see that they must respond to this crisis.

He urged all Jewish organizations in the country to join the boy-cott against German imports. When the older organizations, B'nai B'rith and the American Jewish Committee, said such a strategy would only harm the Jews in Germany, he cited the statements of refugees who had told him that the boycott actually was restraining Hitler from greater violence. The leaders of the older Jewish organizations, who were predominantly Reform Jews, thought that Wise, who was Orthodox, was more interested in showmanship and political advan-tage than in the need to balance the delicate American situation against the problems in Europe. He, in turn, charged them with consistently misreading the situation in Germany. "I do not know how we can afford to be governed by their counsels now," he concluded.[19]

But with the "uptowners," as the leaders of New York's Jewish elite were often called, openly denouncing his warnings that something must be done, Wise was powerless to sway the government from its restrictive policies. Desperate, he approached Franklin Roosevelt. The two men had not spoken to one another since Wise had criticized FDR's cautiousness as governor of New York. But now Roosevelt, wanting Wise's support in the 1936 election, was all charm and flattery: but of course he would press State for more visas. Wise, seeing the president as the best hope for greater social justice, wanting to believe his vague promises, said he would be "entirely happy" in standing for Roosevelt. But after FDR's election landslide, the State Department's wall against immigrants was lowered not an inch. Of 154,000 slots available worldwide under the 1937 quota, only 18,000 quota vias were granted. Roosevelt did help him in negotiations with the British when, four months after their wobbly reconciliation, he went to London as a member of the World Zionist Organization to discuss the admission of more Jewish refugees to Palestine. The British Foreign Office wanted to stop further Jewish immigration to the Holy Land, but a word from FDR to the British ambassador in Washington persuaded them to keep the door open for the time being. Wise took heart in the British concession on Palestine. He also busied himself helping individual Jews get to the United States, signing dozens of affidavits for this purpose. He used his own home to house a number of refugees, while his wife headed a successful effort by the Congress's Women's Division to transform three New York town houses into temporary shelters for more; in all, some four thousand men, women and children started their lives in America in these homes.[20]

In these efforts, Wise received extensive help from ordinary Jewish families as well as from small business owners, who by the hundreds sent small donations to the American Jewish Congress for the purpose of helping refugees in the United States. Entire congregations, as well as small groups of individuals, collected funds for this purpose. In some cases, they also undertook to sponsor one or more individuals for visas. This happened at the University of Minnesota, where the local chapter of the Sigma Alpha Mu fraternity sponsored a young physicist from Germany. "It was a very successful thing," one of the fraternity brothers later recalled. "He lived with us at the fraternity house." Congregations in Minneapolis and St. Paul took responsibility for similar sponsorships, while the Orthodox congregation in Grand Forks, North Dakota, sent both money and clothing to refugee organizations in New York. In Iowa, a local unit of the American Friends Service Committee sent aid and sponsored individual refugees and ultimately raised funds to build a hostel for several Jewish men. Other Christian groups performed similar acts of decency, but, overall, the volume of such effort was unimpressive.[21]

But then the entire world had done little to help those trying to escape from the Nazi persecutions. In addition to expressing a wish to close the doors to Palestine, the British had firmly maintained its own imperial barriers against any meaningful Jewish immigration. In Poland, the government was threatening to do the Germans one better and physically expel all of its "surplus Jews." Most countries outside of Europe refused to accept any refugees, Jewish or otherwise. In Europe, France and Austria had accepted the largest part of the some 100,000 Jewish refugees to leave Germany by the beginning of 1937. But, as Gustave Stern's letter to Stern had noted, many of the French were beginning to protest the acceptance of many more.

As for Austria, the 200,000 Jews living in that remnant of the old

Hapsburg Empire were becoming very anxious by the end of 1937. Hitler was making no secret of his intention to annex Austria, as a first step toward the creation of his vision of a "Greater Germany."

No one, in Europe or elsewhere, appeared willing to stop him.

Notes

1. Cole, *Gerald P. Nye and American Foreign Relations,* pp. 60-76. See also the committee's *Report on Activities and Sales of Munitions Companies*, Senate Report 944, Part 3, 74th Congress, 2nd session, (Washington, Government Printing Office, 1936) pp. 3-13.

2. Fredrecka Straus' application for a visa, April 28, 1937, Jonas Family file, Stern Papers; Jonas interview transcript, pp. 7-8.

3. Solomon Reichenberg to Herman Stern, May 3, 1936, January 6, 1937, and February 11, 1937, all in Erich Reichenberg file, Stern Papers.

4. Affidavit by Stern for Haas family [1937], Herman Stern to Sigmund Steeg, June 26, 1937, and Steeg to Stern, August 4, 1937, all in Julius Haas file, Stern Papers.

5. Adolf Stern to Herman Stern, August 22, 1936 and December 27, 1936, and Gustave Stern to Herman Stern, February 1, 1936, all in Adolf Stern file, Stern Papers.

6. Cole, pp. 98-107. See also Manfred Jonas, *Isolationism in America, 1935-1941* (Ithaca, NY: Cornell University Press, 1966), pp. 144-48.

7. Geoffrey S. Smith, *To Save a Nation: American Countersubversives, the New Deal, and the Coming of World War II* (New York: Basic Books, 1973), pp. 72-73; Susan Canedy, *America's Nazis: A Democratic Dilemma* (Menlo Park, CA: Markgraf Pubs., 1990), pp. 54-55.

8. Robert S. McElvaine, ed., *Down and Out in the Great Depression: Letters from the 'Forgotten Man'* (Chapel Hill: University of North Carolina, 1995), pp. 198-99.

9. Louis B. Ward, *Father Charles E. Coughlin: An Authorized Biography* (Detroit: Tower Publications Inc, 1934), pp. 149-60; Alan Brinkley, *Voices of Protest: Huey Long, Father Coughlin, and the Great Depression* (New York: Alfred A. Knopf, 1982), pp. 269-73; Lipstadt, *Beyond Belief,* p. 127. The opinion poll, cited in Lipstadt, also showed that 51% of those who listened to Coughlin "occasionally" also approved of remarks that they took to be anti-Jewish.

10. David H. Bennett, *Demogogues in the Depression: American Radicals and the Union Party, 1932-1936* (New Brunswick, NJ: Rutgers University Press, 1969), esp. pp. 237-38, 245-47, 263-91; Edward C. Blackorby, *Prairie Rebel: The Public Life of William Lemke* (Lincoln: University of Nebraska Press, 1963), pp. 193-95, 217-32; Smith, pp. 38-52.

11. Catherine McNicol Stock, *Main Street in Crisis: The Great Depression and the Old Middle Class on the Northern Plains* (Chapel Hill: University of North Carolina Press, 1992), pp. 21-25. Stock, pp. 103-5, also discusses the drought in connection to the famous controversy over FSA photographer Arthur Rothstein and his much reproduced cow skull photograph.

12. Gustav Stern's letters discussing the idea of emigrating to South America are in the Adolf Stern file; see the Stiefel transcript, pp. 32-33, for the Schwarz-Kann voyage to New York. Tea Eichengruen Stielfel believed that Regina Kann was able to move money to Holland with the help of Herman's nephew Julius Stern, but that cannot be confirmed.

13. H. J. L'Heureux personnel file, obtained from the State Department through the FOIA; L'Heureux to Samuel Honaker, March 15, 1937, attachment to Stuttgart Dispatch 788, Honaker to Cordell Hull, March 16, 1937, 125.8853/440, U.S. Department of State, Central Decimal Files, Record Group 59, National Archives.

14. Herman Stern to Honaker, April 16, 1936, Nye to Stern, May 2, 1936, Stern to Honaker, February 15, 1937, all in Adolf Stern file, Stern Papers.

15 All the relevant letters and affidavits, including L'Heureux's letter to Stern, June 14, 1937, are in the Falkenstein-Kuhrau file, Stern Papers.

16. Lore Moser, interview with Tenessa Gemelke, April 23, 2001, transcript, p. 1-16; Stern affidavit in Moser file, Stern Papers.

17. Sally Stern (no relation) to Herman Stern, October 1, 1935, Julius Stern file, Stern Papers; Lotte Ullman transcript, p. 40.

18. Martin Weil, *A Pretty Good Club*, p. 91.

19. Melvin I. Urofsky, *A Voice that Spoke for Justice: The Life and Times of Stephen S. Wise* (Albany: State University of New York Press, 1982), pp. 264-68, 302; Gulie Ne'eman Arad, *America, Its Jews and the Rise of Nazism* (Bloomington: Indiana University Press, 2000), p. 115.

20. Urofsky, *A Voice that Spoke for Justice*, pp. 256-59, 282-84, 302-5. The divisions among American Jews over the German crisis were so extensive that even those who wanted to help the refugees could bitterly disagree. In 1933, journalist Dorothy Thompson, a fierce critic of Hitler, chided the American Jewish Congress for focusing too strongly on the German Jews while ignoring the suffering of the *Ostjuden*. But when Wise visited Poland three years later, Polish Jews cheered him and the Congress for speaking out. See Thompson and Benjamin Stolberg, "Hitler and the American Jews," *Scribner's*, September 1933, pp. 124-40; Urofsky, pp. 274-75.

21. Myer Shark transcript, pp. 18-19; Michael Luick-Thrams, *Out of Hitler's Reach: The Scattergood Hostel for European Refugees* (np, 1997).

Chapter Nine
"I Would Gladly Spare the World Another World War"

In 1934, Jacob Rader Marcus, one of America's premier scholars of Jewish history and culture, attempted to persuade his countrymen that Adolf Hitler was not just a danger to the Jews or Germany, he was a danger as well to all of Europe and the entire world. After making a thorough review of Jewish life and history in Germany in his book, *The Rise and Destiny of the German Jew,* Marcus noted that Jews had no choice but to reject Hitler's plan for Germany: Judaism by its humanitarian nature, must oppose "Hitlerian fascism because it threatens to reduce him to the status of a merely tolerated second-class citizen." In the same manner, Marcus warned, Nazism would inevitably try to reduce all other peoples to the same sub-human status – "If Hitlerism succeeds in encouraging other states to adopt its type of government then constitutionalism of the French, British, and American type is doomed."[1]

For almost four years, Americans chose to ignore the warnings by Marcus and many others that Nazism was a threat to the New World as well as the Old. In 1936, while Hitler, having repudiated the Treaty of Versailles, was building his vastly enlarged army and new air force, American magazines and newspapers were filled with statements by public figures to the effect that the tensions in Europe were no threat to the United States. In March of that year, Hitler ordered German troops to march into the Rhineland – the section of the Rhine that had been demilitarized by the Versailles Treaty – and begin building fortifications. The *Fuehrer* was gambling that the French would not react to this provocation and it worked. France and Britain debated the possibility of ordering troops to mobilize and demanding that Hitler withdraw. But this posed the possibility of a war that neither country was prepared to fight. Even if Hitler did withdraw his troops (he had in fact ordered the generals to retreat if the French crossed the border), what then? France did not want to occupy the Rhineland again as they had after the Great War. Nor were they or the British at all certain that they wanted Hitler's government to collapse, for that would present the possibility of a communist government in Germany, and no one, outside of Stalin, wanted that. Perhaps the Nazis would be more amenable to a peaceful relationship if the victors of 1918 let the Rhineland provocation go. Or so they reasoned. France and Britain did nothing, Versailles had been effectively repudiated, and Hitler's popularity in Germany rose to new heights.[2]

In the months that followed, Hitler joined Italy in sending arms, aircraft and "volunteer" troops to Spain to help the insurgents in that nation's civil war. In May 1937, while the civil war in Spain raged, America's Congress by a close vote altered the neutrality law slightly, permitting warring nations to purchase "peaceful" goods like foods and medicine from the United States. In order to reduce the danger of American ships being sunk trying to deliver such materials, the buyer would have to pay cash, in full, for the purchases and also would have to transport the goods in non-American ships.

This was as far as the American public was willing to go at that time. The traditional suspicions of European intrigues remained so strong that many leading public figures refused to see any difference between Germany and its neighbors. Idaho Senator William Borah, one of the leading figures of the emerging isolationist movement, told his fellow senators during the neutrality debate that as far as he could tell "there is no difference, in law or morals" between the actions of Germany and those of Britain or France. As a friend of Rabbi Stephen Wise, Borah had on several occasions written to Wise that the treatment of German Jews was "appalling." But, when it came to suggesting what the United States could do to help Hitler's victims, Borah could "only express my deep sympathy."[3]

But by the end of 1937, Hitler's iron grip was secure enough to allow him to turn his gaze beyond Germany's borders. He had pledged to restore the borders of the nation as it had been before 1918, and then go on to build his *Grossdeutschland* – his Greater Germany. He

This photograph of Hermann Stern was taken in 1902, in Mainz, where he had an apprenticeship with a tailor. Just weeks later the 15 year old Stern sailed for America, where he immediately Anglicized his name to Herman.
Courtesy of Edward Stern

The Stern home in Oberbrechen, Germany, where Hermann Stern spent his early life. His parents, Minna and Samuel Stern, are looking out of the lower windows; the identities of the young man and woman in the upper windows are uncertain.
Courtesy of Edward Stern

Lore Moser, in this photograph with her mother Bette, taken about 1930, was one of the children that Stern helped to get out of Germany. In 1937, the Mosers came to America and made their new home in New York.
Courtesy of Lore Moser

After learning the clothing trade at Straus's Casselton shop, Stern was sent in 1910 to Valley City to run a second store. The Valley City store was in the ground floor of the Kindred Hotel, here preserved by a local sketch artist. *Courtesy of the Barnes County Historical Museum*

The Straus Clothing store in Casselton, North Dakota, around the turn of the century. A cousin of the Sterns, Morris G. Straus (second from the left) offered Herman a chance to work in America. *Courtesy of Edward Stern*

Around 1912, Stern returned to Germany to visit his parents, brothers and sisters. From left to right, in rear: Dora Stern and her husband Adolf Stern, Salli Stern and wife Rosa, Julius Stern and wife Frieda. Middle row, left to right: Gustav Stern and sister Dora, parents Minna and Samuel Stern, sister Jettchen and brother Moses.In front: Gustave Stern (son of Adolf), Herman, Julius, son of Adolf, and "Little Gus," son of Julius and Frieda.   *Courtesy of Alan Ullman*

Hugo Henlein, future husband of Herman's sister Jettchen, in uniform during the Great War. Almost all of Herman's brothers also served in the German Army during the war, and later refused to believe that the National Socialists would ever persecute anyone who fought for the "fatherland" in World War I.
Courtesy of Alan Ullman

Adeline Roth, on the day she married Herman Stern, June 4, 1912. The local newspaper noted that "the handsome couple was much admired by all who saw them."
Courtesy of Edward Stern

Stern soon had sons of his own, and posed for this Valley City newspaper photograph with Adeline, Richard, born in 1913, and Edward, born in 1914. The photo was likely taken in 1916 or 1917. *Clipping from Straus Clothing files, as printed in a store flyer.*

Jettchen Stern Henlein (sitting at right) with her infant daughter, Lotte, around 1925. The Henleins owned a small green-grocery in Bad Schwalbach.
Courtesy of Alan Ullman

Lotte Henlein (second from right) with school friends, including the young boy Dieter Ackermann (later Thomas Maier), in the mid-1930s. Once Nazi anti-Semitic policies were taught in the schools Lotte and Dieter became targets for abuse by many of their classmates.
Courtesy of Thomas Maier

This photograph of Julius Stern, the son of Herman's brother Adolf, was taken in the late 1920s in Valley City, where Julius briefly worked for Straus Clothing. Not particularly interested in business, Julius would have preferred to be a singer. In the 1930s he was one of the first persons that Herman Stern helped to get out of Nazi Germany.
Courtesy of Frank and Larry Stern

Bad Schwalbach, where Hugo Henlein, his wife Jettchen Stern Henlein, and their daughter Lotte lived. The townspeople knew little of the Nazi movement before 1933. But within months of Hitler's taking power, Nazis were pressuring Jewish merchants to give up their businesses.
Courtesy of Thomas Maier

Two others who Stern sponsored for residency in America were his niece Alice and his nephew Gustav, the children of Stern's brother Julius. Alice is seen in this photograph (taken about 1915) with Gustav, younger brother Ludwig, and their mother, Frieda. Ludwig, Frieda, and Julius Stern all perished in the Holocaust.
Courtesy of Joan Stern Mazza and Francis Stern Furgiuele

Hilda Levy Jonas, standing with her husband Solly Jonas, in mid-1937. Their infant son, Walter, is on the lap of Hilda's stepmother Hedwig, followed by Hilda's sister Ruth and her father Samuel Levy. The Jonases were one of the first families to be sponsored by Herman Stern for immigration to America. The Levys were unable to leave Germany and died in the Holocaust
Courtesy of Walter Jonas

Tea Eichengruen (standing, left) was not related to Stern, but he sponsored her immigration from Germany anyway. She posed for this photograph in 1938, just a few days before leaving for America. She later helped get her parents out of Germany. Her brother Erwin (seated on right) was less fortunate.
Courtesy of Tea (Dorothy) Eichengruen Stiefel

Herman's sister Jettchen fled Germany with her family in 1936. They lived in the Stern home for more than five years. Stern helped Hugo Henlein purchase a scrap business at the edge of Valley City, while young Lotte finished her schooling in the community. *Courtesy of Alan Ullman*

Stern was approaching his fiftieth birthday when this photograph was taken in the late 1930s. But unlike others of that age who began to slow down and look back on a successful career, Stern was involved in a dozen new projects, including a plan to help German refugees settle on farms in North Dakota. *Courtesy of Edward Stern*

Several of the refugees that Stern helped lived for a time at his home in Valley City. Note "Eddie" Stern, Herman's youngest son, posing in front of the house. *Courtesy of Edward Stern*

Senator Gerald Nye was the object of considerable national attention when this photograph of him was taken in the mid-1930s. Praised across the nation for his advocacy of neutrality laws to "prevent American involvement in another European war," Nye was also quietly helping Stern obtain immigration visas from the US State department for his German relatives. *Courtesy of the Institute for Regional Studies, North Dakota State University*

War prevented many Jews from leaving Europe, but some families found a way of getting out. Dieter Ackerman, Lotte Henlein's friend and Bad Schwalbach neighbor, was able to get to America with his family after his mother obtained a temporary visa to live in Colombia and then managed to talk their way into the US-controlled Panama Canal zone. *Courtesy of Thomas Maier*

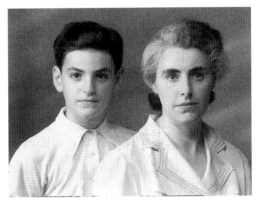

Rosi Klibanski Spier, a cousin of Stern, noted on this photograph that "soon after we arrived [in New York, 1939] we visited our beloved uncle Herman when he was on a business trip." Rosi's son, Wolfgang, soon changed his own name to William. *Courtesy of William Spier*

This farmstead, located west of Grand Forks, North Dakota, was one of several unoccupied farms (ceded to a bank during the depression years) that Stern was hoping to purchase and use in his plan to help German refugees move to the state. The beginning of war in Europe in September 1939 put an end to his dream.
Courtesy of the Elwyn B. Robinson Department of Special Collections, Chester Fritz Library, University of North Dakota

Erika Kann's family, also related to Stern, failed to get out of Europe before the shooting began. Erika's father and uncle died in one of the extermination camps, but she and her mother survived by hiding with this family of Belgian farmers from 1940 to 1944.
Courtesy of Erika Bachar-Kann

Julius Stern, Herman's nephew, was one of at least six Jewish refugees sponsored by Stern who served in the American armed forces. Stern's son, Eddie, also served in the Army's 8th Air Force. *Courtesy of Frank and Larry Stern*

Tea Eichengruen barely managed to get her parents to America aboard this Spanish steamer, the *Navemar,* which crossed the Atlantic and arrived in New York in September 1941. Tea's brother Erwin was unable to get out and died in Auschwitz in 1942. *Courtesy of the Mariner's Museum, Newport News, Virginia.*

After the war, Lotte Henlein met and married Irwin Ullmann, another German refugee. It would not be until years after this 1958 photo was taken, that their children (Alan, age 5 and Elyse, age 2) knew anything about the dangers their parents had survived in order to make a new life in the United States.
Courtesy of Alan Ullman

Herman Stern in about 1975. Active up until the last months of his life, the always forward-looking Stern seldom wanted to talk about the past. Few of his contemporaries ever knew how much he had done on behalf of Jewish refugees.
Courtesy of Edward Stern

In the late 1990s, Margaret (Greta) Steiner, appeared in a local television news segment, telling her story of how she was able to leave Vienna and eventually make her way to the United States. Her parents (inset) were unable to leave Austria and were murdered in the Holocaust.
Courtesy of KVRR TV News, Fargo, N.D.

meant to begin the task now, starting with Austria. His generals warned him that the German armed forces were not strong enough to win if the western powers decided to go to war to stop him. But he contemptuously dismissed their warnings. When he had decreed the formation of a much-enlarged German army in March 1935, in defiance of the Versailles Treaty, France and Britain had responded with nothing more than diplomatic protests. When he had created the new German air force, which was expressly forbidden by the Treaty, the former Allied powers of the Great War took no action. Hitler, who saw a bold, aggressive move as the quintessence of diplomacy, decided he could go much further before provoking Britain or France into actually *doing* something.

On November 5, 1937, Hitler briefed the heads of his armed services on his plans for the future. Germany, he told them, needed "living space" to "secure and to preserve the racial community." This space, he had decided, could only be obtained "by force," singling out Austria and Czechoslovakia as the first nations to be annexed into the Greater Germany, because he suspected that France and perhaps also Britain had "already written off" those two states and would not fight to save them. After securing these two eastern states, Hitler then planned on expanding further eastward at the expense of Russia. He also made it clear that at some point he wanted to settle accounts with the other victors of the last war. He ordered his military chiefs to make their plans according to this general strategy and develop scenarios for marching into Austria and Czechoslovakia when suitable opportunities arose.[4]

As it worked out, the opportunity came first in Austria. Like Germany, Austria had fought on the losing side in 1918. In defeat, the old Austro-Hungarian empire had collapsed, with Hungary breaking away to form its own nation, and other parts of the empire taken by the victorious allies, adding to Czechoslovakia, Yugoslavia, and Romania. Just as the Versailles Treaty had antagonized most of the German people and turned many of them against the new German republic, so the Treaty of St. Germain, with its own war guilt clause and reparations demands, had cost the new Austrian state the support of

millions of its citizens. The treaty also prohibited Austria from form-
ing a unified state with Germany, something that many Austrians had
fervently wanted. This provision angered most of the German Austrians, including the Jewish writer Stefan Zweig, who asked why
Austria was to be denied the right of self-determination that Poles,
Czechs and many others were granted. "It was the first instance in
history, as far as I know," he wrote, "in which a country was saddled
with an independence which it exasperatingly resisted."

Willingly independent or not, the Austrian Republic went through
much the same difficulties as Weimar, then enjoyed a period of prosperity and peace in the latter part of the 1920s. Once Nazism arose in
Germany, it was imitated in Austria, which was after all Hitler's native land. While smaller in numbers compared to their neighbor,
Austrian Nazis were able to tap into a strong tradition of anti-Jewish
feeling within much of the population. Austrian anti-Semitism was,
if anything, even more vicious than that in Germany; Hitler himself
had absorbed much of his hatred from the rhetoric of Germanic nationalist Georg Ritter von Schoenerer.[5]

Jews in Austria did not take the local Nazis very seriously at first,
but after Hitler came to power that began to change, as Margarethe
(Greta) Grunhut ruefully remembered. Greta was born in Vienna in
1906. At the time she grew up, Vienna was recognized as one of the
world's grandest cities. As a little girl she loved it when her father
took her into the heart of the city to see the magnificent government
buildings, the stately edifices of what Stefan Zweig termed Vienna's
"Golden Age of Security," when "everything in our almost thousand-
year-old Austrian monarchy seemed based on permanency." Greta's
father, Julius, owned a grocery in one of the Vienna's working class
districts. "We rented an apartment [near the shop], we didn't own an
apartment. You know, in Vienna not many people had their own
homes. Only the very well-to-do [had homes], lived on the outskirts
in a villa."[6]

Grunhut and his wife took care of the store with the help of a
clerk-apprentice. Their stock mostly was of the kinds of things working families needed for their evening meal – flour, sugar, fruits, rai-

sins, apples, grapes from Yugoslavia, and oranges from Spain. It was not a business that would make them rich, but they did well enough when Greta was little. Then, in July 1914, Greta and her parents were on a train, returning from Bohemia after a visit to her grandparents, when the conductor walked through the train carriage and announced that "the heir [Archduke Franz Ferdinand] and his wife had been assassinated in Sarajevo." "It was so unbelievable. I was eight years old." Life for Greta and her family began to change a few weeks later, when Austria marched on Serbia, setting off the Great War. Julius Grunhut was called to the colors. He spent the war as a guard in the prison camp filled with captured Russian soldiers. Olga Grunhut, Greta's mother, kept the shop going with the apprentice and another clerk she hired. But as the British navy tightened its blockade of Austria and her ally Germany, many of the fruits they had obtained from other countries became little more than a fond memory to most of the workers. Over time, the war's destruction in the countryside reduced the supplies of wheat and sugar to an ever-thinning trickle. By 1916, the year that old emperor Franz Josef died, Greta recalled that "there was a great food shortage. You had empty shelves [in the shops]."

It only got worse. By 1917, Greta's mother could only find clothes "woven out of paper." There was meat only in the countryside, and the shop's new clerk, whose parents had a farm, helped them by bringing "half a calf back for us." As for other foods, they made trips into the countryside to bargain for fresh produce, for vegetables, feathers for lining their worn winter coats, for anything. "The farmers did very well. You went out on the train and bought beans or whatever, in exchange for jewelry or anything." Without these transactions and the meat from the clerk, the Grunhuts could have starved to death. Hundreds in Vienna did die of starvation or disease as the national system began to collapse. Greta and her mother and brother watched as the other nationalities in the empire began to press for their freedom. "The Czechs and Slovaks, they never wanted to be a part of Austria. And the Hungarians, Hungary was [already] a separate state really. The emperor of Austria was also the King of Hungary."

The imperial government collapsed in November 1918. Karl, the emperor of Austria, abdicated the throne. But unlike Germany, the Germans in Austria did not embrace a myth that they had been "stabbed in the back." The defeats in the field and the troubles at home had been too palpable for such a myth to take hold. Consequently, the new republic started out on a much sounder foundation than that of their western neighbor. The republican government was dominated from the first by the Christian Social Party, which drew its support largely from the predominately Catholic countryside, those who hoped that someday the monarchy might be revived, and the shopkeepers of Vienna. The Christian Socialists' major opposition was the Social Democratic Party, which most of Grunhut's working class neighbors fervently supported. While the Grunhuts remained cordial with their Social Democratic neighbors, they feared that the militant unions could eventually break up the country. As for the Austrian Nazis, with just four thousand members in 1928, they were barely noticed.

Austria's precarious political balance was stable through the more prosperous years. It was during this time that Greta Grunhut finished her schooling and began to learn a trade. "I had a cousin and she was a milliner, making hats. I waited half a year and became an apprentice in the store where she worked. It was a big store, very exclusive, called Gaby. I was there two years as an apprentice. I had to take a written test and then make a hat. Of course, I passed the tests. Then I worked for some other stores [for some years] and then I decided to open my own little studio."

She made a down payment on a small building where she could open her shop and live upstairs. Since it was close enough for her parents to walk to their own grocery, they moved in with her. Having accumulated a long list of happy customers, Greta did not need to advertise in order to get new business. But as the worldwide depression spread across the land in the 1930s, the Grunhuts had to work hard to make ends meet.

The depression also wrecked the delicate political balance in Austria. The Social Democrats, the Communists, and Austrian Nazis all gained new members as unemployment grew. The Austrian chancellor Engelbert Dollfuss, fearing that a deadlock in the government would lead to a revolution, suspended the Austrian parliament and tried to maintain control with emergency decrees. He outlawed the Austrian Nazis, then tried to suppress the unions, which triggered a workers uprising in Vienna and the other larger cities. Greta vividly remembered the bloody fighting that ensued. "There was a lot of shooting, and you couldn't get in close to the interior of the city because [the streets] were all blocked out. I remember it lasted some days." Dollfuss brought army units into Vienna and authorized the troops to use machine guns and heavy artillery against the huge working class apartments. Over two hundred men, women and children were killed. Thousands more were injured before the rebelling workers surrendered.

In July, 1934, six months after his bloody victory, Dollfuss was himself murdered. A small group of Austrian Nazis stormed into Dollfuss's office and shot him down. Greta Grunhut learned of the killing while on a hiking trip with some friends. "We were up in the Alps and we heard it in one of the hostels, Dollfuss was assassinated. Everybody was upset." Greta packed and returned to Vienna, afraid she would find German soldiers in the streets when she got there.

The Nazi plotters had counted on sympathetic aid from the Austrian army, or if that failed, on Hitler's help. But Germany, which had been sending steady assistance and directions to the Austrian Nazis from its party office in Munich, did not dare to intervene after Mussolini sent troops to the Italian-Austrian border. German radio suddenly ceased its anti-Austrian broadcasts. Hitler quickly disavowed the coup attempt, which collapsed. The Austrian Nazis were quickly rounded up and the murderers of Dollfuss went to prison. Moving to cover his embarrassment, Hitler replaced his ambassador to Austria with the ubiquitous Franz von Papen, who was given the job of pacifying "the regrettable misunderstandings that has arisen between the two countries."

Kurt von Schuschnigg, Dollfuss's successor as chancellor, continued his predecessor's policies. By dangling an iron fist over the Social Democrats, he kept them from interfering with his courtship of Mussolini, who he hoped would continue to protect his country from Germany. At the same time, he tried to ingratiate himself with Hitler by increasing trade with Germany and quietly granting amnesty to some of the Austrian Nazis. As he confessed in his memoirs, Schuschnigg "knew that in order to save Austrian independence I had to embark on a course of appeasement." But Hitler saw Schuschnigg's actions as a sign of weakness, nothing more. In 1936, the Fuehrer accepted an agreement in which the two nations promised not to "interfere in the domestic arrangement" of one another's countries and promised that Germany recognized "the full sovereignty of the federal state of Austria." He had no intention of keeping these commitments. He was simply biding his time until another opportunity presented itself.

By the end of 1937, Hitler was convinced that the moment had arrived. When Italy had been condemned for the conquest of Ethiopia in 1935, he had courted Mussolini assiduously. In 1936, with the two dictators cooperating in mutual support of the Nationalist forces in the Spanish Civil War, he had seen to it that the Duce heard of every success of the German planes flown by the Kondor Legion's 'volunteer' pilots. Impressed with Germany's military rebirth, alienated from Britain and France, Mussolini cast his lot with Germany. He would not stand in the way of an *Anschluss* a second time.

Nor it seemed would Britain. In November, 1937, the British foreign minister complimented Hitler for his efforts to make Germany a "bulwark in the West against Bolshevism," and congratulated Hitler for using his influence in eastern Europe to check the growing power of the Soviet Union. A month later, another British diplomat candidly told the German ambassador in London that the British recognized that an *Anschluss* was probably inevitable but hoped that "a solution by force [could] be avoided." This, as one German historian has written, was "all that Hitler needed to know before tightening the noose around Austria's neck." He ordered his generals to accelerate preparations for annexing his hapless neighbor.[7]

The Austrian Nazis had spent much of 1937 agitating for a merger with Germany. Using money that came to them in a steady flow from Germany, they staged noisy demonstrations and organized literature campaigns. They also set off bombs in Vienna and elsewhere, then blamed these acts of terror on communists or socialists and called on Germany to intervene in order to protect the country from the Red threat. At the beginning of 1938, Austrian police uncovered a cache of documents in a Nazi-owned office that indicated that there would soon be another coup attempt. When apprised of the documents, Schuschnigg decided he must make a try at negotiating with Hitler. He told Franz von Papen that he would go to Germany and meet Hitler, but only if Hitler reiterated his 1936 promise not to interfere in Austria's internal affairs. With consummate cynicism, the German chancellor sent word that he merely wanted to discuss some "misunderstandings and points of friction" in German–Austrian relations. Reassured, Schuschnigg set off to meet Hitler at the latter's mountain retreat at Berchtesgaden.

When he arrived at Berchtesgaden, Schuschnigg soon realized how foolish he had been to expect that he could simply have a talk with Hitler, statesman to statesman.

No sooner had the two chancellors sat down in Hitler's study, with its huge picture window providing a breathtaking view of the mountains, than Hitler launched into one of his histrionic performances. First he attacked Schuschnigg for Austria's failure to follow a "friendly policy" with Germany: "You quite complacently remain a member of the League of Nations, in spite of the fact that the Reich withdrew from the League [in 1935]," Hitler charged. "And you call that a friendly policy?" Before Schuschnigg could complete his reply, Hitler launched another salvo: "Austria has never done anything that would be of any help to Germany. The whole history of Austria is just one uninterrupted act of high treason. I can tell you right now, Herr Schuschnigg, that I am absolutely determined to make an end of all this. The German Reich is one of the great powers, and nobody will raise his voice if it settles its border problems." A few moments later, he cut off Schuschnigg again to threaten that he would "solve the so-called Austrian problem one way or another." And so it went, with the Austrian chancellor vainly attempting to talk about peaceful solutions and the Nazi Fuehrer going on about Austrian men and women, starving and in rags, beseeching him to save them, then making menacing remarks about the sadness of Germans having to shed the blood of other Germans.

This first exchange ended and was followed by a light lunch, during which Hitler, who had told Schuschnigg he was a man of action, not words, rambled on about motor cars, art, and his plan to show the Americans that Germany could build "bigger and better houses." Several German generals who had come in to dine with the two chancellors said almost nothing; their presence was purely to convince Schuschnigg that Hitler meant business.

After the meal, Hitler disappeared for a rest. Schuschnigg sat down for a smoke and tried to compose his thoughts, but looked up to see Papen and Ribbentrop, the German Foreign Minister, coming over with grim looks on their faces. Ribbentrop handed Schuschnigg a draft statement of Germany's demands. The key provisions in this short document were that Arthur Seyss-Inquart, one of the Austrian Nazis, was to be made the Minister of Public Security "with full and unlimited control of the police forces of Austria," Nazis in jail were to be released, and any officials who had lost their positions because of Nazi sympathies must be reinstated. In return, Germany promised to continue to recognize Austria's "sovereignty and independence." After a few moments to ask questions, Schuschnigg was again shown into Hitler's study, where he found "the Fuehrer pacing excitedly up and down." Hitler demanded that Schuschnigg sign the document at once. When the latter sought to reopen a dialogue by saying that he would have to confer with Austria's president, Hitler appeared "to lose control" and shouted for his military staff commander. As Hitler stalked from the room, the Austrian Foreign Minister, who had accompanied Schuschnigg on this journey, walked in and said he thought they might be "arrested within the next five minutes."

In the end, Schuschnigg agreed to take the document back to

Vienna and get his cabinet and the Austrian president to accept it. Hitler gave Schuschnigg three days to get the job done. He also advised the by-now tired and shaken Austrian that only he - Hitler - could assure Europe of peace: "I would gladly spare the world another world war, but I don't know whether it can be avoided if no one believes me."[8]

Schuschnigg returned to Vienna, where, with some difficulty, he persuaded Austria's President Wilhelm Miklas into accepting the document. By now, as he admitted in his memoir, Schuschnigg felt that total appeasement was the only hope for Austria to keep some measure of its independence. He also hoped that Italy might yet provide him with some statement of support that would make Hitler pause.

But within a few weeks, it became clear that the nation could easily fall into chaos. Austrians who wanted no part of being a province of Germany began their own demonstrations while the Nazis countered by displaying the party flags and portraits of Hitler. It was still illegal to display the swastika in the country, and Hitler had explicitly promised to accept this in the recent agreement, but Schuschnigg quickly realized that Seyss-Inquart had no intention of ordering the police to take the swastikas down. Instead, he went to Graz, where the Nazis had taken so much control that a British correspondent noted that "boys in the street were greeting each other with the Hitler greeting." At Graz, Seyss-Inquart reviewed a fully organized Nazi torchlight parade.

By the end of February, Schuschnigg had decided that if the Nazis were allowed to swagger in this manner, the country would before long drop into Hitler's pocket. So in desperation, he decided to call for a plebiscite on the question, "For a free and independent, German and Christian Austria." As he explained it later, Schuschnigg felt that most Austrians were still anti-Nazi and would vote for independence. As for Hitler, Schuschnigg reasoned that "Hitler either meant sincerely what he had proposed in the agreement [to accept closer ties but not annexation] . . . or he was merely waiting for an opportunity to solve the question by force. In that case, it was better

to end the undignified cat-and-mouse game as quickly as possible."
He announced the plebiscite for March 13. A pro-Nazi editorial writer
in Vienna immediately denounced this as a step toward "democracy
and bolshevization." Some of the Austrian Nazis were worried that
Schuschnigg might get a two to one vote in favor of Austrian independence and so begged Hitler to intervene.

Schuschnigg learned two days after announcing the plebiscite just
what Hitler meant to do. On March 11, Austrian Nazis began marching in the streets with sound trucks announcing "the Anschluss was
at hand." A few hours later, Schuschnigg began a series of meetings
with Seyss-Inquart and emissaries of Hitler, who warned him that
the German army would march if the plebiscite was not called off.
He resisted until he received a message from Goering, demanding
that the plebiscite be cancelled and Seyss-Inquart be made chancellor. Otherwise, Goering promised, "the German armies will move
into Austria." By then Nazi bands had seized public buildings in several cities. The game was up and Schuschnigg, for all he tried to
delay, knew it. He turned in his resignation and then used the radio to
urge the people not to resist a Nazi takeover – Germans, he said,
must not shed "German blood." When Miklas still hesitated to appoint Seyss-Inquart in Schuschnigg's place, a hastily cobbled force
of German divisions called the "Eighth Army" marched in on March
12; Hitler wanted the world to see his triumph and mull over the
threat of his new army. No shots were fired. Crowds greeted the German soldiers so enthusiastically that William Shirer, present to cover
the event for CBS radio, could still vividly remember the spectacle
decades later. "I had often seen the Vienna police break up Nazi demonstrations in this spot. But now they were standing with folded arms.
And most of them were grinning. Some of the young women in the
crowd began to take off their hooked-cross armbands and tie them on
the sleeves of the police. More grins. Obviously, the Vienna police
were going over to the Nazis."[9]

Poor Schuschnigg would have seven years in a concentration camp
to ponder how he might have done things differently. The Jews of
Austria were not given nearly so much time.

While Hitler and his cronies swallowed Austria, France and Britain looked on passively. The British and French governments could not claim that the *Anschluss* had taken them by surprise. The French government received a detailed account of Hitler's meeting with Schuschnigg at Berchtesgaden within a day of the event, and on March 9, a French military attaché in Berlin warned that the German army would move on Austria in about three days. But when the French ambassador in London suggested that the two nations make a strong statement that forceful annexation was intolerable, the British foreign minister scotched the idea of making an issue over a matter that was, in his view, "between Germans." France and Britain thus contented themselves with issuing protests of Hitler's "unilateral" actions, which the Nazis simply ignored. In the House of Commons, Prime Minster Neville Chamberlain denounced rumors that anyone in his cabinet had done anything to indicate "consent or encouragement to the idea of the absorption of Austria by Germany."[10]

On March 13, C. Michael Palairet, Britain's ambassador in Vienna, sent a cable to the Foreign Office to inform the government that mistreatment of "Jews and anti-Nazis [was] already beginning here." The depredations proceeded so quickly in fact, that one scholar refers to the next few weeks as a *Blitzverfolgung* – a lighting persecution. Most of the terror was perpetrated by Austrian Nazis, who could now freely vent their anger on their enemies. A shameful number of "ordinary citizens" joined in to help the usual bullies however, and the results were horrifying. In Vienna, elderly Jews were dragged from their homes and forced to clean pro-Schuschnigg slogans off the walls of buildings; others, including one of the city's premier rabbis, and was seventy-six, were made to clean the sidewalks with toothbrushes. Orthodox women were humiliated by being forced to remove their wigs in public and burn them in the streets. A foreign visitor reported having seen a group of young SA troopers pushing a blind Jew around from one to another, laughing when he fell down again and again. Several Jews, along with a number of Schuschnigg supporters and Social Democrat leaders, were shot down, then more were rounded up and sent to concentration camps. Later about two thousand of the most prominent Jewish businessmen were arrested and taken to a particular street. Adolf Eichmann, wearing his Gestapo uniform, then walked up to the group and asked, "Who volunteers for Dachau?" They were then forced into wagons and sent off to the notorious camp.

As in Germany, the ambitious and greedy rushed to grab Jewish-owned businesses. A favorite method of doing this was for some Nazi to secure an appointment (or simply announce himself) as an "Aryan Commissioner" of a particular shop or industry and then proceed to loot the business. This hurt the economy of Vienna so much that Goering appealed to Hitler to put a stop to it until a more formal method of "Aryanization" could be put into place. In the meantime the small fry of the SA satisfied their avarice by forcing their way into Jewish homes and, while the inhabitants looked on helplessly, simply pocketed jewelry or whatever else they wanted. Outside Vienna, some towns, with or without the connivance of local office-holders, simply ejected their Jewish populations wholesale.[11]

Since the Nazis followed up the military occupation by organizing their own plebiscite, in which the Austrians overwhelmingly approved joining the Greater German Reich, Britain and France did little to protest the anti-Jewish rampage. Once again, the British took the stance that, with the annexation of Austria, this was a matter between the German government and its own citizens. But a sizeable part of the British public was outraged enough by the *Anschluss,* and this may have contributed to Chamberlain's government being willing to show a little more sympathy for Jews trying to emigrate.[12]

The British change of heart lasted long enough to save Greta Grunhut's life. As Greta and her parents watched the German troops enter Vienna, she knew that the persecutions would begin before long. She also expected that her parents would be targeted for intimidation because they were members of the large Humboldt Temple, which had contributed thousands of Austrian schillings to Schussnigg's causes. So it did not surprise her that about a week after the *Anschluss,* Austrian Nazis walked into her father's grocery and simply threw him out. "They poured water on the sidewalk and my father had to go out of the store and on his knees scrub [pro-Schussnigg slogans off] the sidewalk. He lost the business after that, he had to close it. Somebody else took over the store with some other merchandise. He was about sixty-seven then and he couldn't run the store."

Greta herself was left alone for the time being. But when she saw an acquaintance in her neighborhood come down her street one day wearing a storm trooper's uniform she realized it would only be a matter of time before she too lost her shop. It was then she began to think of a way to leave Austria. She had an aunt living in the United States who might help. But with thousands of Jews in Vienna lining up outside the American embassy to apply for visas, it was obvious that an emigration process would take months, perhaps even years. Greta filed her papers and just hoped for the best, that the paperwork would find its way through the system and that she and her parents could meanwhile stay out of the Nazis's way.[13]

That same March, while Hitler coerced his way into Austria, Tea Eichengruen found her escape from Germany. Tea had nearly given up on her dream. After the possibility of going to Israel with some of the orphans from the Dinslaken orphanage faded, she contacted a third cousin who lived in Missouri and asked him if he would sign an affidavit on her behalf. The man turned her down, explaining that he had already given "a number of affidavits for some of his family." Tea found no solace in his offer to sponsor her later on, in perhaps two years, "because I knew, even then, there were no two years" left for Jews in Germany. The suggestion her Aunt Dora had made, that Herman Stern might be able to help her, was perhaps her last chance.

But could Stern help Tea, who was not really a relative? The existing letters he had exchanged with his brother Adolf and sister-in-law Dora do not contain anything to indicate when he decided to try and sponsor Tea, but it seems probable that he made the decision sometime in the fall of 1937. Tea was seventeen by then, and Stern may have thought at first that he could bring Tea over in the same way he had helped Klara: enroll her as a student at the local college.

Toward the end of the year, Stern sent an affidavit to the American Consulate in Stuttgart, asking the consulate to "visa the passport of . . . Tea Eichengruen." Stern swore that he would "receive and take care of her, [so] that she [would] at no time become a public charge upon any [American] community." He also claimed that Tea was his second cousin. This was not strictly true, and the consulate staff, knowing that Stern had already sponsored almost thirty people by then, showed every sign of taking their time on this application.

Sensing the weakness of his affidavit, Stern came up with a second strategy for securing the visa – something that no one but he and a couple of other men knew about for over half a century. Eddie Stern, Herman's son, got the story from a member of Gerald Nye's staff in the early 1950s. "I ran into him in Washington, and the fellow said to me, 'Hello Ed, how's your wife?' I didn't think he'd ever met my wife." The man laughed and explained that back in the late 1930s he and Nye had contacted the State Department to tell them that Tea wanted to come to America to marry Eddie. This subterfuge, however harmless it may have seemed at the time, was in reality very risky, especially for any further Jews in Europe who would turn to Stern for help. For if the State Department had concluded that Stern and Nye were lying to them, further affidavits by Stern would almost certainly have been rejected.

But most Americans were still firmly committed to a foreign policy of strict neutrality in 1937. That meant that Nye, the man most closely identified with the 1936 neutrality laws, was still a man of considerable influence. In December 1937, the Stuttgart consulate informed Stern that "Thea Eichengruen" would be invited to appear at their offices to take tests to determine if she was physically and mentally fit to receive "an immigration visa."[14]

Tea remembers her journey to Stuttgart vividly. She went there on the train alone, in order to show that she was capable of looking after herself. She was more than a little afraid: "I had to stay at a hotel. I didn't know a soul [in Stuttgart]. But I did what I had to do. There were physical examinations to prove that you were healthy, and there were mental tests. I remember being asked to count backwards by threes. Why I remember that I can't tell you, but I do know that I was asked to do that and I did it. As long as you met the requirements, you were entitled to a visa. By that time there were quotas, and you were only called when your [quota] number came up." She obtained her document and returned to Dinslaken to pack.

Her mother had already planned her departure very carefully. She wanted Tea to have everything she needed to set up her own home in America. "My mother had a [large] wooden crate built into which she put as much as she was allowed to pack," for the Nazi government had devised strict limits on how much material an emigrant could take out of the country. "My mother had clothes made for me. My father had a fur coat made for me, so that I wouldn't have to buy anything for quite a long time. When this crate was packed to be shipped, there was an SS man sitting in a chair in our house, watching what went into this crate. I often think he didn't watch very carefully, and I'm sorry that I didn't insist on packing more, because Mother did have beautiful things. In retrospect, I don't blame her for not trying to put more in, because it would have endangered our lives to do that."

As it was, the crate had room for some lovely crystal and dishes, and a complete set of silverware engraved with her initials. Elly Kann had thought the matter out very well – the silverware and dishes, and the fur coat, could be sold in America if necessary. Nazi law also limited the amount of money someone could take with them. But Elly chose carefully for another reason. These small treasures could be the last thing she would ever do for a daughter she would never see again.

In early March, Tea visited Dinslaken's synagogue for the last time. In the service there was a tradition in which people would read from the Torah and ask a blessing and pledge a certain amount of money for the orphanage. "Normally, you would do this in the name of someone who was ill. But this time, everyone pledged something for me. Dr. Rothschild, who was sort of our unofficial rabbi, gave a sermon about my leaving. This still does make me cry." Then her father took her to Hamburg. There, as Tea said goodbye to him and began to board the ship, she could feel the awesome weight of what she was doing in the pit of her stomach. Each step she took up the gangplank brought her that much closer to freedom. But each step also took her further away of all she had ever known. Even more, the awesome responsibility of what she had to do in the coming months became ever clearer and more dreadful. She had to find a place to live, secure a job, save money. Most of all she had to make it possible for her family to join her. She and her mother had already discussed this. "What my mother would have liked to do, but it just couldn't be done, was to send my brother with me. But he was fourteen, and I didn't know how I was going to support myself." But the hopes for Erwin, for all of them, now rested on this seventeen-year-old whose childhood was at an end.

After a quiet crossing of the Atlantic, which gave her time to think about just how final her parting from her family could be, Tea arrived in New York. Eugen Schwarz, her cousin's husband, met her there. As noted already, Eugen and Hanna had been living in New York since the end of 1936. Eugen met her at the customs office. "You filled out first papers right there and then to become a [U.S.] citizen. And [Eugen] said to me 'Tea is no name here. Nobody will understand it.' I said, 'well what should I do?' He said, 'we'll change it to Dorothy.' I thought, not Dorothea, not anything I recognized, just Dorothy. Well, I was totally overwhelmed and frightened, and right then wished I were back where I had come from, so I really couldn't argue. I became Dorothy, although the name somehow doesn't suit me. I'm more of a Tea than I am a Dorothy."

Eugen took Tea/Dorothy to the Schwarz's apartment in Washington Heights, which had become the neighborhood of choice for the German-Jewish refugees. It was a small apartment, just one bedroom. Eugen and Hanna had lived in a larger apartment at first, but had moved to the cheaper place after Hanna's mother returned to Europe. Hanna was waiting at the apartment, and showed Dorothy how to make the couch into a bed. Hanna also told her that "tomorrow you won't have much to do, but the following day you will have to go to work. You have two choices. I know of a position as a nanny, but you should know that the last person who was there had a nervous break-down. Or you can work in my brother-in-law's millinery factory."

Tea decided to take the millinery job. It did not take her long to discover that the work was very difficult and the pay was quite low. She also quickly realized that the Schwarzes had almost no money left. Even worse, for Tea, they were actively looking for better jobs, and if they found what they wanted outside New York City, then she would not be able to stay in the apartment. She was terrified of the prospect of having to live in this city with no real friends, no one she really knew. But then Herman Stern came to New York. "I met him probably no more than six weeks after I arrived. He was coming on a buying trip in the spring, which he did frequently. [When he arrived,] he called and told me I was to come to the New Yorker Hotel at six o'clock. I had no problem recognizing him because of his resem-blance to Adolf Stern. He had also asked his nephew, Little Gus, to come. Gus came with his girlfriend, later his wife. I knew Gus be-cause he, too, had lived in Duisburg."

She was afraid that Stern might decide she would not be able to take care of herself. "That first encounter went much better than I feared, I was incredibly scared." Knowing something of the diffi-culty that had existed between Herman and Julius years before, she was frightened that he might not like her, might even send her back to Germany. "But he did like me, and I think the fact that Little Gus was there did help with the awkwardness. Herman was, I wouldn't say a lady's man, but very charming, very nice, very easy how he put me at ease. He said, 'I can probably help you get a better job.' Shortly thereafter, I did get a better job in a hat factory, where I had to join the union." Then, when Eugen and Hanna found other work, "as counselors in a children's camp, she was to be a nurse and he was the doctor," they sublet their apartment. Tea had to move. "Where did I go? To other friends of Herman Stern, where else?"[15]

Specifically, Stern arranged for her to have a room in the apart-ment of Julius Blumenthal, yet another of the ubiquitous cousins he had sponsored. Blumenthal, together with his wife and mother-in-law, had come to America the same month as Tea (Dorothy), and had practically arrived in New York on the same day. With the help of a friend who manufactured heavy coats, Stern had helped Blumenthal find a job selling fur coats in New York. Because this work provided Blumenthal with better pay than many of the refugees from Germany, he also had better housing. "They had a large apartment," Tea remembered, "and rented three rooms to people whom Herman had sponsored. They were lovely people [who] had these boarders and I was one of them. That actually was a very good time in my life in New York."

Stern managed to visit Tea and many of the others he sponsored about twice a year, when he made his buying trips. Tea remembered one occasion, about two years after she left Europe, when she received a glimpse of Stern's sense of rigid propriety. Stern took her and several others to a nightclub for dinner. "His suppliers were always trying to do things for him and recommended this place in New Jersey. We went in to this building and found there was a door with a little peephole, and inside was a casino. I didn't know what a casino was. These people who were with us started gambling. Somehow, it irritated Herman very much, it made him angry that they were losing money when money could be spent so much better elsewhere, so we left."[16]

Slowly, Tea began to accept America as her new home. She found a better job at a larger hat-makers, sewing labels for Sak's and Macy's into the hats. She made twelve dollars a week, using five of that for rent, and managed to save two or three dollars each time. But, she found it difficult to feel secure, not so much because of the tightness of the money, but because years of Nazi persecution had left her feeling that she could be in danger at any moment. It took her years before the sight of a policeman no longer frightened her; her instinct told her someone in a uniform might strike her or arrest her rather than help her. She came to see Stern almost as a second father, someone she knew would protect her and help her whenever she might need it. Above all, he promised her he would work to get her parents and brother out of Germany.

However, tensions in Europe were rising to fever pitch. Following the annexation of Austria, Hitler set his eyes on the Sudetenland in western Czechoslovakia, where, Nazi propagandists swore, the Germans living there were clamoring for protection within the Greater Reich. Hitler told his generals that he was prepared to go to war to get what he wanted. If Stern was to help the Eichengruens or anyone else get out, he would have to hurry.

Notes

1. Jacob R. Marcus, *The Rise and Destiny of the German Jew* (Cincinnati: Union of American Hebrew Congregations, 1934), esp. pp. 319-20.

2. Several works discuss the possibility that the German Army would have removed Hitler if France and Britain had mobilized over the Rhine provocation, but the evidence for this is sketchy and the bulk of the German officer corps remained loyal to Hitler throughout the worst of the 1939-45 war. In retrospect, an upheaval in central Europe in 1936 was preferable to the devastation of World War II, but retrospect is always favored with such clarity.

3. Jonas, *Isolationism in America,* pp. 110-18; Urofsky, *A Voice that Spoke for Justice,* p. 303. "Isolationist" was a term disliked by most of the leading advocates of strict neutrality in foreign policy matters during the 1930s, but it is the label that history has placed upon them and is used as such here.

4. Joachim C. Fest, *Hitler* (New York: Harcourt, Brace Jovanovich, 1973), pp. 561-63; Gerhard L. Weinberg, *The Foreign Policy of Hitler's Germany: Starting World War II, 1937-1939* (Chicago: University of Chicago Press, 1980), pp. 34-53.

5. Evan Burr Bukey, *Hitler's Austria: Popular Sentiment in the Nazi Era, 1938-1945* (Chapel Hill: University of North Carolina Press, 2000), pp. 6-16; Deborah Dwork and Robert Jan van Pelt, *Holocaust: A History*, p. 94.

6. Margaret Steiner, interview with Shoptaugh, December 1997, transcript, pp. 3-5; Zweig's memory of old imperial Vienna, from his 1943 memoir *The World of Yesterday,* is quoted in David Fromkin, *Europe's Last Summer* (New York: Alfred A. Knopf, 2004), p. 14.

7. Bukey, pp. 15-16; Alvin Finkel and Clement Leibovitz, *The Chamberlain-Hitler Collusion* (Suffolk, England: Merlin Press, 1997), pp. 114-17; Fischer, *Nazi Germany,* pp. 415-16; Kurt von Schuschnigg, *Austrian Requiem* (New York, G. P. Putnam's Sons, 1946) pp. 3-7.

8. Schuschnigg, pp. 11-27; Noakes, *Nazism: Foreign Policy*, pp. 700-1; Thomas Weyr, *The Setting of the Pearl: Vienna Under Hitler* (Oxford University Press, 2004), pp. 8-25, adds additional details from German sources.

9. Scuhschnigg, pp. 28-55; Bukey, pp. 25-27; William L. Shirer, *The Nightmare Years: 1930-1940* (New York: Little, Brown and Company, 1984), pp. 295-96. Weyr, pp. 18-19, notes that Goering later claimed credit for persuading Hitler to send in the army and formally annex Austria.

10. May, *Strange Victory,* pp, 145, 149-50; *Documents on British Foreign Policy, 1919-1939,* (London: H.M.S.O., 1949) Third Series, vol. 1, pp. 44-48.

11. George E. Berkeley, *Vienna and Its Jews* (Lanham, MD: Madison Books, 1988), pp. 259-63; Bruce F. Pauley, *From Prejudice to Persecution: A History of Austrian Anti-Semitism* (Chapel Hill: University of North Carolina Press, 1992), pp. 277-84.

12. As Gerhard Weinberg has noted, the *Anschluss* was the first time "the threat of force was used by Hitler in direct talks with another country . . . and its success would inspire repetition." Weinberg, *The Foreign Policy of Hitler's Germany*, p, 292-93.

13. Steiner transcript, pp. 16-18, 21-23.

14. Stiefel transcript, p. 60; H.S., "Application for a Visa for Tea Eichengruen" [1937]; H.J. L'Heureux to H.S., December 1, 1937, Eichengruen file, Stern Papers. In German culture, particularly among German Jews at that time, Tea, as the daughter of the cousin of Dora Stern, Herman's sister-in-law, could have been seen as a relative of sorts, a part of his extended family. But the Stuttgart Consulate would almost certainly never have accepted that argument.

15. Stiefel transcript, pp. 25-35.

16. Charles Harris [of the Harris (Coat) Manufacturing Company] to Herman Stern, July 22, 1938, regarding a job for Julius Blumenthal, Blumenthal File, Stern Papers; Stiefel transcript, pp. 35-37.

Chapter Ten
Into the Maelstrom

When Hitler became Chancellor of Germany in 1933, the American columnist Walter Lippmann offered the opinion that the Nazis' anti-Semitic policies might actually work in Europe's favor. He did not for a moment doubt that Hitler was interested in expanding German territory. But he seemed to hope that Hitler would settle for victimizing the Jews instead. As he put it, "by satisfying the lust of the Nazis who feel they must conquer somebody" [Germany's Jews could be] "a kind of lightning rod which protects Europe." It did not take long for Hitler to demonstrate that he could intimidate all of Europe while still reducing the Jews within his grasp to a state of utter ruin.

By 1938, Hitler's followers had killed or incarcerated thousands of Germans who he had deemed unfit to live in his Reich. These included, in addition to the Jews, a great many socialists, communists, liberals, and intellectuals whose sole "crime" had been to warn the world of the dangers of Nazism. Many thousands more, including some one hundred and thirty thousand Jews, had left Germany by the beginning of 1938. Many of these refugees had yet to find anything resembling a real home.

France had accepted several thousand German refuges during the ministry of Premier Leon Blum. But this generosity had also inflamed the anti-Semitism of right-wing parties like Action Francaise. Blum's government fell, and the governments that followed were wary of internal divisions that could further weaken the country. These administrations began to turn away refugees. While Britain accepted a small number of German refugees and a few hundred Austrian Jews after the *Anschluss*, London's process for granting an entry visa was painfully slow. The United States had admitted an average of about six thousand nine hundred immigrants from Germany each year since

1932. But despite a tabulation by the American Jewish Committee that concluded "more people emigrated from the United States than came in as immigrants," critics of immigration still complained that the nation was being "flooded" with undesirables, a belief that America public opinion overwhelmingly accepted. Outside of America and Europe (and a handful of Asian and South American diplomats who sold legal visas to those who could afford the prices) there were almost no other havens. By 1938, a full-fledged refugee crisis was beginning to affect the entire continent.

The League of Nations had been created to deal with emergencies like this. So far, however, the League had proven itself unequal to the task. It established a High Commission for Refugees in 1933 that many hoped would deal with the problem. But since the Commission was actually an independent agency, it lacked any real authority, and it had almost no funding. James G. MacDonald, the American professor who served as head of the Commission from 1934 to 1936, became so frustrated with the job that he resigned the post with a twenty-seven page indictment of the world for its indifference to the fate of the refugees. He called on the League to make "a determined appeal to the German Government in the name of humanity" to cease its persecutions of its Jewish population. The League turned a deaf ear to MacDonald's call.[1]

With the Commission powerless and the League impotent, Franklin Roosevelt yielded to pressure from some of his supporters after the *Anschluss,* and announced on March 25, 1938, a plan for an international conference to discuss the refugee crisis. The conference took place in Evian, France in July, with representatives of thirty-two countries on hand to discuss how the world might "facilitate the settlement in other countries of political refugees from Germany (including Austria)." It turned out to be a remarkably cynical gathering. The participants had expected a concrete proposal from the United States, which after all had called for this conference. But Roosevelt had not even sent any of his State Department to it, or anyone else armed with the power to offer anything but rhetoric in the face of the problem. Myron Taylor, the retired businessman who FDR had asked to head the American mission, simply urged the assembled delegates to "act promptly" to avert the "catastrophic human suffering" that would otherwise occur. That was it.

To be sure, the rest of the nations at the conference expressed great sympathy for Hitler's victims, but only one country, the Dominican Republic, offered to take in any of the refugees, and those must be "agriculturalists with an unimpeachable record." Observing the silence that followed this announcement, one of the League staffers present quietly concluded that while none of the nations at Evian were particularly "anti-Jewish [in] feeling," they feared that accepting "any large-scale scheme of [Jewish] migration would only arouse hostility" in their own peoples. After some more speeches, the delegates agreed to the creation of an Intergovernmental Committee on Refugees, which would receive a minimal amount of funding from the United States. Then everyone packed and went home.[2]

While the world talked at Evian, the Jews in Hitler's growing empire faced their Hobson's choice. They could try and flee Germany, or they could stay and hope for the best. The Evian conference suggested that they stood to be treated as pariahs in either case. The scholar Walter Laqueur, who himself left Germany at this time, later explained just how difficult it was for German Jews to contemplate leaving in these circumstances: "emigration meant a poorer life not just materially but also culturally." Outsiders could never truly understand how hard it was to turn one's back on their *heimet,* Laqueur emphasized, and writers who in later years would wonder, in such disapproving tones, how so many Jews could have chosen to remain in Germany, were offering opinions "based on ignorance and the benefit of hindsight, and leave a bitter taste" in those who had been there.[3]

Those who chose to leave the *heimat* behind almost immediately entered a world of desperate anxiety. The future journalist Peter Wyden, then a child in Germany, later described the tensions among his family as they searched for a way to immigrate. They began to talk endlessly of what he called the "three new guideposts" of their future: "'the quota' — the total number of German refugees permitted to enter the United States under the miserly immigration laws; 'the affidavit' — the document from an umpteenth cousin guaranteeing that he would support us if we became destitute; and 'the visa' — which would be our stamped admission ticket into the promised land."[4]

Even children found it horribly hard to get out. During the entire decade, the United States allowed fewer than a thousand Jewish children (under age sixteen) to enter the country and live with a host family. Laqueur pointed out that Americans imported more purebred dogs from Britain than refugee children during this time. In an effort to ease their misery and improve their chances of emigration, more and more young men and women joined Jewish groups (*Juden Buende*) after 1933. After Hitler's government decreed at the end of March 1938 that the public status of Jewish organizations was revoked, stripping them of tax exemptions and any community funding, these organizations still grew to record enrollments. One appeal of the Jewish organizations was the special *Umschichtung* (retraining) classes that many groups provided, so that young people could obtain skills that might induce another country to accept them. The Zionist *Blau Weiss,* for example, provided intensive training in agriculture, in hopes their students could get into Palestine. All each person could do was learn and do all he could and hope that fortune would somehow smile upon him.

In newly occupied Austria, some three thousand Jews each day were applying for papers to leave the Reich. The Reich office for "racial matters" tried to frighten more into leaving by proclaiming on April 26 that "no Jew may have the opportunity to earn money" in Germany. Jews were being forced by the government to give up their businesses to new owners, receiving in return just fractions of their true value. Hundreds of Jewish families were left destitute as a result. In May, Adolf Eichmann, who had been ordered by Berlin to make Austria *Judenfrei* as rapidly as possible, informed Berlin that he had issued to the Jewish community a demand that at least twenty thousand Jews must emigrate from Vienna by the first of May, 1939. No one could doubt that if Eichmann's quota was not met, the Nazis would begin a new cycle of violence.

Desperation was almost endemic. In August, a group of fifty-three Austrian Jews sailed to Helsinki, clutching entry visas given to them by a Finn in the Vienna embassy. They were in good spirits, happy that at last they had escaped from the Nazi horrors. But when the ship reached Helsinki, the Finnish government had repudiated their Vienna official's goodness: the Austrian refugees were not allowed to leave the ship, not even those who simply wanted to pass through on their way to America. As the ship returned to a German port, three of the refugees gave way to despair and drowned themselves.[5]

Gertrude Stern, the wife of Herman Stern's nephew Gustave, wrote to Herman at the beginning of 1938, describing their recent trip to see her mother in Holland. "You cannot imagine how much red tape there is to travel from one European into another European country since we are now stateless," she wrote. "My mother has aged a lot. The concerns for the rest of [our] kin do not let her sleep anymore. She is in the same position like you, Hermann. From morning to night, she is sitting at her writing desk, and for months, she has always somebody staying at her house, emigrants. For the time being, Dr. Hausbacher, for whom you sent the affidavit, is with her, as well as a son of a cousin of hers who was hiding for two weeks because of the Nazis, otherwise he would have ended in a concentration camp. Then he fled to Holland from where he has to flee soon. China is the only country that gives a visa, thus he is forced to go there, and from China he will try to travel to the Philippine Islands where he has friends. It is so depressing how those people barely escape with only their life."

Gertrude asked Herman to try "to find some suitable persons to come up with two more affidavits." One was for a son of a neighbor of hers in France. The boy had remained in Germany, working at a German cemetery in Leipzig. But his mother had not heard from him in weeks, and was afraid that he might have been arrested. An "affidavit in this case should cause the Gestapo to set him free and to persuade the French government to provide him with a residence permit, at least temporarily." The other man, a Dr. Schneider, was giving Judaic instruction to Gertrude's son. A native of Alsace-Lorraine, he had become a German citizen after the region was ceded back to France in 1919. His fervent wish to be German had now become an ironic, "dumb mistake! This step now has the fateful consequence, that the French government denies him [another] residence permit here. It is almost running out and it will not be renewed. He *has* to leave here as soon as possible. Perhaps you can procure an additional affidavit with the help of friends."[6]

Gertrude's sense of urgency was all the greater because at the time she wrote, her husband's parents, Adolf and Dora, were now living in Paris. The manner by which Herman Stern's brother had come to be in Paris was somewhat roundabout. And it could have been fraught with great danger. In September 1937, Adolf made a request to the *Staatspolizei* (State Order Police) in Duesseldorf, asking for two travel permits (*tryptiks*), so that he and Dora could make visits to Holland and Belgium. It is notable that in the meticulously arranged file the Duesseldorf office of the *Staatspolizei* kept on Adolf Stern there is no mention of France as part of Stern's travel plans. After checking with the Gestapo in Berlin that there were no records showing Stern had any tax problems, criminal violations or "political offences" on his record, the *Staatspolizei* granted Stern his travel permits.[7]

Adolf and his wife then set off on their trip, the details of which are unclear. But it is probable, in the light of subsequent events, they saw some of their relatives who had immigrated to Holland and visited Adolf's partner, Sally Kann, in Belgium, to see how their dairy business was progressing. Then in the last weeks of 1937 they went to Paris to see Gustave. The Sterns had not, apparently, informed the *Staatspolizei* of a side journey to Paris, but now Adolf must have been thinking about abandoning Germany altogether – a supposition strengthened by a remark he made to his son a few weeks later. As Gertrude relayed it to Herman, Adolf said that life in Germany had "become impossible."

In Paris, Gustave evidently tried to convince his parents to remain in France. Adolf admitted that the situation in Germany was terrible but still resisted the idea of leaving behind all he had known for sixty-five years. Dora, too, was uncertain. To leave Germany would mean leaving her home, which she had proudly decorated and maintained for so many years. After considerable hesitation, the couple decided to go off to America and see their younger son, Julius. But before they left Paris, Adolf was struck by a car and suffered a broken leg. It was not until April or May that Adolf recovered sufficiently to travel. He and Dora then went on to America. In Chicago, they stayed with Julius and his new wife Herta, who was also a German refugee. Julius had had several bouts of illness since the end of 1937, and Dora had become very worried about him.[8]

After some weeks in Chicago, the couple went on to Valley City to see Herman and Adeline. There, Herman made his own effort to convince his brother not to return to Germany. At one point he thought he had them convinced because he wrote to the nearest American consul and asked for the necessary papers they could fill out to "become permanent citizens of the United States." In the end, Adolf and Dora decided to secure a temporary French visa, return to Paris, and live, at least for a while, with Gustave and Gertrude. It is interesting to note that Adolf went to the German Embassy in Paris in August and asked for his and his wife's passports to be extended, explaining that he wished to stay on "temporarily" in Paris while he recovered from "an accident." He also said he and Dora would "return to Duisburg" as soon as he had recovered. He did this in part because the German government had begun calling in all Jewish-held German passports. Referring to his leg injury (which had not kept him from traveling to the United States and back) allowed him to buy some time. Perhaps he still hoped that the situation in Germany – which he had defended as soldier in the Great War – might improve. Such was the hold of the *heimat* on many of his generation.

The embassy forwarded the request to the Gestapo in Berlin, which forwarded it in turn to their Duesseldorf office. There, after some consideration, the Gestapo allowed the passport to be extended, but added that "preliminary arrangements" were being made to "dispossess" Gustave Stern of his German citizenship.[9]

There is a certain irony in this exchange of letters between the Paris Embassy and the Gestapo. The embassy staff in Paris did not mention in their cable to Berlin that Stern and his wife had just returned from America, which could easily be seen in their passports. The Gestapo may have ignored this information if they had been given it; which they would receive anyway in due time. They may just as easily been suspicious of this trip, which Adolf had not indicated when applying for his travel permits. They were always looking for signs of "disloyalty," especially within the Jewish population. They may have wanted to have Adolf come home and answer questions about his visit to America. The diplomatic staff might have left this tidbit of information out of the cable sent to the Gestapo because they regarded it as unimportant. But it was equally possible that they left it out deliberately, for many of the German foreign services despised the Nazis, found the Gestapo distasteful, and wanted little to do with the campaigns of vilification against the Jews.[10]

If this was indeed the motive in the case of Adolf Stern, then it was a true irony. In just a few weeks, the Paris embassy was to be the setting for an incident that would trigger the Nazi's worst violence yet against the Jews.

Having digested Austria, Hitler was now anxious to gobble up Czechoslovakia, which he saw as the next step to achieving German dominance in eastern Europe. He directed Goebbel's propaganda machine to begin a systematic campaign of agitation, bemoaning the mistreatment of Germans living in the Czech Sudetenland. Only the cession of the Sudetenland, the small nation's most defensible ground against invasion, would satisfy Hitler's desire to protect "his volk." The Nazi chancellor rebuffed Czech offers of negotiation. He meant to emasculate Czechoslovakia and then destroy it, telling his generals, "it is my unshakable will to wipe Czechoslovakia off the map." When his Army Chief of Staff warned him that the army was not yet ready for a war with France, which had signed a treaty to defend Czechoslovakian independence, Hitler promised that France would not fight without Britain by its side, and Britain would negotiate rather than fight.

Once again, Hitler had read the situation correctly. Some of the members of the House of Commons urged Neville Chamberlain, Britain's Prime Minister, to seize this chance and stand up to Hitler before he became even stronger. And a few of the leading figures in Chamberlain's ruling Conservative Party, most notably Winston Churchill, suggested that the government explore reaching an agreement with the Soviet Union in order to threaten Germany with a two-front war. But Chamberlain had decided months earlier that there was "nothing France or we could do, [that] could possibly save Czechoslovakia from being overrun by the Germans if they wanted to do it." He was convinced Hitler would not back down, and he distrusted Joseph Stalin more than he did Hitler, noting that although the Russians made statements about standing in support of the Czechs, they did nothing to mobilize their military. Perhaps Hitler could be brought down in a war, but at what cost? And what would replace him in Germany? Reasoning that it was better to accept the devil he knew, Chamberlain was ready to give Hitler what he wanted if in return he could receive a promise of peace.

After a series of face-to-face meetings with Hitler in Germany, Chamberlain agreed that Britain would sanction the transfer of the Sudetenland to Germany. France, with little reluctance, went along with Chamberlain. In return, Hitler signed a note in which Germany and Britain promised that they wanted "never to go to war with one another again." Chamberlain waved this note in his hand when he returned to England, telling the cheering onlookers that he believed he had fashioned "peace in our time."[11]

There was nothing to cheer about on the other side of Europe. Abandoned, the Czechs acquiesced. As the German Army marched into the Sudetenland, William L. Shirer of CBS Radio was again on hand, this time to witness the muted death throes of the Czech Republic. "It was a very peaceful occupation," he broadcast the next night. "Not a shot was fired. . . . The whole thing went off like a parade, even to the military bands and regimental flags and Sudeten girls tossing bouquets of flowers at the troops and throwing kisses at them . . . from across the fields between the woods the peasants started to emerge, jumping into the air, raising their hands in the Nazi salute and screaming at the top of their voices 'Heil Hitler!'" Privately, Shirer felt sick over the sacrifice of Czechoslovakia, writing in his diary "called [CBS colleague] Paul White in New York, but he said the crisis was over and people at home wanted to forget it and take a rest. Which is all right with me. Can stand some sleep and a change from these Germans, so truculent and impossible now. Phoned Ed Morrow in London. He as depressed as I. We shall drown our sorrows in Paris day after tomorrow."

With the world heaving a sigh of relief that war had been averted, Hitler saw no reason to act any more responsibly. Three weeks after his Sudeten triumph, he told his diplomats that he would find a way to occupy the rest of Czechoslovakia in the spring of 1939. In December, he instructed the army to prepare for the occupation as "merely an act of pacification and not a warlike undertaking."[12]

There had been about twenty thousand Jews living in Sudetenland when the Nazis took over. Within weeks, all but a handful fled east, to what remained of Czechoslovakia, and many tried to get even further away from Hitler's reach. Back in Germany, the Fuehrer ordered a similar number of the *Ostjuden* deported to Poland. One of these pitiful souls, Zindel Grynszpan, had been living in Germany since 1918. He later described how SS troops drove them across the border on the night of October 27, 1938: "No more than ten marks [per person] could be taken out of Germany. The Germans said, 'You didn't bring any more into Germany and you can't take any more out.' . . . we walked two kilometers on foot to the Polish Border. They told us to go – the SS men were whipping us, those who lingered they hit, and blood was flowing on the road. . . . [At the border] a Polish general and some officers arrived, and they examined the papers and saw that we were Polish citizens, that we had special passports. It was decided to let us enter Poland." They were admitted but not welcomed, for the Polish soldiers marched them to hastily arranged camps where, a British witness remembered, they were "herded together in the most inhumane conditions."[13]

Soon after being expelled from Germany, Zindel Grynszpan wrote an account of his ordeal to his son Herschel, who was living in Paris. The younger Grynszpan, who had fled Germany earlier and was living illegally in France, decided that his family, that all Jews, had endured enough. On November 7, he went out and bought a cheap pistol that could easily be concealed. Then he went to the German embassy and talked his way in with a story that he had some "intelligence" to give to a high diplomatic official. Shown to an office that could very easily have been the same room Adolf Stern was in while getting his visa renewed, Grynszpan quietly waited until an assistant secretary named Ernst vom Rath walked in and asked what he could do for Grynszpan. Grynszpan pulled out his pistol and fired five shots, hitting vom Rath twice and mortally wounding him. Grynszpan then surrendered himself, calmly telling the French police that he had shot vom Rath to avenge his parents and all Jews, who had "a right to exist on this earth."

News of the shooting of vom Rath reached Germany within a few hours. Hitler learned of it while eating dinner in Munich, where he was attending a Nazi Party rally to mark the fifteenth anniversary of his 1923 attempt to seize power in Bavaria. The Fuehrer could have cared less about vom Rath, who would soon die of his wounds. But Hitler knew an opportunity when he saw it. He turned to Goebbels and said, very unemotionally, that the government should not try to impede "the volk" or the Party if they "spontaneously" attacked Jews for this outrage. A couple of other leading Nazis at the dinner later testified that they heard Hitler say, "the SA should be allowed to have a fling." Goebbels and the SA leaders quickly set about organizing the "spontaneous" violence, while Heinrich Mueller, the chief of the Gestapo, sent a telegram to all German police groups, ordering them that "actions against Jews and especially their synagogues" across the nation were "not to be interfered with." The pogrom was minutely planned.[14]

Just before midnight on November 9, bands of SA toughs stormed out of party offices across the whole of Germany. Armed with torches and clubs and lists of Jewish residences and businesses, they set off like jackals in search of wounded prey. They attacked thousands of Jews in the streets and in their homes, and nearly a hundred were killed; at least that was the official toll. Stormtroopers burned some two hundred synagogues to the ground. So too were many Jewish homes and a large number of Jewish-owned businesses. German firemen were called out, not to stop the blazes, only to make sure that the flames did not spread to "Aryan" property. Because of the millions of glass shards scattered about the streets from the destruction, this night would ever after be known as *Kristallnacht*, the night of broken glass.

The SA smashed and looted so wantonly that Goering complained it would hamper his newest plan for economic development. The Gestapo and the SS chose their targets more cunningly by arresting thirty thousand Jews who still had significant amounts of property to confiscate. Having expended so much in the rearming of Germany, Hitler was delighted to have these confiscations for his treasury. The depredations against the Jews also diverted the people from the privations they had to accept while the military was being enlarged. In the last hours of *Kristallnacht*, the mob mentality took hold to the point that many ordinary people were helping the uniformed troopers assault and humiliate their Jewish neighbors. The correspondent for the London *Daily Telegraph*, who witnessed some of this, termed what he saw "nauseating." "Racial hatred and hysteria seemed to have taken complete hold of otherwise decent people . . . respectable, middle-class mothers held up their babies to see the 'fun'."[15]

The Jews in Vienna suffered as much as those elsewhere. The SA came to the apartment of Greta Grunhut and helped themselves to whatever caught their eye. "My father had a safety [strong] box, you know a big one," she recalled. "He had to open it and they took all the valuables and money." Greta lost her hat-making shop. "I had to sell everything, what I could sell. Of course, people were just waiting to grab it for no money, for peanuts. I had a permit for my business. I had to give it back."

Then she and her parents had to move, as the Jewish families were crowded together into one section of the city. "They put three families in this one apartment. Each family got just one room, we all had [to share] one kitchen." Jews could find virtually no work at all after *Kristallnacht*. The Grunhuts could easily have starved. But there were still many decent Germans, and one of these, a butcher who had lived near them before November 10, had warned them to prepare for worse days. As Greta remembered, "he said to my father, 'please, if you have some valuables or money, we can save it for you.'" So Julius Grunhut had given some of his money to the butcher. In the months after being forced from their home, the butcher kept his word to help by quietly using the money to provide them with some food.

Thousands of Jews now began crowding the entrances of foreign consulates, begging for a permit to another country. But chances for soon finding a refuge were worse than ever. Four months after *Kristallnacht*, Greta married Felix Steiner, a man she had known for several years. Steiner had been an accomplished tailor in better times, but of course had lost his business along with every other Jewish shop owner. Worse, three of his brothers had lost not only their businesses but their freedom as well. Two were incarcerated at Buchenwald, while the third was at Dachau. A fourth brother had obtained a permit to go to Australia. Felix held out hope that if he could not also go to Australia then perhaps he could get permission to go to the United States.

It is possible that Greta and Felix married in order to help them find a country that would take them in together – many younger Jews believed that married couples would get preference. It was by no means true that such a move would actually enhance their chances. Often it hurt a couple's prospects. Many of the consuls, particularly among the British and Americans, were very suspicious of recently married couples applying for visas, referring to these as likely cases of a "marriage blanche," a union of convenience. In fact, a few months after their marriage, Greta and Felix received word that Felix would be allowed to enter Britain with a "transit visa," where he could stay in a refugee camp while awaiting word from America or Australia.

Greta, however, was not awarded a permit. So in June Felix left for Britain and Greta remained in Vienna. Fortunately, Felix met a man living in Kent named Anton Gruber, himself an Austrian expatriate. Gruber was a member of Britain's German Jewish Aid Committee, and after hearing Felix's story he agreed to provide Greta with a job in his home. Gruber's very kind act cleared the way for Greta to obtain a domestic service visa and by the late summer of 1939 she was able to leave.[16]

At least two of the families that Herman Stern was trying to help were also swept up in the violence of *Kristallnacht*. Fritz Kann, one of the cousins of the Eichengruens, was among the thousands of Jews who were arrested on November 10. Together with many others, he was sent to Dachau. Stern learned of Fritz's arrest a few months later, from the Sterns in Paris. He managed to send an affidavit to Germany, promising that he would secure an American visa for Fritz. On the basis of this document, Fritz was released, but ordered to leave Germany immediately. In a letter Fritz later wrote to Mr. Stern, he said he had gone through "an insane experience [in the camp], unbelievable for human beings. Many I knew there did not endure it. . . . You do not believe how difficult it is for the [Jewish] people here." In January 1939, harassed by the German police because he had not yet left Germany, Fritz Kann fled to Wommelgem, Belgium, and joined his brother Sally on the farm that the Kanns owned with Adolf Stern.[17]

In Dinslaken, Elly Eichengruen, Sally's and Fritz's cousin, had known that trouble was coming right after vom Rath was shot in Paris. She immediately began to fear for the safety of her son Erwin, especially when a group of SA men marched into the town during the evening of November 9. As soon as it grew dark, a handful of SA men made directly for the Eichengruen home, forced their way in and seized Elly's husband and Erwin, taking them to a school where the other Jewish men were being held. Before leaving, the stormtroopers helped themselves to some of the valuables in the house, including some of Elly's silverware, brooches and other jewelry. One of the young thugs tore up a tapestry mounted on one of the walls, but fortunately left alone a painting by the artist Max Stern, which Elly was particularly fond of.

Standing at the windows after the SA left, Elly watched the SA begin to wreck the remaining Jewish shops in the town. Elly was appalled to see how quickly some of the townspeople joined in the destruction, their faces twisted in grimaces of hate and excitement. The worst moment came when the mob rushed to the synagogue and Jewish orphanage and began smashing the windows. After forcing the orphans and staff out into the street, they set torches to the synagogue and continued to ransack the orphanage. As for the orphans, the younger ones were forced into a cart that one of the SA troopers had brought up. Then, as the horrified Elly later told her daughter Tea (Dorothy, as she became in America), "some of the older Jewish boys were forced to pull this cart through the streets" while members of the crowd threw rocks and jeered at the children. As the burning synagogue crashed down in ruin, the crowd began to disperse. Later in the day, the orphans were sent off to Duisburg, just a way stop on the road to the inevitable concentration camp. Leopard Rothschild, the director of the orphanage who had been so kind to Dorothy before she left for America, was also sent to a camp, together with some of his assistants.

Most of the Jewish men, including Hermann Eichengruen and his son, were released later on the 10th. After seeing her neighbors raging at the helpless orphans, Elly Kann decided she had to get Erwin out of Germany before he too was harmed. Dorothy later described her mother's determination: "she sent my brother to Holland illegally. The border was so close. And for the rest of her life, she carried around this enormous guilt [over it], and yet she did the right thing. She thought she was going to save him." Young Erwin went to live with family friends in Amsterdam. He remained there for over three years, eventually entering a training program at Werkdorp Nieuweslius, a camp for educating Jews who wished to enter Palestine.[18]

Soon after Erwin fled across the German-Dutch border, his father lost all his property. Herman Eichengruen was forced to sell his home and business to pay his share of the large fine that the German government imposed on the Jews in Germany for the damage *they* had caused to Germany from *Kristallnacht*. The Eichengruens received only a fraction of what their property was really worth. They then moved to Essen, crowded with hundreds of other families into an apartment building in which food was scare and heat almost non-existent. In America, Dorothy and Herman Stern began to push harder to arrange to get Dorothy's parents and brother out of Europe. But the paperwork, already slowed to a snail's crawl by the State Department's red tape, proceeded even more slowly due to the complication of Erwin's being in Holland.[19]

Stern's willingness to make so much effort for the Eichengruen's was an indication of how much anguish he was feeling over the refugee crisis. After the Munich debacle and *Kristallnacht* he was receiving appeals for help every week, sometimes two or three letters a day asking if he could do something to help someone get out of Germany. His oldest brothers Julius and Moses, who had not been particularly worried about their safety before, were now thoroughly alarmed by the growing violence against the Jews. Julius wrote to ask Herman to try and get visas for himself, his wife Frieda, and Moses as soon as possible. Herman sent affidavits to Samuel Honaker in Stuttgart, noting in his letter that his three relatives hoped to be able to move to France "as temporary refugees."

In Paris, Gustave Stern and his father Adolf had been shocked by the violence of *Kristallnacht*. Adolf's decision the previous summer to stay in Paris may well have saved him from ending up in Dachau, but he was nevertheless deeply depressed at the possibility that he would never see his home again. Gustave thought that a war between Germany and France was now very likely. He wanted to get his family to America as soon as it could be arranged.[20]

That was the predicament, however – how soon could it be arranged, for the Sterns or anyone else? When Tea Eichengruen had applied for her American visa, she had waited about three months for her quota number to come up. *Kristallnacht* had come six months later and changed everything. With many thousands more men and women lining up outside American consulates to file immigration papers and obtain a quota number, consulate staffs were becoming overwhelmed by the sheer volume of paperwork. Now it could take more than a year for an applicant to receive a visa.

Would Europe be able to remain at peace for another year? Veteran observers of the European situation were beginning to express doubts that war could be postponed for more than another six months.

Back in America, Herman Stern was afraid that his loved ones in Europe, perhaps all the Jews on that continent, were running out of time. He realized that he had almost reached the limit of what he could do through his own individual efforts. If he was to save many more, then it was time to ask others for their help.

Notes

1. Ronald Steel, *Walter Lippmann and the American Century* (New York, Little, Brown, and Co., 1980), p. 330; Zucker, *In Search of Refuge*, pp. 47-48; Dorothy Thompson, *Refugees: Anarchy or Organization* (New York: Random House, 1938), pp. 42-55.

2. Paul Webster, *Petain's Crime: The Full Story of French Collaboration in the Holocaust* (Chicago: Ivan R. Dee, 1991), pp. 16-23; Anthony Read and David Fisher, *Kristallnacht: The Nazi Night of Terror* (New York: Random House, 1989), pp. 191-207; Wyman, *Paper Walls,* pp. 43-51.

3. Laqueur, *Generation Exodus* (Hanover, NH: University Press of New England, 2001) p. 12, 22.

4. Peter Wyden, *Stella* (1992), p. 48.

5. Laqueur, pp. 4-6, 129-30; Weyr, *The Setting of the Pearl,* pp. 86-94; Martin Gilbert, *The Holocaust* (New York : Holt, Rinehart, and Winston, 1986), p. 65.

6. Gertrude Vasen Stern to Herman Stern, January 6, 1938, Adolf Stern family file, Stern Papers.

7. The correspondence between the *Staatspolizei* and Gestapo, dated September 9 and 11, 1937, is contained in the file *Akten der Geheimen Staatspolizei, Duesseldorf, uber Adolf Israel Stern,* which is preserved at the National Archives. Michael Stern, grandson of Adolf Stern, kindly provided me a copy of this file. Later correspondence from the *Staatspolizei* and Gestapo refer to Stern as "Adolf Israel Stern," in keeping with the August 1939 decree from the German Ministry of the Interior to the effect that Jews in Germany who did not have "recognizable Jewish names" (Absalom, Ahab, etc) were required to "add the first name Israel or Sara to their names." See Saul Friedlander, *Nazi Germany and the Jews,* pp. 254-55, who notes that this decree not only served to further degrade the Jews in Germany, it also made them easier to identify for "relocation to the east."

8. Julius's sister-in-law was less sympathetic toward Julius's health in her January 6 letter to Herman Stern. In a remark indicative of the great strain that the crisis in Europe was beginning to have on everyone, she wrote "It really is high time that Julius return to work on a regular basis, in every respect. Most of our acquaintances found work, and here is Julius who speaks English so well, much better than most of the people. He does not seem to find a job that suits him or where one keeps him, and all this goes on for months. Just tell me the truth, whether the cause does not lie in Julius himself."

9. Michael Stern interview, p. 3; Tea Eichengreuen interview, p. 22; Edward Stern interview, p 6; Herman Stern to George D. Hopper [American Consul in Winnipeg, Canada], letters of June 28 and July 9, 1938, Adolf Stern family file, Stern Papers. Many family members related in later years that Adolf Stern broke his leg after visiting the United States, but Gertrude Stern's letter of January 6, 1938 makes it clear that this occurred prior to the trip to America.

10. See for example Francis R. Nicosia, "A German Diplomat and the Fate of German Jews: The Case of Heinrich Wolff," in David Scrase, et al, eds., *Making a Difference: Rescue and Assistance During the Holocaust* (Burlington, VT: Center for Holocaust Studies at the University of Vermont, 2004), pp. 127-56.

11. Weinberg, *The Foreign Policy of Hitler's Germany,* vol. II, pp. 313-17. Weinberg points out that Hitler's "major issue was the destruction of Czechoslovakia, while the Sudeten Germans, far from being the focus of his concern, were to serve merely as a tool to broader aims." See also Toland, *Adolf Hitler*, p. 633; Max Beloff, *The Foreign Policy of Soviet Russia, 1929-1941* (London: Oxford University Press, 1949), vol. II, pp. 147-66.

12. Shirer, *"This is Berlin": Radio Broadcasts from Nazi Germany* (New York: Overlook Press, 1999), pp. 34-37; Shirer, *Berlin Diary*, (New York: Popular Library Edition, 1961), p. 114; Ernest May, *Strange Victory,* p. 85.

13. Gilbert, *The Holocaust*, pp. 66-69.

14. Read and Fisher, *Kristallnacht*, pp. 3-8, 45-48, 58-63. See also Gerald Schwab, *The Day the Holocaust Began: The Odyssey of Herschel Grynszpan,* (New York: Praeger, 1990), pp. 1-23.

15. Read and Fisher, *Kristallnacht*, pp. 68ff; Schwab, pp. 23-32.

16. Steiner transcript, pp. 21-29.

17. See Herman Stern to "American Consul, Stuttgart, January 26, 1939, "Kahn [sic] file;" and Gertrude Stern to Herman Stern February 25, 1939, in the Adolf Stern file. See also Fritz Kann to Herman Stern, March 7, 1939, German Language Letters file; all in Stern Papers. The Gertrude Stern letter also reveals that Herman Stern tried to sponsor another person arrested by the Nazis, one Erich Selz, but the papers did not arrive before Selz's "parents were informed of his death, but they never learned the cause, nor the circumstances of his death." For an account of how the German police threatened to again arrest those they released from the camps, see Gloria and Manfred Kirchheimer, *We Were So Beloved: Autobiography of a German Jewish Community* (Pittsburgh: University of Pittsburgh Press, 1997), pp. 76-77.

18. Information about Erwin Eichengruen in Holland is taken from a telephone conversation Shoptaugh had with George Shelton of San Francisco, California in 1998. Mr. Shelton was born in Germany, went to the Holland in the early 1930s and met Erwin at Werkdorp Nieuweslius. The German occupiers of Holland closed the camp, which was organized and funded by the Committee for Jewish Immigrants in Amsterdam, in March, 1941.

19. Stiefel transcript, pp. 48-50.

20. Herman Stern to "American Consul General" [i.e. Honaker], February 11, 1939, Julius Stern file, Stern Papers.

Chapter Eleven
Bringing Refugees "Into the Wide Open Spaces"

A few months before Adolf Hitler took power in Germany, he agreed to be interviewed by an American journalist, Hans V. Kaltenborn. The son of nineteenth-century German immigrants, Kaltenborn tried to open the interview by asking Hitler "why does your anti-Semitism make no distinction between the Jews that flooded into Germany during the postwar period [that is, after World War I] and the many fine Jewish families that have been German for generations?" Hitler was clearly delighted with the opening that Kaltenborn had given him to turn the tables on the Americans. "All Jews are foreigners," he retorted. "Who are you to ask me how I deal with foreigners. You Americans admit no foreigner unless he has good money, good physique, and good morals. Who are you to talk about who should be allowed in Germany?" From that moment, the Nazi line about America and the "Jewish question" was set: every time an American reporter asked about why the Nazis persisted in repressing their Jewish population, Goebbels and his propaganda machine would point to American immigration policy and say "see, you don't want them either."[1]

American reaction to *Kristallnacht* seemed to bear out Hitler's rejoinder. Just a week before the Nazi rampage on November 10, a nationwide poll showed that over three-quarters of the respondents opposed permitting "a larger number of Jewish exiles from Germany to come to the United States." Polls taken after *Kristallnacht* showed that, while Americans expressed sympathy for the German Jews, they were no more willing than before about admitting Jewish immigrants. The bulk of the American press was only a little more sympathetic. Almost all the major American newspapers expressed shock and disapproval of the Nazis' brutal atrocities; virtually none of them expressed an opinion that the United States should alter its immigra-

217

tion restrictions or provide any real aid to the Jews being driven from Germany. Not even the major religious publications in the country would go that far.[2]

Many newspapers in the upper Midwest generally gave perfunctory attention to the Nazi atrocities, if they gave them any attention at all. The *Daily News* in Moorhead Minnesota was an exception. It provided front-page coverage to *Kristallnacht* and its impact in Europe for nine days. The Fargo *Forum* gave considerable attention to *Kristallnacht* and in an editorial urged the American government to express "official concern" about the persecutions. The *Grand Forks Herald,* where the largely Orthodox Jewish community continued to thrive, also published some detailed stories. None of these papers, however, made any editorial suggestions in favor of a more generous immigration policy.[3]

In Washington, Franklin Roosevelt reacted to *Kristallnacht* by recalling the American ambassador to Germany. Given the desultory state of American opinion in regard to the plight of the Jews, it was probably the strongest action he could take. How much the recall influenced the American consulates at a time when they were being swamped with applications for immigration visas is an open question. In any event, the consulate staff did little to alter their methods of dealing with the applications. As Henry Morgenthau, Roosevelt's Treasury Secretary, noted in his diary, the consulate staff handled "human lives at the same bureaucratic tempo and with the same lofty manner that they might deal with a not very urgent trade negotiation."

None of which deterred Herman Stern in the least. He continued filing further affidavits and treating each immigration case as if it alone was the one that mattered. In March of 1938, he had sent affidavits to Stuttgart on behalf of Gustav Strauss, a nephew of his late employer and friend Morris Straus. He also sent affidavits for Strauss's sister Bette Besmann, and her husband Seigfried. Because Strauss and the Besmanns lived in Chemnitz, the papers had been forwarded to Raymond Geist, the American Consul General in Berlin. Geist must have known something already of Stern's friendship with Gerald Nye. He also showed more sympathy for the plight of Germany's Jews than most other State Department consuls. But in this case, he assumed a very aggressive tone with Stern from the first communication.

Writing to Stern, Geist said that he could take no action on the Strauss applications because Stern had "not satisfactorily corroborated your statement regarding your income." Puzzled, because his previous statements of solvency had been sufficient before, Stern sent Geist an affidavit showing that his 1937 income had exceeded seven thousand dollars. Geist rejected this affidavit and demanded a certified copy of Stern's income tax filing. Stern then sent both his personal tax report and that of Straus Clothing and added a letter attesting to his reliability from the North Dakota representative of the Democratic Party National Committee. He also secured a further affidavit on behalf of Strauss from his neighbor Karl Olson, the owner of the Fair Store, Valley City's major department store. Olson corroborated everything Stern had said, and promised that, if it were necessary, he would use his own resources to help Stern take care of Strauss and the Besmanns. Stern concluded his cover letter with a solemn statement that he had "properly taken care of" all thirty-three of the men and women he had sponsored to date. He also induced Senator Nye to write a letter to Geist, and probably thought that would be the end of the matter.[4]

He was wrong. Geist now wrote to Gustav Strauss and told him that unless Stern provided a detailed accounting of those who Stern had sponsored for visas – where they lived and worked, how often Stern checked on them – Geist would regard Stern's affidavit as useless. An alarmed Strauss sent this information on to Stern.

Stern's reply to these demands was prompt and annoyed. He then listed how "the relatives I have sponsored previously are getting on":

• Klara and Erich Stern were working in Chicago, where their parents, Gustav and Selma, had joined them in 1936;

• Little Gus, the son of Herman's brother Julius, was working in New York, as was Tea (Dorothy) Eichengruen, who had arrived just a few weeks before;

• Trudl Herman was also in New York, "giving voice lessons and singing in churches and temples";

• Hans Lion was living with his family in Cincinnati, where "his [medical] practice is growing and he is more than self-supporting";

• Hugo Heinlein's and his family were living in Valley City; "Mr. Henlein has established a business for himself and [is] doing nicely";

• Hans Benjamin was working in a clothing factory in Virginia;

• Erich Falkenstein was in dental school, with Stern probably paying the tuition, while his wife's job in a dental lab "takes care of household expenses";

• Julius Haas and his family were living with relatives in New York; he and his two sons were working as bakers;

• Manfred Reichenberg was working in a hospital in Brooklyn;

• Herman Jacob had a photographer's job in Chicago, "and is more than making his way."

In all, the letter accounted for twenty-four people. Stern mentioned neither his nephew Julius nor Leon Hayum. He also failed to mention the more recently arrived Moser family or a young man named Felix Falkenstein, a cousin of Erich who he helped get to America in 1937 and who now worked in the kitchen of the Jewish hospital in Brooklyn. In closing, Stern frostily told the consul, "I assure you any relative for whom I have assumed sponsorship are worthy of my confidence." So absorbed was Stern in this argument, he barely noticed the arrival of another family in New York, who he co-sponsored and helped to find work.[5]

Geist still took no action on Strauss's applications for visas. In August, Nye wrote another letter to Geist, which he hoped "may expedite matters in behalf of Gustav Strauss." Geist did not reply to Nye's letter for two full months and when he did, he told Nye that he was not satisfied with Stern's assurances, nor the evidence submitted for his income. He insisted that since Stern had already sponsored so many "aliens in connection with visa applications," the Consul General would not approve any further visas unless he received "evidence to show whether or not the aliens for whom Mr. Stern previously made affidavits are as yet self-supporting." He did not explain what kind of evidence he would find "satisfactory" for this purpose.[6]

The standoff continued. The Nazis introduced a new passport for Germany, one marked with a large "J" (for "Jude"), intended to mark the document's bearer as a social pariah. Then *Kristallnacht* came, and in its wake Stern briefly vented his frustrations in a rather sharp letter to Nye. When he read in the newspaper that Nye and several other senators had said that they did not see any need to revise the American immigration rules because of the anti-Jewish violence in Germany, he fired off a letter to Nye to say he was "rather confused" by Congressional stiffness on the issue. "I do appreciate as you do that to open the gates for immigration without any control or without a planned program would be against the best interest of America and its Jews, but I was rather disappointed to see such a short severe statement from you without further explanation."[7]

After receiving this rebuke, Nye continued to help Stern. But Stern also reached out to another old friend for help in his quests. Ever since he had worked with James Milloy in the Greater North Dakota Association, Stern had held the younger man in high regard. Milloy had left his position as secretary of the GNDA in 1931 to become a reporter the *Minneapolis Tribune.* His skills at the *Tribune* were impressive enough for the paper to send him to Washington DC as its permanent correspondent. Milloy also acted as a lobbyist in Washington, representing from time to time the interests of a variety of northern plains businesses. He had developed a number of contacts in the nation's capital and had kept in touch with Stern.

Just a few days after *Kristallnacht,* Stern wrote to Milloy. To better appreciate Stern's frustration, the letter is worth quoting in some detail: "I am giving you a big order today," he wrote, "in connection with many affidavits that I have furnished for German relatives in order to permit them to come to this country. I have encountered one very difficult case. It is the case of Gustav Straus [sic] of Chemnitz, Germany." After explaining the situation as he saw it, Stern commented, "I have complied with every request that the Consul has made and have even gone a step further by furnishing [an] additional affidavit of support from Karl J. Olson, proprietor of the Fair Store in

Valley City. So far, all my efforts have been to no avail. I might state that I have furnished papers for relatives, which were presented to the Consuls at Stuttgaart [sic] and Hamburg, and in every instance these cases were given very prompt attention. For that reason I feel positive that the papers submitted to the Consul in Berlin are correct, and I cannot account for any reason why they should not be recognized." He noted that Strauss, as a goods importer, had "several thousand dollars [deposited] in this country" and would never become a charity case.

Stern believed that Strauss may have "got off on the wrong foot" at the Berlin office and so may have angered one of the assistants to the point that "his case is being deliberately delayed for some minor technical reason." As a man who carefully supervised his own staff at Straus Clothing, Stern was appalled by the capriciousness he discerned in the handling of visa applications. So he told Milloy that he was "inclined to believe that the only way the case [of Strauss] can get a speedy and fair consideration is by appealing to the State Department Secretary Hull. This is where you can do the job. . . . You will perhaps be informed by the State Department that the American Consul is the sole and only judge in deciding these cases – but I do know that the State Department has the power and the jurisdiction to intervene."

He noted that Nye had already sent a couple of notes to Geist, and told Milloy that he should talk to Nye if he wanted to, "but I am inclined to think that you can crash [sic – crack?] this case better yourself." He closed with an appeal to Milloy's sense of decency and friendship: "Jim, you would do a real charitable act if you can get immediate action on this case. . . . I hate to bother anyone as busy as you are. But I also like to go to a man who can get results." Stern had taken Milloy's measure perfectly, for the man cabled him that he would "move on the Strauss matter" immediately.[8]

This communication with Milloy marked a turning point in Stern's mission to help German Jews. In asking Milloy to talk to the State Department, Stern showed that he knew Nye's influence with Franklin Roosevelt's administration was on the decline. True, Nye had just won re-election to the Senate for a third full term, but Roosevelt's supporters had grown tired of Nye's growing conservatism on domestic issues. Whereas FDR once restrained North Dakota Democrats from excoriating Non-Partisan Republicans, this time Nye's Democratic opponent had attacked Nye repeatedly as a "reactionary." Nye "yeses the progressive people of North Dakota [at home]," he charged, "then goes down to Washington and 'noes' them at every chance." Roosevelt was also becoming worried that the neutrality laws Nye had helped create would hamper the American government's ability to react to Hitler's aggressive moves. Stern decided that the charming Milloy would have better luck this time. And indeed, Milloy was able to report within a week that the State Department had cabled Berlin to ask for "a report on Strauss's visa application."⁹

In addition to obtaining Milloy's help, Stern decided that he needed to reorganize the paperwork he had kept on those he had already sponsored. He did this by hiring a new assistant at Straus Clothing, a young man named James Hetland. Hetland was a student at Valley City High School. As he explained years later, Hetland knew Herman Stern only from shopping at the store. Then one day, he learned at school that Stern had called and asked about him. "They told me, 'Herman wanted to know if you were good with a typewriter and could write,' and so on. And they told [Stern], 'He's on the newspaper at school, and he's going to start writing a column for the *Times Record* in sports. So he's pretty handy with putting things together.' And I think that was it."

Stern asked Hetland to come down to Straus Clothing. "So I trotted up the stairs [to Stern's office]. 'Sit down, Jim,' he said, 'and we've got to talk a little bit.' He said, 'You know, when I got my education I didn't learn to use a typewriter, and I didn't have the opportunity to do some of the things that I understand you do very well. And I'd like to have you help me along the way, because I've got a project that I've taken on that is really sort of an overwhelming thing, but I think if you'll help me, we can get some good done.'" Stern told young Hetland that he was "'trying to rescue some of my family from Germany. They're trapped, more or less. It has become very difficult for them to get out. So I'm trying to work from this end to make it possible for our system of newcomers to provide the right answers [on visa applications] so that some of these people can come out.' And that really began a tremendous experience, the experience of the man's thoughts and his hopes and his desires to help other people."

Hetland reorganized Stern's papers regarding his affidavits and put together files on each family Stern had sponsored as well as each person or family for whom he was preparing new affidavits. He also drafted Stern's letters to the consulates and to Washington. He admitted that the hardest tasks were dealing with the spelling of German personal names and place names. Hetland would type the letters and Stern would say "'Gosh, I wish I had learned to use the typewriter. I just never had the chance.' Then he'd pat me on the back and we'd keep going." Stern hoped that with a better system his relatives might get visas more quickly. He could sense that their danger was growing greater with each day.[10]

Sometimes people hit a rock in the road and decide they have to slow down. Faced with Geist's roadblock over the Strauss visas, Stern could easily have done the same. Having already done more to help German Jews than any other single person he knew, perhaps he had done enough. Business conditions had grown better, and his son Eddie was suggesting that now would be a good time to consider expanding, perhaps by opening a store in Fargo. Stern could do with less strain on his finances if he was to try this idea. He had turned down a request from an associate in New York that he help another family, explaining that he worried about "shoulder[ing] any more sponsorships in these depression times."[11]

But slowing down was not Stern's way. He soon decided he was going to try and help even more Jewish refugees. For some time, he had been gathering information about available land in North Dakota, land that might be used to provide small farms to refugees. He had done some calculations concerning how much it would cost to help families from Europe buy small farms in the state. Now, armed with this information, this remarkable man was ready to make a bold proposal to Stephen Wise.

On November 16, 1938, less than a week after *Kristallnacht*, Stern sat down and presented his idea in a letter to Wise. He wrote that he had met Wise "some years ago" when he went with Gerald Nye to an American Jewish Congress gathering. "It was my intention to discuss this matter with you personally when attending your services on October 23ʳᵈ," Stern wrote, "but time did not permit it." Instead, Stern had talked to a mutual acquaintance, about "the deplorable condition of the German-Austrian Jews." This man had urged him to write to Wise. After summarizing for Wise his own efforts to sponsor Jewish refugees, Stern got to the heart of his proposal:

"While I was in New York, I could not help but notice that too many of the immigrants stay in New York not knowing where else to go. No one knows better than you do that sooner or later this will create a serious condition because New York cannot continue to absorb the constant flow. There might even be a revolt among our American born Jews whose jobs are being jeopardized by immigrants, not even mentioning the danger from gentile labor. Here is the plan I would like to submit to you for consideration. I realize that many immigrants are not the type by nature or training to pursue the work I have in mind, but there are hundreds of families having lived and still live in small country districts of Germany who have been closer to the soil and agriculture, who might be brought into the wide open spaces of the West where they could establish homes for themselves, would become producers and consumers without taking away jobs from others in the congested districts."

Stern noted that land in "a great many fertile valleys" in North Dakota could be had for "$20.00 to $35.00 per acre at long deferred payment plan[s]." He knew of land "in the famous Red River Valley" which would be suitable, for it was part of "the most productive farm section in America." The land was available, he noted, because it belonged to an insurance company that had acquired it "through foreclosures" in the 1930s, and would be willing to sell it on the right terms. On such land, he noted a family could "make a good livelihood" on an eighty acre tract, which meant a section could provide homes for eight families. In order that these families would not live alone, he thought it best to acquire land sufficient for sixteen families to live close to one another.

Stern had worked with the Greater North Dakota Association to calculate that "$500,000 would make a very fine start for 75 to 100 families" by purchasing equipment, and other necessities. The land, he expected, would cost an additional "$2,500 per family." He asked if "Jewish Philanthropic Organizations" might not be able to help raise the funds for this, and noted that eventually the refugees could pay back some of the money after they began to make profits from their crops. He also noted, in an oblique reference to the State Department's regulations, that such families would be regarded as "self supporting." He also believed that the spreading of Jewish refugees into the rural parts of America could "avert the constant growing danger of anti-Semitism in America."

Stern closed the letter by assuring Wise that he had "no selfish motive in proposing this plan," that his motive was to try to give a "way out for a small part of the poor unfortunate souls who are looking for peace and happiness" away from Europe.

This letter to Wise clearly marked a turning point in Stern's efforts to help battle against the persecutions of the Jews. Having admitted in his letter to Wise that his "own limit [to help] was to the exhausted stage," he was now reaching out to "other friends to furnish affidavits." Now he wanted to develop a full-fledged campaign among the Jews in the northern plains to help dozens of German Jewish families, perhaps hundreds if things went well. This was also the first time Stern referred in his correspondence to a fear that the influx of Jewish refugees would fuel "the growing danger of anti-Semitism in America."[12]

Not coincidently, Stern was now embracing his own Judaic heritage. Eddie Stern remembered that it was at this time that his father began to attend Temple on a more regular basis, attending services of the Fargo Reform Congregation. Ed acknowledged Hilda and Solly Jonas as the ones who "brought my parents back to the Temple," by describing to them how Jews were being persecuted whether or not they practiced their faith. "If there's any credit to be given for inspiring a person to start being more religious as they got older, that credit certainly goes to the example set by Solly and Hilda."[13]

Herman and Adeline probably received some comfort from their renewed faith, especially as it grew more difficult to get refugees out of Europe in the coming months. Stern's first disappointment came when Stephen Wise replied to his letter, for, while congratulating Stern on sponsoring refugees and agreeing that "many of the people could be brought into the west under some such plan as you suggest," Wise thought the cost of "$5,000 per family would make it impossible even to consider the question of large and wide transportation [of refugees]." Stern replied with a suggestion that the costs could be reduced by having two families "live in the same building," and assuring Wise that the monies raised toward his proposal would not simply be donations – "if the right families are selected the investment will pay out." There is no indication that Wise replied to this second letter.[14]

However, soon after this, Stern pursued his plan by contacting other Jewish organizations. He contacted the Hebrew Sheltering and Immigration Service in December and, in return for their interest in his idea, agreed to act as an agent for HIAS in raising money for the "assistance of refugees in dictator-controlled nations." He also agreed to help the United Palestine Appeal, which was trying to raise ten million dollars to help a hundred thousand European Jews immigrate to Jerusalem. A week before Hanukah, Stern traveled to Bismarck to speak to members of the Temple about both the HIAS campaign and his own resettlement plan. He followed this up in the early weeks of 1939 with trips to Grand Forks and Fargo, where he solicited help from the Jewish communities in those cities. As his son Ed later noted, Stern found at these visits that "Orthodox Jews – I mean the Russians and the others who had [in Europe] felt a little more persecution – were a little more generous than the German Jews." As it was, fundraising proceeded slowly, possibly because Stern was not well known to many of the people he talked to.[15]

Stern also continued to gather information about land for his re-settlement plan. In this he was aided by his contacts through the Greater North Dakota Association, which had been collecting information on the state's farms for years. He ultimately decided that the best site for what would be in effect a new Jewish colony was land northwest of Grand Forks, taking up significant portions of five townships: Wheatfield, Strabane, Gilby, Agnes, and Inkster. The National Life Insurance Company, the current owners of the land, provided Stern a detailed description of the farms, whose owners had lost them to taxes during the worst of the dustbowl era in the mid-1930s.

"These tracts of land," National's representative wrote Stern, are "largely in the immediate vicinity of the little town of Orr" and were within thirty-five miles of Grand Forks by both rail and "a good, hard-surfaced road" which most of the farms could reach by gravel roads. Many of the farmsteads had electricity, the representative assured Stern. As for the land quality, the company agent noted that since National Life had taken title of them, the fields had been planted largely in alfalfa and sweet clover, for "feeding livestock and putting something back into the land, and it shows the results." He promised Stern that the black silt-loam soil was excellent for all manner of grains and cited the example of a neighboring farmer whose "famous Elk Valley Farm" had regularly shown "a record of production that is almost tops in North Dakota." He also predicted that the soil would be excellent for sugar beet production if the farmers could "get a sugar beet acreage allocation" from the American Crystal Sugar Company plant in Grand Forks. The agent sent Stern a full map of the quarter sections in this block of land and told him that "our company would entertain a price of $20 per acre for these tracts aggregating 6240 acres" in a fifteen year mortgage.

After again doing some calculations with the help of the GNDA, Stern asked the insurance company to give him an estimate of how much it would cost for sufficient land and equipment and supplies for twenty-five families. He also asked Bert Groom, the chairman of the GNDA's Agricultural Committee, to go look over the land in question. The National Life Insurance Company drew on data from the

New Deal's Farm Security Administration in submitting its costs for adding such additional buildings as "a small henhouse, granary and hogbarn and a well" to some of the farmsteads. They also included costs for cows, sows, horses, cultivators, plows, and a host of other necessities, for a total cost of $144,540 to give Stern what he requested. They further included complete sets of photographs of some of the farms and recommended to Stern that, inasmuch as he was aiming to build "more or less of a co-operative farming proposition" he should consider "obtain[ing] the services of a well trained farm manager" to assist the refugee families in getting started.

Bert Groom added a summary note to the company's figures, telling Stern that the 3840 acres of this revised scheme was good soil that for the asking price of $73,350 was "the cheapest tract of land that I have seen in the Red River Valley in many years." He further thought some of the additional necessary buildings could be had by buying already standing ones on other properties and moving them to the site. He advised Stern that, if he decided to make the deal, he should try and close it before July 1 because National would then throw in half of its current crop harvest for the costs of growing the hay and clover.[16]

Stern was by now very enthusiastic about the prospect of making his idea a reality, the more so because he had caught the interest of the National Coordinating Committee. Established in 1937 to organize assistance for refugees as they arrived in the United States, the National Coordinating Committee was delighted with Stern's plan to create a colony of Jewish immigrants in North Dakota. Jacob Kravitz, the assistant director of the Committee's Resettlement Division, urged Stern to meet with Robert Herbst of Fargo and help him organize a resettlement plan for their state. He also informed Stern that "there are new plans afoot – as far as agricultural placements [of refugees] are concerned – which involve a very close working relationship with the Jewish Agricultural Society." Stern had already explained his scheme to the Society, and held out hopes that they could help him as well.

By now, Stern was touting his twenty-five-family colony as a model not only for wresting greater numbers of German Jews from the Nazis' clutches but also for making them over into the best of citizens. In a letter to another officer in the Coordinating Committee, he painted his vision in the brightest of agrarian populist hues: "farm opportunities are to be found many places, but they must be sound. That is the reason the location of my experiment is the Red River Valley, one of the most fertile sections of the world. . . . I realize there are hundreds of farmers who are failures, the same as in any other line, but those who are set up and operate on a business like basis can and always will be able to enjoy the comforts of an average American family." He went so far as to forecast that if most refugees continued to live in urban America, immigration might be further tightened, asking "who can tell if these laws will not be restricted if the refugees are to continue to clamor for the larger centers?"[17]

In like manner, he proposed another plan, this one designed to help refugee physicians who had come from Europe only to discover that they would not be allowed to practice medicine in America. Stern knew well that, thanks to the American Medical Association's lobbying the states to deny licenses to physicians who were "not American citizens," foreign doctors like Eugen Schwarz and Hans Lion often had to settle for low paying jobs. Stern saw such restrictions as a foolish waste of talent that could readily be placed in service for small town America.

Once again he found the principal cause for the prejudice against the German Jewish physicians in the crowds of refugees living in urban America. "Because of the 1500 or more refugee doctors in New York and vicinity," he wrote to the Coordinating Committee, "the medical profession all over the United States . . . has made it impossible for refugee doctors to settle in most states because of the requirement of citizenship. We in our own State could furnish location for fifty doctors if the restrictions can be lifted."

Stern set out on a year-long campaign to find places for immigrant physicians in some the region's small communities. He wrote letters of inquiry to the secretaries of state in North Dakota, South Dakota and Minnesota as to the rules for obtaining a medical license and assembled a list of doctors who were active in his own state's Medical Association, and opened a correspondence with yet another of the immigrant aid agencies – the Central Committee for Resettlement of Foreign Agencies. After collecting and reading a number of articles on the subject of medical needs in rural America, he began writing the "prominent doctors all over the State to see if we can in some way influence these men so they will gradually recommend modifying the rules and attitude of the [AMA] National Organization."[18]

Even with all this, Stern continued to work to find jobs for several of the men and women he had sponsored. He had his best success in the greater clothing industry, locating jobs at Kuppenheimers and elsewhere. But he wanted to find employment in North Dakota for at least some. "Dad knew all these people and he was twisting arms to get jobs," his son remembered. Stern persuaded some of the Jewish storeowners in the state to take on one or two refugees, sometimes in temporary positions. In one case a storeowner in Minneapolis wrote Stern that he "can't guarantee you that he will get a job, but will *promise* you that we will try our very best to place him." Other attempts failed when the refugees lacked adequate skill in English or simply would not be welcomed in the community. "A Jewish boy here won't do as the town is very small and the people just won't take to them," a store owner in Fessenden told Stern. "It took me a long time until I grew in their hearts."[19]

Stern persisted in this and in all his other endeavors to get more German Jews out of Europe and to safety in America. But he knew he was running out of time.

In Europe, decisions being made in London and Berlin were leading Europe inexorably into war. The British public had greeted the Munich settlement in 1938 with boisterous relief. But just below the surface there was also shame that the British Empire had walked away from its commitment to Czechoslovakia. The shame was then mixed with anger over the savagery of *Kristallnacht*. Many British leaders both in the government and the House of Commons, who

had resisted calls for the nation to seriously rearm, now reversed themselves and supported measures for enlarging the Royal Air Force,
modernizing the navy and even exploring the possibility of conscrip-
tion. The British also urged the French government to strengthen its
own defenses, particularly in the air.

Then in early 1939, rumors reached the British Foreign Office
that Germany might suddenly make an attack on Holland. In something like a panic, the British cabinet pressured Chamberlain to agree
that Britain would go to war if Germany did indeed invade Holland.
They then warned the Belgians that Germany intended to "dominate
Europe by force," and prepared an "appreciation" in which Britain
and France would go to war to stop Germany. But, having come to a
determination to begin standing up to Germany, the government chose
not to share this determination with Hitler.[20]

Hitler meanwhile continued to be a step ahead of the rest of
Europe's guesswork. Having decided to seize control of the remnant
of Czechoslovakia, he employed agents to encourage a separatist
movement among the Slovakians and then threatened the Czech government: Germany would bomb Prague unless the Czechs "placed
the fate of the Czech people and country in the hands of the Fuhrer of
the German Reich." Abandoned by the west, the Czechs gave in and
on March 15 German troops marched into Bohemia and Moravia.
Hitler marched into Prague with his troops and proclaimed the German annexation of these provinces. In Munich, Bill Shirer noted he
"could not help recalling how Chamberlain said [the Munich Agree-
ment] not only saved the peace but had really saved Czechoslovakia."[21]

A week later, Hitler coerced Lithuania into returning the province of Memel to Germany. Soon after, he squeezed major oil concessions from Romania and demanded from Poland the return of
Danzig and the lands between it and the German border. When the
Polish foreign minister declined to agree and sent extra troops into
the "Danzig Corridor," Hitler ordered his troops to prepare for war
while the German press unleashed a campaign of vitriolic abuse, the
worst aspects of which Shirer recorded: "POLAND LOOK OUT!

warns the *B[erliner] Z[eitung]* headline, adding: ANSWER TO POLAND, THE RUNNER-AMOK (AMOKLAUFER) AGAINST PEACE AND RIGHT IN EUROPE! ... WARSAW THREATENS BOMBARDMENT OF DANZIG – UNBELIEVABLE AGITATION OF THE POLISH ARCH-MADNESS (POLNISCHEN GROSSENWAHNS)!"

Whether Hitler really intended war or simply wanted to frighten Poland into acquiescence will forever be debated, and in many ways it does not matter, for Chamberlain's government now chose to take its stand against Hitler. In a cabinet meeting held three days after the annexation of the Czech provinces, Chamberlain said "he had now come to the conclusion that Herr Hitler's attitude made it impossible to continue to negotiate on the old basis [of appeasement]." Chamberlain had decided to warn Hitler that Britain would not accept German domination of Europe, and that "if Germany were to proceed with this course after warning had been given, we had no alternative but to take up the challenge." On March 31, the Prime Minister told the House of Commons "in the event of any action which clearly threatened Polish independence, and which the Polish Government accordingly considered it vital to resist with their national forces, His Majesty's Government will feel themselves bound at once to lend the Polish Government all support in their power." A similar pledge was made to Romania. France soon after joined Britain in these guarantees, making what was in essence a defensive alliance with Poland and Romania.

If Chamberlain hoped that by doing this he could make Hitler back down he was mistaken. In May, Hitler told his highest ranking commanders that "we cannot expect a repetition of [the diplomatic victory over] Czechia. There will be war." He said he still hoped to "isolate Poland" but even "if it is not definitely certain that a German-Polish conflict will not lead to war with the West then the fight must be primarily against England and France." In order to be able to concentrate his forces against the two western European powers, Hitler was even willing to conclude a temporary arrangement with his mortal enemy, Russia.[22]

Europe's drift toward war had little impact on Jewish immigration. In Germany, the Jewish families continued to line up at the various consulates, beg for visas and go away empty handed or obtain visas but wait weeks on end for a chance to enter the United States under the quota system. Jews who had left Germany years before and were living in France or Holland or elsewhere debated whether or not to stay and hope for the best or to try and immigrate again. They understood that these could well be life and death decisions, but who could say what was the right thing to do?

The case of Gustav Strauss was a fine example of this. Stern had gathered a set of "letters of [self-]support from all the immigrants who have been sponsored by myself" and forwarded these to Raymond Geist in Berlin. Despite these, and the help of Jim Milloy and Gerald Nye, neither Strauss, nor his sister and brother-in-law had yet been granted visas. Strauss thought of leaving for Cuba and waiting there while the American visas were approved. He had written to Stern in November 1938 that "many people took the step via Cuba. After a short stay there, it was possible [to proceed to United States]. Now I have heard there are difficulties at this time. Perhaps you could find out, and let us know, what is going on there."

But during *Kristallnacht*, Strauss was briefly incarcerated and then warned to leave Germany, soon. He decided that he and his sister and her husband should sail for Latin America, where he hoped they would buy temporary visas until they could get into the United States. He sent Stern a letter the day he and the Besmanns boarded ship in Antwerp. The letter is worth quoting in full:

"We are already on the ship in Antwerp. In spite of numerous inquiries either in person or in writing or by phone, we did not get any information [from the Berlin Consulate]. One is speechless how those people at the consulate work. One should expect that letters *are* being answered, even after some weeks, but at least answered at all. These people do not care at all. Even with the telegram from Nye in Washington, up to this day we have heard nothing. It does not make any difference to those people. In any case, we did not want to wait any longer. You know how long we were waiting. As far as I am concerned, we should not have to wait so long. We had planned to travel to Trinidad. However, three days before the departure, the entry there was blocked. Now the ship plans to land in British Honduras. This is a culturally deprived country. We hope in any case, for only a short stop. As soon as we land there, I'll go to the American consulate to request the papers from Berlin. Please, keep on trying, [so] that the waiting time won't be so long. As I can see, due to the delay of the last inquiry, the waiting period again has gotten longer, for an acquaintance has been already notified to be at the consulate in May. Please, inform us, if you have positive news for us. You will be able to find out the timetable for our ship. In my opinion, we will be in four weeks in Belize.

"For you efforts, dear Hermann, thank you very much, and we will hope that we have after our trip some spirit left. Probably we will need some money to live on, since the deposited money will be temporarily confiscated. I will let you know. In this case, be so kind and take care of it promptly."

Strauss and the Besmanns ended up in Venezuela rather than Honduras. While the reason for this is not explained in the correspondence, it was most likely because Strauss had learned he could get temporary residence papers more readily in Venezuela (at least at that moment, for several of the Latin officials were by now doing a brisk business in selling temporary haven to refugees who could afford it). They spent nearly four months in Venezuela, rather than the four weeks Strauss had hoped for in his letter to Stern. After dozens of letters and telegrams, exchanged among Stern, Strauss, Nye, and the State Department the visas were finally awarded. Their quota numbers were also advanced, because the "Berlin Consulate [was] glad, upon the receipt of a request from the Consulate at Caracas, to transfer quota numbers for the use of the applicants to the latter office." Strauss and the Bessmans left for New York around the end of May 1939. Once again, Stern's friends in Washington had given him priceless help.[23]

Another family who fled Germany by way of Latin America was that of Erich Vasen, Gertrude Vasen Stern's brother. Like the Gustave

Sterns, Vasen and his wife Hetty had left Germany earlier than most, living briefly in England, where their son was born, then moving to Switzerland. Late in 1938, Erich Vasen had decided they should leave Europe. He contacted Stern for help on how he could enter Cuba. After receiving details that Stern had obtained from HIAS, Vasen wrote again, informing Stern that, "because the general situation in Europe is getting more and more dangerous now, I decided to emigrate. Already last October, I applied for the visa for the United States at the American Consulate in Zürich. I was informed I could not receive a quota number before the middle of 1939, and that the visa could not be granted within the next two years – too many immigration applications. From you and from others have heard that, by way of Cuba, [we can] get sooner to the United States. I arranged for the immigration visa for Cuba." He asked Stern to help from his end and told him to pay his expenses by drawing upon nearly twenty thousand dollars that Vasen had transferred into American banks over the previous five years.

Stern filed affidavits for the Vasens in January 1939, and kept in touch with the family. He soon learned from Vasen that the family had arrived in Cuba, where they discovered that "people [are] not allowed into Havana itself, unless they paid $360 [per person]." After some time spent in an immigration camp, Erich learned at the United States consulate of "the waiting period of two years, only 18 visas granted monthly for German Jews." Fearing they might be deported back to Germany, they suggested that their son, having been born in London, might be able to leave for America by claiming British citizenship, but this idea was quickly quashed. It would take Vasen more than a year, and an interim stay in Chile, before he and his family were able to enter the United States.[24]

So it went in the first half of 1939, as war clouds deepened and families scampered toward any shelter from the coming storm.

Notes

1. H. V. Kaltenborn, *Fifty Fabulous Years* (New York: G. P. Putnam's Sons, 1950), pp. 186-187.

2. Hadley Cantril, ed., *Public Opinion, 1935-1946* (Princeton, NJ: Princeton University Press, 1951), vol. 1, p. 385; Lipstadt, *Beyond Belief*, pp. 98-109; Robert Ross, *So It Was True: The American Protestant Press and the Nazi Persecution of the Jews* (Minneapolis: University of Minnesota Press, 1980), pp. 109-121.

3. *Moorhead Daily News,* November 8-12 and 14-17, 1938; Melva Moline, *The Forum: First Hundred Years* (Fargo: The Forum, 1979), p. 153.

4. Geist to Stern, March 15 and May 3, 1938, Stern to Geist, April 11 and June 2, 1938, and Geist to Gerald Nye (referring to Nye's letter of May 3), May 28, 1938, all in Strauss-Besmann file, Stern Papers. For an analysis of Geist's sympathy for the German Jews, see Zucker.

5. Stern to Raymond H. Geist, July 22, 1938, Strauss-Besmann file; Stern to Charles Harris, July 21, 1938, Julius Blumenthal family file, Stern Papers. Information on Felix Falkenstein from the Falkenstein-Kurau file and from Stanley Falkenstein, Felix's son, in a letter to Shoptaugh, December 7, 1998.

6. Nye to Geist, August 26, 1938 and Geist to Nye, October 29, 1938, Strauss-Besmann file, Stern Papers. By this point, Stern had received an angry letter from Gustav Strauss in which Strauss rebuked him for "not send[ing] in the beginning the complete papers and if one item is not working out, so the whole process is delayed enormously. . . . Perhaps you cannot quite understand how it feels when one has to wait for one thing such a long time." (Gustav Strauss to Stern, September 2, 1938, German Correspondence file, Stern Papers). Overall, Strauss's letters are peevish and arrogant, and it is clear that, in his fear of being denied a visa, he made a bad impression at the American consulate. It is also a testament of Stern's dedication that he persevered in Strauss's case.

7. Stern to Nye, December 3, 1938, Political Correspondence file, Box 10, Stern Papers. There is no reply to this letter in either Stern's papers or the papers of Nye in the Hoover Presidential Library.

8. "Milloy, Once Minoter, Who Became Look Officer, Dies," ca. March 1971, undated obituary in "James Milloy" file, Stern Papers; Stern to Jim Milloy, November 13, 1938, and Milloy cable to Stern, November 17, 1938, both in Strauss-Besmann file, Stern Papers.

9. Cole, *Gerald P. Nye*, pp. 133-49; Milloy cable to Stern, November 25, 1938, Strauss-Besmann file, Stern Papers.

10. Gerald Nye to Stern, August 26, 1938 and Raymond Geist to Nye, October 29, 1938, in Strauss-Besmann file Stern Papers; Michael Morrissey, interview with James Hetland, August 4, 1999, transcript, pp. 1-5.

11. William Wolff to Stern, June 1, 1938, Albert Kahn family file, Stern Papers. Later letters in the Kahn file reveal that the Kahns immigrated to Italy in mid-1939. In November of 1939, Stern secured an affidavit for the family from Max Goldberg of Fargo and asked Jake Levitz to provide a supporting affidavit, but reiterated to Albert Kahn that he could not provide any financial commitment of his own. The file does not indicate the ultimate outcome of this case.

12. Stern to Stephen Wise, November 16, 1938, Dr. Stephen Wise file, Stern Papers.

13. Edward Stern, Eulogy for Solly Jonas [1992], copy in Shoptaugh's possession.

14. Stephen Wise to Stern, November 21, 1938, Wise file, Stern Papers.

15. Stern to Asher Katz, December 18, 1938 and Stern to J. C. Taylor, December 29, 1938, Jewish Resettlement file, Stern Papers; "Bismarck Campaign to Aid Political Refugees Planned," *Bismarck Tribune*, December 14, 1938; Edward Stern transcript, p. 15.

16. H.A. Schnell, letters to Stern, February 24 and April 19, 1939, along with Bert Groom's undated note, all in Jewish Resettlement file, Stern Papers.

17. Jacob Kravitz to Stern, May 29, 1939, and Stern to J. W. Pincus, June 12, 1939, in Jewish Resettlement file, Stern Papers.

18. In addition to the Pincus letter above, which is quoted, see Stern to Charles Jordan, July 1, 1939 and numerous other letters in the Foreign Doctors Placement file of the Stern Papers. See also "A Program for the Refugee Physician," *The Journal of the American Medical Association,* May 13, 1939, for a contemporary summary of the issue.

19. Edward Stern conversation with Shoptaugh, July 1998; Walter Lesser to Stern, October 15, 1938, Foreign Doctors Placement file, and Ben Oser to Stern [ca. September 1939], Jewish Resettlement file, Stern Papers.

20. Weinberg, *The Foreign Policy of Hitler's Germany*, pp. 518-26.

21. Noakes, ed., *Nazism, 1919-1945*, vol. 3, pp. 725-28; Shirer, *Berlin Diary*, p. 122.

22. Weinberg, *The Foreign Policy of Hitler's Germany,* pp. 535-47; Shirer, *Berlin Diary*, p. 132; Noakes, ed., *Nazism,* vol. 3, pp. 736-39.

23. Strauss to Stern, November 5, 1938 and January 17, 1939, German Correspondence file. Among the voluminous letters in the Strauss-Besmann file, the most important are Eliot Coulter to James Milloy, January 17, 1939, Milloy to Stern, January 18, 1939, Stern to Nye, January 22, 1939, A. M. Warren to Stern, February 15, 1939, A. M. Warren to Nye, March 20, 1939, and A. M. Warren to Nye, April 18, 1939. Later letters in the file indicate that in 1940 and 1941 Strauss became alienated from some of his American relatives over money matters.

24. Erich Vasen to Stern, January 9 and February 25, 1939, German Correspondence file, Stern Papers; Isaac Asofsky [of HIAS] to Stern, December 15, 1938, and Stern to American Consul General, Havana, January 27, 1939, Erich Vasen file, Stern Papers.

Chapter Twelve
"Each Day Lost May Mean the Loss of a Life"

Greta Steiner held her breath when the train stopped at the German-Belgian border. The train car was filled "mostly with women who were in the same situation as I was," wives and daughters of Jewish men who had already left Germany. When they boarded the train in Vienna, a few passing civilians remarked how happy they were to be rid of so many "Juden." As they passed through Germany, they saw a lot of soldiers. Hitler was gathering his troops for conquest. Like Greta, all the women had their proper permits to leave Germany and their visas to live in Belgium or Great Britain. But at the border stop, they waited and wondered, would something go wrong now, here just yards away from their freedom? They waited. Then the train moved forward again and crossed the border and they felt better. "Everybody was happy when we left Aachen and were out of Germany."[1]

It was mid-July. Just a few weeks later, Hitler made a bargain with Josef Stalin: Germany could attack Poland and the Soviet Union would remain neutral and collect the eastern provinces of Poland as its reward. German troops invaded on September 1st, its tanks and aircraft crushing the Polish armies in a few weeks. After some hesitation, Britain and France declared war on Germany. The horror of the Second World War had begun. "I was very lucky to get out," Greta realized when the shooting began. "It was a question of luck."

After crossing the English Channel, Greta boarded another train, this one bound for Kent, where the family who had promised her a job had a country home. "The name of the town was Bexley, where I was. It wasn't very far from London." She went to work as a domestic, doing "everything that was to be done in a house, cooking and cleaning. They were nice people, but it was very lonesome. It was like a big estate. It wasn't connected with the town; it was up on

241

the hill. It was in a piece of woods, you know. It was very isolated. I'd see only the milkman and the mailman, that's all."

Her husband Felix was nowhere near Bexley, he was in Camp Kitchener, a refurbished military base, along with some three thousand German men, all refugees. All of these men had been granted temporary asylum in England. Chamberlain's government expected them to move on as soon as they received papers to emigrate somewhere else. Many of them had been beaten by Nazi thugs, not a few had been in concentration camps, but the British feared some of them might be spies sent to perform sabotage or steal secrets, and so they would remain in the camp until they were ready to move on to another country. Greta was happy that her employers invited Felix to see her at Christmas. "They had to invite him and he had to get a permit to leave the camp. He came to the house for three days."

In January 1940, Greta obtained an American visa to go the United States. Her aunt Francisca, her father's sister, who had gone to America in 1907, had sponsored her. Felix then found a sponsor with the help of his sister, who lived in California. In February, Felix and Greta boarded the *SS Britannic* for a special voyage across the Atlantic. "You know, it took ten days to go from Liverpool to New York, because we couldn't take the regular [shipping] route on account of the German U-boats. I remember it was painted all gray, and we didn't know when we were leaving. They didn't tell us. We were on the boat a day or two, and then we felt the movement, you know. We were mostly refugees on that boat."

Evading the U-boats, which had sunk over half a million tons of British shipping since the war began, the *Britannic* docked in New York. The Steiner's went to live with her aunt in New Jersey. Felix went to the National Refugee Service in New York for help in finding a job. "My husband registered there, you know. That's how you could find a job. My husband was really a custom tailor. You know, he had gone to designing schools, he learned to make a suit from scratch, it's like building a house. And he couldn't find a job for that. He could have found a job maybe if he would have been a union member. How could he be a union member with him just arriving here? So that job in Fargo was offered to my husband as a simple tailor, you just do alterations."

The job in Fargo was at the newest Straus Clothing store, which opened in 1939 with Ed Stern as its manager. Ed Stern had said he would be happy to give a job to a refugee. The Steiners went to Fargo on a Greyhound Bus and arrived on St. Patrick's Day. Ed Stern was surprised when he met them, for somehow he had missed the fact that Felix had a wife. He recovered quickly however and found a room for both of them to live in at the home of Jacob Zimmerman. Having just arrived in a new country, Greta was uncertain about moving halfway across a continent for Felix's job, but her aunt said, "If you don't like it, you can come back." As it happened Greta lived in Fargo for more than sixty years.[2]

Very few of the men and women who Stern helped chose to live in rural America for any length of time. Erich and Klara, and eventually their parents Gustav and Selma, lived in Chicago, as did a few others. A few, like Hans Lion, ended up in Cincinnati, while a few others went to work in clothing industries in the south Atlantic states. But the largest number stayed in New York, mostly in the Washington Heights neighborhood on the north end of Manhattan. Washington Heights was in some ways a natural choice for recent immigrants from Europe. It was filled with large apartment buildings that had been built for middle-class use but were only sparsely filled during the hard years of the depression, which allowed the first Jewish refugees from Germany to take an apartment and rent out the extra rooms to other refugees, often relatives, as they arrived in America.

During the decade, Washington Heights became something of an American outpost for those who had chosen exile over Hitler's New Order. The refugees built for themselves the appropriate institutions for an émigré enclave: kosher delis, singing groups, reading rooms with German newspapers and magazines, and a Hebrew school. Then there were the larger elements for an emerging German-Jewish-American refugee culture – a synagogue founded in 1935, in which the services contained an adroit blend of German Conservative and Orthodox elements, a society, the Deutsch-Judischer Club, and its attendant newspaper, *Aufbau*. Over time the residents studied copies of *Aufbau* with as much fervor as rabbis did the Torah, for it regularly carried announcements of new arrivals and inquiries about the fate of relatives or friends back in Germany.[3]

In 1939, one of Stern's relatives added another badly needed service to the neighborhood. Rosi Spier was thirty-eight years old when she arrived in New York in February of that year. She had married in the latter 1920s, to a lawyer named Klibanski, but the union began to collapse after the death of their first child. Rosi divorced her husband just after the birth of their son, Wolfgang, in 1934. Taking back her maiden name, Rosi went to Berlin where she placed her son in an orphanage while one of the Jewish organizations trained her in social work and helped her find a job. As she explained to an interviewer in 1981, "I became the social worker of a school founded in Bad Nauheim by the Reichsvertretung der deutschen Juden for children who could not attend the country schools anymore on account of antisemitism. . . . I lived there with the teachers and children, and by then I had my boy with me. We lived in the same building with a kindergarten teacher and the son of the head nurse of the school."

Soon after she began her job, Rosi received a letter from her second cousin in America, Herman Stern. He told her, "all of our relatives ask for an affidavit. Why don't you?" It was the middle of 1938 by then, so Rosi decided she should emigrate for Wolfgang's sake. Stern sent his affidavit, and, aware that his ongoing visa struggle with Raymond Geist in Berlin was well known in Stuttgart, took the precaution of adding a carefully written letter to Samuel Honaker. "Every immigrant [I have sponsored] has received a proper home, not alone through my own efforts, but also through the assistance of my friends. You may be satisfied without any doubt whatsoever, that I shall continue to carry out the pledge and that none of the immigrants sponsored by me will become a public charge but on the contrary will become useful citizens."[4]

Rosi Spier received her visa, but not before she witnessed the destruction of the school she worked at: "the Nazis from Bad Nauheim came into the school and broke everything and they threw us out into the street with the kids. I think it was right after Kristallnacht." The Burgermeister of Bad Nauheim protested against the action of the stormtroopers but the violence continued and the school was closed. In some cases, their parents had been arrested and sent to camps, so "Jewish organizations took care that the children were somehow looked after. Some of them were [later] sent to Switzerland. Some were deported." The police chief of Bad Nauheim, who had joined the Nazi Party, told Rosi she was lucky to be able to get out. He added, "I wish I could go with you."

Rosi and Wolfgang came to America early in February 1939, but they had to endure some tough months in New York. Rosi was unable to find any work for weeks because her English skills were limited. Leaving four-year-old Wolfgang with a former teacher who like her was a refugee, she went out to find whatever work she could. At first, the only job she had was as a maid to a middle-class family in Brooklyn. Because she lived in the home with the family, she only saw "Wolfi" once a week.

She arranged to place him in another home closer to Brooklyn so she could see him every night. "He misses me a lot," she reported to Herman Stern. The woman who took care of the boy told her that she had explained to him that "at night when you sleeping, [your mother] comes and lies down right next to you, and early in the morning, when you are still asleep, then she leaves for work. Wolfi lay down very close to the wall and said 'then I want to leave room for my Mami, so she can sleep well.'"

While this arrangement continued, Rosi was unable to save any money. She was making thirty-five dollars a month but was paying twenty of that for Wolfgang's care. Stern sent her some money, but other relatives helped her as well, including Little Gus, Julius Blumenthal, and Ludwig Hammerschlag, all cousins who had also been helped by Stern. Rosi was worn out by the commuting and hated being away from her son, but still realized how fortunate she was by comparison. "I do not believe that any one in this country can imagine what one feels when one arrives here, knowing that happy feeling to have escaped all the sadness and hardships over there [in Germany] and the grief and the pain . . . All the people [there] are so worn and powerless, I cannot find peace of heart, I do not find it fair, indulging in all the good things." Wanting to give something back to the families in Washington Heights, she began to plan a combination school and day care that she could operate for the children of hard-pressed Jewish refugees.[5]

With her struggles with English, her confusions about getting around the city, and her reliance on a handful of close friends, Rosi Spier was a fair representative of almost every German Jew who came to America in the late thirties. Rejected by their own country they feverishly tried to fit in to their new home and adopted American ways as fast as they could, all the while clinging to a few vestiges of what they had left behind. There was much to learn – and unlearn, for it took time to accept that the police in New York were not eager to crack them over the head. As Dorothy (Tea) Eichengruen had remarked, a policeman was "not somebody to be feared, but somebody to be trusted, somebody who is there to protect you." Many of the new arrivals were puzzled by the lack of uniforms in American society, not just Nazi uniforms, but military uniforms (American army officers made a point of traveling "in mufti" in the 1930s in order not to appear militaristic in this troubled time).

Would they ever be able to understand American customs, let alone begin to practice them? When she first arrived in New York, little Lore Moser pointed out to her parents something she had never seen before. "As we were walking down the gangplank, I said, 'Oh, look,' in German, because I knew no English, 'a black man.' This man who picked us up, a relative, said, 'Oh, in America, you must never say a black man. You must say 'a Negro.'" The strangeness continued when she began school. "My mother knew nothing about how children lived in America. The first day she sent me to school with an apron and the same thing we had in Germany, a little pencil box and a stylus that you used to write on the blackboard. That's how it was in Germany. People laughed when I got there." The fear of being laughed at, or worse, was a prime reason why many crowded into the Washington Heights neighborhood and never left.[6]

Trite as it is to say it, it is important to note that the German Jews who came over in the decade of the thirties adapted to America in different ways. From all accounts, Little Gus began to fit into his new surroundings quickly, while poor Julius found the adjustments so difficult that he was for a time made physically sick by his strange and challenging new world.

For most of those who came over courtesy of Herman Stern, it is important to remember they had lived in quite comfortable circumstances in Germany before the coming of Hitler. Many of the men had been physicians or other professionals, most of the rest had owned their own businesses. Being forced to flee their homes, they had come to a country that was said to be full of promise, only to find mostly low-paying jobs and limited opportunities to better their circumstances. A refugee from Germany, a woman in New York noted in her diary, had "to work three times as hard for a third of the salary that a so-called American would get. Who or what exactly is an American? I often scratch my head over that."[7]

Having grown up in poorer circumstances and emigrated decades earlier, Stern had strong feelings about thrift. He helped each of them as best as he could. He made efforts to find better jobs for several, lent money to several of the families, and helped the Henleins as well as others to establish their own businesses. But he also chided them to save money at every opportunity, and sometimes the recipient of this advice did not appreciate it. As one of the people he sponsored explained, off the record, "he really didn't grasp just how little we had when we arrived, and thought we spent money just to have a good time. We went out at night in order to meet people that might help us get ahead."[8]

Adeline Stern also tried to help some of the new arrivals become accustomed to American culture.Knowing that her husband had invested a good deal of himself and his reputation in sponsoring so many men and women, Adeline was quietly determined that those he helped would do their best to fit into American society. Dorothy Eichengruen later treasured memories of how Adeline helped her adjust to American ways. "I was intimidated [by Adeline] at first, but it didn't take me very long to get over it, and she taught me so much that first year I knew her, about certain foods and ways of doing things. I remember distinctly, I'd never eaten cantaloupe, and she served this cantaloupe with French dressing or something. I didn't like the taste at all, but I ate it. And she taught me how to clear the table, that one did not stack [dirty] dishes to carry them, that one carried them one at a time in America. Things of that nature."[9]

For his part, Herman urged each and every one of his relatives to "become American" in mind and heart. Each time Stern sent in another affidavit, he thought about how that person might be received in America. He gave a copy of his "Pride of Accomplishment" booklet to every person he sponsored. He pressed every parent to send his or her child into scouting, another of his own great loves. He was confident that the scouts would help the children learn English and better understand American mannerisms. Lore Moser's parents put her into Girl Scouts as soon as she was old enough to join: "our relatives in Yorkville had a daughter, a little older than I. She had outgrown her Girl Scout uniform. So that's how I got to be a Girl Scout. It was wonderful, wonderful. I learned English, and the Scout leader was just a lovely, lovely gal who really taught me a lot."

While Lotte Henlein also joined the Girl Scouts and adapted quickly to the behavior of the American teens she met at Valley City High School, she and her parents made major efforts to practice their Jewish faith as they had in Germany. They always traveled to Fargo to attend the synagogue at the High Holidays. "They had that beautiful synagogue which stood on Front Street. And they had a big congregation at the time. On the holidays it was full. They came from all around, God knows, from all around. It was packed." But Lotte knew her parents missed some of the more Orthodox forms of worship they had known back home. They also attempted to follow a kosher diet "as much as we could. We couldn't get the kosher meats, so what could we do?"[10]

Stern continued to find ways to help others escape by persuading friends to sign affidavits in his place. In the first months of 1939, he got Max Goldberg to sponsor a cousin of Hilda Levy, and himself sponsored Jakob and Selma Jonas and their daughter, relatives of Hugo Henlein. He persuaded furniture store owner Jake Levitz to sponsor a young couple named Erich and Hertha Landsberg, and then talked Alex Rosen, a businessman in Bismarck, into helping him sponsor two relatives of Ludwig Hammerschlag. He also told his friend Manny Sgutt that he planned to return to Fargo to "see if we can get a few more affidavits signed"[11]

The list of those who wanted Stern's help continued to grow. Arthur Spier, the brother of Rosi Klibanski, wrote to Stern, anxious to get a copy of the affidavit Stern had already supplied for him. "According to the waiting number [i.e. quota number] I received already," he wrote, "the waiting period might be two years, and under the current situation, I do not have a choice but to go to a temporary country, which would be for me either Holland or Sweden. Both countries demand the proof of a sponsorship for the [eventual immigration to the] USA." Spier had asked the American consul in Berlin for a copy of the affidavit, but this request had been turned down on the grounds that such a document was "confidential" until the consulate called on Spier for further information – "had I known what kind of a person the local consul is, I would have asked you from the very beginning to send the affidavit directly to my address."

Soon after this communication, Gertrude Stern sent Herman another letter concerning the situation in Paris. "With the last affidavit again you have done such a great, good deed. Dr. Schneider will be leaving soon with a French quota number, while the others will have to wait a while," Gertrude wrote, continuing with a recitation of the frantic efforts of others to get out as war drew closer. "Fritz Kann has fled without a passport or any luggage across the border into Belgium. There he can stay until his emigration to America. As I wrote already, the sponsorship paper [sent] for Erich Selz became invalid, since the parents were informed of his death [while being held in detention], but they never learned the cause nor the circumstances of Erich's death. Could you ask the gentleman, who wanted to procure this affidavit, to have it issued now for another protégé of mine? Perhaps you are considering me as impertinent. I do not know what else to do. It is about the son of a cousin of my mother, an especially very fine young man, who fled a few months ago to Holland, where my mother took him in, but he did not get a longer residence permit for Holland. If you cannot help him, the only way out is to go to China, and I would like to prevent him from going to China. Enclosed is his letter. See what you can do. Besides him, my mother is still working for my dear grandmother, my Uncle Hans Wertheimer and Dr. Mausbacher, to come live at her house. Dear grandfather Adolf has to go back to the hospital next week. He still cannot walk too well, and while he was in such pain, we ordered ex-rays for him, took him to the best specialist. You are right, politically it looks very bad for Europe."[12]

It was undeniably bad. In January of 1939, Hitler marked the sixth anniversary of his appointment as chancellor by giving a speech at the Reichstag. In it, Hitler warned "international Jewry" that if it somehow succeeded "in plunging mankind into another world war" then it would result in "the annihilation of the Jewish race in Europe." These were the strongest words he had used yet about a desire to initiate mass murder of the Jews in his growing empire. Many more now took this seriously and began to seek any way out they could find. From the end of 1938 to the beginning of November 1939, the American immigration quota for Germany and Austria had been completely filled for the first time in the decade.[13]

In America, many of the Jewish organizations stepped up their work to help the Jews still living in the fast-growing Reich. HIAS and the Joint Distribution Committee continued their campaigns to find new sponsors for Jewish refugees, while the Distribution Committee was trying to unify all the major fund-raising efforts (for the support of incoming Jewish refugees and for assistance to those who remained in Germany) into one large campaign. A Joint Distribution Committee report in December 1939 indicated that about one-third of the Jewish men had been sent to concentration camps after *Kristallnacht* and that Jews in smaller German communities were now being forcefully moved into larger cities to live in ghetto conditions; thousands of Jews were being fed only because public kitchens had been set up with foreign donations.

Once again, the major organizations could not agree on what tactics to follow in pressing the Federal government to liberalize its refugee policy. While the American Jewish Congress quietly lobbied Congress and the State Department, the American Jewish Committee organized rallies to publicize the crisis and urge people to continue boycotting German exports. Meanwhile, prominent American and British Jewish leaders, including Stephen Wise, were trying, with the State Department and Foreign Ministry help, to negotiate a new plan for mass Jewish emigration from Germany in exchange for *increased* purchases of German exports. But these talks with German representatives went on for months, too long for many of the poor souls in Germany.[14]

In Europe, Hitler harbored the hope that Chamberlain would back down from his pledge to defend Poland against German aggression. But while there is evidence that Chamberlain indeed did have second thoughts about his promise to Poland, British public opinion had been aroused by the betrayal of the remnant of Czechoslovakia and felt that this time the Empire must stand up to Germany. Members of Chamberlain's own government had also decided that the nation had to take a stronger line. Duff Cooper, a member of Chamberlain's cabinet, resigned from his post after Munich and spoke publicly on the need to stand firm against the Nazis. "A regime that begins by the public burning of books," he warned, "which continues by abolishing freedom of thought and speech, which persecutes religion and which seeks by cruelty to exterminate an ancient race that gave Christianity to the world among other benefits, is barbarous in the worst meaning of the word and is the enemy of true civilization." Faced with the possibility that enough Conservative leaders might turn away from him, and perhaps call for new leadership under Winston Churchill, Chamberlain rebuffed German offers to negotiate the Polish boundary question. The British intransigence infuriated Hitler. He told the League of Nations Commissioner for Danzig, "if the West is too stupid and blind to grasp [the chance for peace he offered at the cost of Poland] then I shall be compelled to come to an agreement with the Russians, beat the West, and then after their defeat turn against the Soviet Union with all my forces." The British Foreign Office thought it impossible that Hitler and Stalin could come to any agreement and so completely missed signs that agents for the Reich and the Soviet Union were already dickering over terms.[15]

Stern meanwhile made a frenzied effort to snatch a few more relatives and friends out of Hitler's grasp before war began. Once again, friends came forward to help him. In the last months of peace he found a farmer outside of Valley City who agreed to provide employment to both of Herman's brothers, Moses and Julius, and sent this information on to Stuttgart in the hope it would advance Moses's application for a visa. A young woman named Friedel Bein, whose relationship to Stern is unclear, was given an affidavit by Maurice Aved, one of the salesmen of the Fargo branch of New York Life. Bein used this document to migrate to Britain in the last month of peace, and remained there during most of the war. Robert Herbst contributed another affidavit to help the family of Hans Wertheim to obtain their own temporary visa for Britain, where they, too, would remain after the shooting began. From the correspondence it appears that Stern had never met Wertheim, but had still arranged to help him.[16]

By contrast Herbst knew Alice and Arthur Stern very well. Alice was the daughter of Herman's brother Julius. She left Montebaur about the time the Nazis required her parents to leave their town and move to one of the larger cities, where they had begun to concentrate their Jewish population. Stern invited Alice to live with him and Adeline in Valley City, but she declined the offer and stayed with her brother, Little Gus, before getting her own apartment. Later in 1939, a neighbor of Alice warned her uncle that Alice was having a difficult time making ends meet. Herman thanked the woman and said he would call Gus to check on her, commenting that the problem was likely due not to intentional neglect by her brother but rather to Alice being too proud to ask for help. Stern also attempted to sponsor a young man named Erich Reichenberg, who he identified as a distant cousin and also as Alice's fiancé. Sadly, the war blocked this last-minute effort.

Similarly, Stern's first cousin and boyhood friend Arthur Stern, who had lived near the Henlein's in Bad Schwalbach, arrived in New York and went to work in yet another of the clothing industries Stern did business with. Toward the end of the year, Stern agreed to help Arthur find sponsors for his own parents.[17]

Then there were the members of the Goldschmidt family of the village of Niedertiefenbach. Siegfried Goldschmidt, a second cousin on his mother's side of the family, was one of the last persons Stern was able to help without obtaining a co-sponsor. After receiving his visa, he arrived in New York sometime in late 1938 but did not get in touch with Stern. The next Stern heard of him was in January 1939, when the Jewish Welfare Society of Philadelphia notified him that, after doing farm work in upstate New York for several months, Goldschmidt had come to Philadelphia without any funds and with a serious hernia that would require surgery – could Stern help him? Stern hesitated, partly because Goldschmidt had relatives in New York who Stern had believed would help him. But he sent funds to pay for part of Goldschmidt's expenses in Philadelphia and then arranged for Goldschmidt to meet Little Gus in New York. Gus by then had a fairly decent job with one of the men's stores on Fifth Avenue. He promised his uncle to see to the problem and talk to Goldschmidt's cousins: "leave that case to me and I [will] do everything to get him work." A few months later, learning that another member of the family, named Ludwig Goldschmidt, was trying to get into Britain, "pending his re-emigration to the U.S.A.," Stern informed the German Jewish Aid Committee of London that he would try "to enlist some of my friends to do something."[18]

In a similar case, Stern had to deal with a problem dropped in his lap by one of the men he had helped years before. Leon Hayum had left Stern's employ in 1937 and returned to the east coast. That same year he and Stern had filed affidavits for the family of Leopold Schlafheimer, one of Hayum's relatives. Stern had signed an affidavit as a favor to Hayum, and clearly considered the Schlafheimers to be Hayum's responsibility. But in July of 1939, he received a letter from the National Refugee Service asking him to provide some money for Schlafheimer and his wife and daughter, who were still having "difficulty getting started in this country." Hayum had already explained that he could provide no help. Nonetheless Stern was disappointed and felt that, just as he had honored his promise to help Hayum, so Hayum should have been man enough to stand by his responsibility. Thus, when he sent a money order to Schlafheimer, he dryly commented in a note to Hayum that if Schlafheimer (or by implication Hayum) "wants to repay when he is able he can do so."[19]

There were others doing their part as well to help some of these refugees. David Naftalin, one of the most prominent members of Fargo's small Jewish community, used his influence to help find jobs for several of the men Stern brought to America. It was through him that Sally Jonas was able to get a job as a butcher in Fargo. He also helped others get work in the meat packing businesses in West Fargo and in his own hide and fur business. At one point Naftalin wrote to Stern suggesting that he speak to a couple of the men working in Fargo. "The recent arrivals for whom I get jobs have a superior complex with men that they are working alongside of . . . Mr. Levitz told me confidentially that one man is making too much trouble with the rest of the help," which could have meant one of the émigré's was urging his co-workers to organize in an area that was not friendly to unions. Naftalin and Jake Levitz nevertheless continued to co-sponsor some of Stern's affidavits. Middle America may have been identified with rampant isolationism so far as the situation in Europe was concerned, but there were quite a few who extended themselves and their resources to help Europe's increasingly despairing refugees.[20]

Myer Shark vividly remembered the young man that his Sigma Alpha Mu fraternity sponsored at the University of Minnesota. "This student that we sponsored, his name was Rolf Landshof, and he was a physicist. There was a letter of recommendation in his file from Albert Einstein, and Albert Einstein said in his letter that they should be sure and not reveal his letter, because if the Nazis heard that he recommended the young man, they'd never let him out." When Landshof was approved and arrived in Minnesota, he lived at the Sigma Alpha Mu house. Years later, Shark "got in touch with the national fraternity and I told them about Rolf Landshof and wondered if they knew about his whereabouts, and they came up with his address. He was retired now, but he was at a school. He was a scientist at a school in California someplace. I corresponded with him briefly, and he remembered me and, of course, I remembered him." Some other colleges in Minnesota arranged similar sponsorships.

Another man who made it to St. Paul because he was fortunate to have a cousin living there was Wilhelm Mueller. Mueller lived in the village of Lechenich. He was just a few weeks shy of his fortieth birthday when Hitler became chancellor in 1933. Like Stern's brothers, Willi Mueller was a veteran of the Great War, which meant nothing to the Nazis who drove him and his seventy-eight-year-old father out of their horse-trading business. Soon after, one of their neighbors gave the Muellers some friendly advice. "My mother had gall bladder colic, and we called the doctor. It was in the evening by the time he came in the house, the doctor, who was Gentile, and he was sitting there and waited until we were alone, and all of a sudden he said, loud, 'Get out of here!' So we got up [to leave].   And he said, 'No, no, I don't mean that.' Then he asked my mother if she had relatives in America, and then it came to us, you know he wants us to go to America. That doctor saved our lives."

Willi's mother had a cousin who lived in St. Paul, "a man named Henry Weiler. He was born in Switzerland. My mother wrote a letter to him, and within two weeks he got the affidavit ready and sent it to us." Weiler sponsored both Willi and his brother Ludwig, who was two years younger. They were able to obtain their visas and leave Germany in June of 1938. Weiler owned several businesses and was able to give both men a job in one of his St. Paul stores. When he found that they did not like living in a larger city he agreed to help them move to Fargo and go to work in one of his other investments – a stockyard in West Fargo. Weiler also helped the brothers fill out papers to sponsor their parents, who soon after *Kristallnacht* left

Germany for France.[21]

Jake Levitz, one of the businessmen in Fargo, filed an affidavit to sponsor someone independent of Stern's list of relatives, a woman named Heti Lowenstein who wanted to come to America and marry one of Levitz's furniture store employees. After having some difficulty getting action on the affidavit, he asked Stern for help. Stern sent the file on to Gerald Nye, asking if the Senator could do something about the "most unusual and unreasonable" demands of the State Department. Nye obliged by contacting Herve L'Heureux in Stuttgart and together they worked out a satisfactory arrangement, leading Stern, just a few weeks before Germany attacked Poland, to thank Nye once again: "your intervention always seems to bring the desired results."[22]

There was also the case of Erwin Stiefel, a young man from Duisburg who Tea Eichengruen had known before she left Germany. "There was a Jewish athletic club in Duisburg and I joined it, and that's how I met him. He was actually the instructor for gymnastics or something like that." Stiefel was also related to close friends of Tea's parents, so she saw him in passing from time to time until she left Germany. Then in the summer of 1938, a few months after she arrived in New York, she received a request from a family named Ruben in Kansas City. "Erwin had relatives who got to America sometime earlier. The family by the name of Ruben. They wrote to me and said they knew of me, because they knew my parents. Would I please go to the pier [in New York] on such-and-such a date and meet Erwin? I rented him a room somewhere near where I lived. I was still working for this nasty woman from Berlin and had to ask her for a few hours off to go and get him. It was terribly hot. I was not used to the heat."

Erwin Stiefel was himself in a poor mood when he disembarked. "Unfortunately, he had had a very terrible experience. His father had committed suicide. It was connected to Erwin's leaving. Erwin's sister had gotten married and left Germany immediately. Erwin left a week later, so this man was left by himself. He was an Eastern Jew. So what was there for him to look forward to? His wife [Erwin's mother] had died very early on. She was forty-two when she died of breast cancer in 1929, I think. So he was left alone, and he committed suicide right after Erwin left." Young Stiefel was given the news while on board his ship to America. Shocked, probably guilty at having left his father alone, Erwin and Tea "just did not get along at all, and I really couldn't wait for him to leave to go to Kansas City." Three years would pass before Tea saw him again.[23]

More help might have been possible, but there was still a great deal of economic hardship in the rural parts of the region. A memoir of one young Jewish woman living in the western part of North Dakota underscored this sad fact with poignant detail about her father's farm and small store in the town of Halliday. "Even our business competitors who operated a store across the street from ours . . . gave a helping hand during one particular period of stress. They were not just competitors but very good friends as well. . . . Farm loans were made available under President Franklin Delano Roosevelt's New Deal programs to farmers. Although we today complain loudly of governmental bureaucracies, these farm agencies were nonetheless the means by which we and countless others were able to keep our land and maintain our farming operations. . . . The year after my family left Dakota [due to her father's failing health], it was as Dad had predicted. After seven years of drought, in the fall of 1941, western North Dakota produced its first bumper crop. Unfortunately, Dad did not live to see this."[24]

Mindful of the difficulties that still existed, Stern asked his friends to tread lightly when talking to people about affidavits or donations to his rural resettlement idea. "I am still flooded with requests for affidavits," he wrote a friend in Grand Forks, but warned him "do not push the matter too hard if you sense that it is not a popular subject." His friend responded that there was "a certain lack of initiative on the part of certain persons here," but that he intended to "do my share" to get some more signed affidavits. Stern thanked him and commented, "Each day lost may mean the loss of a life [in Germany]." Stern pressed his colony idea on groups in New York well into that last summer of peace.[25]

As August began, few doubted that war was coming. German troops were already massing on the Polish border and the Poles had begun calling up their reserves. Hitler still hoped that he could draw Britain and France into another agreement that would give him what he wanted in Poland, but he was equally prepared to do a deal with Stalin if he had to. In April, Stalin had replaced his foreign minister and French diplomats had warned Chamberlain's government that this move indicated that the Soviet dictator was willing to treat with Hitler. Chamberlain still doubted such a bargain was truly possible. As a consequence, the military mission he sent to Moscow to talk about joint defensive measures was given no real power to make any binding arrangements. The talks dragged on slowly; by mid-month Stalin was convinced he could get nothing substantial from the British. Hitler made up his own mind at about the same moment. On August 20, he sent a personal telegram to Stalin, asking him to receive his foreign minister, Ribbontrop, to discuss matters of "grave importance."

Stalin knew a firm offer when he saw one. Ribbontrop went to Moscow on August 23, and the two nations concluded a non-aggression pact within a matter of hours. A secret protocol to the treaty gave Russia a "free hand" in relation to Finland and the Baltic States, Germany disclaimed any interest in parts of Romania, and Poland was divided between the two along the Vistula, San and Narev rivers. In return, Stalin tacitly agreed to stand aside while Poland was overrun by the German armies. No shot had yet been fired but the Second World War had begun in a Russian parlor.

Or had it? Hitler postponed the planned attack on Poland for five days in the hope that Britain and France would now come forward with a proposal for a negotiated settlement. France refused to move until Britain did, and Chamberlain may have been tempted to negotiate, but British public opinion was now dead set against another Munich-style retreat. When Germany attacked Poland in the early hours of September 1, 1939, by sending their tanks roaring across the border and using their vastly superior air force to blast the Polish planes into piles of debris, Chamberlain continued to hesitate. Then on September 3, pressured by members of his cabinet, he sent Hitler an ultimatum stating that Britain would declare war if German troops did not withdraw from Poland. Hitler rejected the warning. A reluctant and depressed Chamberlain used BBC radio to tell the British people that they were now at war. Although he admitted that Britain was now committed to fighting an "evil thing," his was hardly a fighting speech. "You can imagine what a bitter blow it is to me that all my long struggle to win peace has failed," he said in the most telling passage. "Yet I cannot believe that there is anything more or anything different that I could have done that would have been more successful."

In Berlin, the German citizens appeared no happier than Chamberlain. Bill Shirer, still covering Germany for CBS News, watched a group of men and women on the Wilhelmplatz listen to the loudspeakers announce Britain's declaration of war. "When it was finished, he later wrote, "there was not a murmur. They just stood there as they were before. Stunned. The people cannot realize yet that Hitler has led them into a world war."

There were some who did realize the gravity of the war, however. In Dresden, Victor Klemperer, a scholar forcibly retired because of his Jewish ancestry, recorded the news of the expanding violence in his diary. Many Germans were acting "ten thousand times more arrogant than in [19]14," he wrote, and he was certain the war would only make the plight for him and the rest of Germany's Jewish population worse than ever: "as I lie down to sleep, I think: Will they come for me tonight? Will I be shot, will I be put in a concentration camp?"[26]

The outbreak of the war hit Herman Stern and those who he had helped very hard. In New York, Tea Eichengruen worried that war meant her parents would be trapped in Germany and wondered what might happen to her brother in Holland. In Valley City, Lotte Henlein thought how sad it was for her father to have been forced out of his country and then be in America watching it at war again. In Chicago, Julius Stern worried about his family in Paris, while in New York, Alice wondered if her parents would be safe in Germany.

As for Herman, he was saddened to see Germany once again at war, but unlike 1914, this time he had no confusions about who was at fault for causing the conflict or who he wanted to win. He knew Hitler and the Nazis had to be destroyed before his family could be safe. What would happen to his relatives now, he wondered. Adolf and Dora and Gustave's family were still in Paris, which could be attacked at any moment by the *Luftwaffe*. He was not certain where in Germany his brothers Julius or Moses were, making it all the more difficult to continue trying to get American entry visas for them. And what about the others he had filed affidavits for, could they get out? All he knew for certain was that he was still unwavering in his determination to help them all.

Notes

1. Here and below, Steiner transcript, pp. 25-34.

2. Dorothy Spielberg [of the National Refugee Service] to Edward Stern, March 4, 1940, Jewish Refugee Resettlement file, Stern Papers. The letter specifically notes that Steiner had a wife and that both he and Greta had "fair command of English."

3. Steven M. Lowenstein, *Frankfurt on the Hudson: The German-Jewish Community 0f Washington Heights, 1933-1983* (Detroit: Wayne State University Press, 1989), esp. pp. 35-56.

4. Gloria DeVidas Kirchheimer and Manfred Kirchheimer, *We Were So Beloved: Autobiography of a German Jewish Community* (Pittsburgh: University of Pittsburgh Press, 1997), pp. 35-37; Herman Stern to Samuel Honaker, June 13, 1938, Rosi Klibanski file, Stern Papers. The State Department used Rosi Spier's married name in all their records and correspondence.

5. Kirschheimer, *We Were So Beloved,* pp. 38-39; Rosi Klibanski letters to Stern, February 5, March 7 and 17, 1939, all in German Correspondence file, Stern Papers.

6. Stiefel transcript, p. 45; Moser transcript, pp. 7, 12.

7. Hertha Nathorff, "An American Life," in Mark M. Anderson, ed., *Hitler's Exiles: Personal Stories of the Flight From Nazi Germany to America* (New York: The New Press, 1998), p. 301.

8. Information on Gus Stern from his daughters Joan Mazza and Frances Furgiuele; information about Julius Stern from Lotte Stern, his second wife. The remark about Stern's views on how his relatives should be frugal comes from someone who asked not to be identified.

9. Stiefel transcript, p. 41.

10. Ullmann transcript, pp. 28-31.

11. Affidavits for Jakob and Selma Jonas in Jonas family file; Bertha Levy to Herman Stern, January 9, 1939, German Correspondence file; Stern to Alex Rosen, February 8, 1939, Vasen family file; Stern to Emanuel Sgutt, February 28, 1939, Landsberg family file. All these are in Stern Papers, as is the Hammerschlag file which has brief details on Fritz and Edith Hammerschlag, sponsored by Alex Rosen and Stern. In her January 9 letter, Mrs. Levy thanked Stern for obtaining an affidavit for her son Alfons, but noted that her son "unfortunately is not at home, but since November 1938 is in a [concentration] camp in protective custody." Alfons younger brother was also in the camp. The two boys apparently never got out of Germany.

12. Arthur Spier to Stern, January 5, 1939, and Gertrude Vasen Stern to Stern, February 25, 1939, both in German Correspondence file, Stern Papers.

13. Dwork and van Pelt, *Holocaust: A History*, pp. 259-60; Richard Breitman and Alan Kraut, *American Refugee Policy and the Crisis Among European Jewry* (Bloomington: University of Indiana Press, 1987), p. 112.

14. Yehuda Bauer, *My Brother's Keeper* (Philadelphia: The Jewish Publication Society of America, 1974), pp. 254-78; Breitman and Kraut, *American Refugee Policy*, p. 96.

15. H. Agar, *The Darkest Year: Britain Alone, June 1940-June 1941* (Doubleday and Co., 1973), p. 33; Noakes, ed., *Nazi Germany,* vol. 3, p. 739.

16. Stern to American Consul Stuttgart, April 6, 1939, Moses Stern file; Frank Heimes to Julius Stern, April 5, 1939, Julius Stern file; Maurice Aved to Stern, February 15, 1940, Freidel Bein file; Hans Wertheim to Stern, January 13, 1939, Hans Wertheim file, all in Stern Papers.

17. Stern to Mrs. L. Weinberger, July 28, 1939, Alice Stern file; Berte Taubenblatt (for National Council of Jewish Women) to Stern, June 12, 1939, Reichenberg file; Stern to American Consul, Stuttgart, December 8, 1939, Arthur Stern file, Stern Papers. Additional information on Erich Reichenberg from Fran Furgiuele and Joan Mazza, daughters of Gus Stern and nieces of Alice Stern, in letter to Shoptaugh, February 23, 2004. This states that Erich Reichenberg apparently died in Europe and that "Alice was devastated for the rest of her life."

18. Stern to Jewish Welfare Society of Philadelphia, March 20 and March 25, 1939, Gustav Stern to Herman Stern, [March 1939], and Stern to Jewish Aid Committee (London), March 13, 1939, all Goldschmidt file, Stern Papers. The letters in this file concerning Ludwig Goldschmidt, and his desire to emigrate to Britain, are incomplete, but it is evident that the man had not emigrated by the time the war began.

19. Charles White to Stern, July 24, 1939 and Stern to Leo Hayum, August 21, 1939, Hayum-Schlafheimer file, Stern Papers.

20. David Naftalin to Herman Stern, July 17, 1939, Jonas Family file, Stern Papers.

21. Myer Shark transcript, pp. 18-19; William Mueller, interview with Shoptaugh, May 18, 1999, transcript, pp. 1-10. Like so many others, Mueller changed his given name to William when he took out his American citizenship papers.

22. Stern to Nye, May 17, 1939 and July 17, 1939, Lowenstein file, Stern Papers.

23. Myer Shark transcript, pp. 17-18; Stiefel transcript, pp. 21-22, 46-47.

24. Toba Marcovitz Geller, "Our Family," (1976) printed family history The Geller Collection of the North Dakota Jewish Project, Upper Midwest Jewish Archives, University of Minnesota.

25. Stern to Dr, Irvine Lavine, January 21 and February 1, 1939, and Lavine to Stern, [January 1939] in "Dr. Irvine Lavine" file, Stern Papers. See also Erich Warburg to Stern, June 20, 1939, Stephen Wise file, Stern Papers.

26. A. J. P. Taylor, *Origins of the Second World War* (London: Penguin Books ed., 1991), pp. 302-36; Shirer, *Berlin Diary,* p. 150; Victor Klemperer, *I Will Bear Witness: A Diary of the Nazi Years, 1933-1941* (New York: Randon House, 1998), p. 307.

Chapter Thirteen
Trapped

Michel Stern was barely four when the British bombers began their nocturnal flights over Paris in the late summer of 1940. He could still vividly recall the drone of the aircraft engines sixty years later. "I recall being in the bomb shelters and although I know there were no bombs [deliberately] dropped in Paris, there were air raids and bombs dropped nearby. I recall specifically going down to the basement of the apartment and sitting sideways [against the wall], and listening to the air raids. You could hear boom, boom, boom, whatever that was."[1]

Like young Michel, most of the French had difficulty grasping how quickly their world had come crashing down. Ever since 1918, the French Army had been considered the best in the world, and although experts predicted that the German Army, with their powerful air force and armored divisions, would be a formidable opponent, no one thought that a quick German victory was possible. Indeed, most military writers predicted that when Germany finally attacked, the situation would become a stalemate, a bloody battle in the trenches similar to that of the Western Front in the Great War. As Bill Shirer noted in his diary, the Allied leaders "made the fatal mistake of thinking that this war would be fought on the same general lines as the last war." So did practically everyone else.

Then the whole world was shocked when, in mid-May, the German tanks had roared into Belgium and northern France, blasted the French forces in front of them out of the way, and within weeks had thrust to the English channel, cutting off the cream of the French and British forces to the north. Within another week, Britain began evacuating its defeated army from Dunkirk. The French Army hastily tried to regroup and keep the Germans from smashing through the rest of their defenses and seizing Paris. But despite everything they tried, it made no difference. When the Germans broke through again, the French government declared Paris an open city and fled south, with thousands upon thousands of Parisians following in their wake, clogging the roads, jamming the trains, fleeing the onslaught of "the Boche." When German forces did enter Paris on June 14, the city was half-empty. The Sterns had remained in the city because Gustave, who in addition to being a German exile, was a father of two, and forty years old, had been called up for military service in the last days of the fighting. As Michel remembered, "my father was drafted into the French army and he served in a colonial regiment as a cook. He told many stories of his adventures as a cook at the particular camp that he was at." Fearing that Gustave would never be able to find them again if she left with the children and Gustave's parents, Gertrude had decided to stay in Paris.

The government of Reynaud fell two days after the Germans took over Paris. A new Premier, Henri Petain, asked Hitler for an armistice on June 16. Six days later, the Germans imposed their humiliating terms on the French: Germany would occupy the northern half of France, including Paris, and all of the channel coast; several hundred thousand French prisoners of war would remain in German hands until a final peace treaty was concluded; France would pay all of the costs of the German occupation and in addition would turn over to the Germans any "German subjects living in France." With resistance impossible, the French had little choice but to accept.[2]

In Paris, Gertrude and her children waited for Gustave to return home. "When the French capitulated," Michel remembers, "he was interned with his battalion. Sometime after the capitulation he was released and came back to our apartment in Paris." I remember I came into my parents' room. My father was wearing blue and white pajamas. That was the first time I'd seen him in months." The Gestapo already had begun seizing the property of German Jews living in Paris, in some cases entering their homes and taking jewelry, paintings and any other valuables they found to their liking. But Michel did not recall such an intrusion into their home. The sausage casing business that Gustave had managed was all but ruined by the war, but the family had managed to hide some money. The challenge now facing the Sterns was to keep out the way of the arrogant victors. A number of German Jews in Paris chose to commit suicide in the weeks following the armistice.

In Vichy, the capitol of the unoccupied parts of France, the American ambassador studied the armistice terms and talked to some of the more pro-German members of the new French government. He informed the State Department that he expected Petain and his followers to willingly collaborate with Hitler: "their physical and moral defeat has been so absolute that they have accepted completely for France the fate of becoming a province of Nazi Germany." Vichy would show greater independence than this assessment feared, but they would make no effort to protect the Jews in France from Hitler's wrath. Petain's government willingly adapted the German anti-Semitic policies as their own. One month after accepting the armistice, Vichy repealed a statute prohibiting the press from attacking ethnic and religious groups. French newspapers soon released a flood of anti-Jewish vitriol. In October, Vichy banned Jews from most public service jobs, from teaching, and from being part of the French media. Then they gave the local districts of southern France carte blanche to intern any foreign-born Jews the local authorities deemed suspicious. The French variant of the Holocaust was beginning.[3]

In Paris, young Michel knew little about the persecutions of the Vichy regime. But he understood that the Nazis, who had driven his family from their home in Germany, were now in Paris and could hurt him any time they wished. Watching them from his home, strutting along the streets, eating and sipping wine at the sidewalk cafes, he also noticed that food was soon more meager in their apartment, a consequence of the large amounts of grain and other victuals being exported to Germany. "So we lived in the apartment, me, my brother, my grandparents, and my parents for something like six months during the occupation." His brother, who was six years older and remembered his German, picked up some much needed cash for the family by running errands for German soldiers. "I also know that my parents were very concerned about me because I also spoke German fluently at that time, childish German and French, and they were concerned that I would blurt something out about us in German. They instructed me never to speak German in front of any German," for fear he might draw too much attention to the family.

While still in Paris, the Sterns had visitors: the wife and daughter of Sally Kann. Erna and her daughter Erika had been to hell and back. When Germany attacked Belgium in May of 1940, the Belgian government immediately rounded up all of its German refugees, which included Fritz and Sally Kann and Sally's wife and daughter. Erika Kann was then about twelve years old. "The Belgian government had decided that we were Germans and thus enemies of Belgium," she recalled. The Kanns, with many others, were first sent to a prison in Antwerp. "There the men were separated from the women and children. That is when I saw my father and his brother for the last time. Three days later we were sent to the French-Belgian border, where we were handed over to the French Authorities." Belgium was collapsing quickly under the German onslaught, so the Kanns and many other German Jews were taken south, escorted by French soldiers. "For 10 days we traversed France in cattle wagons," on roads filled with hundreds of others who were fleeing the advancing German troops. "Our guardians were mainly Sengelese soldiers." Passing through to the south of France they went on toward the Mediterranean coast. "We arrived on the 23rd of May, 1940, in the Camp de Gurs."[4]

Gurs, a town in the Pyrenees, was the site of internment camps where the French had decided to hold foreign-born Jews. The camps had been built for refugees from the Republican forces of the Spanish Civil War. The French now herded into these compounds anyone they thought might be a threat – communists, political "undesirables," German and other foreign-born refuges. Sally and Fritz Kann were sent to a men's camp, Erika and her mother to a camp for women. About two-thirds of the total population of the camps was Jewish. The conditions in the camps were disgraceful, overcrowded and lacking most of the necessities for a healthy or even clean existence. The huts were surrounded by seas of mud. Water was available at only a few facets, requiring people to stand in line for hours in order to get a small pan of the brackish liquid. The food given to the refugees was little more than a thin gruel made up of chickpeas boiled with animal bones, a few potatoes and vegetables and, on occasion, some unidentifiable meat. The huts were almost bereft of wood or coal for heating until well into the winter of 1940-41 which, when combined with the malnutrition, dysentery, pneumonia, and other illnesses in the camps, caused the death of over eight hundred men, women and children by the coming of spring. This did not stop a Petainist newspaper editorial from asking "how long shall we house and feed these undesirables," and suggesting that they be handed wholesale over to the Germans.

The guards at the camps ranged for the most part from indifferent to brutal. It was reported that the commandant of the women's camp at Gurs was drunk for days on end during the summer and fall of 1940. It was also reported discipline among the guards was poor and that many of the woman found it fairly easy to steal or forge release certificates or simply walk away when no one was paying attention. Walking away is exactly what Erna and Erika did. "My mother and I were able to escape from the camp early one morning when no one was paying attention to us. Gustav[e] Stern had let us know, through a letter from the Red Cross, that if we could get to somebody, an associate of his, that there would be money waiting for us so as to enable us to continue our journey." Making their way to Paris, paying for food and shelter along the way with the money from Stern's friend, they briefly saw the Sterns and then went on to Belgium, crossing the border late at night. In a 1936 letter to his son Julius in Chicago, Adolf Stern had commented that he thought Erna Kann "cannot speak one reasonable word, makes no sense, only stupid nonsense." Yet four years later Erna had found her way out of Gurs and managed to get her daughter and herself back to Belgium without detection, an achievement of considerable daring and level-headedness.

Reaching Wommelgem the Kanns found "there was nothing left of our farm." It could have ended right there had not their Belgian neighbors decided to help them hide from the Germans. In order to decrease their chances of being discovered, Erika and her mother separated. Erna Kann hid in a farmhouse near Wommelgem. "My mother did not go outside for 28 months." Erika was taken to a village near Bruges, where the in-laws of one of her former neighbors had a farm. "I was taken there to the house of Theodore Saelens. He and his wife had 14 children, seven were already married and the family [living on the farm] consisted at that time of 35 people." Erika simply disappeared into the throng. Saelens and his wife had never met Erika and knew that she was Jewish and to hide her could mean the death for all of them. But he took her in. "From that moment I became their 15th child. Today I am myself a grandmother of eight, and I don't know whether I would have the courage to give shelter to an unknown girl and thus endanger my whole family." But Saelens accepted the risk and Erika survived.[5]

Back in Paris, Gustave was worried that the Kann's visit may have endangered his own family. The Germans might come looking for him or perhaps for his father. Perhaps they would begin rounding up all the Jews in Paris and force them into a ghetto, or worse. He decided that the family needed to make its way into Vichy territory and wait there for the visas that his Uncle Herman was trying to get for them. Michel never learned the details, but somehow his father learned of French men who, for a fee, would sneak people around the German guard posts at the border between the occupied territories and Vichy France. Gustave understood that it could be dangerous to hire someone to take them across these "escape lines," because the Germans were also paying French men and women to betray those who tried to flee. But he felt that they had to take the chance. Adolf Stern sent his brother in North Dakota a telegram explaining that the family intended to leave Paris because the Germans "are putting people in concentration camps on very short notice."[6]

Michel, not yet five, described "the first time we tried to get out, [which] was in early 1941. My father had hired some guides to take us across the demarcation line. We drove our car up to a point, left the car there at this point, and the guides started taking us through the woods to the demarcation line, but the Germans knew that people were coming [through the woods south of Paris]. There were guard dogs that my parents heard; and that I may have a recollection of, although I'm not sure. When that happened, the guides disappeared; they just fled. So my parents and my grandparents and brother and I had to come back. My father carried me back. Somehow we got back to the car and went back to Paris."

The Sterns waited for several months before making a second attempt to cross the boundary line in May, this time by dividing the family among different guides. "My father arranged to have us smuggled out," Michel recalled, "but when I mean smuggled out, we didn't go together. My father and mother had one guide, my grandparents had another guide, and my brother and I were taken [by a third guide] by bicycle across the demarcation line. We had a little sidecar with the bicycle hooked on to it. The guide put a blanket over us [in the sidecar]." This time, the late night journey was not interrupted. Their guide took Michel and his brother into Vichy. "We were to meet everyone [at a rendezvous, possibly at Briare] on a certain date over the demarcation line. We got to the place, but no one else was there. The guide stayed with us there overnight and the next day my parents showed up and my grandparents showed up. My parents had been delayed because their guide's father was concerned that the Germans were having [military] maneuvers that night and they shouldn't go [until the next night]. Ultimately, we met and we took a train to Marseilles. I remember the train very well."

Marseilles, France's principal port on the Mediterranean, was already a crossroads for refugees who hoped to stay out of German hands. Former German labor leaders, socialist leaders, modernist writers, musicians and artists, scientists and journalists, and countless numbers of Jews, all came to Marseilles in the hope that from there they might find a way out, to Spain or Portugal or North Africa, or perhaps to England or Canada or America. As the exiles and refugees came to Marseilles, so too did representatives of the groups dedicated to helping them, including men and women from HIAS, the International Red Cross, and various churches and private charities. The Joint Distribution Committee, which already was spending over three million dollars a year on Jewish refugees across Europe, began sending substantial amounts of aid to the large numbers of Jews in Vichy, France.[7]

The Sterns crowded themselves into a tiny apartment, the rent for which was paid, Michel believed, by the money his father had managed to bring along from Paris, with additional funds sent by Gertrude's mother, who had already immigrated to Chile with other members of the Vasen family. "My guess is that [my parents] weren't impoverished, but I'm sure that everything that my grandmother sent supplemented whatever they had taken with them. They had left everything in Paris in the apartment in the care of a man by the name of Schiffman. He stored all the goods in a warehouse including my father's musical library, his piano, everything, even our gas masks. Ultimately it was shipped to the United States in 1949, gas masks and all."

At Marseilles, Gustave did some volunteer work for the American HIAS office, which may have afforded him some protection from the Vichy state police who seemed to enjoy hassling Jews in the city. Through HIAS, Gustave attempted to find out the condition of Fritz and Sally Kann, who were still incarcerated, but his questions were rebuffed by the French authorities. He decided not to try again for fear he would only harm their situation. In the meantime, he learned that Vichy was not permitting many refugees to leave France, even if they had all their proper papers and permits. Freda Kirchwey, a correspondent for *Nation,* explained the tragic dilemma: "Only the other day it was learned that Germans and persons from conquered territories can no longer obtain exit visas from the local French authorities. Applications for exit visas are sent to Vichy, and it is believed the Petain government submits them to the armistice commission at Wiesbaden. This means not only that applications by known antifascists will be turned down; that is certain and only relatively tragic. It means, much more crucially, that every application will reveal to the Gestapo the whereabouts of one of its victims. . . . Many antifascists who have already secured that most precious of all documents – an American visitor's visa – are trapped."[8]

Another American who watched the calamity unfolding was a mercurial, difficult, and stubborn young American named Varian Fry who had been sent to France by a coordinating group in New York, called the Emergency Rescue Committee, in order to help "prominent" refugees get to the United States by using special visas obtained from the State Department through Eleanor Roosevelt. While he carried out this task, Fry made notes about the camps. These notes contain heartbreaking glimpses of what life was like for those trapped there. In his notes about Gurs, made from a visit to it in the last days of 1940, Fry noted that on a typical day fifteen to twenty people died, commonly from pneumonia or illnesses associated with malnourishment. He noted that the barracks for the internees had almost no windows, few had any lights except for small kerosene lamps, stoves and fire wood were nonexistent, and the roofs of most of the buildings leaked. The daily food ration consisted of 350 grams of bread, soup, and tiny handfuls of rice and macaroni. Meat was added to the soup only once each week. One internee told him that they welcomed the rats that proliferated in the camp because these could be caught and eaten. The French had tightened their security since Erika and her mother had escaped; the only time a person could leave the camp now was to attend one of the frequent funerals. Fry also noted that the American Rescue Center was distributing blankets and clothing to many people in the camps, which was very important because many had been interned with nothing more than what they were wearing. Similar reports from the Joint Distribution Committee corroborated Fry's observations.[9]

Just days after the Stern family arrived in Marseilles, the German Central Office for Emigration in Berlin sent an order to all its consulates directing that no more documents should be issued permitting Jews to leave Germany or its occupied territories. Further immigration of Jews, the order concluded ominously, was being curtailed in preparation for a "doubtless imminent final solution" to the Jewish question.[10]

Soon after their arrival in Marseilles, Adolf sent a telegram to his brother Herman to inform him of their new location. But Herman was to be bitterly disappointed if he thought this would somehow expedite the issuing of visas to his relatives. The threat of war had made several of the consuls even more uneasy about the visa process. In Stuttgart, Samuel Honaker spent the last months of peace dealing with charges that some of his clerks had accepted bribes from German Jews in return for giving their visa applications preferential treatment. As he informed the State Department, at the very end of 1938, he learned that one of his "German clerks," a man named Emil Friesch, had been arrested by the German authorities on the suspicion that Friesch was "conniving with Jews to get money out of Germany in contravention of the German foreign exchange laws."

Honaker at first hoped this might be an isolated incident, that Friesch had been "denounced by some neighbor endeavoring to obtain the favor of the Police by directing suspicion towards him as a person having contact with members of the Jewish race." But he soon realized that Friesch indeed had been peddling favors, for Friesch soon confessed to the German police that he had "accepted money from prospective immigrants" in return for "information which would facilitate their immigration to the United States." Friesch implicated several other German nationals who worked in the visa section. One was Erich Staginnus, another clerk, who had been impersonating Herve L'Heureux and visiting some applicants, telling them that he would advance their applications in return for money. By searching the file cabinets in the consulate, Honaker found envelopes marked as the "private property of Erich Staginnus" and containing over nineteen thousand Reichsmarks. Honaker also uncovered evidence that in return for shares in this loot, clerks working with Friesch and Staginnus had falsified some of the records in applicants' files, causing L'Heureux, taking the information as genuine, to place these applicants higher on the quota list. "This," Honaker was embarrassed to admit, "might have enabled a number of applicants to leave Germany many months, or even years, before their regular turn on the waiting list may have been reached."

In all, Honaker dismissed from their jobs Friesch, Staginnus and four other German nationals who had worked in the visa section. All six ended up in the hands of the Gestapo. This swindle perpetrated within the consulate was a black mark for Honaker's record and he knew it, the more so since most of these clerks "had been employed in the Visa Section for many years." The best he could offer in his defense was to assure Washington that he had acted quickly enough to get rid of the guilty clerks before their scheme took on "the proportions of a 'racket'." He also ordered L'Heureux and Hugh Teller to review some six thousand application files in order to discover if any refugee had actually been able to leave Germany with a visa issued as a result of bribery. So far, Honaker was pleased to note, they had found so such cases – he wanted Washington to know he had stopped the scheme before it became a real scandal. He also made a point of saying that he was "confident" that the larcenous clerks had never approached an applicant who had had the benefit of moving up the quota list as a result of endorsements from "prominent citizens in the United States, including Senators, Congressmen, and Governors of various states."

Finally, Honaker warned the remaining clerks in the consulate to bear in mind that some applicants for visas, particularly those of the "Jewish race." might, out of anxiety and fear of "the persecutory measures to which they were subject," resort to "sacrificing their scruples" in order to get out of Germany as soon as possible. In other words, a clerk who demonstrated zealousness in helping a German Jew would be suspected of venality.[11]

Investigations like this were undertaken in almost all of the American consulates as the signs of war drew nearer, and many German Jews became frantic to escape. Just a week before Germany invaded Poland, Honaker wrote another report in response to claims that some of the consulate personnel were helping "refugees smuggle jewelry out of Germany." This time he was happy to note that the swindle was carried out by German criminals who posed as consular clerks and persuaded some Jewish applicants for visas that, for a fee, they could alter the quota list and also use the consulate to transfer more of the immigrant's money to Switzerland. The Gestapo had moved in and arrested the con men, and Honaker reassured Washington that no one working at the consulate had been involved in this particular scheme.[12]

Incidents such as these only made Washington even more uneasy about admitting large numbers of European refugees, and the coming of the war prompted the State Department to order a tightening of security in the matter of visa approvals. Just days after Germany completed its conquest of Poland, the Department ordered every consulate in Germany to carefully review all visa applications, looking for any sign that an applicant harbored "subversive ideas." The consuls themselves were instructed specifically to reject visas if their investigations led them to have "any doubt whatsoever concerning the alien." It was 1931 all over again, only this time the motivating factor was not hard times but fear of espionage and subversion. The war had made neutral America fearful of any German immigrants as potential saboteurs.

This concern was most evident in the office of Breckinridge Long, a personal friend of Franklin Roosevelt who was appointed in the fall of 1939 as special Assistant Secretary of State in charge of "emergency war measures." Long's job included the growing refugee crisis, and to this task, he brought a specific viewpoint. For he was convinced that a great many of the German refugees seeking entry into the United States were threats to American security and that he should use his office to prevent the "penetration of German agents" who would seek to take advantage of the "courtesy and hospitality of the United States for ulterior purposes."

Long's job made him the primary contact between the State Department and the numerous organizations that were trying to get approval for the immigration of more refugees. In numerous meetings with its members, he became convinced that too many of the groups were naïve about the dangers of German spies entering the country while posing as refugees. When meeting with a group of rabbis in December of 1940, he found their arguments tiresome. "They had another list of persons to whom we should grant [emergency] visas.

I explained to them the policy of the Department . . . [that the persons on the list should be] applying for [regular quota] immigrant visas rather than asking us to start again the issuance of [emergency] visitor's visas when the emergency was not as it had been [earlier in the summer]." In several memos, Long complained that the President's Advisory Committee on Political Refugees, which Roosevelt had created after the Evian Conference, were either deliberately misleading the State Department or were hopelessly naïve, because many of the names they submitted were of people who would use "the courtesy and hospitality of the United State for ulterior purposes."

Members of the President's Advisory Committee responded in kind, complaining that Long was deliberately obstructing the Committee's attempts to obtain emergency visas to use in rescuing intellectuals and political opponents of the Nazis. They pointed out that only fifteen visas were issued from a list of over five hundred persons they had recommended for emergency visas. Their members and spokespersons of other organizations further argued that Long showed distinct anti-Semitic bias in his lack of sympathy for the refugees, a charge that many historian writers have subsequently repeated. Newer research, however, suggests that Long's attitude was little different than that of most senior State personnel who were absolutely convinced that many refugees would either be agents of the Nazis when they arrived or would soon become agents because the Nazis would threaten their relatives back at home.[13]

The suspicion that refugees from Germany or German-held territories would increase the likelihood of espionage and sabotage was widely held. Polls showed that as much as 95 percent of the Americans questioned thought immigration should continue to be tightly restricted, partly out of the fear of saboteurs. Members of the isolationist bloc in Congress reinforced this fear by making speeches warning against the dangers of "foreign agents."

Roosevelt adjudicated the State-Advisory Committee fracas with his usual tactic of placating both sides and then leaving it to them to wrestle with their differences. But he was clearly concerned about potential espionage, or at least the possibility that he could be charged by his opponents with not doing enough to prevent it. For at the time France was collapsing, he expressed concern about "fifth columnists" to several of his inner circle and approved the transfer of the Immigration and Naturalization Service from the Labor Department to the Justice Department, giving the Federal Bureau of Investigation greater oversight over the immigrants as they came to America.[14]

Sensing that the President would not move to stop their Department's restrictive policies, the consuls issued fewer and fewer visas as the war went on. In Stuttgart, Honaker now began to require his visa staff to check information concerning the legal pasts of applicants. Later he warned State that on the basis of intelligence he had received, the German government was giving "good conduct certificates" to "[visa] applicants with criminal records." The barricade of regulations and delays discouraged even the most determined applicants. Visa approvals dropped to new lows. From September 1939 to the beginning of 1942, only 4883 visas were issued under the German quota, about one-seventh of what had been issued between *Kristallnacht* and the beginning of the war. Most exits from France remained similarly blocked, which meant that Fritz Kann and thousands of other applicants for visas would never get any closer to the United States.[15]

The collapse of France caught most Americans by surprise. The sudden crisis that followed as the German occupiers began to establish themselves in France likewise caught American Jewish organizations completely unprepared. Prior to the German onslaught in May of 1940, most American Jewish leaders thought that they had from fifteen or twenty years to help the refugees immigrate to other parts of the world. But now everywhere that the German soldiers marched the Nazi anti-Semitic program followed. Petain's Vichy government was, if anything, embracing the program even more enthusiastically than many Germans. Helping the more than three hundred thousand Jewish refugees in France under such circumstances required the American groups to completely review their priorities. The Joint Distribution Committee, for example, had refrained from sending any substantial funds to Jews in Germany because they feared that doing so would make them appear "guilty of helping the Hitler regime." The new situation forced their policy makers to change their minds. By the end of 1940, the Committee was spending over twenty-five thousand dollars a month in direct efforts to help Jewish refugees and a like amount in indirect aid funneled through other agencies. Other American Jewish groups were expending funds in similar proportions.[16]

Herman Stern might well have shaken his head in frustration. Two years before, he had made his proposal to Stephen Wise about settling Jewish refugees on farming land in North Dakota. Had the plan been implemented and had the level of funds that the Joint Distribution Committee was now expending each month on relief efforts in France been put into Stern's plan, as many as two hundred and fifty more Jewish families might now be safely living on the small farms he had imagined.

But Wise had rejected the plan as unfeasible, and in the atmosphere of 1938, that was probably true. The Jewish families who lived in American cities, and provided the greatest support for groups like the Joint Distribution Committee and the American Jewish Congress, would not have supported the scheme. Parts of the American media would have called it an ill-conceived plan for ransoming the Jews in Hitler's hands. Doubts would have been voiced that Jewish refugees from small German towns could have succeeded on the Dakota prairie. Even in 1940, few conceived the horror that would descend on European Jews over the next three years.[17]

Stern naturally was certain that his plan would have worked. He knew the lands that he had marked for the project and knew the villagers that he was certain could have made the land productive once again. He would have dismissed the perception that the Jews were being ransomed as unimportant, for results were what mattered most to him. But he also knew that he could never prove something that would never happen, and the war, coupled with the lack of support in New York and the State Department's fears of subversives among the visa applicants, now made it impossible to carry out the proposal. Sadly, he released his local supporters from their pledges to help and turned his attention back to those he was still trying to help with affidavits. The situation here, too, was not very encouraging. Only a handful of these men and women were able to obtain visas in 1940 and 1941. Among these were some more members of the Falkenstein family and Erich Vasen and his family, now finally able to take the last steps in their long trek from Europe to Cuba to America. Edith and Ludwig Hammerschlag, together with Margarethe Kahrau, Erich Falkenstein's mother-in-law, were also able to reach the United States in 1940. So, too, did the three members of the Jacob Jonas family, in-laws to Hugo Henlein. In all of these cases Stern received help from business owners in Fargo, who signed supporting affidavits, and help from Jim Milloy and Milloy's redoubtable assistant Ruth Harrison, who kept him apprised of the mood in Washington.[18]

Stern's satisfaction at being able to help these people was dimmed when, three months after the war began, Hugo Henlein died in December 1939. Lotte noted the irony of her father dying because of an injury sustained in the Great War just months after the beginning of a new war. "My father's one lung was gassed during the First World War. He had but one healthy lung, and then he caught a cold, he got pleurisy, it moved to the lungs with pneumonia. And they didn't have antibiotics at that time. It moved to the heart and then he died." The wound he sustained in 1916 in defense of Germany had helped to kill Hugo three years after escaping from the clutches of his ungrateful countrymen. After Hugo's daughter Lotte graduated from high school in 1944, she moved to New York for business school. Lotte's mother joined her in New York a year later.[19]

Stern had difficulty re-establishing contact with his brother Adolf and Gustave's family in France. Ruth Harrison looked into the possibility of trying to get the Gustave Sterns into America as French citizens, but, finding this impossible, suggested to Stern that he explore getting them a temporary visa for Cuba. Stern replied that he would ask "one of our Senators in Washington" for help, but by then Gustave and the rest were already on their way to Marseilles. It took weeks for this news to reach America. The whereabouts of Herman's older brothers Moses and Julius were now a mystery as well. It took him months to learn that they and Julius's wife had been moved from their villages to Frankfurt Am Main where they now lived in a Jewish ghetto. Little Gus, Julius's son, was by now terribly upset about the paucity of information about his parents.[20]

Brooding over these matters, Stern was finding it very difficult to relax and his son was becoming worried about him. Ed was in fact feeling guilty about the strain his dad was under. While he was finishing school, he had "sort of resented" the relatives who had lived with them. First Klara had been there "eating the ice cream before I got to it," then Hugo's family arrived and "moved in and used up [our] hot water." Then in 1938, he had talked Herman into opening a new store, not so much because he thought it the ideal location but because Louise McCutcheon, his high school sweetheart, had moved there and by managing the store he could be near her. Business at the Fargo store had been rather slow during the first year and Ed thought he had only added to his dad's worries. Realizing that he "wasn't very helpful in all Dad's efforts," Ed urged him to spend more time in his garden, maybe listen to some music at home. Later he convinced his father to take a few days off and go to the Minnesota lake country near Park Rapids. After some time in a cabin and walking along the shores of Bad Axe Lake, the elder Stern came back to Valley City refreshed, ready to dive back into the work at the store. He told Ed that he had seen land in the Park Rapids area that would be "just great" for a Scout camp; as soon as he had more time, he would look into the prospect of raising money to buy some of it for that purpose. And, he added, he was going to contact Nye again about getting the rest of his brothers out of France and Germany.[21]

Call it devotion, call it obsession, call it plain mule-headedness perhaps, but Stern was not about to give up.

Notes

1. Here and below, Michael Stern transcript, pp. 3-9. The "boom boom boom" that he refers to was probably fire from German anti-aircraft guns. Like so many of his relatives, Michel had his name changed to Michael when the family arrived in America late in 1941. Likewise his brother, who was born Hans in Germany and used the name Jean in France, became John in America.

2. Ernest May, *Strange Victory*, pp. 383-447; Shirer, *Berlin Diary,* pp. 299-318.

3. Noel Barber, *The Week France Fell* (New York: Stein and Day, 1976), p. 302; Ian Ousby, *Occupation: The Ordeal of France, 1940-1944* (New York: St. Martin's Press, 1997), pp. 97-99.

4. Erika Bachar-Kann, letter to Shoptaugh, September 10, 1998.

5. Andy Marino, *A Quiet American: The Secret War of Varian Fry* (New York: St. Martin's Press, 1999), pp. 73-83; Ousby, *Occupation,* pp. 186-87; Bachar-Kann letter, September 10, 1998. A copy of the November 14, 1936 letter from Adolf Stern to Julius Stern was given to Shoptaugh by Ms. Bachar-Kann.

6. Herman Stern to James Milloy, January 15, 1941, and Stern to American Consul, Marseilles, May 5, 1941, Adolf Stern family file, Stern Papers.

7. Yehuda Bauer, *American Jewry and the Holocaust: The American Jewish Joint Distribution Committee, 1939-1945* (Detroit: Wayne State University Press, 1981), pp. 153ff.

8. Freda Kirchwey, "Nightmare in France," *The Nation*, August 17, 1940.

9. Marino, *A Quiet American*, pp. 44ff; Varian Fry, *Surrender on Demand* (Boulder, CO: Johnson Books, 1997, reprint of 1945 edition); Fry, "The Camps at Gurs (at the end of December 1940)," Varian Fry Papers, Columbia University. I owe a special debt to Bernard Crystal, Curator of Manuscripts at Columbia University for lending me a microfilm copy of Varian Fry's Papers. See also, Bauer, *American Jewry and the Holocaust*, pp. 157-161. Bauer also notes that the JDC avoided working with Fry because their representatives knew he was smuggling some refugees out of Europe via Spain, and the JDC could not "be identified with any illegal activities."

10. The German order banning Jewish immigration is quoted in Gilbert, *The Holocaust,* p. 152, and further avers that this was "the first official reference to any such 'final solution.'"

11. "Dismissal of Six German Clerks Assigned to the Visa Section for Having Received Money from Prospective Jewish Immigrants to the United States," January 17, 1939, 125.8853/503, U.S. Department of State, Central Decimal Files, Record Group 59, National Archives.

12. "Report of Investigation of Alleged Visa Irregularities at Stuttgart Consulate," August 27, 1939, 150.6269/82, U.S. Department of State, Central Decimal Files, Record Group 59, National Archives.

13. Richard Breitman and Alan Kraut, *American Refugee Policy and European Jewry, 1933-1945*, pp, 112-120; Fred L. Israel, ed., *The War Diary of Breckinridge Long* (Lincoln: University of Nebraska Press, 1966), p. 196.

14. Zucker, *In Search of Refuge*, p. 172; Henry Feingold, *The Politics of Rescue,* p. 140.

15. Zucker, *In Search of Refuge,* pp. 166-67; Breitman and Kraut, *American Refugee Policy*, p. 120.

16. Bauer, *American Jewry and the Holocaust,* pp. 24-26, 159.

17. Felix Cole, the American consul in Algiers, brushed against an issue that reflected both class differences and an urban-rural division in the American reaction to the refugee crisis. In a letter he sent to the State Department in regard to the Emergency Rescue Committee's desire to obtain emergency visas for some of the threatened German intelligentsia, Cole asked "Is an 'intellectual' more worthy of consideration [for immigration] than a working man or a small time merchant. . .?" Was the worker to be "refused on L.P.C. grounds while the University professor is welcomed and supported because of his education, his fluent speech or pen, and his appeal to wealthy individuals?" Quoted in Breietman and Kraut, *American Refugee Policy*, p. 133.

18. Details for each of the visa cases in the Vasen, Jonas, and Falkenstein files of Stern's Papers. Jacob Jonas had taken his wife and daughter to Rhodesia in 1938 before, sponsored by Hugo Henlein with support from Stern, receiving papers to enter the United States in 1940. From a letter Samuel Honaker wrote to Stern in September 1940, it is revealed another man named Louis Jonas was also sponsored by Stern and was able to immigrate to England in 1940. Whether or not he subsequently moved on the United States is unclear.

19. Ullman transcript, p. 34.

20. Ullman transcript, p. 60, and conversation with Frances Stern Furguiele, the granddaughter of Julius Stern. See also Ruth Harrison to Herman Stern, March 14, 1941 and Stern's March 17 reply, both in the Vasen file.

21. Edward Stern transcript, p. 11, supplemented with Edward Stern's letter to Lynn Kletzkin, April 5, 1991, copy given to Shoptaugh by Edward Stern.

Chapter Fourteen
"Our People are Getting Desperate"

In the summer of 1941, the war was going Hitler's way. His soldiers occupied over a dozen countries in Europe, ranging from Norway in the far north to Greece in the south, France in the west to Poland in the east. Much of the remainder of Europe had accepted German domination, granting Hitler very favorable trade agreements and in some cases permitting German soldiers to be stationed within their borders. Britain, under the magnetic leadership of Winston Churchill, who had replaced the hapless Chamberlain in May 1940, had survived the vicious aerial onslaught of the German *Luftwaffe*, but their situation was not encouraging. German bombers continued to do great damage to London and other major cities. German submarines were wreaking havoc on British shipping in the Atlantic, threatening the British people with starvation. And a German-Italian army was driving the meager British forces in North Africa back toward Cairo; loss of the Suez Canal would sever the United Kingdom from its empire and possibly force it to sue for peace.

Now the Fuhrer had set his sights on the Soviet Union. In January of 1941, Hitler told his senior commanders why it was time for him to scrap his neutrality pact with Stalin and send his armies deep into the heart of Russia. "The possibility of a Russian intervention [against Germany] in the war is keeping the English going," one of his listeners recorded. "They would only give up the race if the last continental hope was destroyed . . . Until now he [Hitler] had operated on the basis of always destroying the most important enemy position in order to move a step forward. For this reason Russia must be beaten." Like Napoleon in 1812, Hitler hoped to bring down Britain by striking a fatal stab in the opposite direction, and at the same time secure the "living space" he wanted for his German empire.

A small number of the German commanders warned Hitler that he was taking a huge gamble in attacking Russia in 1941. They pointed out that his invasion plan rested on an uncertain estimate of Russian strength, that German industry had not yet been organized for a long war while intelligence about Russian industry east of Moscow was sketchy, that with Britain not yet beaten, the country lacked the resources for a lengthy two-front war. The German forces would be spread too thin in the vast Russian countryside, they said, and there were too few trained replacements on hand if casualties rose beyond the estimates. Nonsense, the Fuhrer replied, the Russian troops had inferior equipment, were poorly trained and, since Stalin's purges of the senior commanders in 1937, even worse led. The sudden attack would shatter the Russian army quickly. Then Stalin's Soviet system, which had no support among his people, would collapse. "We have only to kick in the door and the whole rotten structure will come crashing down," Hitler assured one of his army group commanders. When a few of the doubters persisted, he grew angry and dismissed their reservations with insults. The majority of the generals voiced no objections. Germany's powerful divisions, after all, had defeated every force they met on the field. Their soldiers were rested and confident, even cocky. Russia could not resist the power of their tanks and bombers for more than six or eight weeks.[1]

Hitler also intended his strike at Stalin's empire to go far toward the elimination of his pet hate, the Jews of Europe. As the plans for the attack were being put into shape, he summoned Heinrich Himmler, commander of the SS and Gestapo, for a separate briefing. No record of their talk has come to light, but Hitler revealed a part of his thinking when he met with his generals in March of 1941 to further discuss the invasion. The head of his Combined Forces staff later recorded Hitler as saying that behind the advancing German armies, the SS would exercise "decisive control" over the conquered territories in matters of "politics, administration, law enforcement, and racial policy." The SS task would include "dirty work" that Hitler deemed necessary to "cleanse" the conquered territories, work that would "depopulate the area and re-appropriate it as a space for German settlements."

The "de-population" would mostly result from hunger, because the Russian harvest was to be expropriated and sent to Germany. Himmler told his staff that this would reduce the Russian population by twenty to thirty million people. He also told Reinhard Heydrich, one of his most trusted and ruthless subordinates, that new *Einsatzkommandos* (special action forces) would be needed in Russia. *Einsatzkommandos* had been in action in Poland, where they had murdered tens of thousands of Poles who, because of having higher education or political experience, were considered potential "insurgents." A very large number of the men and women who were executed by these shooting squads had been Jewish. For Russia, the kommandos would have to be enlarged into *Einsatzgruppen* (action task forces) to carry out such killings on a much greater scale.[2]

The killing groups were made up of "officials from the Gestapo... from the Criminal Police, men from the SD and from [Kurt] Daluege's regular [Order] police, soldiers from the *Waffen*-SS and foreign auxiliary policemen." At first, the rank and file of the four task groups organized were told only that they had to carry out tasks of "unprecedented severity." Some of these men had participated in the executions in Poland and probably understood from the first what was expected of them. Heydrich spoke more freely to the *Einsatzgruppen* commanders, instructing them to round up political figures, Communist Party leaders, Russian army commissars, and Jews, and execute them. One later recalled, that Heydrich specifically singled out the Jews for slaughter because, "in the Fuhrer's view," they were the foundation of bolshevism. Himmler later told several officers in the *Einsatzgruppen* that, regardless how difficult it was for men to shoot dozens of people each day, it had to be done because "these orders came from Hitler as the supreme Fuhrer of the German government, and that they had the force of law."

Whether or not Hitler and his inner circle were already discussing an intention to murder all the European Jews in their hands is a question that is still subject to sharp debate. But from the moment that Hitler decided to carry out his design for German *lebensraum* at

Russia's expense in 1941, he also decided that the Jews in Russia – as many of them as the Germans could reach – were to die.[3]

The German assault on Russia began in the early morning hours of June 22, when, after a heavy artillery and air bombardment, two and half million German soldiers began their march eastward. The Russian armies on the German-Soviet border, deployed for a planned attack against Hitler's empire in 1942, were caught unprepared for a full-scale assault. Stalin had ignored multiple warnings of Hitler's strike until the very last moment, too late to allow the Russian soldiers to prepare a proper defense. As a result, most of the Russian air force was destroyed on the ground by German planes, and Russian army communications were completely demolished. Shocked and confused, Russian units suffered heavy causalities and Soviet commanders lost control of their troops. Stalin ordered counterattacks, but these failed and the debacle quickly mushroomed into a rout as large numbers of poorly trained troops deserted or fled into the heavy forests.[4]

These heady days of success seemed to bear out Hitler's confidence that the Soviet system would quickly collapse. The central route to Moscow, by way of Minsk and Smolensk, appeared to be wide open. German units plunged eastward, advancing 350 miles in just ten days. Armored spearheads dashed ahead to surround huge numbers of the retreating Russians, forcing over six hundred thousand of them to surrender after just three weeks of combat. By the end of the year, the number of Russian prisoners exceeded three million, from which the Germans drew massive numbers of slave laborers, leaving the rest to die of starvation and disease in open-air compounds. Many prisoners, especially Ukrainians and Byelorussians who had never supported Stalin's regime, joined special units and fought alongside the German army.

But slowly the Soviet resistance began to stiffen. In the north, the drive to Leningrad faltered when the German armor was forced to crawl along narrow roads through deep forests. Russian units stopped falling back and began launching new counterattacks, using divisions that German intelligence had never identified before. Hitler's high command soon concluded that instead of the two hundred divisions they had expected to fight, the Russian Army, in fact, had over three hundred divisions. Many of these were hastily organized and poorly armed. But some of the fresh units were well-equipped with faster, heavier and better armed tanks than anything the Germans had. Heavy attacks were launched against the German flanks. Because of their greater experience in mobile warfare and their supporting air power, the Germans were able to blunt these attacks and keep pressing on toward Leningrad and Moscow, but their progress was slower than expected, a circumstance made worse by the poor quality of the Russian roads, most of which were little more than dirt tracks that would disintegrate into glutinous mud after any kind of substantial rain. German casualties also rose faster than the planners had anticipated.

Hitler's timetable for victory was coming undone. Rejecting an overture from Stalin for a negotiated peace, he began to interfere regularly in the day to day operations, ordering units to be diverted away from their original objectives and toward ports and industrial areas. When his staff warned him that his new orders would jeopardize the chances of defeating the Soviet Union before winter, Hitler brushed aside their objections, saying that generals did not appreciate the need to secure critical economic resources for the years ahead. By late July, what had been planned as a short war was beginning to turn into a battle of attrition.

Behind the front lines, soldiers and party men, who had sworn their oaths of absolute loyalty to Hitler so many years before, now began to realize just what the promise of absolute obedience could cost them. The *Einsatzgruppen* set about their grisly business as soon as the guns opened fire on the first day. In the tiny village of Virbalis, just across the boundary line, SS men aided by Latvian policemen rounded up the Jewish population and shot them down in a long trench. The first group was killed by machine guns, a witness reported after the war: "Lime was thereupon sprayed upon them and a second row of Jews was made to lie down. They were similarly shot," as were six further groups. The smallest Jewish children were not shot, but brutally beaten and then buried alive. This performance was repeated in countless villages, and in many of them men and women of the local Gentile population betrayed their Jewish neighbors to the executioners. Jews frequently fought back with back with axes or farm tools but were ultimately overcome by the well-armed killing squads. In Bialstok, one of the first major cities taken in the initial invasion, over eight hundred Jews were murdered by members of an Order Police Battalion, either by shooting or by being forced into the city's Great Synagogue which was then burned to the ground. Generally, a Jew survived the *Einsatzgruppen* only by hiding with the help of a friend or running away into the forests and joining the partisan groups that sprang up in the wake of the invaders.[5]

The *Einsatzgruppen* were aided in their grisly chores by a number of ordinary German soldiers. The high command of the German Army had prepared and distributed a document entitled "Guidelines for the Conduct of the Troops in Russia" prior to the invasion. One of the document's proclamations left the average soldier in no doubt as to the manner in which he should treat the Russian population. "This battle," the document noted, "demands ruthless and energetic measures against Bolshevik agitators, irregulars, saboteurs, and Jews and the *total eradication* of any active or passive resistance" to German occupation. In a corollary decree, German officers were told that "acts committed by Wehrmacht [army] personnel or followers against enemy civilians, even if the act is a military crime or offense, may go unpunished." In the field, German units would call upon Russian troops to surrender, advising them to "finish off the [political] commissars and the kikes" before giving up their weapons.

It should have come as no surprise then that units like the 221st Security Division, made up of older soldiers and stationed in the rear of the newly conquered parts of Russia, began executing Jews almost as soon as they entered an area. "The place is crawling with Jews," a 221st officer wrote in a report of the unit's occupation of Bialoviza village. "We're rounding them all up for work, some to sweep streets, some to mend them." Then the Germans made the Jewish population clean the soldier's boots. When "the Jew elder had insisted the job mustn't be rushed," the German soldiers shot him. "That got the bastards moving!"[6]

Although it would not become known until many years later, the British government had detailed information about the crimes of the *Einsatzgruppen* and German army units within weeks of Germany's attack on Russia. British specialists in cryptology (secret codes) had learned how to intercept and break German coded radio transmissions. These transmissions included reports sent from the *Einsatzgruppen* commanders to Berlin. Thus, when an intercepted message from early August 1941 revealed that one of the four main *Einsatzgruppen* had killed over thirty thousand people, the British analyst of these words commented that the commanders of the killing units appeared to be "somewhat in competition with each other as to their 'scores'." Other intercepts spoke of three hundred Jews shot here, five hundred there, over a thousand elsewhere, until the totals began to run into the tens of thousands. In September, a summary of the intercepted German reports, which was seen by Churchill and members of his war cabinet, noted that the actual toll of executions was likely double what had been learned from the messages that could be decoded, and further stated that "the figures [known] are no less conclusive as evidence of a policy of savage intimidation if not of ultimate extermination." Partly because of concerns that their invaluable code-breaking operation could be compromised, the British government concealed detailed knowledge of these facts for the rest of the war and beyond.[7]

As yet, the United States government knew nothing of these atrocities in Russia beyond rumors collected and sent home by American journalists in Europe. These rumors were largely discounted by the mainstream press and radio networks.

In the meantime, America was still clinging on to its neutrality, but the commitment toward taking no sides was not quite as strong as it had been in the mid-1930s. After the German attack on Poland, President Roosevelt used his influence to get enough votes in Congress to further revise the neutrality laws that Gerald Nye had helped create. He wanted the "cash and carry" provision that had been applied to non-military sales in 1937 extended to armament sales, and argued that the United States would be more likely to stay at peace if Britain and France had the weapons they needed to block further German expansion. In this step, the President had measured the current national mood astutely, for a poll taken in late September showed that while four out of five Americans did not want to become involved in the war, four out of five also identified Germany as a major threat to the United States.[8]

In November, Congress agreed by a close vote to amend the neutrality laws and permit cash-and-carry sales of arms and munitions to warring powers. Nye, together with number of other advocates for strict neutrality, fought the proposal vigorously, arguing that the measure violated true neutrality because Germany lacked the merchant ships to carry away any purchases. Nye warned that this was but the first step toward lending money to the Allies and then, eventually, joining them on the battlefield. But despite his opposition, the bill passed. Britain and France began buying millions of dollars worth of military hardware, including a number of light bombers from Lockheed aircraft that were flown to the northeastern-most corner of North Dakota and then "carried" by horse team across the border into Canada, from which point they were flown in stages to Britain.[9]

From then until America entered the war, Nye and those who agreed with him fought a rearguard action against the Roosevelt administration's policy of gradually increasing aid and support to the Allies. They denounced Roosevelt's decision in the late summer of 1940 to trade a number of older American destroyers to Britain in return for leases of port facilities and air bases at various British bases in the western hemisphere. They decried the formation of a group called the Committee to Defend America by Aiding the Allies, which organized public support for additional measures to help Britain against Germany and China against Japan. Many of them questioned the need for the Selective Service Act in 1940, a peacetime military draft for an enormous expansion of the American military. They gave thousands of speeches, published thousands of articles and millions of pamphlets, all arguing that the nation's best hope for remaining at peace was to return to strict neutrality. Despite this, their argument steadily lost favor. Germany's victories in Europe convinced more and more Americans that it would be wisest to help Britain hold out against Hitler than to face him alone after Britain was defeated.

In September of 1940, a large group of the "isolationists," as they were known by that time, formed the America First Committee, an organization which dedicated itself to the proposition that "American democracy can be preserved only by keeping out of the European war." America First enrolled over 800,000 members, the bulk of them in the middle western and plains states. Gerald Nye did not participate in the American First movement at first, partly because he did not want to be associated with the group's strident opposition to Roosevelt's unprecedented candidacy for a third term in the White House, and partly because he sensed that joining the group could hurt him in some parts of North Dakota.

A month after he was re-elected, Roosevelt called for even greater aid to Britain. Let America lend Britain the weapons and supplies they needed to win the war, he argued, and America could remain safe. FDR's proposal brought Nye down off his fence. He agreed to speak at an American First rally in opposition to Roosevelt's Lend-lease plan, and soon was speaking across the country at American First rallies. It was in these speeches that Nye developed what was to become his dominating theme in 1941 – that the American people had been duped by carefully tailored propaganda into supporting measures that would aid the British. "American columnists," he argued, were "feeding us daily with the fear of what is going to be our lot if Britain loses the war." He singled out Walter Lippmann, Dorothy Thompson, and Walter Winchell, among others, and implied that these journalists were engaged in a conspiracy with the Roosevelt administration to bring America into the war on Britain's side. Soon after, Nye added the names of several radio journalists and Hollywood producers to the list of those he charged with stampeding the American nation toward war. None of this did anything to prevent the Lend-lease Act from being approved by Congress in April 1941.

In August, Nye joined John T. Flynn, a member of the America First National Committee, and Missouri Senator Champ Clark in writing a resolution for a Senate investigation of Hollywood and radio for influencing "public sentiment in the direction of participation by the United States in the present war in Europe." The Senate accepted the resolution and a three-man subcommittee was named to undertake the task. Nye did not serve on the subcommittee because he intended to testify before it. [10]

Nye wanted to reap a rich harvest of good publicity for his cause from the "Hollywood investigation." Having gained his national reputation by investigating the "merchants of death," he now hoped to shore up his sagging fortunes with an investigation of a new crop of war mongers. But fate is a fickle muse, for the investigation was a fiasco for the America First movement from start to finish. Before the committee began its work, Nye gave a radio address in which he accused the major studio heads for using movies as "gigantic engines of propaganda" in order to "rouse war fever" against Germany. Because most of those studio heads, who he named, were Jewish, Nye was quickly charged with anti-Semitism by some of his enemies. Nye had been charged with hostility towards the Jews before and always denied the charge. But he often couched his denial in a combative manner that did nothing to reassure his listeners. In the previous May, for example, he had received a telegram from Stephen Wise which implored him not to speak at a certain gathering in New York, because the sponsors of the meeting, Wise said were "virtually fascist [and] certainly anti Jewish." Nye promptly replied that he would keep his speaking engagement and his speech would contain nothing "of encouragement for anti Semitic groups." In a follow-up letter he warned Wise that American Jews were agitating "the European issue" to the point that it could "bring down upon their race a lot of displeasure" from the rest of the nation . . . we are fast approaching the hour when we are bound to deal with this growing racial spirit." He could hardly have chosen poorer words in defending himself to Wise.

After the charges against him were renewed on the eve of the Hollywood investigation, Nye sent a letters to William Stern of Fargo to assure him that the claims that he was "demonstrating anti-Semitic sympathies" were completely ridiculous: "though my patience has been sorely tried by this attitude of the [Jewish] race toward the war, I am no more anti-Semitic today than I have ever been, and I have never been that. . . . when I can do or say anything that will destroy this conclusion in any mind that I am anti-Semitic, let me know about it." But in neither this letter nor a similar one he wrote on the same day to Harry Lashkowitz, a noted attorney in Fargo, did Nye mention the crucial help he had been giving to Herman Stern for so many years. This omission, plus the fact that he asked neither man to make a public statement of support on his behalf, was a deliberate calculation. Nye had stated repeatedly that he believed calls by American Jews for the United States to join in the war against Hitler would spark an anti-Semitic backlash in American society. Nye obviously believed as well that it would harm him, more than help him, among his constituents if he publicly revealed his help to Herman Stern. Whether or not Nye had fairly gauged the mood of his state when he made this choice, it is not without significance that Stern was himself very reticent about what he was doing, both at the time and for years afterward.[11]

On September 9, Nye appeared before the Hollywood sub-committee and reviewed the evidence he had collected on Jewish influence in Hollywood. Dismissing the charge of anti-Semitism as a ploy by the interventionists to distract attention from their own attempts at "pushing our country on the way to war," he said he was, "*as yet at least*, bitterly opposed to the injection of anti-Semitism as a cause or issue in our American way of thinking and acting" and that an America at war might lead to anti-Jewish persecutions. His opponents hastened to use his ill-considered words against him.

Two days after Nye's remarks, another prominent non-interventionist, Charles Lindbergh, fanned the flames with a speech in Des Moines, Iowa. The hero flier of the 1920s had become one of America First's greatest draws on the lecture circuit. And like Nye, Lindbergh blamed specific groups, who swayed public opinion "by subterfuge and propaganda," for the growing sentiment against Germany. Most notable among these propagandists, he said, were agents of the British government, members of the Roosevelt administration, and "the Jewish" in America. Of the last group, Lindbergh said he did not "blame them for looking out for what they believe to be their own interests, but we also must look out for ours . . . No person with a sense of dignity of mankind can condone the persecution of the Jewish race in Germany. But no person of honesty and vision can look on their pro-war policy here today without seeing the dangers involved in such a policy both for us and for them. Instead of agitating for war, the Jewish groups in this country should be opposing it in every possible way for *they will be among the first to feel its consequences.*"

Both Nye and Lindbergh were accused of trying to encourage American rightwing attacks on Jews, of using gutter tactics in "stormtrooper fashion," and of "seeking to destroy liberty through bigotry." Nye did not help matters by defending Lindbergh. Telling reporters that Lindbergh was a "courageous American" who was in no way anti-Semitic, Nye added that "the Jewish people are a large factor in our movement toward war."[12]

In the midst of this, the Hollywood hearings degenerated into a similar round of charge and countercharge, at which point the embarrassed subcommittee members agreed to suspend the proceedings until matters calmed down, then reconvene. But as it turned out, that would never happen.

Men in high places were playing for high stakes that September. Congressmen wrangled and the press debated which courses of action would preserve the peace for America. Meanwhile, Roosevelt pursued his own strategy. However much he may have wanted to keep Americans out of the war, he doubted that Britain could win on its own and correctly guessed that Russia's Stalin would try to negotiate a cease-fire with Hitler. Roosevelt knew that if it came to America having to fight he would need a well trained army. But under the draft legislation of 1940, he knew that those taken into the military by the selective service would soon be released. So in August he twisted arms to get the military draft extended and keep the current servicemen in uniform. It took a mammoth effort to get an extension, which passed by a mere one vote. Roosevelt also had an emergency to deal with in the Atlantic, where a German submarine had attacked an American destroyer. In response, FDR issued an order to the Navy to "shoot on sight" at any German ship seen in American sea defense zones. America was not yet at war, but the drift in that direction was unmistakable.[13]

In the Soviet Union, the stakes were of an entirely different order. There was virtually no place for rules of any kind in the war that was being fought on the Russian steppes. The German troops continued to press eastward, killing and capturing hundreds of thousands of Russians. But as soon as one Russian army was annihilated, another would appear to take its place. By now fighting with his High Command almost as often as the German soldiers were battling at the front, Hitler began interfering with the attack plans on a daily basis. The best troops were sent off on one special mission after another, wearing out both men and equipment in trying to secure too many objectives while succeeding in nothing that struck a mortal blow against their foe. Other troops were pulled out of the lines to help harvest the Russian crops that Germany vitally needed for the coming year. Nervous, angry that the Soviet Union was not collapsing as he had expected, Hitler was beginning to wonder if he might lose his war. He told one of his best field commanders that he had not been properly briefed on the true extent of Russian reserves and tank strength. Otherwise, he said, "I would not – I believe – ever have started this war." Russia was proving to be too big to bring down in a quick campaign.[14]

This state of affairs may have influenced the next step that Hitler ordered in his war against the Jews. The Russian war had descended to the level of a no-quarter contest. Commenting on the activities of the *Einsatzgruppen* and regular German troops who had begun to shoot prisoners, one military historian noted that by late summer "all commissars and Jews knew the fate in store for them if they fell into

German hands, and determined that neither they nor their comrades should surrender." Knowledge of this, plus the reports of the executions by the *Einsatzgruppen*, may have prompted Hitler to order the murders of Jews in Germany. In mid-July, he had told officers and administrators in a meeting for organizing the governing of the conquered territories that it would easiest to "wipe out anyone who gets in our way." Two weeks later, Goering contacted Heydrich and ordered him to make preparations for "a total solution of the Jewish question in those territories of Europe which are under German influence." In September, the first transports of German Jews to the east were organized. Meanwhile, one of the *Einstazgruppen*, whose men were becoming both physically exhausted and emotionally wrought by the constant executions, was experimenting with a gas van for more "efficiently" killing Jews in Russia.[15]

While Hitler and Stalin, Churchill and Roosevelt were determining the fate of millions, Herman Stern was focusing his energies on a handful of souls. Any chances he had in helping some of his remaining relatives in Germany melted away in mid-June of 1941, when the State Department, with Roosevelt's concurrence, ordered all German consulates in America closed because they believed the consulate personnel were being used for espionage. Germany retaliated by ordering all American consular personnel to leave Germany and German-occupied areas. When the consulate in Stuttgart closed, Samuel Honaker was sent to work in the American embassy in Turkey, while Hugh Teller and most of the other American employees were reassigned to countries in Europe that were still free from German occupation. The closing of the American consulates made it all but impossible for thousands of Jews remaining in Germany to obtain American visas, including several men and women that Stern had tried to sponsor.[16]

Stern now accepted that his brothers Moses and Julius would never get to the United States. As Lotte Henlein recalled, "we knew they had been taken to Frankfurt. They took them to Frankfurt into an apartment. I don't know for how long." Herman and Jettchen thought for some years that their brothers had died in Frankfurt during the war. But this was not true. Both of the Stern brothers did indeed die during the war, but in much different circumstances. Moses was sent to the Czech village of Terezin, which had been chosen by the Nazis as a ghetto for a great many of the Jews who had been living in Czechoslovakia when it was dissolved by the Munich Agreement. In November 1941, the SS, using Jewish laborers, converted the village into a ghetto for some of the German Jewish population. Moving the Gentile population of Terezin elsewhere, Himmler's men took steps to present the village, renamed "Theresienstadt," as a "safe haven" for elderly German Jews, sent to the east to "protect" them from British bombing raids. The SS continued this façade by bringing in a film crew and made a carefully scripted documentary that stressed how well the population of Terezin was treated and how happy the inhabitants were. They also permitted agents of the International Red Cross to come and take a carefully staged tour of the main village square, where the shops had been temporarily stocked with ample food.

But once the Red Cross men left, the food was immediately removed, for in reality Terezin was a squalid prison where sixty thousand German and eastern Jews were crammed into a space built for seven thousand. Deliberately starved, denied ordinary medical care or any kind of decent treatment, the death rate rose rapidly, becoming so high that the Germans eventually built a crematorium there to dispose of the bodies. As the men, women and children died, more Jews from western Europe were transported to take their places. Most of those who were rugged enough to survive the conditions were eventually shipped to Auschwitz and murdered in the gas chambers. Seventy-year-old Moses died in Terezin sometime in 1942, possibly from hunger and malnutrition.[17]

Years later, Jettchen Henlein was horrified to learn the real story of Moses from a book about Oberbrechen. "It was written in German, it was all about Oberbrechen," Lotte remembered. "That's when she first saw that [Moses had died in Terezin]. She started to cry one day. I said, 'Mama, what's the matter?' Mama was crying, she said, 'I thought they died in Frankfurt.' She said, 'My brothers.' Oh, I can still see it."

As for Moses' brother Julius, he and his wife Frieda were sent from Germany to the east late in 1941. Their son Gustav learned after the war that both of his parents died in the camps. Julius would have been about sixty-five at the time of his death, Frieda about sixty. As for Ludwig, Gustav's younger brother, he had been living in France in 1940 and like so many others had been interned at Gurs at the time of the German attack. It was there that he died, late in 1941 or early in 1942, of unspecified natural causes at the age of thirty-five.[18]

Herman did not know these things until later, but by the end of the summer of 1941 he was certain that his brother Adolf, with Dora and the family of Gustave, would die at the hands of the Nazis unless he somehow got them out of Marseilles. He tried everything to expedite their passage to the United States. He had provided new forms, detailed listings of his income and properties, and once again turned to his friends in Washington. Both Gerald Nye and North Dakota Congressman Charles Roberts wrote letters to Secretary of State Cordell Hull, attesting to Stern's reliability. Stern himself wrote to Hull, promising that Adolf and the rest would have a "welcome home and support" from him in Valley City. He further offered to place ten thousand dollars on deposit as a guarantee that they would never become a public charge. The letters seemed to have no effect. Gustave, in desperation, sent a cable to Stern saying that it was "impossible" for all six of the family to get out together, so Stern should try to get visas "for my mother and father only."[19]

In New York, Tea Eichengruen was feverishly trying to get her own parents out of Germany and her brother out of Holland. Tea's mother and father had their visas and were waiting for their turn to emigrate under the State Department's quota system. They did not want to leave without Erwin. However, his presence in Holland made a joint departure almost an insurmountable obstacle. In May of 1939, Tea had sent virtually all the money she had, three hundred and fifty dollars, to officials in Cuba in order to secure documents allowing all three of her family to live there while waiting for their America quota numbers to come up. "I had brought a camera to America, which I sold for $100. The rest I had saved. What went wrong was that the money fell into the wrong hands, was pocketed, and the permission to enter Cuba was not given them. So the ship sailed without them." The ship, incidentally, was the *SS St. Louis*, and in the end none of the Jewish passengers were allowed to disembark at Cuba.[20]

The onset of war a few months later made it even more difficult for Tea to help her parents. Even if Jews had entry visas for other nations it was immensely difficult to sail from Europe. The British blockade of Germany left German ships stranded in foreign ports. Shipping lines from most other nations refused to accept German currency for passage. The United States consulates' tougher regulations, which now required documented evidence of paid ship tickets before granting a visa, added to the problems. Herman Stern promised he would help obtain ship tickets for the Eichengruens. He also continued to bombard the State Department with letters asking for action on the case.[21]

In the early spring of 1941, after months of waiting, the Eichengruens finally obtained the precious American documents. In late June, at just about the time Germany and America began to close their respective consulates, the couple took a train to Spain and lived there on a temporary permit while they waited for ship tickets and news about Erwin. Tea sent her parents three tickets to use on a Spanish ship. She had obtained the tickets from Stern, and they were very expensive: "three hundred dollars [per person] was an outrageous price to pay for a ticket. I took the tickets with the understanding that we would repay Herman once they would get here." They expected Erwin to receive his visa from the American consulate in Holland very soon and could then go to Spain and take passage with his parents.[22]

The Eichengruens booked passage on the *Navemar*, a five thousand ton Spanish steamer that had already carried several groups of European refugees to North America. The ship was to leave Barcelona in July. Herr Eichengruen sent a cable to his son with the schedule for sailing. July came and sailing day approached, but still no reply came from Holland. Then, on July 4, Tea received a telegram from her father's relatives in Amsterdam: Erwin would not be coming; he had "been refused his American visa" by the Amsterdam consulate. It was too dangerous to wait any longer. Herman and Elly Eichengruen boarded the *Navemar* and left Spain. The ship was very crowded and there was only a limited amount of food aboard. After a stop in Havana, the *Navemar* arrived in New York on September 12, 1941. Tea was shocked at her parents' appearance. They were worn, quite thin and suffering from exhaustion. "My father was so hungry that – and this I remember very well – I went to get him a sandwich and the only thing I could get was a ham sandwich. I didn't tell him [it was ham] but he didn't ask."[23]

Two days after Tea's parents made it safely to New York, Hitler's government issued a new decree ordering all Jews in Germany to wear the Star of David on their clothing. With this as a readily recognizable mark, the Nazis could round up thousands of Jews on moment's notice.

Herman Stern went to New York a few days later to assure the Eichengruens that he would try to bring their son out of Holland. He bought a Cuban visa for Erwin. (It was in fact already too late; before the year ended Erwin was rounded up with hundreds of others as part of a deportation of Dutch and German Jews "to the east.") One wonders just how Stern felt when he saw the Eichengruens. There was satisfaction no doubt at having helped them come to America, and a certain amount of worry about their deteriorated condition. But as he watched the happy reunion of parents and daughter, it would be understandable if he regarded the moment in some way as bittersweet. The Eichengruens were haggard and worried about their son, but they were safe, while his own relatives were still trapped in Marseilles.

The United States was drifting closer and closer to war. During the week that Tea's parents arrived in New York, the U.S. Navy launched the new battleship *Massachusetts,* Americans were advised that German submarines were making ocean travel very hazardous, and Scandinavian-Americans were horrified to read stories of German soldiers executing civilian hostages in Norway. And while the Chinese ambassador urged the United States to keep up its "economic pressure" on Japan, Japanese negotiators in Washington said that they were "optimistic" that they could work out their differences with the Americans. No one knew that a large Japanese naval task force was already gathering for a surprise attack on the American Pacific fleet.

In early November, Stern wrote to a friend in Washington that "our people [in France] are getting quite desperate, with conditions getting more serious every day." Then, just as he was about to give up hope, the chief of the State Department's Visa Division sent him a letter informing him that the visas had been approved for Adolf and the others. The war had reduced European immigration to a trickle, and the family had no trouble with the quota system, so transportation was now the last obstacle to getting them out of Europe. But Herman had high hopes that they would be able to get tickets for a ship out of Marseilles. The next ship for America was scheduled to leave about December 10, 1941.[24]

On December 6, Adolf Hitler met with his General Staff to discuss the situation in Russia. The news there was grim. Despite having inflicted over five million casualties on the Russian forces, the German army had failed in its attempt to seize Moscow. Cruel winter storms had descended on the troops, most of whom had no heavy clothing. Soviet soldiers were counterattacking in force and the Germans were being forced to give ground. The Fuhrer was nevertheless optimistic. Understating Germany's own losses and lack of preparation for a long war, he ordered his forces to stand fast and outlined plans for seizing Russian oil and coal fields. He ordered a return to the attack within a few days. The Army chief of staff noted ruefully in the headquarters war diary that Hitler refused to accept the true state of affairs: that Germany had shot its bolt and was now facing a two front war that it could well lose.

Forty-eight hours later it became a three-front war. Gerald Nye was in Pittsburgh on December 7, at the Soldiers and Sailors Memorial Hall to give another speech for an America First rally. As he waited for his turn at the podium, a reporter came back stage and told him that the White House had issued a bulletin about a Japanese air attack on the fleet at Pearl Harbor. Nye replied that this sounded like a hoax but asked the reporter to get more information. Then he went on stage and gave his speech. Just as he was concluding a passage about British propaganda in the American press, the reporter returned and handed him a note which said that Japan had declared war against the United States. Clearly disconcerted, Nye read the note to the audience and cut short his speech. He told the press outside that he would certainly vote for war against Japan but still believed in remaining neutral in the war in Europe. That avenue was closed three days later when Hitler declared war against the United States. Nye by then was already the object of derision as the man who spoke of "non-intervention" while Japanese bombs fell on American sailors.[25]

With America's entry into the war, Herman Stern believed that now, "there seemed to be no opportunity for passage" for his relatives. But he was wrong. As Michael Stern later recounted, his father had decided it would be too dangerous to wait until December 10, and somehow got the family on a small ship sailing to Morocco. "I remember we took a small ship from France. I remember quite well being seasick. I can remember very much being seasick. We landed in Oran, I believe, and took a train to Casablanca. I can remember a train. We lived in an apartment in Casablanca and I can remember another thing that no one else remembered. That was that I was playing in a schoolyard and I was going down a slide. My mother was watching me and there were two German soldiers watching me. And I remember that I had asked my mother something [about the soldiers] and she told me not to worry. Ultimately I found out it was an open [i.e. neutral] city and they weren't doing anything anyhow. They were just watching us. I do remember that specifically. I can remember what their uniforms even looked like."

After a few weeks in Casablanca, the Sterns used practically the last money they had to buy tickets on the Portuguese freighter *Serpa Pinto*, another ship that had made several refugee runs across the

Atlantic. The *Serpa Pinto* set sail from Casablanca on Januray 26, 1942, six weeks after Pearl Harbor, bound for New York. The *Serpa Pinto* was one of the few ships that German submarines were under orders not to attack on the high seas, but its captain took no chances and followed a serpentine route toward his destination. "We went from Casablanca on a roundabout way. I remember the ship very well. I remember that it had a little dining room for children. I remember there was a little boy by the last name Alexander, who I played with during the trip. I wasn't seasick at all. I remember stopping in Jamaica because I remember them loading bananas. It was strange because I was watching English soldiers loading bananas. We landed around February 10 of '42 in New York." Like the *Navemare,* this ship was loaded to the bulwarks with passengers, most of them refugees.

"We were picked up by my father's first cousin, Gustav Stern. He was known as "kline Gustav" [little Gus], he was this little guy, 5 foot 1 inch, something like that. He picked us up and we stayed in a hotel called the Woodrow Wilson. I remember that well. I had scarlet fever in New York. I think we stayed in New York for a couple of weeks. Then we went to Chicago where my Uncle Jay lived. My dad got a job selling shoes at Goldschmidt's. I'm not sure whether my mother was working, but we lived in the Hyde Park area for about a year."[26]

Adolf, Dora, Gustave, Gertrude, Michel and his brother John were the last of Herman Stern's family to get out of Europe. They were among the last German Jews to escape Hitler's wrath. Many of those who remained under Nazi control already were being shipped like cattle to their deaths.

Notes

1. Albert Seaton, *The Russo-German War, 1941-45* (New York: Presidio Press, 1993), pp. 43-64, for an excellent analysis of the German invasion plan and its limitations, and Alexander Dallin, *German Rule in Russia, 1941-1945* (Boulder, CO: Westview Press, 1980 edition), pp. 1-19 for Hitler's decision "to eliminate the permanent Bolshevik menace in this war." Hitler's confidence in destroying the Russian forces quickly was echoed by most leading military men in America and Britain.

2. Noakes, *Nazism, 1919-1945: Foreign Policy, War and Racial Extermination*, p. 813; Gerald Fleming, *Hitler and the Final Solution,* pp. 32-37; Dallin, *German Rule in Russia*, pp. 27-29; Richard Breitman, *The Architect of Genocide: Heinrich and the Final Solution* (New York: Alfred A. Knopf, 1991), pp. 145-47.

3. Fleming, *Hitler and the Final Solution,* pp. 43-45; Gunther Deschner, *Reinhard Heydrich: A Biography* (New York: Stein and Day, 1981), pp. 169-77. These two works, together with Breitman's biography of Himmler, Wistrich's *Hitler and the Holcaust,* Christopher Browning's *The Origins of the Final Solution: The Evolution of Nazi Jewish Policy, September 1939-March 1942* (Lincoln: University of Nebraska Press, 2004) are among many studies that wrestle with the question of exactly when the decision was made by the Nazis to exterminate Europe's Jewish population. The issue often turns on what the various Nazi leaders meant when they used the term "Final Solution" at certain points in time. For example, did a letter of 1940 by Heydrich, referring to a "territorial Final Solution" foresee mass murder or was Heydrich referring to "a large-scale deportation" which he also mentions? Likewise, the exact meaning of a July 1941 letter by Goering ordering Heydrich to make plans for "the hoped-for Final Solution to the Jewish question" is disputed by historians. For an excellent analysis of the various deportation proposals (which would inevitably have caused of the deaths of thousands through starvation and disease) see Philip Friedman, "The Lublin Reservation and the Madagascar Plan: Two Aspects of Nazi Jewish Policy During the Second World War," in *Roads to Extinction: Essays on the Holocaust*, edited by Ada June Friedman (New York: Jewish Publication Society of America, 1980).

4. Seaton, *The Russo-German War*, pp. 141-44; See also Richard Overy, *Russia's War* (London: Allen Lane, 1997), and Constantine Pleshakov, *Stalin's Folly: The Tragic First Ten Days of WWII on the Eastern Front* (Boston: Houghton Mifflin, 2005) which draw upon recently opened Russian archives for the Soviet side of the war.

5. Martin Gilbert, *The Holocaust*, pp. 154ff.; Richard Breitman, *Official Secrets,* pp. 46-48. In addition to the killings of Jews, *Einsatzgruppen* and Army units also murdered thousands of Russian prisoners, Communist party functionaries, and various "ideological enemies." Matthew Cooper, *The Nazi War Against Soviet Partisans, 1941-1944* (New York: Stein and Day, 1979) and Alexander Dallin, *German Rule in Russia,* are indispensable studies for this part of Hitler's murderous policies.

6. Ben Shepherd, *War in the Wild East: The German Army and Soviet Partisans* (Cambridge: Harvard University Press, 2004), pp. 52-53, 64-65; Pleshakov, *Stalin's Folly,* p. 212.

7. Breitman, *Official Secrets,* pp. 91-96, which in addition to the items quoted has an excellent analysis of why the British kept these intercept files sealed for decades after the war ended. See also Stephen Budiansky, *Battle of Wits: the Complete Story of Codebreaking in World War II* (New York: Free Press, 2000).

8. Roosevelt, "Repeal the Arms Embargo," *Vital Speeches of the Day,* October 1, 1939, pp. 738-41; Donald F. Drummond, *The Passing of American Neutrality* (Ann Arbor, MI: University of Michigan Press, 1955), pp. 87-110.

9. Cole, *Senator Gerald P. Nye,* pp. 153-67; Shoptaugh, "Borderline Neutrality," *North Dakota History,* Spring 1993, pp. 2-13. See also Cole's *Roosevelt and the Isolationists* (Lincoln: University of Nebraska Press, 1983) for a full examination of the national debate over neutrality.

10. Here and below, Cole, *Senator Gerald P. Nye,* pp. 177-191; John E. Moser, "The 1941 Senate Investigation into Hollywood," *Historian,* Summer 2001.

11. Stephen Wise to Nye, May 20, 1941, and Nye's reply, May 21, 1941; Nye to William Stern, August 29, 1941; Nye to Harry Lashkowitz, August 29, 1941, all in Gerald Nye Papers, Herbert Hoover Presidential Library, West Branch, Iowa.

12. Cole, *Senator Gerald P. Nye*, p. 189-92; Lindbergh, Speech in Des Moines, Iowa, September 11, 1941, text at http://www.charleslindbergh.com/americanfirst/speech.asp.   Italics in both Nye and Lindbergh quotes have been added.

13. Waldo Heinrichs, *Threshold of War: Franklin D. Roosevelt and the Entry of America into World War II* (New York: Oxford University Press, 1988), pp. 146-79. Even though Britain and the Soviet Union signed a mutual pact on July 12 promising not to negotiate separate terms with the enemy, Churchill worried that Stalin would do that until well into 1943. Roosevelt, too, worried about Stalin's dependability and hesitated to send Lend-lease aid before having Harry Hopkins visit the Soviet Union. For a detailed study, see Warren F. Kimball, *Forged in War* (New York: William Morrow, 1997).

14. Seaton, *The Russo-German War*, pp. 145-52; Heinz Guderian, *Panzer Leader* (New York: Ballantine Books abridged edition, 1972), p. 153.

15. Seaton, *The Russo-German War*, pp. 78, 100; Wistrich, *Hitler and the Holocaust,* pp. 96-99. Wistrich, Fleming and many others speculate that Hitler ordered the Holocaust after sensing that Germany might fail in its war against Russia.

16. *Foreign Relation of the United States, Europe 1941,* vol. II, pp. 628-34; Wyman, *Paper Walls,* p. 197.

17. Moses Stern's death recorded in the Yad Vashem Central Database of Shoah Victim's, using information from the Bundesarchiv in Koblenz.

18. Ullmann transcript, p. 60, supplemented by conversation with Edward Stern; deaths of Julius, Frieda and Ludwig Stern recorded in the Yad Vashem Central Database of Shoah Victim's based on information from Frances Stern Furguiele.

19. Charles Robertson to Cordell Hull, July 8, 1941; Nye to Hull, July 8, 1941; Stern to Hull, July 23 and August 27, 1941; Gustave Stern to Herman Stern October 28, 1941, all in Adolf Stern families file, Stern Papers.

20. Stiefel transcript, pp. 52-53. Herman Stern must have written to Wise or someone else in New York concerning the plight of the *St. Louis* passengers because he received from the Joint Distribution Committee a letter explaining the Committee's negotiations with Cuba: James N. Rosenberg to Stern, June 15, 1939, Stephen Wise file, Stern Papers.

21. Wyman, *Paper Walls,* pp. 170-171.

22. Irwin Rosen [of the American Jewish Joint Distribution Committee] to Tea Eichengruen, March 8, 1941, Tea Eichengruen to Joint Distribution Committee, April 26, 1941, in Stiefel papers, copies in Shoptaugh's possession. See also Stiefel transcript, p. 54.

23. Tea Eichengruen to Joint Distribution Committee, July 9, 1941, and Joint Distribution Committee to Tea Eichengruen, July 30, 1941, and notes by Herman Eichengruen concerning his son, made in Seville, Spain, July 1941, all in Stiefel papers, copies in Shoptaugh's possession. See also Stiefel Transcript, pp.55-56. After taking another group of refugees to Cuba, the steamer *Navemar* was sunk in the Atlantic in January 1942 by an Italian submarine.

24. A. M. Warren to Herman Stern, November 22, 1941, Adolf Stern family file, Stern Papers.

25. Seaton, *The Russo-German War,* pp. 208-9; Cole, *Senator Gerald P. Nye,* pp. 197-99. Hitler's formal agreements with Japan did not obligate Germany to declare war on the United States, and his reasons for doing so are still disputed. But as Robert Wistrich notes, the decision had an impact on the Holocaust – "with American entry into the war, the Jews of Europe had lost whatever role they might still have had (in Nazi minds) as bargaining chips with which to effect the behavior of the United States." See *Hitler and the Holocaust,* pp. 111-12.

26. Herman Stern to HIAS, December 14, 1941; Isaac Asofsky [of HIAS] to Stern, December 23, 1941; Stern to HIAS, January 26, 1942; Stern to Ruth Harrison, March 6, 1942 [which notes that Gustave Stern and family have recently arrived in New York, so perhaps Michael Stern's memory is in error on this point]; all in Adolf Stern family file, Stern Papers; Michael Stern transcript, pp. 8-11.

Chapter Fifteen
"Why Then Did No One Draw the Correct Inference?"

Ed Stern was marking prices on men's pajamas at the Straus store in Fargo on December 7, 1941, when he heard on the radio that Pearl Harbor had been attacked. He figured that war with Japan would soon mean war with Germany, and was pleased when Hitler declared war against the United States three days later. Ed was no longer the teenager who thought that refugees helped by his father were just nuisances; he and his brother Dick had heard the stories of many of them and had long since been "in favor of helping Britain, we were in favor of Lend Lease and all that kind of stuff."

Ed decided to enlist as soon as possible. "I was supposed to go to Bismarck to have a [draft] physical about December 10th or something like that, which is right in the middle of the Christmas season and we only had two fellows working in our little [Fargo] store. I told them [at the draft board] if they would wave that physical I would enlist the day after Christmas, which I did. I went down to Minneapolis to enlist and since I could type they grabbed me right away. There I was typing. After about six weeks of typing I got sent to Fort Warren for basic training. Then I got sent to an air base in Spokane [Washington]. By a quirk of fate I got assigned to somebody in a grocery warehouse instead of a clothing warehouse. The reason I was assigned to the grocery warehouse was because the C.O. of that grocery warehouse and I had graduated from Penn [University] in the same class. We didn't know each other, but he had his choice and he chose me. After three months of good brutal work, to make sure I was not a gold brick, they sent me to O.C.S. [Officer Cadet School] and it was Air Force O.C.S." After becoming an officer, Ed asked for overseas duty in Europe. "I wanted to get at those goddam Germans."[1]

With Ed's departure to the military, Herman Stern found it necessary to drive to Fargo to check on the business. Although he was

311

nearly fifty-five by early 1942, Stern still had a tremendous amount of energy and had no difficulty making the journey two or three times each week, to check the inventory and the books. He also continued to drive out to check the farm he and his sons owned near Stanton, made trips on behalf of the Greater North Dakota Association, and continued to be active in the Boy Scouts. In spite of all this, he somehow found time to throw additional energies into war-related activities. Like his son, he wanted to do his part to "get at" the Nazi overlords. He took a leading role in raising money in Barnes County for state and national USO activities. He also accepted the post of county chairman for the War Bond drives, raising more bond subscriptions in Barnes than any other county in the state. "Mr. Stern was able to instill into his corps of workers the same enthusiasm he himself feels," the Valley City newspaper commented. In 1944, Stern became the State Chairman for the National War Chest campaign, which put him on the road even more than before. After all this, he still had energy left over to oversee the preparation of a number GNDA reports sent the U.S. Department of Agriculture, castigating the Agricultural Adjustment Act for its interfering with the independence of Dakota farmers. Never a fan of Franklin Roosevelt, Stern was delighted when the need to feed the Allied nations brought an end to the AAA's acreage reduction efforts and several other New Deal programs.[2]

Felix Steiner had been with the store for about a year. He found Herman to be friendly but also a rather exacting boss. Straus Clothing used Steiner's talents to measure customers and make alterations to the clothes mass produced by Kuppenheimer or one of their other wholesale suppliers. They had no real use for his abilities as a master tailor. Over time he became frustrated with these limitations, but for the moment he was happy, the more so because he was away from the turmoil in Europe.

Greta Steiner, too, was content with life in Fargo. She liked the town well enough and felt they she and Felix were welcomed by the community – "they made us feel at home." But she greatly missed Austria. An avid hiker and downhill skier, she and Felix took an occasional trip up to Lake Itasca or one of the other lakes east of Clay

County to hike the small pine forest trails, but she longed for the Austrian Alps where she had spent her holidays. She never really accepted cross-country skiing as a substitute for the slopes of Austria.

Felix was by nature a "very private" person and was not much interested in socializing. He preferred to stay at home and listen to opera – he enthusiastically collected records – rather than go out in the evenings. But Felix made an exception in the matter of his faith. "We were not very observant Jews" in Austria, Greta recalled. But as a result of the persecutions of the 1930s, Felix "felt an obligation to his own people," and so persuaded Greta that they should regularly attend worship services: "That's where we belonged." In the beginning, they attended the Hebrew Congregation on First Avenue, but both of the Steiners found the "more eastern" style of this Orthodox group too much unlike the services they had known in Austria, because "many of the Jewish people in North Dakota came from Russia and other places east of Austria." Ultimately, they began attending the Reform-oriented services that were organized early in 1942 by Robert Herbst, William Stern, Jacob Levitz and a number of others.

As war continued, Greta feared for the safety of her parents and her brother. In 1940, she and Felix had filed affidavits in the hope of getting her mother and father out of Austria. "We had papers for my parents. Eddie Stern [also] made affidavits for my parents. We wanted to get my parents out, and at that time you still could get boat tickets, and we had no collateral at the bank to get a loan, so Eddie signed for us. I mean the bank loaned us the money [for tickets], but he signed [the loan] for us." However, no action was taken on the visa applications before Germany blocked all further Jewish emigration in 1941. Like everyone else, Greta and Felix would not know the fate of their families for some years.[3]

Willi Mueller and his brother also moved from St. Paul to Fargo in 1942. After living in St. Paul for a little more than a year, Willi married a woman named Erna Baer, who had grown up in a village near Willi's home in Germany. "Her mother and my mother, they were raised together in the same town. [Erna and I] we were friends, we had lived six kilometers apart. She left Germany in 1936 and lived in New York." Erna had met Willi and his brother Ludwig when they arrived in New York and helped them travel on to St. Paul. Willi had kept in touch with her since, and they had married. Both Erna and Willi wanted to live in a town smaller than St. Paul. Henry Weiler had investments in cattle, including a cattle market and feed lot that he owned in the town of West Fargo. One day he sent Willi and Ludwig out to Jamestown, North Dakota, to buy cattle for his lot. When Willi pointed out that his English skills were still limited and asked how he could talk to people, Weiler told him not to worry: "ask for help in German and most of them will answer you in German." The two men went, bought the cows and took them to West Fargo, then returned to St. Paul and told Weiler that they liked the area so much they wondered if they could find jobs there. No problem, Weiler replied, they could get jobs at his feed lot. Willi's father had been a horse trader, but had never dealt in cattle, but they went to Fargo and got into "the beef feeding business," renting land near West Fargo and becoming cattle traders. To supplement this, Willi also took a job at the Armour Packing Company slaughterhouse in West Fargo.

In September of 1942, Willi's mother, Fanni, and Aunt Klara arrived in the United States. After he and his brother left Germany in 1938, Willi's parents and aunt had immigrated to France. In 1940, they had also been detained by the French government and interned in the camps near Gurs. Moses Mueller died in the camp within a few weeks of his internment, but a distant cousin of the Muellers, who was a French citizen, got Willi's mother and aunt released by pledging a bond for them. The two women then lived, under police supervision, in a small apartment in Gurs, their rent paid by the cousin. Henry Weiler had agreed to sponsor both women for American visas and they were among the fortunate few to legally leave Vichy, France in 1942. Fanni and Klara both lived with the Muellers in Fargo, but Willi's aunt died in less than a year because of health problems that had been exacerbated by her incarceration in France.

Willi and Erna also became active in Fargo's Jewish community, and largely because of the encouragement of Solly Jonas. "The funny thing was, I was in the stockyard working, and there were some people that knew that I was Jewish, and they said 'There is a Jewish German family living in Fargo, maybe you want to know them, that you can get more acquainted.' So we went, my wife and I, to their house, and when they opened the door, Erna saw him and she said 'I know you.' His [Solly's] sister and my wife, they had learned to cook together in a hotel in Germany. But we didn't really know them until we met in Fargo." Willi and Erna soon came to know most everyone in the city's Jewish community.[4]

Herman was proud to tell some people that, in addition to Eddie, no less than six of the young men he had sponsored for visas were serving in the American armed services during the war, including Little Gus, Erich Stern, and Julius Blumenthal. But he shared this information only with a select group, for he was still reticent about the scope of his Jewish activities. As one of the other businessmen in Valley City later commented about his sponsorships of Jewish refugees, "I knew of it. I heard about it. He didn't talk about that here in town, because – well, I guess I can't say why he didn't, but maybe because they were of his [Jewish] nationality. But he was very, very careful about the things that he did and talked about. So a number of us knew about it, but it wasn't general knowledge. I doubt if very many people in the community outside the business district were aware of it, and if they were, [it was] very marginal."[5]

Stern's concerns about rousing anti-Semitism may also have influenced advice he gave while visiting Tea Eichengruen and her parents in New York. "He said 'I don't want you to stay in New York. Life is too hard. There are too many young Jews here [to compete for jobs] and your father is sixty-two years old. Go wherever you want to go. I'm not telling you where you should go. Go wherever you want to go, but don't stay in New York.' Naive as I was, I said, okay, if it really doesn't make any difference, why not go to Seattle? It's a beautiful city. I had been there with [Herman and Adeline] that summer and really fell in love with Seattle. I thought it was one of the most

beautiful cities I've ever seen. I knew there were some German Jewish people there. I knew there were some people from our part of
Germany. So my parents would not be so isolated." To help them on
their way, Stern gave Tea several dozen jeweled pins – "flowered
pins, out of silver thread," made by a friend of Stern's – to sell and
"have a little spending money when we got to Seattle."

Tea and her parents arrived in Seattle just a few days before the
Japanese attack on Pearl Harbor and found an apartment at the Cambridge Arms on Ninth Street. "We lived there for some time. Of course,
then 7th of December came, I will never forget that either, there were
blackouts." Because the Eichengruens were by definition "enemy
aliens," they were soon visited by the FBI. "We had to report to the
Army, we were fingerprinted, that bothered me a lot." Stern was so
upset when he learned of this that he persuaded the Governor of North
Dakota to write the Army district commander at Fort Lewis, in Seattle, and attest to the loyalty of the family. This probably had no
influence on the Army whatsoever; they did not release the
Eichengruens from the curfew restrictions until several weeks later,
after the jitters of a possible Japanese attack on the west coast had
faded.

Fortunately, both Tea and her father found daytime jobs in Seattle. Tea worked in a department store during the Christmas season,
then took a job at a millinery store owned by a woman named, oddly
enough, Betty Gruen. Once again, she made hats for sale in the store.
Hermann Eichengruen (who soon shortened his own name to Gruen)
also found a job. "To my dying day I'll give him credit for this. My
father, in all his life, had never worked for anybody else. He became
a janitor in the Washington Athletic Club. After a few weeks, he took
over handling the laundry at the club," probably, Tea thought, because the owners of the club liked the quiet and friendly man and
wanted to give him an easier job by handing out towels rather than
scrubbing the floors and hauling the trash. Elly eventually found a
job in a toy factory, making stuffed animals. "So between the three of
us we were able to pay the bills every month and send a check to
Herman [Stern] for thirty dollars" toward the debt owed for the ship

tickets.[6]

Mr. Gruen spent much of his free time writing letters in an effort to get information about young Erwin, who the family assumed was still in Holland. They could not know that Erwin, together with thousands of others, were already marked for death in Hitler's "final solution" to the "Jewish problem in Europe."

No written order has ever been found wherein Hitler directed Himmler and the SS to begin murdering Europe's Jewish population in their hundreds of thousands. It is probable that the Nazi Fuehrer never gave a written order for the Holocaust, just as he had not given written orders for the murders of the SA leadership in 1934, or any number of other bloody acts for which he did not wish to leave a record. In 1941, Himmler told SS killing squad commanders that the decisions to exterminate the Jews came from a "Fuehrer-order" or "had been personally ordered by Hitler," and later during the war said that the task had been given by Hitler to him because the SS could better keep such wholesale killings a secret than the German Army or the labyrinth of Germany's government bureaucracy. But of course, it did not remain a secret for very long. There were too many witnesses, too many killers. Soldiers returning from the Russian campaign in the fall of 1941 began telling family members and friends about the shootings they had seen perpetrated by the *Einsatzgruppen.* Rumors of the massacre of some seventy thousand Jews at Babi Yar in September were being whispered about Germany by mid-October. By the end of 1941, the death toll of Jews in Russia had reached half a million or more.[7]

Even before that, in September, as the German army's drive toward Moscow began to falter, Himmler wrote a note that sounded the death sentence for German Jews: "the Fuehrer wishes that the *Altreich* [the German state before1938 and Austria] and the [Czech] Protectorate from the east to the west should be cleared and freed of Jews as soon as possible." Several thousand Jews, many of them elderly, were rounded up in the larger German cities and sent by train to Lodz and Riga soon after. Those being transported were told that

they were to be "resettled" in the parts of Poland that had been annexed by Germany in 1939. But thousands were shot immediately
after they arrived at their destinations and the rest were crowded into
ghettoes to await a similar fate. Among those who were immediately
killed may have been Hilda Jonas's father Samuel, her step-mother
Hedwig and her half-sister Ruth, who was then fourteen years old.[8]

More transports of German Jews followed as the Nazis organized
an assembly line for mass murder. After the *Einstazgruppen* performed
experiments in killing people by carbon monoxide poisoning inside
mobile vans, the SS set up a special camp near Chelmno, with gas
chambers in wooden huts for use in mass exterminations. This death
camp was used for the first time on in early December to kill a group
of Jews from the local area. Thereafter, hundreds a day were sent to
Chelmno from the ghetto in Lodz and then murdered.

Meanwhile, the *Einstazgruppen* were sending in reports of their
progress in other parts of the east. A report from *Einstazgruppe* C in
early November stated that wall posters had been used to announce
to Jews in and around Kiev that they were to gather to "be resettled,"
and that the Jews "still believed they were going to be resettled until
just before their execution. . . . up to now around 75,000 Jews have
been liquidated in this fashion." In another report, dated the first of
December, the leader of *Einstazkommando* 3 reported that "there are
no more Jews in Lithuania apart from the work-Jews [slave labor
groups] and their families . . I wanted to bump off these work-Jews
and their families but this brought me smack up against the civil
administration (the Reich Commissar) and the Wehrmacht and
prompted a ban on the shooting of these work-Jews and their families." Some of these reports were transmitted by radio, intercepted
and decoded by the British. While Americans did not yet have privy
to these decodes, the American embassy in Berlin warned Washington in November that Jews in Germany were being deported to work-
gangs in Russia and that SS units were carrying out mass executions.
For obvious reasons, neither the British nor the American intelligence
estimates were made public.[9]

It was partly in order to prevent disputes between the SS and the

Army or various administrators that Heydrich summoned a number of senior Nazi officials to meet with him to obtain a "uniform view among the relevant central agencies of the further tasks concerned with the remaining work on this final solution." The gathering, held in the Berlin suburb of Wannsee on January 20, 1942, included representatives of the Ministries of Justice and Interior, the Reich Chancellery, the Foreign Office, the Race and Settlement Office, the SS, and the Ministry for the Occupied Eastern Territories. The minutes of this meeting elucidate the way in which all of the Jews under Nazi control were now to be murdered. After reviewing the prior actions taken against the Jews, including the attempts at forced emigration, Heydrich told his listeners that all previous attempts to make Germany "Jew-free" had failed; now the Jews in Europe, who he estimated to be about eleven million people, were to be moved enmasse: "The evacuation of the Jews to the east has now emerged, with the prior permission of the Fuhrer, as a further possible solution instead of emigration. These actions, however, must be regarded only as an alternative solution. But already the practical experience is being gathered which is of great importance to the coming final solution of the Jewish question." Everyone at the meeting understood that "final solution" meant mass murder and that the "practical experience" was that of the killing squads of the *Einsatzgruppen.*

Those at the conference then created a rough list of approximately how many Jews lived in each country of Europe (including Germany's allies, the neutral nations, and those that had yet to be invaded, like England and Ireland) and engaged in a discussion of the definition of who was, and was not, a Jew, in order to create a consistent manner of identifying who would be sent to their deaths in the east. In order to quell the possibility of objections over the killing of German men who had fought in World War I, the group agreed that "Jews with war decorations" would be sent to "an old people's ghetto – Theresienstadt is envisaged" and that German Jews over sixty-five would be sent there as well." It was also noted that some of those sent east would be "conscripted for labour in the east under appropriate supervision" and that "a large number of them will drop out through natural wastage." As for those who were tough enough or lucky enough to survive the hard work, "they will have to be dealt with accordingly. For if released they would, as a natural selection of the fittest, form a germ cell from which the Jewish race could regenerate itself." The meeting concluded with some of the participants urging that the program be carried out "as soon as possible" and that steps be taken, particularly in the western European countries, to ensure that the victims were gathered and transported "without upsetting the population."

By this means, the blueprint for extermination was drafted. Once again, those receiving their orders had been told that "the prior permission of the Fuhrer" had been obtained. They thus could put aside any doubts and carry out their duties.[10]

From January through June of 1942, hundreds of thousands of Polish Jews were transported out of their ghettoes and murdered in Chelmno and in additional camps at Majdanek and Belzec. By April, the Slovakian government had yielded to German pressure to allow their Jewish population to be "evacuated" to a new camp at Birkenau, which had been added to a large complex of concentration compounds outside the village of Auschwitz. Large numbers of these Slovakian Jews were among the earliest to be murdered at Auschwitz. Testimony later presented at the trials of German war criminals explained how the camp commandants by then evolved a ruse to put the intended victims at ease: "The victims . . . were led to believe that they had arrived at a transit camp. An SS-man strengthened this belief by announcing that they were to undress and go to the baths in order to wash and be disinfected. They were also told that afterwards they would receive clean clothes and be sent on to a work camp. Separation of the sexes, undressing, and even the cropping of the women's hair could not but reinforce the impression that they were on their way to the baths. First the men were led into the gas chambers, before they were able to guess what was going on; then it was the turn of the women and children."[11]

As more and more Polish, Slovakian and German Jews were transported to the east and disposed of, German occupying troops, with the assistance of Dutch policemen, began rounding up the Jews living in that country. This included Erwin Eichengruen, the younger brother of Tea. Erwin's fate was not known to his sister until 1948, when the Dutch Red Cross sent Herman Eichengruen a record from the German archives confirming that Erwin was deported with many others to Auschwitz on July 15, 1942. Heinrich Himmler was himself at Auschwitz that day to observe how the gassings were conducted. A number of Jews from the train that had carried Erwin were chosen as the victims for this demonstration of the gas chambers. It is recorded that Himmler usually felt uneasy watching the execution procedures, but he expressed satisfaction to Auschwitz's commandant, Rudolf Hoss, on the methods of killing. He said he wanted the camp to be expanded. He then gave Hoss a promotion.

Erwin Eichengruen was not among those done to death for Himmler's sake. The SS had created several "shops" at Auschwitz to manufacture uniforms, boots, even synthetic rubber. Erwin was among those who were selected to work at one of these tasks. That meant that he and the others, usually young men and women, were taken to have their heads shaved and their arms tattooed with an identifying number. Provided with a thin suit of prison garb, they were set to work. They were fed only enough to keep them working, usually a thin soup that consisted of some vegetables and animal bones boiled in water. Workers at Auschwitz generally lost five or six pounds a week. If no disease intervened or the person was not eventually sent to the gas chamber, death by starvation was inevitable. In Erwin's case, sometime around September of that year, the eighteen-year-old boy died. The Dutch authorities who investigated his case were unable to discover the cause of his death, but noted that "experience gathered in the search for missing deportees" suggested that the most likely possibilities were "disease, exhaustion, or asphyxiation."[12]

Throughout 1942, the Jewish communities in Hitler's empire were steadily decimated. Moses Stern was sent to die in Theresienstadt. His brother, Julius, and Julius's wife, Frieda, disappeared into the camps and were never heard from again. Regina Kann, the mother of Hanna Schwarz, similarly disappeared, her decision to return to Europe from America having proved to be a fatal one. Selma Kann, the widow of Rudolf Kann, was deported with her sons Manfred and Herbert, who had lived for a time with Tea Eichengruen in Dinslaken. Where Selma met her fate is unknown, but Herbert died in Sobibor and Manfred was murdered at Auschwitz. Every person that Herman Stern had sponsored lost family in the Holocaust. Alan Ullmann, the son of Lotte Henlein and her husband, Irwin Ullmann (who was also a German refugee) later studied German documents and identified thirty relatives of the Henleins and Ullmanns who perished. Lotte herself related the story of how her husband's parents died. "They were informed in December of 1941 to assemble at a certain spot. They could take a few things along and that's all. I'm going to tell you something very few people know. They had to buy a passage to the concentration camp, paid it themselves. And if you didn't have the money, another had to pay for it. They were sent to Riga, Latvia." Albert Ullmann died of pneumonia and malnutrition. Elsa, his wife, was "shot to death by an open grave" with dozens of others. In the years following the war, Stern heard dozens of such stories about the relatives of those he had helped.[13]

On July 16, 1942, thousands of French policemen conducted a mass raid to round up all foreign-nationality Jews in Paris. There had been previous raids to arrest foreign Jews before, but none on this scale, which was carried out in cooperation with the German occupiers. The police started the sweep before dawn and within two days had arrested almost thirteen thousand people, three-quarters of them women and children under the age of sixteen. About one hundred Jews committed suicide after receiving word of the sweep; in some cases, mothers jumped from their apartment windows while clutching their babies. The prisoners were herded into a large stadium used for cycle racing and held there until transportation was arranged to take them to a French internment camp. The majority were crowded in Drancy, which already had a reputation for brutality and a high death rate. Those that survived Drancy were soon shipped off to the east, mostly to Auschwitz.

The Nazi government was also pressuring Vichy to yield up its

Jewish population. Petain and Pierre Laval, his vice-premier, had approved a vigorous program of "Aryanization" for the new France. Jewish-owned property had been confiscated for the French state, leaving many Jews destitute and foreign Jews particularly vulnerable. But when the Germans demanded that the Jews be transferred to their authority, the French leaders hesitated at first, Laval commenting that he could accept the deportation of foreign-born Jews but felt that the French people would object to the deportation of fellow citizens. But Hitler's representatives to Vichy were insistent and ultimately the French gave way, yielding up the foreign Jews first and the rest later. In August, trainloads of internees from Gurs and the other Mediterranean camps were sent off to Auschwitz. As usual, the poor victims were crammed into cattle cars, with from seventy to a hundred persons in each wagon. Fritz and Sally Kann were apparently separated at this time. Sally Kann was fifty-eight when he died at Auschwitz. Where Fritz died is unknown. Erika, still in hiding at the Saelens farmhouse near Bruges, Belgium, heard rumors of the killing of Jews. But even by the time British and American forces drove the Germans out of Belgium in 1944, she knew nothing specific about her father's fate.[14]

Information about the Final Solution began to leak to the outside world almost as soon as the killings began. On November 19, 1941, a British diplomat in Switzerland informed the Foreign Office that he had been told from a Polish informant that "1 ½ million Jews [who] were living in Eastern (recently Russian) Poland have simply disappeared altogether." Additional information, with detailed accounts of some of massacres carried out in Russia, was forwarded by agents of the underground Polish Home Army. The British by then had confirmation of some of the decoded Order Police radio reports of mass executions by the *Einsatzgruppen*. But in order to protect the vital decoding secrets, the government made no official statements about the mass murders.

In the meantime, American correspondents who had been in Germany warned readers that the Nazis were murdering Jews in large

numbers. Sigrid Schultz of the *Chicago Tribune* wrote of her memories of hearing SS men brag in 1939 of "how they had locked Poles
and Jews into cellars and then thrown hand grenades through windows left open for the purpose." H. R. Knickerbocker predicted in
his 1941 memoir of reporting from Berlin that "five or six million
Jews" would die during the war, although he expected this to be the
result of the "slow death" of starvation. In October 1941, Louis
Lochner stated in his syndicated column that a "fixed German policy"
to murder the Jews was being carried out. Numerous other articles
appeared in American newspapers that briefly reported the mass killings near Kiev, the reports of executions elsewhere, and the onset of
deportations of Jews in Germany to "uncertain fates" in the east. The
bulk of major newspapers, in the words of one historian, "placed the
various stories [of executions of Jews] on inner pages and allotted
them but a few lines," which "left readers free to accept this news as
valid or to dismiss it as unverified information in which the paper
had little faith."

A discerning reader could put pieces together and guess with reasonable accuracy what was happening to the Jews of Europe. The
Roosevelt government avoided any official comment on whether or
not the Germans indeed had embarked on a deliberate plan to exterminate the Jews until July 1942, when FDR himself sent a statement
to a New York City rally sponsored by the American Jewish Congress and the B'nai B'rith. In this, Roosevelt said that Americans
"will share in the sorrow of our Jewish fellow-citizens over the savagery of the Nazis against their helpless victims. The Nazis will not
succeed in exterminating their victims any more than they will succeed in enslaving the world." Roosevelt promised that the Nazis would
be held accountable for any such atrocities after the war. The statement could have been intended as a warning to Hitler that the Allies
knew what was happening. But all the same, the Office of War Information, the American government's official news agency on war
matters, were directed not to highlight "atrocity material,' nor to focus on Jews as special victims of the Nazis.[15]

This reluctance on the part of Britain and the United States governments to openly comment of the extermination of the Jewish population puzzled and angered Jewish leaders in several parts of the world. Richard Lichtheim, a representative of the Jewish Agency in Geneva, Switzerland, gave vent to his frustration in a report he wrote before the end of 1941. With the beginning of deportations to the east, he stated, "the fate of the Jews" [in Germany, Austria and the Czech region] is now sealed. . . . There was a time when the US and the other [South] American states could have helped by granting [additional] visas. But this was obstructed by the usual inertia of the bureaucratic machine and by red tape." In America, Stephen Wise received information from other sources about what was occurring. He passed some of this on to the State Department and urged the officials there to make renewed efforts to help more refugees get out of Europe or Africa. But as little was done, he too became anguished. "The truth is," he wrote a friend, "in the midst of a war, it is very difficult to make anyone see that we [Jews] are most particularly hurt."[16]

Then information came that was difficult to ignore. Late in July, a German businessman traveled to Zurich and told a Swiss associate that he believed a plan was being considered in Germany to exterminate all European Jews with poison gas. This information reached representatives of the World Jewish Congress in Geneva, who in turn asked the American and British diplomats in Geneva to pass the revelation on to Stephen Wise. The State Department in Washington suppressed the information, but the word reached Wise anyway from friends in London. Wise went to Washington and asked several officials at State to seek conformation of the report before he made a public statement. He waited until November, when Undersecretary of State Sumner Welles told him that it was true. Wise then called a press conference and announced that evidence from Europe showed that over two million Jews had already been killed by the Nazis in an "extermination campaign." Most of the major newspapers in America carried the story, but many of them added editorial doubts as to the accuracy of the evidence. Some used words like "asserted" and "claimed" in reporting Wise's remarks. Others noted that the report to Wise came from the World Jewish Congress, and that judgment had to be withheld, because Jews were obviously an "interested party" in the story rather than neutral observers. The State Department issued no statement to clarify the doubts.[17]

A certain callous indifference was certainly present in the way in which reports of the wholesale murders were received by the Allied governments. The war was world-wide in scope, the scale of destruction was vast, and the outcome still in doubt. Millions had already died in the conflict. It was not certain when or how Hitler could be decisively defeated, and, with Japan still to be dealt with, some were predicting that the war could last another ten years. At the level at which Roosevelt and Churchill had to view the war, it was no doubt very difficult to consider the fate of one specific ethnic group as the greatest priority.

Also true was the fact that many people simply could not make themselves believe that even the Nazis would actually set out to systematically kill every Jewish man, woman and child. When Felix Frankfurter met a representative of the Polish underground in Washington in 1943, who told him in detail about how the Jews were being exterminated at the death camps, Frankfurter said he refused to believe him. Frankfurter did not think the man was lying, he simply refused to believe it. The Dutch historian Louis de Jong later commented that many of the Jews in Europe did the same thing: "Hitler had said it plainly: let war come and the whole of European Jewry will be exterminated. And the war had come. Why then did no one draw the correct inference? . . . The gas chambers, however, spelt death – and what death! – not only to individuals but to all those they held dear: their parents and grandparents, their children and grandchildren, their relatives and friends. Small, indeed, must have been the number of those among the millions driven to death, who could face that awesome truth." Certainly few of the young men or women that had made it to America with Stern's help saw the signs with total clarity. Like soldiers who see death all around them and still cling to the notion that it "can't happen to me," so the Steiners, the Ullmans, the Levys and many others still felt that, somehow, those dearest to them in Europe would survive the war. A large part of the reaction of the American press and people to the rumors of the killings rested on this wholly human desire to deny the worst.[18]

From the time of Wise's announcement until the end of the war, Jewish groups appealed to Roosevelt and Churchill to rescue the Jews in Hitler's hands before they were all murdered. Appeals for action were published in the newspapers, including a full-page ad in the *New York Times* that asked readers "How Well are You Sleeping" in the face of the exterminations going on in Europe. The ad urged a major petition campaign asking the U.S. government to establish a special refugee administration, alter the immigration laws, and save some of Hitler's intended victims. Threaten to execute some of the German prisoners or interned civilians, mount a bold rescue operation, ransom the women and children, bomb the rail lines leading to the camps, do something! Always the Allied leaders turned down the pleas, saying the war itself took priority and the best action would be to use the troops and the bombers to defeat Germany and end the war. In January 1944, Roosevelt yielded to pressure from Henry Morgenthau, his Treasury Secretary, and created the War Refugee Board, which issued special immigration permits to some of the Jewish refugees in Africa and elsewhere. By that time, some four million Jews in Europe had already been murdered.[19]

If enough important people had been able to clearly see in 1938 that Hitler would not rest until he had exterminated Europe's Jewish population, would they have done more? If Wise had accepted that inevitability in 1938, would he have embraced Herman Stern's proposal to settle German Jewish families on farms in North Dakota? Could Wise have convinced enough members of the American Jewish Congress to put up five thousand dollars for each family? If the Holocaust had been accepted as inevitable in 1938, would the Congress have acquiesced to a change in the immigration laws and the taxpayers accepted a half billion dollar Federal program to settle a hundred thousand Jewish immigrant families in the Great Plains? Hindsight may be blessed with perfect clarity, but it stretches the imagination to believe that even with absolute clairvoyance such a program may have been undertaken in the America of 1938.

Herman Stern may have sighed "if only" many times, but as the news of the Final Solution was dissected and debated, he kept his custom of keeping quiet. Once his brother Adolf, with Gustave and the others, arrived in America in early 1942, Stern stopped his ongoing correspondence with members of the State Department and with Gerald Nye. He had accepted at the outbreak of the European war in 1939 that his brothers Julius and Moses were probably not going to get out, and probably saw little point in speaking out on the immigration issue thereafter. As someone who had stated several times that he was worried about an eruption of anti-Semitism in the United States, he likely thought that it would be improper and foolish to say anything on a matter as divisive as the news of the Final Solution was becoming in America.

Instead, he focused his attention on matters close to home. Ed had worried about how "this poor old man was going to run two stores in Valley City and Fargo," but they did not become a problem. "He moved into the rooming house that I had lived in, he kept a place [for overnight stays] and he drove back and forth. He just had pep." In 1944, after persuading Gustave Stern to move with his family, and Adolf and Dora, from Chicago to Fargo and work at the store, Herman made trips to Fargo mainly to visit them. He found the visits especially comforting after his other brother, Gustav, died of heart failure later in the same year.

In addition to this and the war bond campaigns, he spent time on the North Dakota Winter Show in Valley City, which the Greater North Dakota Association sustained with a volume of advertising. In his free time he drove out to the farm he owned, to see to the expenses, and just walk out in the fields; just as with his garden at home, the time he spent studying the soil and the crops was a great comfort.

The failure to save his brothers hurt him deeply. The rumors of mass murders were increasing in volume by 1942, when Felix Steiner told him that the Fargo store needed more help. Steiner complained that he was putting in too many late night hours in order to alter suits and Stern needed to hire someone to reduce the load. Stern replied that he did not care "how many hours" the work took – "I consider the accomplishments!" Compared to many others, Steiner should count his blessings. Similarly when Ed prepared to leave for overseas duty, his father told him to be careful, make him proud, and remember that he was fighting for a better world than there would be if Hitler won the war. He made similar remarks at bond rallies.[20]

In the meantime, encouraged by Solly and Hilda Jonas, he and Adeline continued to attend services at Fargo's Reform Congregation. Early in 1942, the congregation purchased a large home in Fargo at the intersection of Second Avenue and Nineteenth Street South, and remodeled it into a formal Temple. On February 16, 1942, they incorporated as Temple Beth El. In 1945, Stern formally became a member of the congregation.[21]

Throughout the war, the members of Temple Beth El Sisterhood contributed time and money to the Red Cross, USO, and other war-related activities. Neither the minute books of the Sisterhood nor the congregation board ever spoke of the devastation of the Jewish population in Europe. This was not unusual. The records of the older and more Orthodox Congregation B'Nai Israel in Grand Forks, contain similar notes about Red Cross and war charities but no mention of *Kristallnacht* or the mass killings of Jews in Europe. Such silence in the face of the Holocaust rested on many factors: the sheer horror of it, the desire of the immigrant refugee to "fit in" rather than call attention to his or her foreign-ness, fear that a wave of anti-Semitism could be kindled in the United States, internal differences over the cause of Zionism, the fact that with eleven million American men and woman in the armed services it would be considered "selfish" to dwell on the devastation being wrought on a foreign people – all these played a part. Greta Steiner later commented that Temple members seldom spoke of the killings during the war or in the early years following it, partly because it was "just too horrible to want to think about." Doubting by then that her own parents would survive the war, Greta, like thousands of others, came to know the feeling of being more than just a refugee, of being one of the few who survived.[22]

By the summer of 1944, further eyewitness accounts of the death camps appeared in the American press. By the end of the year, with Germany's defeat all but inevitable, American polls showed that about three-quarters of the people believed that the Nazis had been murdering Jews and political prisoners, but still doubted that the numbers of the victims ran into the millions. Only when American, British and Russian troops overran Auschwitz and the other death camps in 1945 did the public finally accept the full scale of the horror. But the story was soon dwarfed by victory. Ed Stern was happy when Germany fell and Hitler committed suicide in the ruins of Berlin, because he wanted some measure of retribution for the murders that Hitler had ordered. But he was happier with the end of the war because that meant he could go home. People wanted to get back to their normal lives and forget the horrors.

One man who played little part in the victory celebration was Gerald Nye. In 1944, running for re-election, Nye could not overcome his isolationist label or the humiliation of his appearance in Pittsburgh the moment Pearl Harbor was being attacked. In a three-way race he was defeated for re-election by the Democratic Party candidate, who won by a thirty thousand-vote plurality. Although he talked about running for office again, Nye's political career was really over. He went into private business in Washington DC and later held a post in the Federal Housing Administration.

Nye lived until 1971. His part in helping so many of Stern's relatives obtain American entry visas remained unknown during his lifetime. He himself may never have regarded the matter as very important. There is no record that he ever commented on it. But the fact remains that without his help over a period of six years, and his intervention at key moments with letters to the State Department, Gustave Stern and his father Adolf, Hermann and Elly Eichengruen, Gustav Strauss, the Besmanns, and many others would surely have died in the camps.[23]

Notes

1. Edward Stern transcript, pp. 15, 17, supplemented by additional conversation in August 2005.   While Ed Stern and his brother openly favored aid to Britain prior to Pearl Harbor, their father never said anything on the subject, but proudly wrote to may people of his son's enlistment in the Army Air Corps.

2. See the War Loan Bond Drives, USO Fund Drives, and North Dakota War Chest files, Stern Papers, and the Valley City *Times-Record,* October 19, 1943. The GNDA files contain the reports of complaint that the AAA program was hampering "farm solvency and stable business conditions."

3. Steiner transcript, pp. 38-40, 45, supplemented by an earlier recorded interview between Mrs. Steiner and Max Liebowitz, [1975-76?], copy of tape in the Nathan and Theresa Berman Upper Midwest Jewish Archives, University of Minnesota.

4. Mueller transcript, pp. 8-13.

5. Roy Sheppard transcript., pp. 6-7.   This statement clearly referred to Stern's Judaism rather than his German background, as did a second statement when Shepard, responding to a question about anti-Semitism, said he could not recall "anyone making any disparaging remarks about him [Stern] because of his nationality."

6. Stiefel transcript, p. 56-59; Stiefel letters.

7. The issue of how much the German people knew about the Holocaust is covered in Daniel Goldhagen's rather sensational account, *Hitler's Willing Executioners: Ordinary Germans and the Holocaust* (New York: Knopf, 1996), but this work should be supplemented by the more judicious research of Eric Johnson and Karl-Heinz Reubard, *What We Knew: Terror, Mass Murder, and Everyday Life in Nazi Germany* (New York: Basic Books, 2005), which concludes (p. 397) that about a third to a half of German adults "had some level of awareness of the Holocaust."

8. Fleming, *Hitler and the Final Solution,* pp. 50-53; Walter Laqueur *The Terrible Secret,* pp. 89, 152, 196-97; Deschner, *Reinhard Heydrich,* p. 177. The Yad Vashem database of Shoah Victims records Samuel, Hedwig and Ruth Levy as having died in Lodz.

9. Noakes, ed., *Nazism,* vol. 3, pp. 1094-96; Breitman, *Official Secrets,* pp. 91-99, 124. Despite the objections of the German Army (Wehrmacht) against the executions of Jewish men and women being used for labor, other reports praised the Army for its full support in the gruesome deeds of the *Einsatzgruppen.*

10. Noakes, ed., *Nazism,* vol. 3, pp. 1127-34; Wistrich, *Hitler and the Holocaust,* pp. 102-107. See also the excellent analysis by Mark Roseman, *The Wannsee Conference and the Final Solution: A Reconsideration* (New York: Metropolitan Books, 2002).

11. Breitman, *Official Secrets,* pp. 112-114; "Operation Reinhard: The Extermination Camps of Belzec, Sobibor and Treblinka," edited by Aharon Weiss, Yad Vashem Studies XVI, and the Jewish Virtual Library website (http://www.jewishvirtuallibrary.org/jsource/Holocaust/reinhard.html#6).

12. Richard Breitman, *The Architect of Genocide: Himmler and the Final Solution*, pp. 236-37; J. Van de Vosse to Herman Gruen, March 16, 1948, in Steifel Papers. During the war, the Eichengruens changed their last name to Gruen.

13. Ullmann transcript, pp. 41-42; Alan Ullmann communication to Shoptaugh, July 30, 2002.

14. Ousby, *Occupation,* pp. 187-92; Paul Webster, *Petain's Crime: The Full Story of French Collaboration in the Holocaust* (Chicago : I.R. Dee, 1991)*,* pp. 115-19; Erika Bachar-Kann to Shoptaugh, January 24, 1999.

15. Laqueur, *The Tragic Secret*, p. 83, 109-110; Lipstadt, *Beyond Belief,* pp. 144-56, 162-64 (on the placement of stories in newspapers); Breitman, *Official Secrets,* pp. 122-36.

16. Laqueur, *The Tragic Secret,* pp. 174-75; Urofsky, *A Voice that Spoke for Justice,* p. 327.

17. Breitman, *Official Secrets,* pp. 137-42; Lipstadt, pp. 180-83. See also Laqueur and Breitman, *Breaking the Silence* (New York: Simon and Schuster, 1986) for fuller details. Two months after the stories based on Wise's announcement appeared, Breckinridge Long directed the American consulates not to forward further reports of murders of Jews to any private citizens.

18. Laqueur, *The Tragic Secret,* pp. 154-56.

19. *New York Times,* November 24, 1943; David Wyman, *The Abandonment of the Jews: America and the Holocaust, 1941-1945* (New York, Pantheon Books, 1985), pp. 144-55, 183-87.

20. Stern to Felix Steiner, September 21, 1942, Personal Correspondence File, Stern Papers; Conversation with Edward Stern in 1998 and Ed Stern transcript, p. 21. The rift with Steiner was brief, for Stern encouraged Steiner to open his own tailor shop in 1944, gave him advice, and sent a number of customers to him for special work.

21. *Temple Beth El: The First Fifty Years,* pp. 7-8; Max Goldberg to Herman Stern, December 29, 1945, Max Goldberg File, Stern Papers.

22. Sisterhood Minute Books and Board Minutes at Temple Beth El, Fargo; Sisterhood Minute Books, Congregation B"Nai Israel Records, Elwyn B. Robinson Department of Special Collections, Chester Fritz Library, University of North Dakota; Steiner transcript, p. 29. See also Peter Novick, *The Holocaust in American Life* (New York: Houghton Mifflin Co., 1999), pp. 19-59, 103-9.

23. Lipstadt, *Beyond Belief,* pp. 233-43; Cole, *Gerald P. Nye,* pp. 214-23.

Chapter Sixteen
"They Didn't Owe Me Anything"

November 15, 1950 was one of the happiest days in Stern's life. It was the day that he opened his new store in Valley City. Building a new store was something he had wanted to do for several years. The venerable old Kindred Hotel, where he had operated for so long, had seriously deteriorated during the 1930s. Stern had bought the dilapidated thing and wanted to tear it down after the war, but the shortage of construction materials during the postwar housing boom had forced him to wait. Finally in late 1949, he was able to begin. Moving his store into a leased space further north on the street at the beginning of 1950, he had the Kindred demolished and erected in its place a modern store of tan brick and glass. The store was fronted by several windows for displays. A basement for the store's inventory also contained a meeting space for the town's Boy Scouts, which Stern still served as the troop's leader.

The new store opened the morning of November 15 with a "grand opening sale," drawings for numerous prizes (including a prize for the person who could most closely guess "the number of stitches in a huge pair of Oshkosh overalls" hung on the side of the building), refreshments, and free "orchids for the ladies." Commenting about the attractiveness of the store, a business friend from Fargo told an announcer for the local radio station that the store's design and layout reflected the owner's desire for the best – "I know that Herman Stern wouldn't have anything else but the finest." In a letter to her friends and family, Herman's wife Adeline noted that over two thousand people visited the store that day, including some old timers who had bought clothes at the old Sternberg's store before M. G. Straus bought it and renamed it. Noting that the current governor and the governor-elect were among the many V.I.P.s to come by to congratulate them, she added that for her "the high spot" of the day was when

335

her son, Dick, arrived from Washington State and "could spend a few days with us." Typically, Stern himself initially shied away from talking to the local radio announcer and had his son Ed do the talking. Cornered by the same announcer later in the day, he thanked all of his friends and customers for their "kindness and thoughtfulness" in coming for the dedication and quickly turned the microphone again over to Eddie.[1]

The war and immediate postwar years had been fairly good ones for the Straus business. True, Stern had not enjoyed having to abide by the regulations of the government's wartime price regulation for various types of clothing. He had to work hard to maintain a decent inventory in the midst of shortages. "We had to buy merchandise where ever we could," he told a business audience some twenty years after the war. "We went to the black market to supply work shirts. I used to go to New York, down on Picardy Street," where little shops would sell a great many things outside the rules. "We used to go down there and buy work shirts and overalls and gloves . . . They didn't want to take our check, they wanted cash, but we wanted to be sure our merchandise went out of the store." Stern also checked the even smaller stores on Fifth Avenue, which had a "piece good market." "We'd buy a piece of goods here and a piece of goods there ... [and] take them out to small [garment] manufacturers who didn't have big war contracts and get them made into suits so that we'd have a few suits to sell in our stores." Because women's clothing was somewhat easier to obtain, Stern added a ladies line in the Fargo store.[2]

At war's end, Stern noted that his "stocks [of merchandise] were practically depleted." But the stores did very good business once the postwar economic boom began to satisfy pent up American demand for new homes, appliances, clothes, and other consumer goods they had done without during the conflict. When Eddie returned home at the end of the war, Herman offered to help stake him in a different occupation, saying "you don't have to go back to Fargo, there are many other places to do business." But the younger Stern and his wife Louise, who he had married before going overseas, wanted to remain in North Dakota, and Ed went back to managing the Fargo store.

For a brief few months, he and his cousin Gustave worked at the store together. But Gustave was "absolutely miserable" in trying to sell clothes. "He would stand there near the door, his hands tightly gripped together behind his back, and just stare into space. He hated the clothing business." Gustave later admitted that he "was not content in North Dakota." He had had a stroke of luck when he was hired to play the organ for one of Fargo's Congregational Churches, but he missed his larger musical career terribly. In 1945, Gustave took his parents and family, with Adeline, to Seattle for a vacation. "We fell in love with Seattle, especially when we went by Lake Washington and the southern part [of the state], we were reminded of Zurich." Since his brother-in-law Erich Vasen also lived in Seattle, Gustave, encouraged by Herman, decided to move there with his wife and sons and try his luck in a dry cleaning business with Vasen. This did not work out very well either.[3]

But then Gustave's fortunes took a turn for the better. Oddly, this happened because his father, Adolf, was in failing health by the time the family moved to Seattle. "My father had gotten cancer," Gustave later recalled, "and he said 'I want a doctor who speaks German.' That was Doctor Irving Wirth." Wirth, himself an immigrant from Wurzburg, was a general practitioner at the time. Although he was able to do little for Adolf because the cancer was already advanced, Wirth and Gustave quickly struck up a friendship over their mutual love of music. The two men had dinner at Wirth's home one evening. Gustave also played Wirth's piano. After listening to Gustave for "a little bit," Wirth said to Gustave, "'I know some people at the Seattle Civic Opera, I want you to meet them.'" Gustave met several of the Opera's patrons over the next few months. And, with one thing and another, he managed to get a job conducting at some of the Opera's performances. Before this, America had been a refuge. Seattle now became for Gustave a real home.[4]

As the postwar prosperity continued, some of the former refugees saw their chance to grab a piece of the American dream. Eric

Stern spent several years working for stores in Chicago, learning the intricacies of the clothing trade. Then, in March 1950, he wrote to Herman Stern about "an opportunity" to lease "a space in Hyde Park" where he and a partner could open a store for "made to order clothes." After describing the space and the potential market, he asked Stern about the prospects for success. Eric would need to sell "250 garments a year," Stern replied, suggesting the store's mainstay should be suits that cost about $44.50 to make and sold for $65.00. It would take "at least a year" before the store would begin to show a profit, he concluded. But, with the right choices and aggressive advertising he thought the store could succeed in Chicago if Eric had "the determination to stick to it." For several years thereafter, Stern reviewed the financial statements of Cohn and Stern and gave advice. The store succeeded. The partners added more off-the-rack clothing with shoes and accessories as the years went by, and in the mid-1960s, opened a new store in one of Chicago's prestigious shopping centers on Michigan Avenue. When Stern wrote Eric of how proud he was at the store's growing success, Eric replied "we consider your praise a high compliment."[5]

In similar vein, Erwin Stiefel started a business with advice from Stern. After marrying Tea Eichengruen, Stiefel served in the U.S. Army, most of the time at Fort Leavenworth, Kansas. Leaving the service in 1945 with a master sergeant's rank, Erwin worked in a variety of jobs for a time, then in the 1950s established a business in wholesale jewelry with his sister's husband in Kansas City. Tea thought he "would have liked to have become a physician as he started, but by that time his brother-in-law was here and so they started this jewelry business together. He would have been a much better doctor than he was a businessman, no question about that." The couple put up five thousand dollars, borrowed from Herman Stern, for their share of the business. He sent Stern regular reports of the business and of course, Stern sent him advice in return.

During these years, Tea and her father tried to discover the circumstances surrounding the death of her brother and also the fate of a number of others. Herman Gruen wrote dozens of letters to authorities in Holland to learn what had happened to Herbert and Manfred Kann, the two boys who had lived with them for a time in the mid-1930s. The boys' mother had taken them to live in Holland before Tea left for America. From letters sent to her before the war, Tea knew that Mrs. Kann had worked as a sales clerk in Holland and that "the boys were, for a brief time, in a school in Italy, I do believe. Now, who paid for that, I don't know." During the war all contact had been lost with the family and it was not until after the war that Herman learned that Mrs. Kann had "trusted a man, paid him for helping them to escape, to get out to Switzerland. The man denounced them. They were picked up the next day." Dutch authorities confirmed that Herbert died in one of the camps, Manfred in another. But Tea's family never learned "what happened to my aunt, nobody knows."

Tea's father also worked to obtain restitution from the postwar government of West Germany for the property he had lost in the 1930s. He wrote letters detailing the extent of his property and business in Dinslaken and listing the jewelry and artworks the Nazis had seized from their home during *Krystallnacht*. There was some confusion in the exchange of letters because Herman had changed his last name to Gruen. But after this had been resolved, it took years for the family to receive restitution payments. By then Elly had passed on, her life shortened, Tea believes, by the guilt she felt over sending her son to Holland in 1938.[6]

Americans enjoyed the 1950s as a decade of almost uninterrupted prosperity, and Stern's business benefited as much from the era as any other. The boys raised and on their own, he and Adeline sold their house on the east side of town and moved to a new house in the new development on the northwest edge of town. One of the first things Stern did after moving in was plant a large garden in his back yard. Gardening remained one of his greatest pleasures to the end of his life. The rest of America may have enthralled with television in the 1950s but Herman proved to be immune to its charms. Aside from the kinds of music he could find on variety shows and Lawrence

Welk's show, he scarcely noticed the television set. He continued to devote hundreds of hours to civic causes and walked to the store every morning and home every night.

In these happy times, the subject of the Holocaust was almost never mentioned. Although he enjoyed listening to Eddie talk about his experiences with the American air forces in Britain, Herman would generally only talk about the war's affects on the business. In regard to the deaths of his brothers Julius and Moses, or the murders of the millions of other Jews by Hitler's minions, he remained silent. He did not hold the ordinary German people to be in any way responsible for their deaths. When a German woman whose parents had known Stern as a young man wrote to him after the war asking if "German people in America" could send food to help the children in her town, Stern once again responded in kindness by sending the family CARE food packages from America and school bags for the woman's daughter and her friends. "It's impossible for you to imagine how the children rejoiced [to] your package with the school bags," related the mother of one of the children. Stern continued to send packages over a period of two years.[7]

Back in America, Stern helped some of his extended family obtain a measure of justice for their losses by obtaining restitution payments from the German government. Tea Stiefel's father, as noted, obtained some restitution for his lost property. Jay Stern's wife, Herta, wrote to Stern explaining that Jay (Julius) was seeking restitution for his losses in Germany. Because the German authorities wanted information about the income he had earned in America, Herta asked Stern if he would write a statement concerning "the time when Jay worked at your store, what his position was there and that he did his work satisfactorily." The fact that Herta made the request, rather than Jay, suggested that Stern and his nephew were still on poor terms. Stern's reply, listing the dates that Jay worked at Straus from 1922 to 1926 and that "his services as salesman and assistant were satisfactory," does nothing to counter that impression. He said nothing about Julius's second employment from 1927 to 1930. Gustave Stern also sought and received some restitution, as did many of the others.[8]

But even the letters that Stern exchanged in regard to restitution never touched directly on the subject of the nightmare that had engulfed Europe's Jewish population. Stern's reticence on the subject of the Holocaust probably rested in part on the fact that, as a pre-Great War immigrant, a man who was German by birth, Jewish by faith, and an American by choice, he had difficulty accepting that the German people *he* had known could have been complicit in the murders of so many. He was not alone in this. Fredrecka Straus sent Stern a letter in 1948, marking "the anniversary of [Stern's] first stepping on American soil, 45 years ago." She wrote Stern that the nation would be "a greater, better U.S. than it is," if more would emulate Stern's "qualities of heart & understanding, unselfishness & tolerance." She and her husband had "recognized what you stood for, early in your career," Rickie wrote, and had taken great pride in Stern's work and "unselfish creations of [organizational] movements which put the State on the map." She had been prouder still of all Stern had done to help his and her own relatives, but never specifically mentioned the German persecutions that had made Stern's assistance so important.[9]

This was not unusual. The destruction of Europe's Jews went unspoken among hundreds of thousands of America's Jewish people for almost two decades. Jews with German ancestry were particularly reticent on the issue. They seemed to readily accept the assertions of "ordinary Germans" who claimed that they had been ignorant about the murders of the Jews by Hitler and his henchmen. When the United States welcomed the Federal Republic of Germany into its NATO alliance, some American Jewish organizations protested the "forgive and forget" attitude they discerned in the gesture, while other groups argued that it was necessary to "put aside" the past and move on. The Cold War contributed to the latter argument. Few in the 1950s wanted to be seen as "soft" on the question of communism. An official in the American Jewish Committee noted privately in 1950 that the failure to remind others about complicity of the German people in the "6,000,000 Jews exterminated" was lamentable, "but that is past, and we must deal with the [international] facts today." As a result, the scholar Peter Novick has concluded, during the

1950s "to a considerable extent the Holocaust was a private, albeit widely shared, Jewish sorrow."[10]

One way Jews in America expressed their true feeling was in their support of the new nation of Israel. Herman Stern contributed frequently to fund raisers for Israel, purchased bonds issued by the new nation and for several years agreed to coordinate efforts for the United Jewish Appeal. Virtually all of those he had helped flee Germany contributed as well, ranging from Stern's nephew Eric, who lent his growing success in Chicago to a special fundraising dinner for Israel, to Felix and Greta Steiner and Solly and Hilda Jonas, who, despite always having to carefully budget their money, gave as much as they could. Greta supplemented Felix's income by continuing to design and fashion hats. She became well known in and around Fargo for the delicacy of her creations. Her hats adorned many a bride in North Dakota until well into the late 1970s.

Erika Kann decided to make her home in Israel. While hiding in Belgium during the war, she had continued her education by walking from the Saelens' farm in the dead of night to borrow books from nuns at a nearby convent. After the war ended, she received some further education at the convent, then took a secretarial course and "worked for 2 years as a steno-typist" in Belgium. Her mother had agreed to marry the farmer in whose house she had hidden from 1940 to 1944. They had to wait for about a year for her husband Sally, killed at Auschwitz, to be declared dead by the Belgian authorities. In March 1948, Erika immigrated to the United States. She "visited Gus Stern [Little Gus] in New York," who told her about how his own parents had been killed by the Nazis, then went on to Chicago to see Jay and his wife, then on to Seattle to visit the Sterns there.

Finally she went to Houston where her mother's brother lived, and found a job there as a secretary. But she did not find America as welcoming as it had been to others. When she told a clerk that she appreciated his help, her boss "explained to me that in Texas you don't say 'thank you' to an office boy." She retorted that the boy "had his nose in the middle of his face just like you and me," and soon had to look for a new job. When she applied for a shorthand-typist position at Shell Oil, the interviewer "asked whether I was Jewish, he's still waiting for an answer." Soon after, her uncle "explained certain facts of life to me" about being Jewish in America and Erika decided to return to Belgium. "I decided to join a group of friends to go to Israel. In October 1949, we left and joined a kibbutz on the Lebanese border near the sea." In a letter Erika wrote to friends in the United States soon after arriving, she said "it was a wonderful feeling to debark in a Jewish harbor [of Haifa]. Although it was very primitive in comparison to other ports, the fact that the workers, employees and most of the most of the people you see are Jewish, gives you a free feeling."[11]

In August of 1957, Stern celebrated his seventieth birthday by walking from his home to the store to see that new suits that had arrived were being unpacked and displayed the way they should be – his way. He had never been much of a person to mark his own birthdays. Parties and elaborate celebrations generally did not interest him. But this time, many of his family were determined to mark the occasion. Knowing that Herman was not particularly interested in fancy presents, Eddie collected various sums of money from about sixteen of the families that had escaped from Europe in the 1930s and combined in into a check for his father. He found a calligrapher to design a scroll in honor of his father, which read in part "To you who unselfishly devoted precious time and money in order to answer our prayers from across the sea, we shall forever be indebted. Through your love of fellow-man we have been able to once again live in Peace, Security and Happiness. The enclosed check is only a token of our affection and gratitude. Let us contribute to one of your humanitarian projects . . . God bless you for many, many years to come." Among others, the scroll was signed by Arthur Spier and his sister Rosi, Gustave and his family, Little Gus, Jay Stern, the Ullmanns, Jonases, Henleins, Blumenthals, Hass family, and Felix Falkenstein.

Naturally delighted by the gesture, Stern gave the money to his oldest and most favored cause, the Boy Scouts. But the passage of time saddened him, too. Most of his siblings had been dead for more than a decade. Brother Gustav had died of heart failure before the end of the war, Adolf's cancer had killed him in 1946, and Dora died in Seattle in 1955. Jettchen, the only sibling left, had moved to New York, where she lived with Lotte until her death in 1977. Back in Valley City, blessed with good health, still enjoying an overabundance of energy, Stern must at times have felt like a stately old oak standing in the midst of young saplings.

Nor surprisingly, he liked to keep his remaining family very close. He made buying trips to New York, not so much because he thought he had to select the merchandise as because he wanted to see Jettchen and Lotte and her husband, and Little Gus and the others. He was always disappointed that almost none of his relatives from Germany had made their homes in North Dakota. Having lived among the far more emotional Parisians, Michael Stern thought that his uncle was something of a puzzle. Admitting that he thought Herman was very reserved, "a real North Dakotan," he also admitted that "people have different recollections of him. Even my wife remembers him quite well. She thought he was very warm. I think that he had a duty, an overriding duty to take into the United States all these people. I don't even know what he did it for. I mean, family was very important and he wanted to make sure that we got here. He was a classy guy." But Michael would never for a moment have considered living on the Great Plains, where he felt people kept too tight a rein on their feelings.[12]

By 1960, Eddie Stern was handling most of the day-to-day management for Straus, both in Fargo and in the Valley City store. It was during the 1960s that Americans began to pay more attention to the Holocaust. This was due in part to the publicity that was given in 1960 to the abduction of Adolf Eichmann by Israeli agents, who had found him living under an assumed name in Argentina. More than a hundred people, a great many of them former prisoners at the Nazi camps, testified at Eichmann's trial in Jerusalem, an event that Hannah Arendt, herself a refuge in the 1930s, assessed in a book that questioned the roles played by many people and groups in the efforts to save Jews from Nazi maltreatment. Now that enough time had passed to make the Holocaust an historical event, other books began to appear raising many of the same questions broached by Arendt. By the beginning of the 1970s, a great many books and articles were asking questions about how serious the Roosevelt government had been in its desire to save more Jewish refugees.

As serious examination of America's role in the Holocaust grew, so too did the efforts of anti-Semites, cranks and crypto-fascists to deny that the Holocaust ever happened. Father Coughlin had dismissed the murders of the Jews as "Hebrew propaganda" in 1942. Soon after, the Postal Service stopped the distribution of Coughlin's magazine *Social Justice* on the grounds that his pro-Nazi remarks violated the Espionage Act. The Church in Rome decided to muzzle him too. He was ordered to cease his radio broadcasts. He returned to the tasks of his parish and kept silent for the rest of his life. Not so Gerald L. K. Smith, Coughlin's old ally and one of the stalwarts of the America First movement. Smith had begun calling the Holocaust a hoax in the 1950s. He spread his vitriolic poisons in a series of articles and pamphlets to a small number of follows who continued his campaign of hate. By the time of Smith's death in 1976 the Holocaust-deniers were a well-organized group.[13]

The debate over the Holocaust and America's role in it led many of the people Stern had helped to seek out more information about their lost relatives. Gustave Stern received help from American Jewish organizations in order to find out more about the property his father had lost to the Nazi confiscations. In the process he discovered the existence of the police file that had been kept on Adolf Stern. Gustave's son Michael still has a copy of the file. Lotte Henlein Ullmann sought out information about the fate of her Bad Schwalbach neighbors and her father's relatives. Other members of the family began to do the same.

Herman Stern's reaction to the growing volume of questions concerning America's responsibilities in the Holocaust is unknown. When scholars and others argued that more European Jews could have been rescued had there not been divisions within the American Jewish community, particularly the rifts between Orthodox and Reform groups, Stern ignored the controversy. His sons do not remember him reading any books about the Holocaust or making any comments about the American government's refugee policy of the 1930s. He seldom mentioned Gerald Nye after 1945. Nye returned for a brief visit to North Dakota in the late 1960s, during which he gave a talk at the University of North Dakota calling American military actions in Vietnam the kind of foreign policy "error" he had warned against in the 1930s. There is no indication that Stern and Nye met then or had any other contacts in which they reflected on what they managed to achieve.

When Stern gave interviews to various people about his history, he played down his own role in saving so many lives. In a 1974 interview he said that he and Adeline had made the joint decision to help as many as they could, and that his wife had helped him every step of the way in getting his relatives to "this great country." He praised Nye for everything he had done to help. He also gave credit to the men in Fargo who had agreed to act as co-sponsors in order to allow more men and women to escape. Stern's son Edward later remembered that his father had more than once remarked that, though the Jews in North Dakota who were the founders of the Reform temple had strong differences of opinion with those who were part of the Orthodox congregation in the community, both groups had set aside their differences during the 1930s to provide help for Europe's Jewish refugees.

Stern wrote in notes he made as part of a 1976 project to collect Jewish history in North Dakota, "A great regret brother Julius and Moses did not heed the danger of concentration camp. Brother Julius, so well liked, always said 'die tuen uns nichts' (meaning they are not going to harm us). It was too late much to our sorrow." A man who much disliked those who went around placing blame, whatever the circumstances, Stern said nothing in the interview to criticize the performance of the Stuttgart consulate staff of the State Department. He would not make accusations against the country that had been so good to him since his arrival nearly seventy years before.[14]

In 1972, the Sterns embarked on a four-week trip to Germany

and Israel with Ed's son, Richard. Stern visited his home town of Oberbrechen and was happy to discover living there a classmate from his school days. The man "was quite overcome with joy" to see Herman, Adeline wrote in an account of the trip, "and mentioned several times that Herman had been the leader of their 'gang,' which Herman had forgotten. Stern visited the graves of his parents and eldest sister, finding they had not been desecrated as so many other Jewish graves had been during the Hitler period: the community "had taken it upon themselves to keep this cemetery in very good condition with a paid caretaker." Stern also met with a local historian and provided the man with information about himself and his families for use in a town history that was later published.

Although by that time almost eighty-five years old, Stern was remarkably energetic in Germany, showing Adeline the places where he had walked the fields and tended to the cows as a boy and the streets he had walked in Mainz during his unhappy apprenticeship before leaving Germany and going to America. Adeline, Herman and Rick visited Wiesbaden, Heidelberg and Frankfurt, taking a brief outing along the Rhine. Adeline noted on several occasions that her husband found everywhere the same decent, kind German people he had known in his youth.

Adeline herself found Israel to be the highlight of the journey. From examining the farmland near the home of Erika Bachar-Kann and her husband, who was a veteran of the Six Day War of 1967, to touring the holy sites in Tel-Aviv, she made copious notes of everything she saw. She described in some detail their visit to the Golan Heights region. "The valley is occupied by several Jewish Kibbutz and much damage was done [here] before the Six Day War ended. We saw the underground bunkers of the Syrians and many discarded wrecked tanks, etc. Our guide told us that the Israeli Army had to build the roads under fire for the troops to move forward. They had few guns and went through hell; he said that they won the Six Day War through grit and determination." In Tel-Aviv, Adeline was impressed with another guide, a veteran of the American Army in the Second World War. He had fought in "Italy and later in Germany where he met his wife. She was in a Nazi Labor Camp, where she saw her parents cremated." Both the man and his wife still served in the Israeli reserves. "Serving in the army is an unpleasant task," Adeline noted, "but it is part of their way of life to preserve their dearly won freedom, which they are ready and willing to defend at all costs." After leaving Israel in early May, the Sterns spent a few days in London before returning to the United States. In ending her travel diary, Adeline noted that she and her husband had formed the "deepest respect and admiration" for the people of Israel.[15]

While Stern's visit to Oberbrechen seemed to have ignited a flood of nostalgia for the homeland of his youth, Germany evoked very different emotions in his niece Lotte Henlein Ullmann. Lotte's husband, Irwin Ullmann, who she had met in New York after the war, had been incarcerated in Nazi labor camp. "My husband had a request to go over from the German consulate." Irwin had witnessed a camp guard select Jewish prisoners for execution. "In other words, [the guard had pointed and said] 'you live and you die.' If he thought you were capable of working, you probably lived. Irwin was in the background and he had seen that." In 1985, the government asked Irwin to come and be a witness at a war crimes trial. Irwin had horrible memories of Germany and insisted he would only travel if Lotte accompanied him. Neither of them enjoyed the trip; as Irwin testified in court, Lotte relived her own persecutions. They left Germany as soon as possible. Lotte and Irwin returned to Germany a few years later to see Bad Schwalbach, this time with their son, Alan. At Bad Schwalbach Lotte tried to find out if any of the Jewish neighbors and friends she had had survived the war. She learned nothing. "A woman told me when I was there, that the Nazis just told everyone to pack up and put them on the cattle car. There was no one that I know from that whole area who was alive anymore."

At the cemetery outside Bad Schwalbach, Lotte was shocked to find the Jewish gravesites defaced and vandalized. At "every single grave, the stone was [knocked] down, never picked up." When she and her family returned to New York, Irwin told her that he never wanted to see Germany again: "He said many times, 'our faith in

God may have faltered, but our faith in people was almost gone after those times'" in Germany.[16]

Tea Stiefel's return to Germany was a little more pleasant. She made no trips to Germany before the death of her husband. "Erwin – everything German for him was totally forbidden." Stiefel refused to read anything in the German language. Nor would he speak the language. "He and I never spoke German to one another. Never." Although the Stiefels traveled to Europe in the 1970s, Erwin would not go to Germany. "He asked his cousin to come to Switzerland to see him on our first trip to Europe. He would not have set foot into Germany."

After Erwin's death, Tea did go to Germany in 1995, and returned to Dinslaken. In a similar way to Lotte Ullmann's second trip to Germany, Tea was invited back to Dinslaken by the German authorities, together with other Jewish survivors from the community. There was a ceremony held to commemorate a monument for the Jewish orphans who had been pulled in a cart through the streets while a crowd, urged on by Nazi storm troopers, had hurled stones and insults at them. The monument, a bronze replica of the cart, was dedicated by the mayor of Dinslaken, who also issued a formal apology to Tea and the others who had been able to flee Germany. None of those who returned had been children at the Jewish orphanage in 1938; so far as is known, none had survived the Holocaust.

Up to the last moment of the ceremony, Tea had not been sure of the wisdom of returning to Germany. "I truly felt that their atonement, or their effort to atone, was genuine. Because I had told my daughter before going, 'If anyone says one wrong thing, I'm leaving. I'm not staying.' And they could not have treated us better than they did. They made every conceivable effort." But after the ceremony, Tea found it "unnerving" to talk to some of the people who remembered her. "A lot of people recognized me because I look a lot like my mother. Marsha [her daughter] and I were walking in the street one time, and I think the people probably had been alerted to the fact that we were coming in newspaper, radio, and television." Several people came up to talk to her. One was her old friend Liselotte Schulze, the girl whose snub of her had fired her determination to leave Germany. Now in her seventies, Liselotte was happy to see Tea, and wanted to apologize for her rudeness of sixty years before. Tea, thinking that had Liselotte not acted as she did all those years ago, she might have stayed in Germany and died in one of the camps, told the woman that she had no hard feelings.

A day later, Tea visited a school where many of the students were the children of Turkish immigrants hired to work in the mines near Dinslaken. She answered questions about her own experiences as an immigrant. Suddenly one of the boys asked her something that startled her. "The question was, 'How does it feel to come back to your homeland?' And just without thinking, I said, 'I need to correct you. I was born here, but my homeland is America.' This is very strongly as to how I feel." Soon after, Tea told her daughter that she was ready to go home.[17]

Stern's ninetieth birthday came and went in 1977 and still he showed the energy of a man at least thirty year's younger. True, he drove very seldom. When he and Adeline, who was just four months younger, wished to leave Valley City, to visit friends in another town or go to services at the Temple in Fargo, they called Eddie or used one of the employees at Straus as a chauffeur. But Stern still walked to many places in town, still retained an excellent memory, still kept up with much of the minutia of the business.

Like many elderly men, he worried more about his offspring than about himself. All of his siblings were dead by the late 'seventies and now some of the refugees who had been so young when he helped them, were dying, most notably his nephew, Julius, in 1972. He feared something might happen to one of his grandchildren. On one occasion his grandson, Rick, was driving his grandfather's car and was rear-ended on the road. Worried, he took the car back and apologized for the damaged vehicle. "That's not important," Herman said, "so long as you're all right." But when Rick's brother, John, stopped off to see a friend while driving back from Minnesota, and arrived a couple hours late, he found Herman "pale and shaking," both angry and afraid that something horrible had occurred to the boy. "I'm disappointed in you, John," he said. "I felt just terrible for worrying him so much."

Stern did not want to outlive any more of his family. But in 1979 he lost Adeline. Diagnosed with leukemia a few years before, she died in December, a few days before Hanukkah. She was buried in the Hebrew Cemetery in Fargo. To the outside world, the Sterns had been formal and generally reticent; only those who knew them well were aware of just how much her love had meant to him. Her death crushed him. Herman insisted in staying on in his home, but in his loneliness, he brooded and soon began to decline. He would not survive without her for long.

Lee Isensee, a young man who went to work at Straus in the mid-1960s, was running errands for him by then, and noted that he was becoming depressed. "We had a lot of good talks. At the end he had kind of a change in philosophy. He had told me that, 'Lee, your family is the most important thing in life.' All I've done with my family is talk about work. That's all we know, and that's all we ever talk about. Don't let that happen. Go spend some time with your family.'" Isensee also realized that Stern did not want to hear praise about the many things he had done for the Boy Scouts, the Greater North Dakota Association or any of his other community activities. He remembered the time years before when the city government had decided to name the arena for the Winter Show in his honor. "He was very upset when he went up to the Winter Show and saw the sign that said 'Herman Stern Arena.' He didn't want that recognition." Stern left the ceremony early because he was so uncomfortable with the attention. "Of course, he accepted it and it went on, but he didn't want that. Mr. Stern was very, very humble, and he never really talked about his accomplishments or the things that he had done. He didn't want credit for a lot of different things."

Eddie, too, tried to cheer his father up by pointing out to him the awards he had received and telling him how proud he was to have a father who had saved so many people back in the days before the war. But Stern waved away the compliments. Eddie persisted, pointing out that Stern had risked his business in order to pledge to support so many refugees. It was no sacrifice, the old man replied, they had all made good, and "they didn't owe me anything."

Still very alert but physically worn out and heartbroken, Stern entered the hospital in Fargo in June of 1980. Tea Steifel, learning that he was failing, traveled to Fargo to see him one more time. "When I got there, he really surprised me. I walked in and he looked up and started speaking to me in German. He had never done that before."[18]

Stern died in the hospital on June 20, about six weeks shy of his ninety-third birthday. At the memorial service for Stern, held at the local Methodist Church in Valley City, North Dakota Governor Arthur Link said that Stern's life had been "a life of devotion" to his adopted state. While others saw the problems of life as walls blocking them from what they desired, Link concluded, Stern had converted the blocks into "stepping stones" over which he found new paths to make a better life for himself, his family, his town and state. One of the two former refugees who had traveled to North Dakota for the funeral also spoke, and it was here that many of Stern's friends and neighbors, who had turned out en masse to honor him, learned for the first time of the extraordinary efforts he had made to rescue so many.

Dressed in one of his best Kuppenheimer suits and his prayer shawl, Stern was buried in the Jewish cemetery in Fargo, next to Adeline, the graves of his sister, Jettchen and her husband Hugo, just a few yards away. Robert Seltzer, the husband of Stern's granddaughter, Cheryl, and a rabbi, spoke briefly at the graveside on how Stern's life exemplified the best Judaic, and human, qualities. In keeping with his wishes to have something simple, Stern's grave is covered by a flat stone on which was carved his name, birth date and death date, nothing more. Numerous obituaries were published announcing his death, giving him the praise that he had repudiated in life. The obituaries noted his part in Scouting, in promoting the state of North Dakota, in the Winter Show and many other contributions to his state. None remarked on the part he had played in saving more than a hundred lives at a desperate time.

"Be humble in the eyes of God," he had written in the little pamphlet he gave to young men and women over the years. "Be more than tolerant, be understanding. Judge an individual not on his race, creed, or economic standing; judge him for what he is." Judged by his own beliefs, by his character and by what he had done, Herman Stern had been someone very special indeed.

Notes

1. Adeline Stern to "Dear Ones," November 19, 1950, New Store Opening file, Stern Papers; "Grand Opening of Straus Clothing in Valley City," KOVC broadcast on November 15, 1950, tape 946 from Sound Archives of the Special Collections, University of North Dakota.

2. Herman Stern, transcript of a 1968 speech made at a marketing seminar in Fargo, Marketing Seminar file, Stern Papers.

3. Edward and Richard Stern, videotaped interview with Wes Anderson, July 24, 2004, Barnes County Museum; Gustave Stern interview transcript, pp. 7-9. According to Michael Stern his father and Vasen "opened a cleaners and a clothing store called Atlas Cleaners and Clothing. That went for about a year until my father punched out my uncle and the police came and separated them," Michael Stern transcript, pp. 10-11.

4. Gustave Stern interview transcript, pp. 8.

5. Eric Stern to Herman Stern, March 29, 1950 and undated [mid 1960s]; Herman Stern to Eric Stern, March 31, 1950, together with brochures and financial statements of Cohn and Stern, Eric Stern file, Stern Papers.

6. Stiefel transcript, pp. 62-63.

7. Elisabeth Dawes to Stern, March 1948, Elisabeth Dawes file, Stern Papers. The Dawes file and the file of Agnes Heinrirhl (Dawes' mother), contain further details on Stern's aid to German children. Dawes' husband was a prisoner of war in Russia from 1945 until 1949.

8. Herta Stern to Herman Stern, March 18, 1958; Herman Stern to "Whom it May Concern," April 3, 1958, in Jay Stern file, Stern Papers.

9. Rickie Stern to Herman Stern, October 16, 1948, German Relatives file, Stern Papers.

[10] Peter Novick, *The Holocaust in American Life* (Boston: Houghton Mifflin, 1999), pp. 90-98. See also interviews in Eric A. Johnson's and Karl-Heinz Reubard's more recent *What We Knew: Terror, Mass Murder, and Everyday Life in Nazi Germany*.

11. Erika Bachar Kann to Shoptaugh, January 24, 1999; Erika Kann to "Dear Folks," November 12, 1949, copy in Trip to Israel file, Stern Papers.

12. Michael Stern transcript, pp. 13-14.

13. In addition to Arendt's *Eichmann in Jerusalem* (1963), significant works published in English (and thus available to most Americans) during this period would include Raul Hilberg's *The Destruction of the European Jews* (1961), Gerald Reitlinger's *The Final Solution* (first American edition in 1961) and Arthur Morse, *While Six Million Died,* which appeared in 1967 and was in use in American schools after appearing in an inexpensive paper edition in 1968. David Wyman's *Paper Walls* (1968) and Henry Feingold's *The Politics of Rescue* (1970) were being widely used in college-level American history classes throughout the 1970s.

14. Herman Stern, interview by Duane Crawford, March 21, 1971; undated notes in the Jewish Historical Project file, both in Stern Papers.

15. Adeline Stern, "Special Note" on Trip to Germany and Israel, 1972; copy of typed manuscript given to Shoptaugh by Edward Stern.

16. Ullman transcript, pp. 16, 27, 57-60. After her trips to Germany, Lotte found information about a few Jewish neighbors from her home town who had survived the Holocaust. It was only in the last year of her life that she learned that her Bad Schwalbach friend Dieter Ackerman (Thomas Maier) had survived to reach America with his mother.

17. Stiefel transcript, pp. 64-66.

18. Lee Isensee, interview with Michael Morrissey, July 21, 1999, transcript, pp. 14, 17; Shoptaugh conversation with Tea Steifel, June 1998.

Herman Stern's List of "People sponsored to come to America"

During the 1930s, Mr. Stern kept a small notebook in which he recorded the names of those for whom he prepared and sent affidavits of sponsorship to the U.S. State Department. In addition, he kept an untitled list of individuals and families sponsored by other members of the North Dakota Jewish community and a list of German physicians that he hoped he could help immigrate to North Dakota and receive a license to practice medicine.

Stern omitted some names on his list. For example, he did not list Solly and Hilda Jonas, one of the first couples. Mrs. M. G. Straus had signed the affidavit Stern prepared for her because Solly Jonas was her cousin. Stern listed some individuals twice and occasionally misspelled some of the names. The author has altered the spelling of some names in accordance with the spelling a person used in his or her correspondence. The family relationship of the person to Herman Stern (H.S.) has also been added when this is definitely known.

Herman Stern's list of people he helped are listed roughly in chronological order of filing of each affidavit.

- Klara Stern (niece of H.S., the daughter of Gustav Stern)

- Erich Stern (nephew of H.S., the son of Gustav Stern)

- Trudl Hermann (a second or third cousin of H.S.)

- Leon Hayum and Ida Hayum (Leon a cousin of H.S., his wife a cousin of Klara Stern)

- Solly and Hilda Levy Jonas (Solly Jonas was a cousin of H.S.)

- Hugo Henlein (the husband of H.S.'s sister Jettchen)

- Jettchen and Lotte Henlein (sister and niece of H.S.)

- Manfred Reichenberg (the son of a personal friend of H.S.)

- Hans Lion, his wife and two children (a physician, Lion was a distant relative of Adeline Stern)

- Julius Stern (nephew of H.S., son of Adolf Stern)

- Gustav Stern (nephew of H.S., son of the elder Julius Stern; known as "Little Gus")

- Hans Benjamin (apparently a cousin of one of H.S's sisters-in-law)

- Tea Eichengruen (a cousin of Dora Kann Stern, H.S's sister-in-law, not related to Stern)

- Gustav Stern (brother of H.S., not to be confused with "Little Gus" noted above)

- Selma Lewisohn Stern (Gustav's wife and H.S.'s sister-in-law)

- Erich and Ruth Falkenstein (relatives of Hugo Henlein, but not related to Stern)

- Morris Mosser, his wife Bettie, and daughter Lore (cousins of H.S.)

- Arthur and Gerta Oppenheimer and two children (Arthur a second cousin of H.S.)

- Herman Jacob and wife (a second cousin to H.S.)

- Alfred and Ruth Leske (Ruth a second cousin of H.S.)

- Felix Falkenstein (related to Erich Falkensten, but not to H.S.)

- Julius and Meta Haas and two sons (second cousins of H.S.)

- Marg. Kuhrau (sister of Ludwig Hammerschlag)

- Ludwig and Edith Hammerschlag (related to both the Falkensteins and Henleins)

- Rosi Spier Klibanski and son Wolfgang (Mrs. Klibanski was a cousin of H.S.)

- Julius Bumenthal, his wife and mother-in-law (Julius a second cousin to H.S.)

- Siegfried Goldschmidt (a second cousin of H.S.)

- Louis and Frieda Behr (parents of Ruth Leske)

- Irmigard Naftaniel and husband (related to Leske family)

- Arthur Stern and family (cousins from Bad Schwalbach)

- Alice Stern (niece of H.S., daughter of Gustav Stern)

- Leopold Schlafheimer family (Leopold Schlafheimer was the brother-in-law of Leon Hayum)

- Gustav Strauss (a second cousin to H.S., from Stern's mother's side of the family)

- Jacob and Betty Bessman (Betti Strauss Bessman was Gustav Strauss' sister, and Jacob was her husband)

- Jacob, Selma and Dora Jonas (all cousins of Herman Stern and Solly Jonas)

- Hermann and Elly Eichengruen (parents of Tea Eichengruen, but not related to H.S.)

- Eric Vasen, his wife and son (brother of Gertrude Vasen Stern, Eric and his family were not related to H.S.)

- Arthur Spier (brother of Rosi Klibanski and cousin to H.S.)

- Adolf Stern and his wife Dora Kann Stern (Herman Stern's older brother and his wife)

- Gustave Stern, his wife Gertrude Vasen Stern, sons Hans and Michel (Gustave was the nephew of H.S., son of Adolf Stern)

- Dr. and Mrs. Jonathan Schneider (not related to H.S., one of the German physicians that he hoped would practice medicine in North Dakota)

- Moses Stern (brother of H.S., never emigrated, died in Theresienstadt, Czechoslovakia)

- Julius Stern and his wife Frieda Falkenstein Stern (brother and sister-in-law of H.S., never emigrated, died in concentration camps during the war)

- Ludwig Stern (nephew of H.S., son of Julius and Frieda Stern, never emigrated, died in Gurs internment camp, France, 1942).

In addition to these eighty-seven people, Stern co-sponsored fifty or more other individuals with the assistance of several prominent men from the Jewish community of Fargo. Stern's list naming these immigrants is sketchy, often listing just a last name. Files in the Herman Stern Papers are equally thin; in some cases no information has been found beyond the names. Since Stern always said he had brought "about 125" people to America, it is likely that all were not able to emigrate from Europe.

Co-sponsored by Robert Herbst:
- Wertheim family
- Dr. Maurbacher (one of physicians that Stern wanted to bring to North Dakota)
- Kopfstein family (all friends of Stern before he immigrated to U.S.)
- Marcus family
- Albert and Friedrich Kann and families (friends of Stern before he immigrated to U.S)
- Seigfried Stern family (friends of Stern before he immigrated to U.S.)
- Sol Falkenstein family

Co-sponsored by Max Goldberg:
- Ludwig Falkenstein
- Alfons Levy (related to Hilda Levy Jonas)

Co-sponsored by "Paper" (probably Joseph Paper, owner of Fargo Iron and Metal):

- Kurt and Werner Benjamin (brothers of Hans Benjamin, Kurt died in Auschwitz; Werner emigrated and lived in his later years in California. A sister also emigrated but may have had a different sponsor.)

Co-sponsored by Jacob Stern:

- Frankels family
- Albert Winter

Co-sponsored by William Stern:

- Hilda Falks family

Co-sponsored by "Avid" (Maurice Aved, New York Life insurance agent in Fargo):

- Friedl Bein (a friend of the Adolf Stern family in Duisberg)

Bibliography

The main sources for this work are of course the papers of Herman Stern, deposited at the Elwyn B Robinson Department of Special Collections, Chester Fritz Library, University of North Dakota, and the interviews I conducted with individuals who had lived through the experiences. Those interviews, both in tape and in transcript, are now deposited at the Northwest Minnesota Historical Center, Minnesota State University Moorhead.

In addition to these, the endnotes to each chapter cite the numerous published books and articles I used, together with other archival records from the National Archives and other repositories. Scholars can easily retrace any of these items, and general readers would not be interested in a full accounting of them here. What follows is a basic bibliography of works on the Holocaust, America's role in the refugee crisis, and the life of Jewish refugees in the United States.

Aly, Gotz. *'Final Solution': Nazi Population Policy and the Murder of the European Jews* (New York: Oxford University Press, 1999)

Anderson, Mark, editor. *Hitler's Exiles: Personal Stories of the Flight from Nazi Germany to America* (New York: The New Press, 1998)

Arad, Yitzhak, et. al., editors. *Documents on the Holocaust* (Lincoln: University of Nebraska Press, 1999)

Bankier, David, editor. *Probing the Depth of German Antisemitism* (New York: Berghahn Books, 2000)

Barkai, Avraham. *From Boycott to Annihilation: The Economic Struggle of German Jews, 1933-1943* (Hanover: University Press of New England, 1989)

Bauer, Yehuda. *American Jewry and the Holocaust: the American Jewish Joint Distribution Committee*, 1939-1945 (Detroit MI: Wayne State University Press, 1981)

Breitman, Richard and Alan Kraut. *American Refugee Policy and the Crisis Among European Jewry* (Bloomington: University of Indiana Press, 1987)

Breitman, Richard. *The Architect of Genocide: Himmler and the Final Solution* (New York: Alfred A. Knopf, 1991)

Breitman, Richard. *Official Secrets: What the Nazis Planned, What the British and Americans Knew* (New York: Hill and Wang, 1998)

Broszat, Martin. *The Hitler State: The Foundation and Development of the Internal Structure of the Third Reich* (New York: Longman, 1981)

Browning, Christopher. *The Origins of the Final Solution: The Evolution of Nazi Jewish Policy, September 1939-March 1942* (Lincoln: University of Nebraska Press, 2004)

Dawidowicz, Lucy S. *The War Against the Jews, 1933-1945* (New York: Bantam Books, 1975)

Dippel, John V. H. *Bound Upon a Wheel of Fire: Why So Many German Jews Made the Tragic Decision to Remain in Nazi Germany* (New York: Basic Books,1996)

Dwork, Deborah and Robert Jan van Pelt. *Holocaust: A History* (New York: W. W. Norton, 2002)

Feingold, Henry L. *Bearing Witness: How America and its Jews Responded to the Holocaust* (Syracuse NY: Syracuse University Press, 1995)

Feingold, Henry L. *The Politics of Rescue* (New Brunswick, NJ: Rutgers University Press, 1970)

Friedlander, Saul. *Nazi Germany and the Jews* (New York: HarperCollins, 1997)

Daniel Goldhagen. *Hitler's Willing Executioners: Ordinary Germans and the Holocaust* (New York: Alfred Knopf, 1996)

Jaekel, Eberhard. *Hitler's Weltanschauung: A Blueprint for Power* (Middletown, CT: Wesleyan University, 1972)

Johnson, Eric and Karl-Heinz Reubard. *What We Knew: Terror, Mass Murder, and Everyday Life in Nazi Germany* (New York: Basic Books, 2005)

Kaplan, Marion A. *Between Dignity and Despair: Jewish Life in Nazi Germany* (New York: Oxford University Press, 1998)

Kirchheimer, Gloria and Manfred. *We Were So Beloved: Autobiography of a German Jewish Community* (Pittsburgh: University of Pittsburgh Press, 1997)

Klemperer, Victor. *I Will Bear Witness* (New York: Random House, 1998)

Laqueur, Walter. *Generation Exodus: The Fate of Young Jewish Refugees from Nazi Germany* (Hanover, NH: University Press of New England, 2001)

Laqueur, Walter. *The Terrible Secret: Suppression of the Truth about Hitler's 'Final Solution'* (New York: Little, Brown and Co., 1980)

Lipstadt, Deborah. *Beyond Belief: The American Press and the Coming of the Holocaust* (New York: Free Press, 1986)

Lowenstein, Steven M. *Frankfurt on the Hudson: The German-Jewish Community of Washington Heights* (Detroit MI: Wayne State University Press, 1989)

Michalczyk, John J., editor. *Resisters, Rescuers, and Refugees* (Kansas City, MO: Sheed & Ward, 1997)

Milfull, John, editor. *Why Germany?: National Socialist Anti-Semitism and the European Context* (Providence, RI: Berg, 1993)

Novick, Peter. *The Holocaust in American Life* (Boston: Houghton Mifflin, 1999)

Ousby, Ian. *Occupation: The Ordeal of France, 1940-1944* (New York: St. Martin's Press, 1998)

Pulzer, Peter. *Jews and the German State* (Oxford: Blackwell, 1992)

Richard Rhodes. *Masters of Death: The Einsatzgruppen and the Invention of the Holocaust* (New York: Knopf, 2002)

Roseman, Mark. *The Wannsee Conference and the Final Solution* (New York: Metropolitan Books, 2002)

Ryan, Donna. *The Holocaust & the Jews of Marsellie: The Enforcement of Anti-Semitic Policies in Vichy France* (Urbana: University of Illinois Press, 1996)

Seltzer, Robert M. *Jewish People, Jewish Thought: The Jewish Experience in History* (New York: Macmillan Publishing Co., 1980)

Soumerai Eve Nussbaum and Carol D. Schulz. *Daily Life During the Holocaust* (Westport, CT: Greenwood Press, 1998)

Wistrich, Robert S. *Hitler and the Final Solution* (New York: Modern Library, 2001)

Wyman, David. *The Abandonment of the Jews: America and the Holocaust, 1941-1945* (New York: Pantheon Books, 1984)

Wyman, David. *Paper Walls: America and the Refugee Crisis* (New York: Pantheon Books, 1985 ed.)

Zucker, Ami. *In Search of Refuge: Jews and US Consuls in Nazi Germany, 1933-1941* (London: Vallentine Mitchell, 2001)

Index

Note: In cases where a relative of Herman Stern had the same given name as another relative, a short explanation of the specific relationship has been provided. Similarly, a name change following immigration to the U.S. is also noted.

Ackerman, Dieter (Thomas Maier): 140, 146n, 355n.

American Jewish Committee 68, 70, 71, 116, 117, 123n, 166, 198, 341.

American Jewish Congress 68, 116, 117, 158, 165, 167, 171n, 225, 251.

American Medical Association (AMA) 230.

Anschluss (annexation of Austria): 174-175, 179, 180-184.

Anti-Semitism: in Austria: 176, 186; in France: 154, 197, 267, 278-279; in Germany: 42-44, 53-56, 59n, 67-68, 83-86, 87, 89-92, 94-95, 97, 101n, 113, 125, 127-129, 142, 217, 221 (see also Holocaust); in the United States: 19n, 29-30, 31-32, 69, 116-117, 120-121, 156-159, 169n, 226, 244, 277-278, 294-296, 315, 328, 329, 331n, 345-346.

Aved, Maurice: 252, 361.

Bein, Friedel: 252.

Benjamin, Hans: 151, 220, 358, 361.

Besmann, Bette: 218.

Besmann, Siegfried: 218.

Blumenthal, Julius: 191-192, 245, 315.

B'nai, B'rith: 117, 166, 324.

Boycotts: of German trade, by U.S: 115-117, 165-166, 251; of Jewish trade, by Nazi Party: 83-85, 94, 101n, 125-126, 141, 156-157.

Borah, William: 174.

Bruening, Heinrich: 51.

Chamberlain, Neville: 185, 205.

Churchill, Winston: 205, 251, 285, 291, 298, 326, 327

Clark, Bennett: 294

Cooper, Duff: 251